Contents

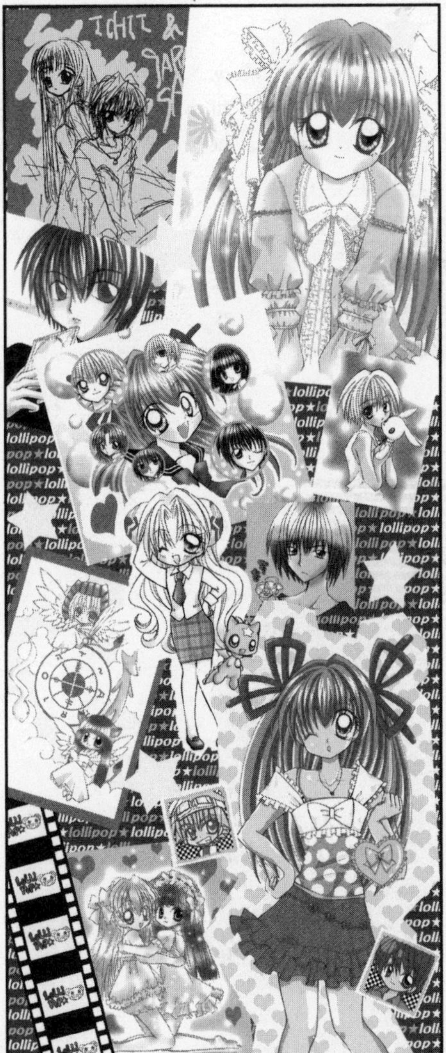
ICHII &
lollipop★lollipop

Honorifics Explained

Throughout the Del Rey Manga books, you will find Japanese honorifics left intact in the translations. For those not familiar with how the Japanese use honorifics and, more important, how they differ from American honorifics, we present this brief overview.

Politeness has always been a critical facet of Japanese culture. Ever since the feudal era, when Japan was a highly stratified society, use of honorifics—which can be defined as polite speech that indicates relationship or status—has played an essential role in the Japanese language. When addressing someone in Japanese, an honorific usually takes the form of a suffix attached to one's name (example: "Asuna-san"), is used as a title at the end of one's name, or appears in place of the name itself (example: "Negi-sensei," or simply "Sensei!").

Honorifics can be expressions of respect or endearment. In the context of manga and anime, honorifics give insight into the nature of the relationship between characters. Many English translations leave out these important honorifics and therefore distort the feel of the original Japanese. Because Japanese honorifics contain nuances that English honorifics lack, it is our policy at Del Rey not to translate them. Here, instead, is a guide to some of the honorifics you may encounter in Del Rey Manga.

-san: *This is the most common honorific and is equivalent to Mr., Miss, Ms., or Mrs. It is the all-purpose honorific and can be used in any situation where politeness is required.*

-sama: *This is one level higher than "-san" and is used to confer great respect.*

-dono: *This comes from the word "tono," which means "lord." It is an even higher level than "-sama" and confers utmost respect.*

-kun: *This suffix is used at the end of boys' names to express familiarity or endearment. It is also sometimes used by men among friends, or when addressing someone younger or of a lower station.*

-chan: *This is used to express endearment, mostly toward girls. It is also used for little boys, pets, and even among lovers. It gives a sense of childish cuteness.*

Bozu: *This is an informal way to refer to a boy, similar to the English terms "kid" and "squirt."*

Sempai/
Senpai: *This title suggests that the addressee is one's senior in a group or organization. It is most often used in a school setting, where underclassmen refer to their upperclassmen as "sempai." It can also be used in the workplace, such as when a newer employee addresses an employee who has seniority in the company.*

Kohai: *This is the opposite of "sempai" and is used toward underclassmen in school or newcomers in the workplace. It connotes that the addressee is of a lower station.*

Sensei: *Literally meaning "one who has come before," this title is used for teachers, doctors, or masters of any profession or art.*

-[blank]: *This is usually forgotten in these lists, but it is perhaps the most significant difference between Japanese and English. The lack of honorific means that the speaker has permission to address the person in a very intimate way. Usually, only family, spouses, or very close friends have this kind of permission. Known as yobisute, it can be gratifying when someone who has earned the intimacy starts to call one by one's name without an honorific. But when that intimacy hasn't been earned, it can be very insulting.*

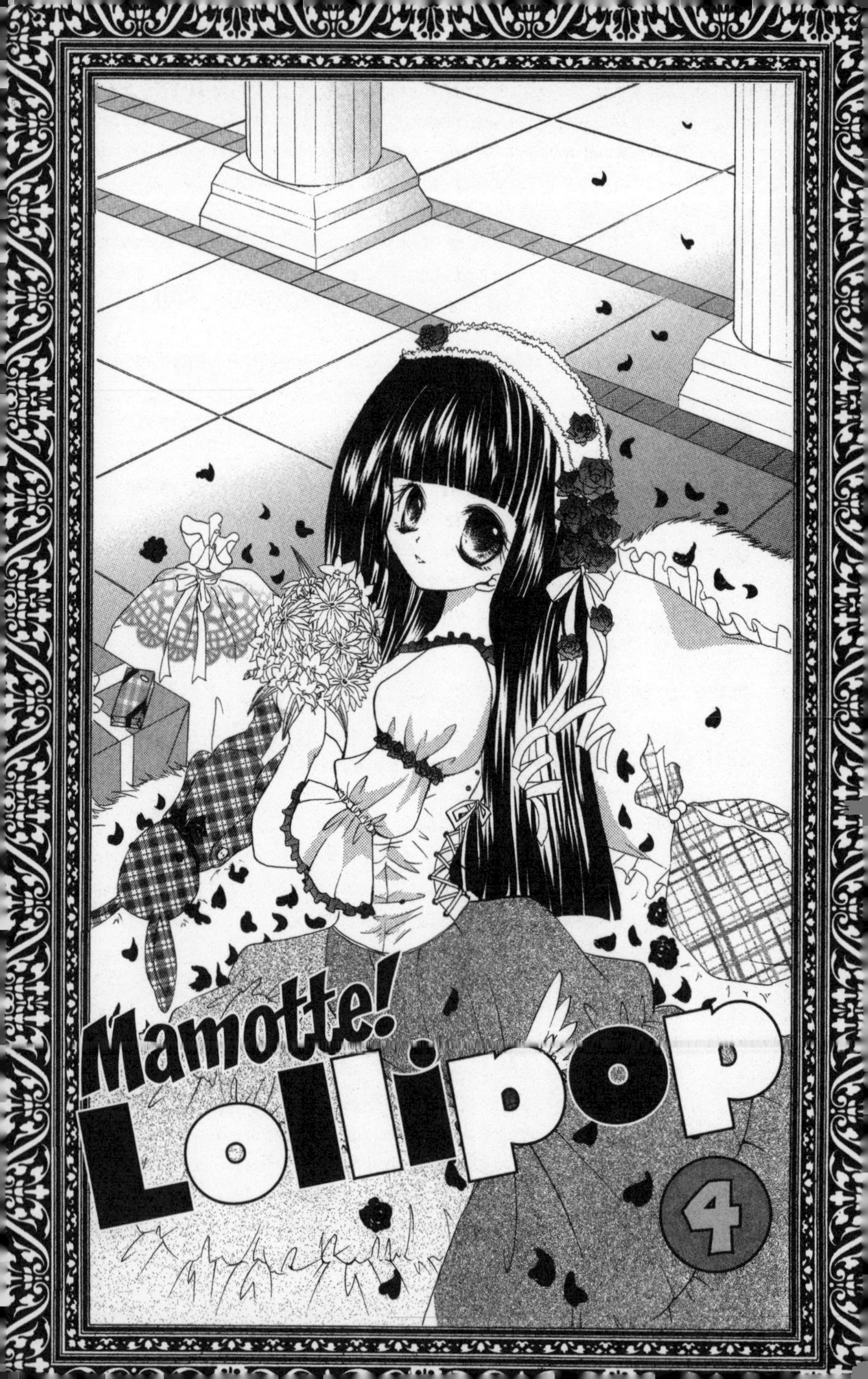
Mamotte! Lollipop
4

CONTENTS

MAMOTTE! LOLLIPOP

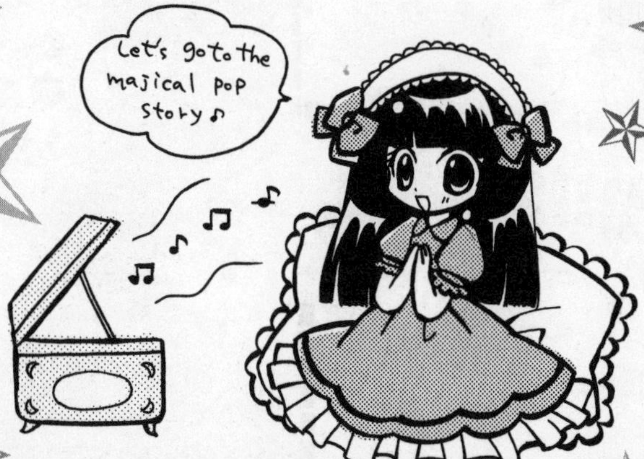

Let's go to the majical pop story♪

TELL ME! LOLLIPOP

1 Nina accidentally swallowed the Crystal Pearl for the Magic Exam.

→ Like this one

Nina
Likes boys who are strong, kind and good-looking.

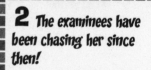

Zero
Simple, but has a strong sense of justice.

Ichi
Kind and a bit grown-up.

2 The examinees have been chasing her since then!

3 But Zero & Ichi promised to protect her all the way until the end of the exam. ☆

Sun
Usually easygoing, occasionally turns frightening.

Forte
Sun's friend, likes to cross-dress?!

Gô
Rokka's servant, does anything she wishes.

Rokka
Actually is five years old, loves Ichi.

4 Love and trouble just never end with these two cool boys around!!

◀ And now the exciting magical pop story begins.

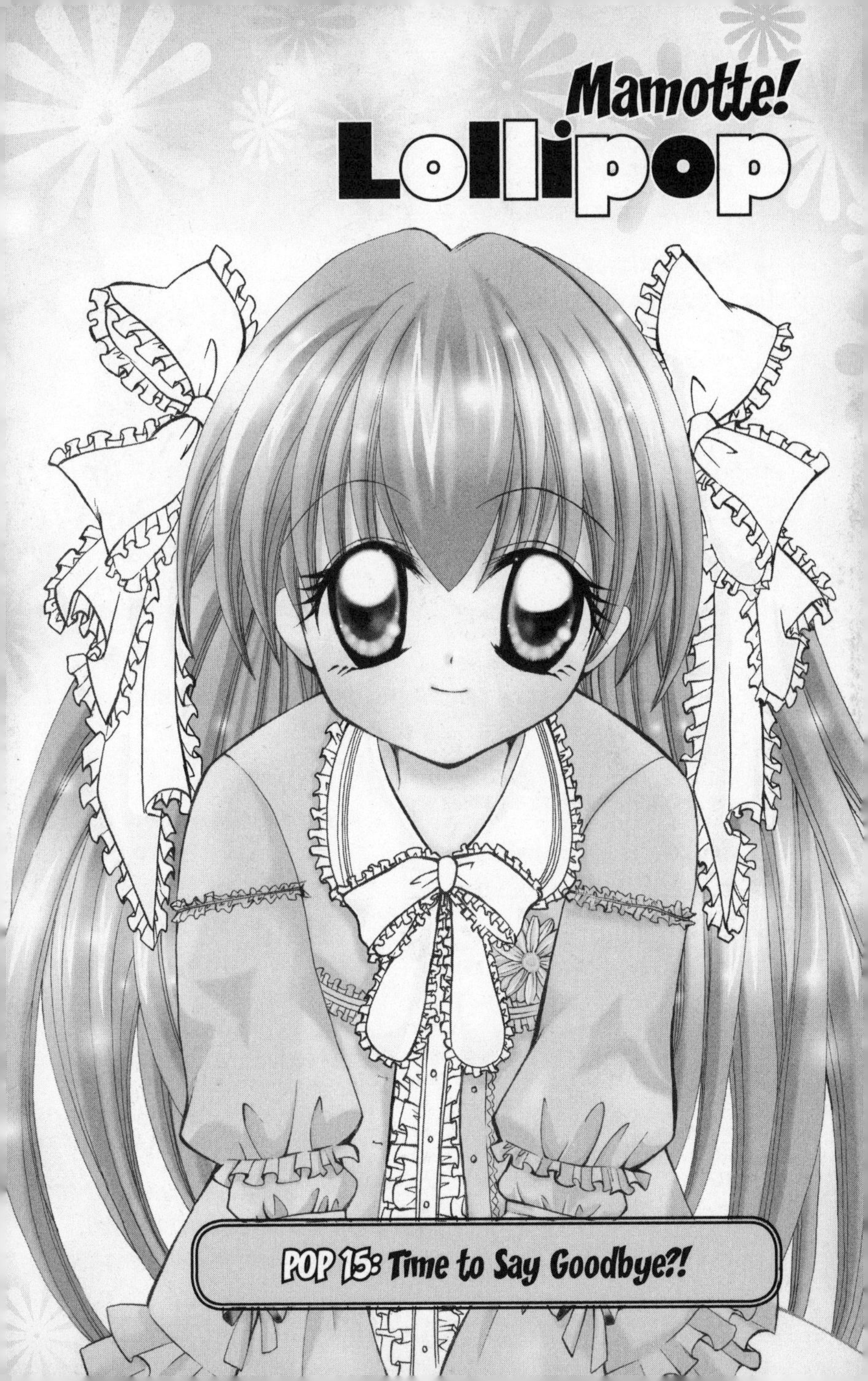
Mamotte!
Lollipop
POP 15: Time to Say Goodbye?!

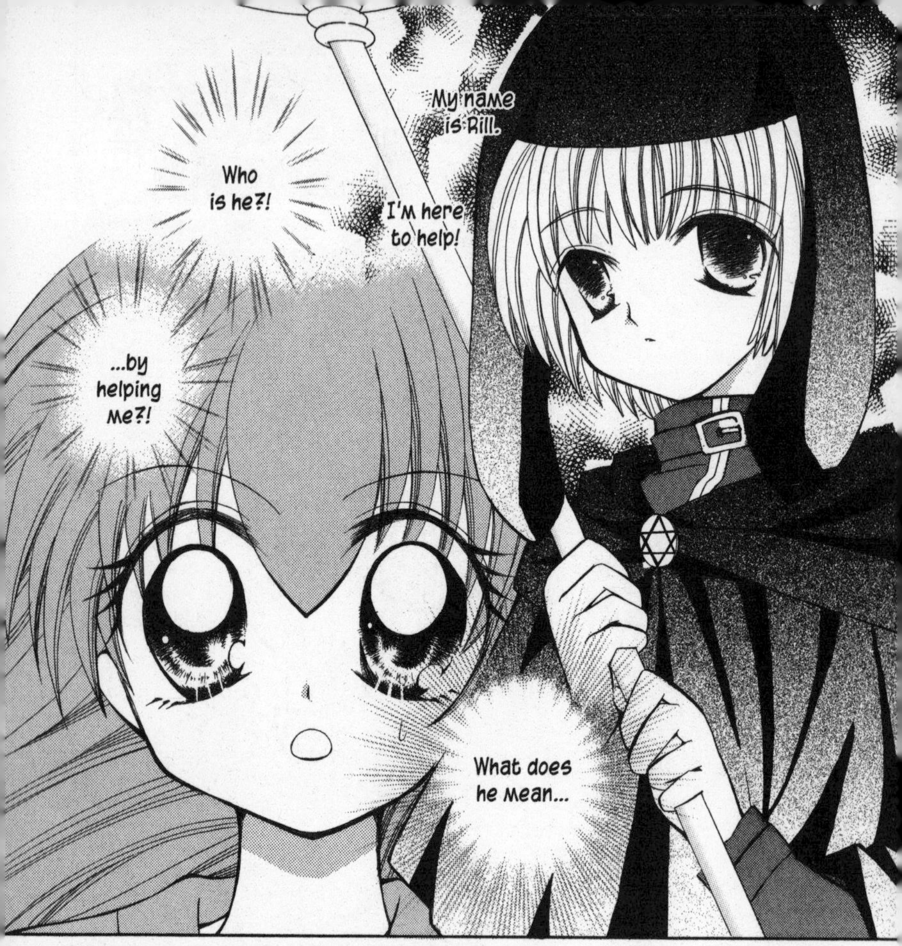
My name is Rill.
I'm here to help!
Who is he?!
What does he mean...
...by helping me?!

PoP15 Time to Say Goodbye?!

I never imagined I'd draw the one-day event over three episodes. I'm getting a little sick of having everyone in the same outfits. (Laughs) Rill has finally made his appearance. I'm glad that I was able to draw him to my satisfaction. It feels like the story is unfolding more rapidly as it comes closer to its end. Of all the new examinees, the little sister, Sis, is my favorite. I also had fun drawing Rokka in her school uniform in this episode. The cover page was done digitally. Since this was my first time using the digital graphic program on a cover illustration, I felt nervous. I designed Nina's outfit based on Pink House Ltd. → A brand name. All frilly . . .

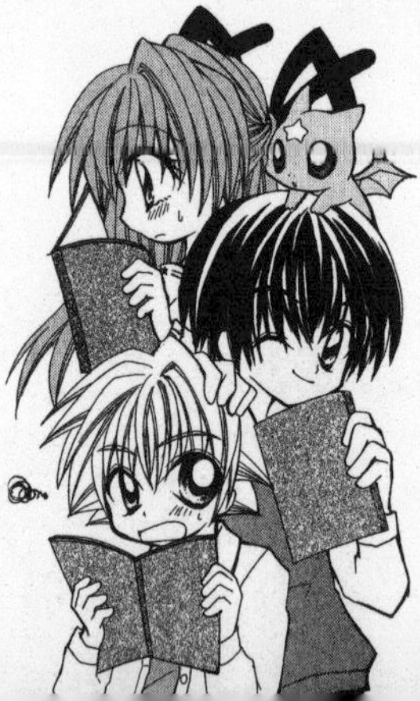

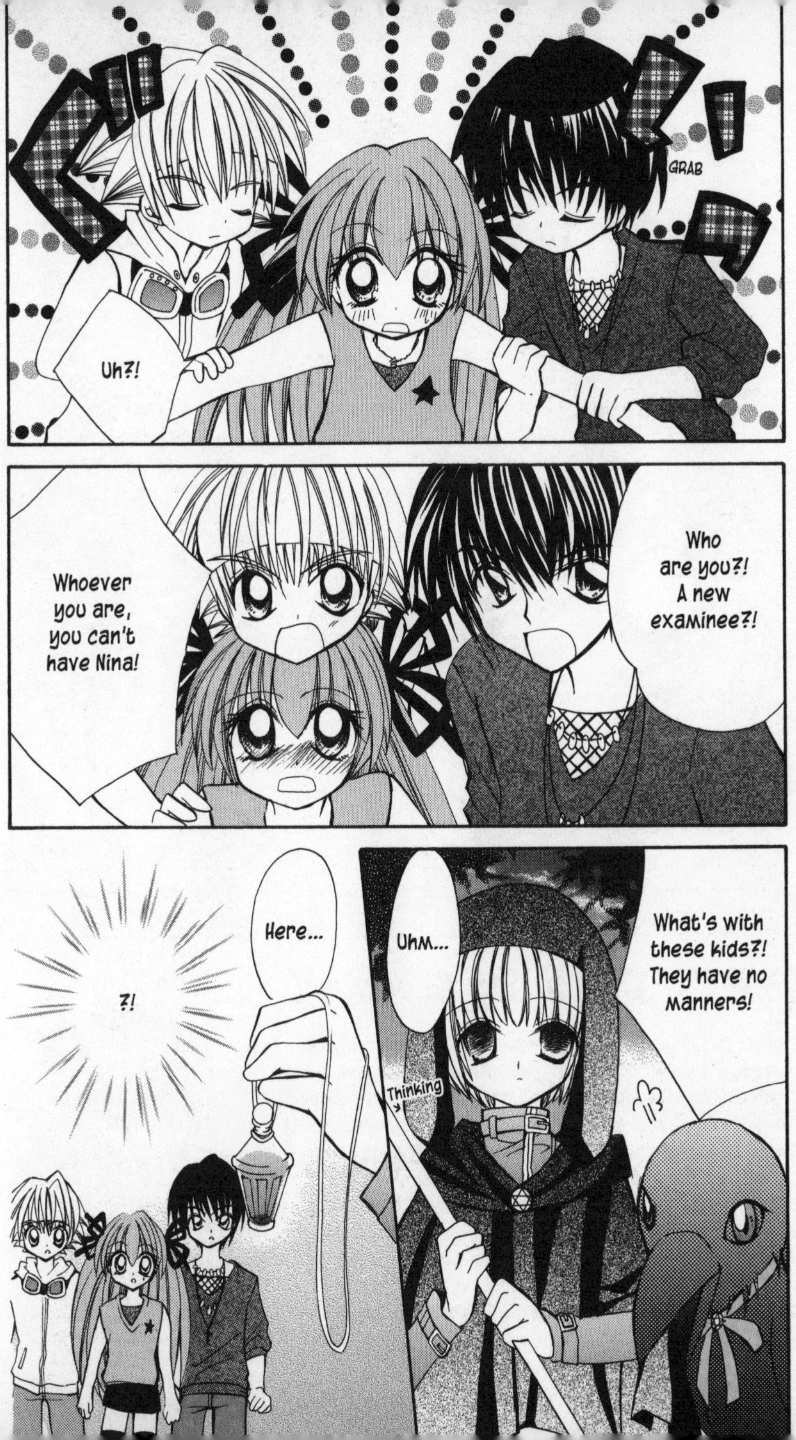
GRAB
Uh?!
Who are you?! A new examinee?!
Whoever you are, you can't have Nina!
What's with these kids?! They have no manners!
Uhm...
Thinking
Here...
?!

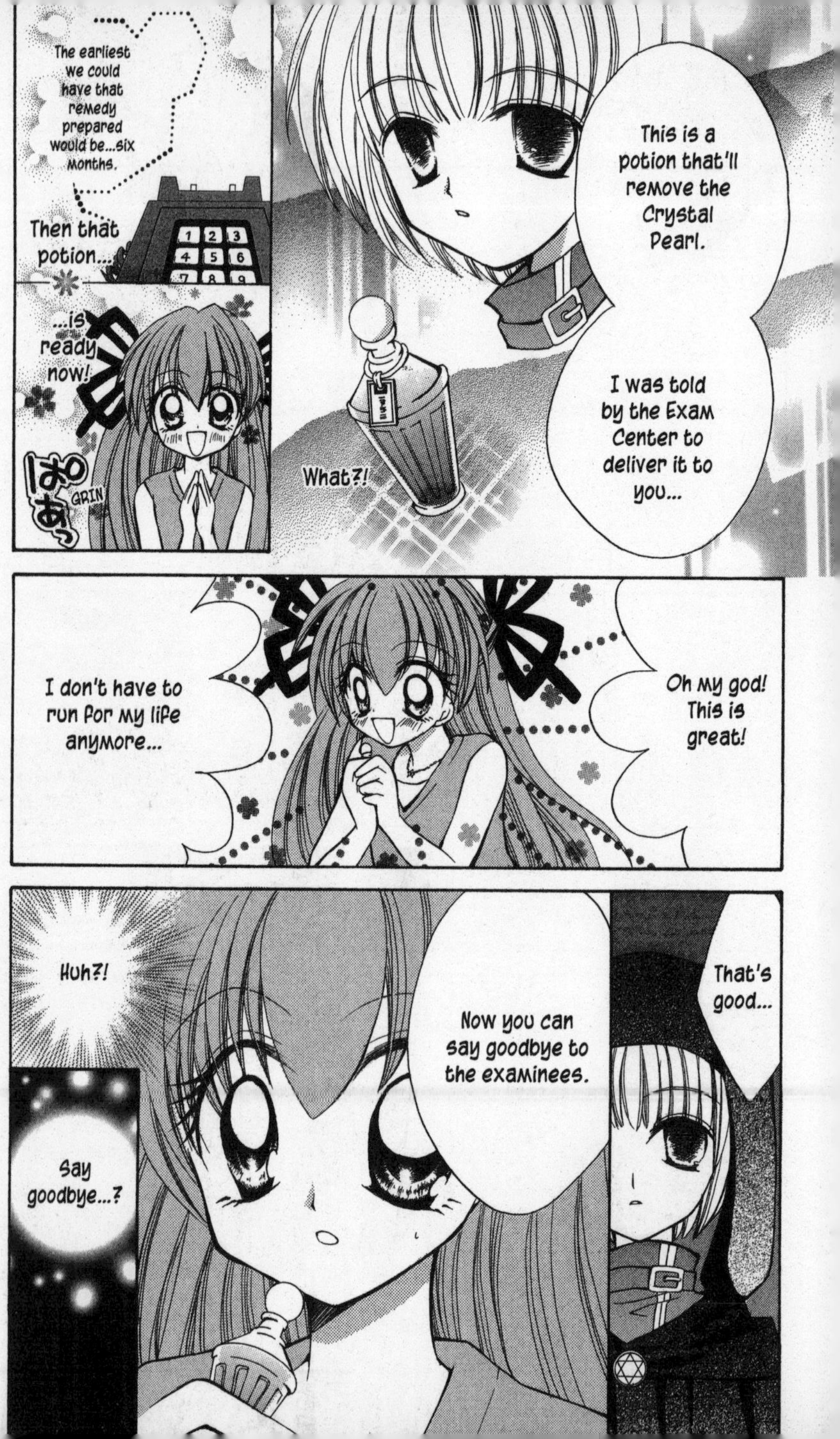
This is a potion that'll remove the Crystal Pearl.
I was told by the Exam Center to deliver it to you...
What?!
.....
The earliest we could have that remedy prepared would be...six months.
Then that potion...
...is ready now!
ぱあっ
GRIN
Oh my god! This is great!
I don't have to run for my life anymore...
That's good...
Now you can say goodbye to the examinees.
Huh?!
Say goodbye...?

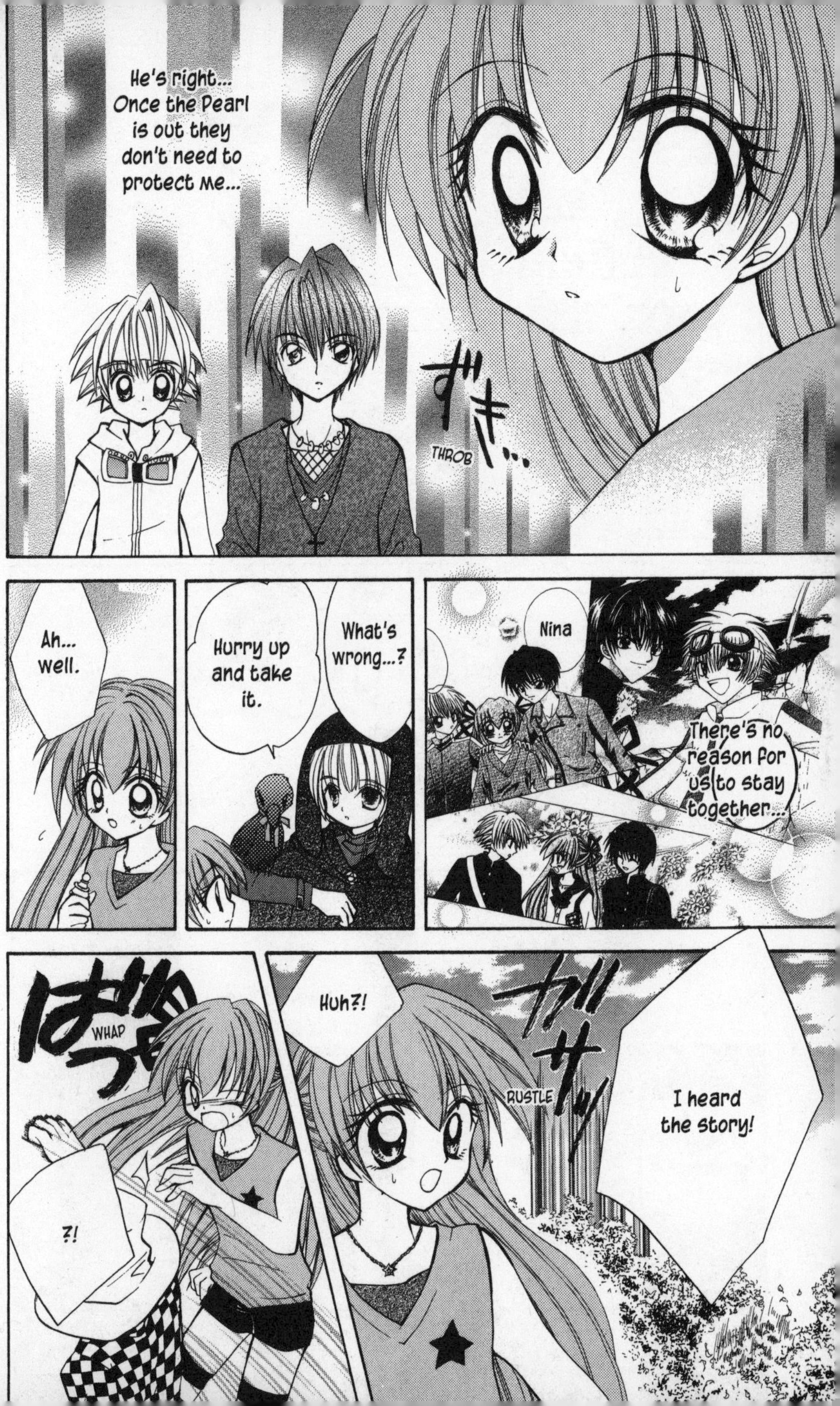
He's right... Once the Pearl is out they don't need to protect me...
THROB
Nina
There's no reason for us to stay together...
What's wrong...?
Hurry up and take it.
Ah... well.
I heard the story!
RUSTLE
Huh?!
WHAP
?!

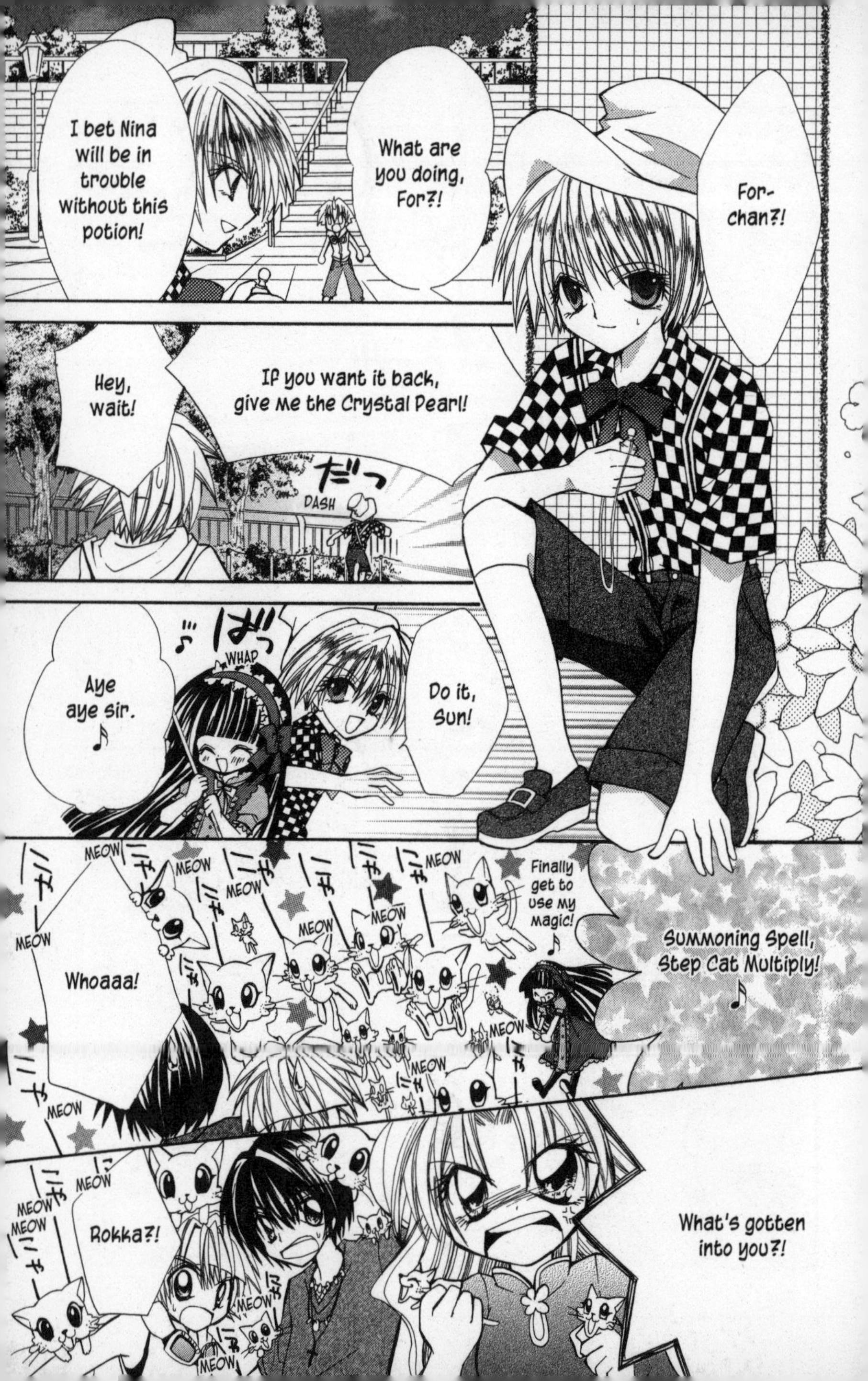
For-chan?!
What are you doing, For?!
I bet Nina will be in trouble without this potion!
If you want it back, give me the Crystal Pearl!
DASH
Hey, wait!
Do it, Sun!
WHAP
Aye aye sir. ♪
Summoning Spell, Step Cat Multiply! ♪
Finally get to use my magic! ♪
MEOW
MEOW
MEOW
MEOW
MEOW
MEOW
MEOW
MEOW
MEOW
MEOW
Whoaaa!
MEOW
What's gotten into you?!
MEOW
MEOW
Rokka?!
MEOW
MEOW
MEOW

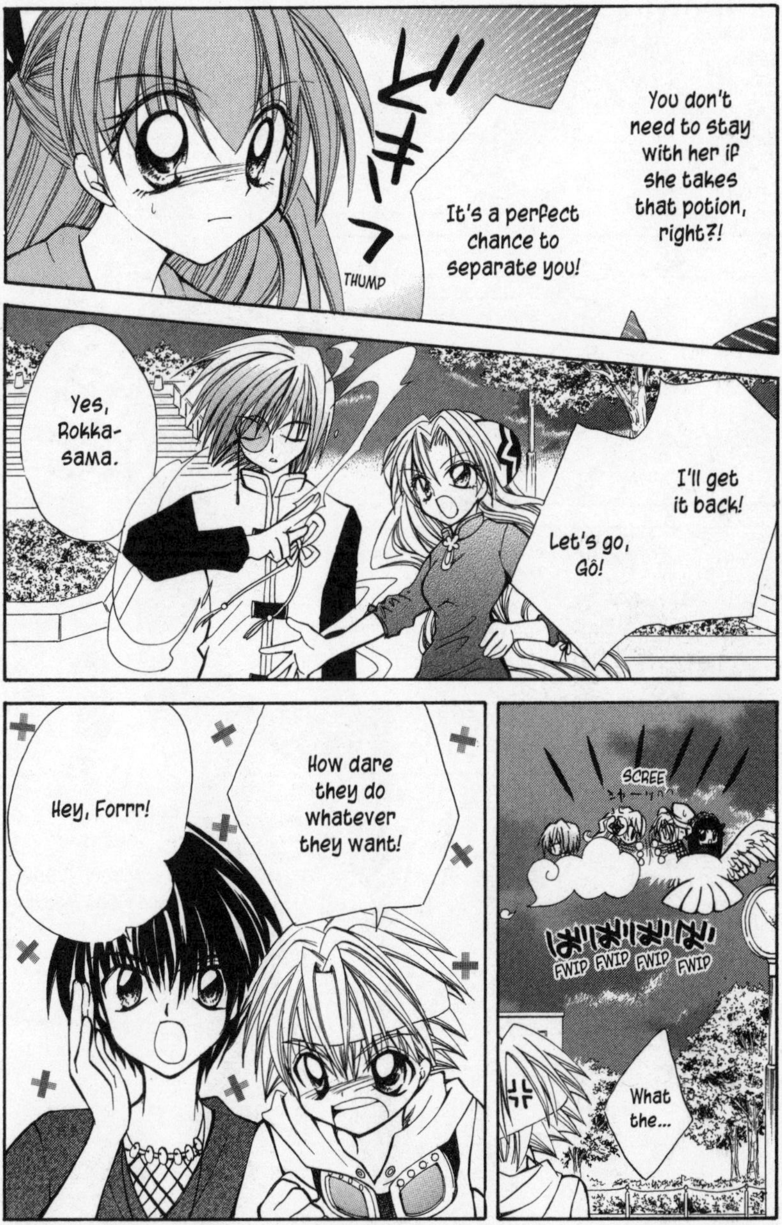
You don't need to stay with her if she takes that potion, right?!
It's a perfect chance to separate you!
THUMP
I'll get it back!
Let's go, Gô!
Yes, Rokka-sama.
SCREE
FWIP FWIP FWIP FWIP
What the...
How dare they do whatever they want!
Hey, Forrr!

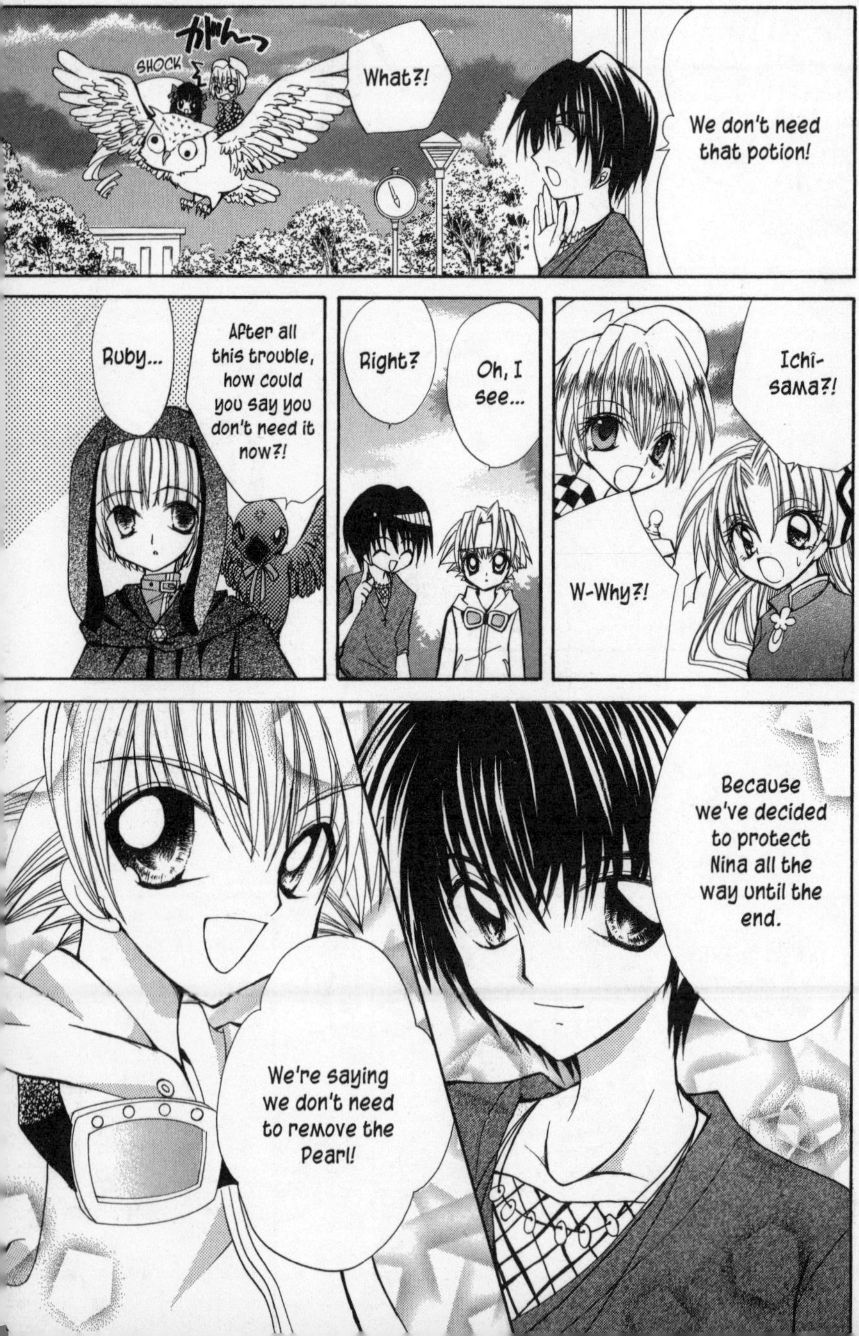
We don't need that potion!
がんっ
SHOCK
What?!
Ichi-sama?!
W-Why?!
Oh, I see...
Right?
After all this trouble, how could you say you don't need it now?!
Ruby...
Because we've decided to protect Nina all the way until the end.
We're saying we don't need to remove the Pearl!

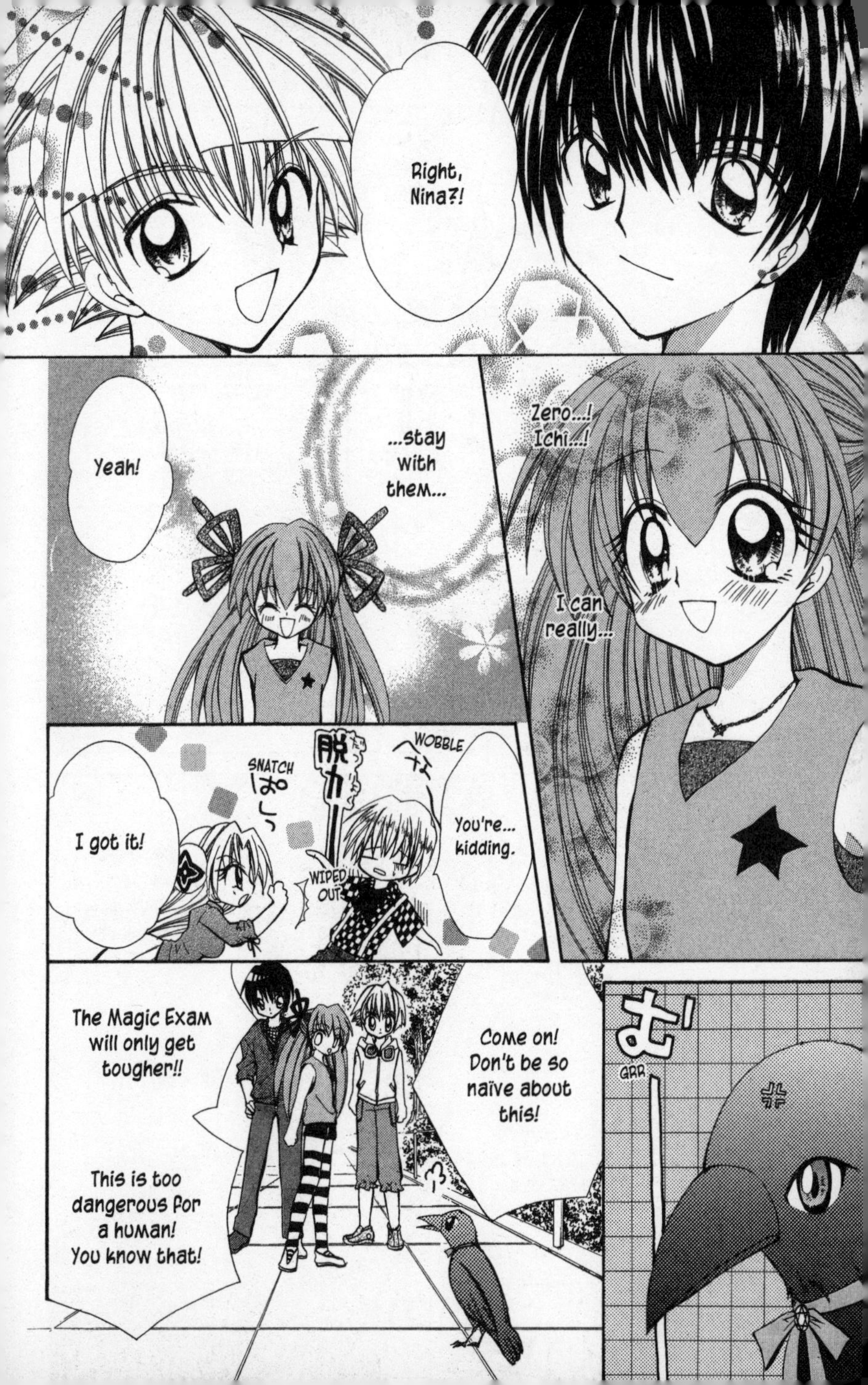
Right, Nina?!
Zero...! Ichi...!
I can really...
...stay with them...
Yeah!
WOBBLE
You're... kidding.
脱力
WIPED OUT
SNATCH
I got it!
むっ
GRR
Come on! Don't be so naïve about this!
The Magic Exam will only get tougher!!
This is too dangerous for a human! You know that!

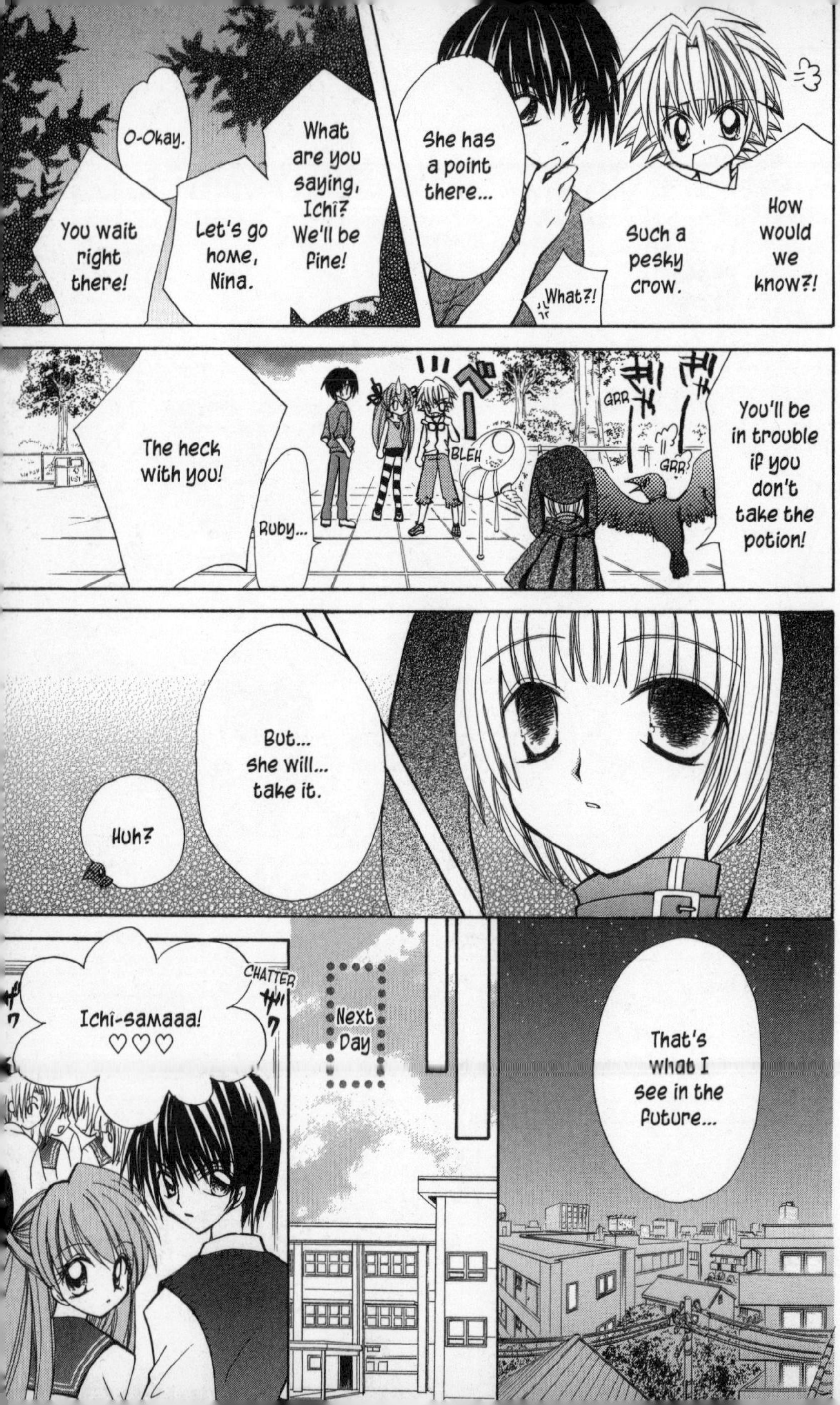
How would we know?!
Such a pesky crow.
What?!
She has a point there...
What are you saying, Ichî? We'll be fine!
Let's go home, Nina.
O-Okay.
You wait right there!
You'll be in trouble if you don't take the potion!
GRR
GRR
BLEH
Ruby...
The heck with you!
But... she will... take it.
Huh?
That's what I see in the future...
Next Day
CHATTER
Ichî-samaaa! ♡♡♡

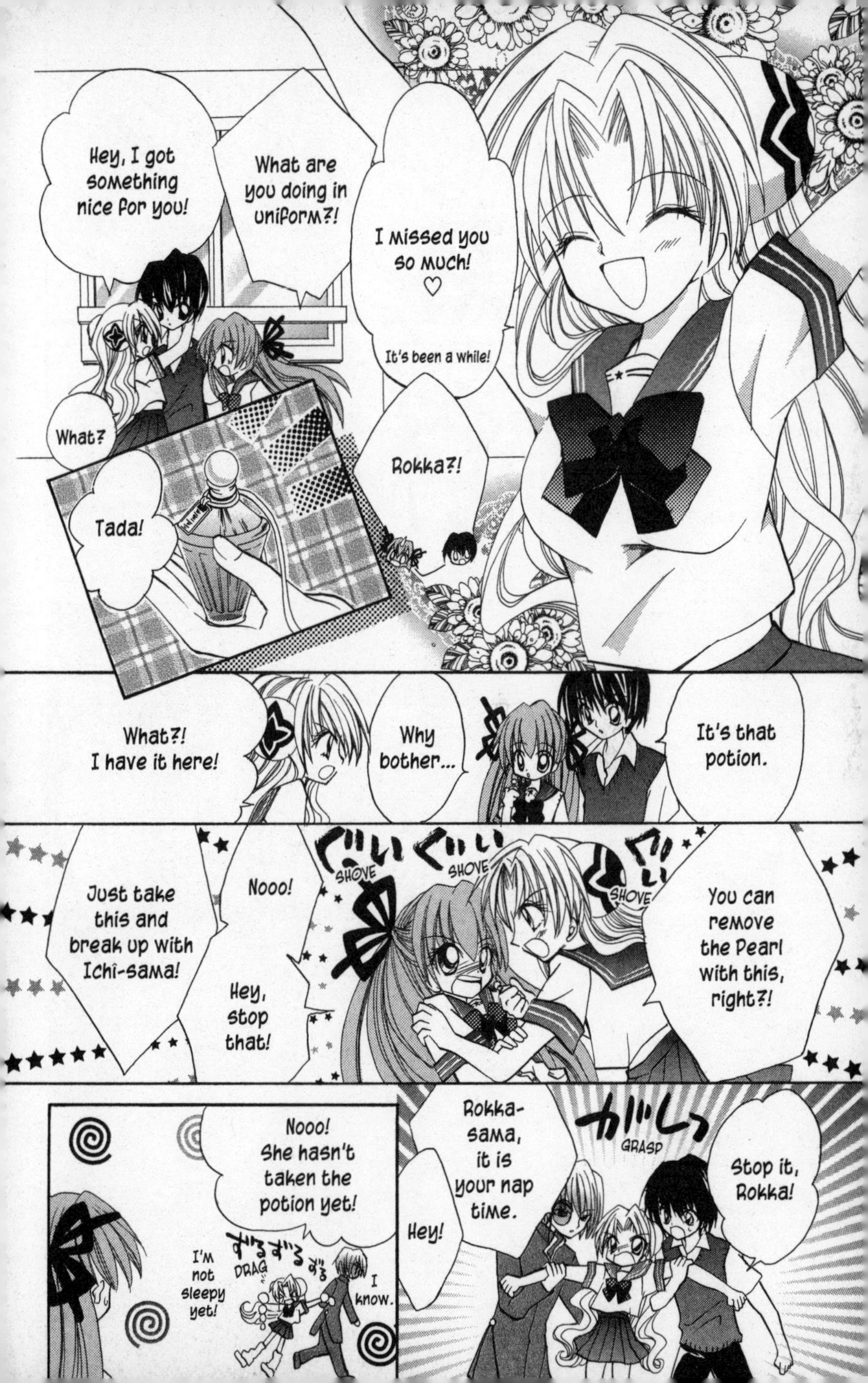
I missed you so much! ♡
It's been a while!
Rokka?!
What are you doing in uniform?!
Hey, I got something nice for you!
What?
Tada!
It's that potion.
Why bother...
What?! I have it here!
You can remove the Pearl with this, right?!
SHOVE
SHOVE
SHOVE
Nooo!
Hey, stop that!
Just take this and break up with Ichi-sama!
Stop it, Rokka!
GRASP
Rokka-sama, it is your nap time.
Hey!
Nooo! She hasn't taken the potion yet!
I know.
DRAG
I'm not sleepy yet!

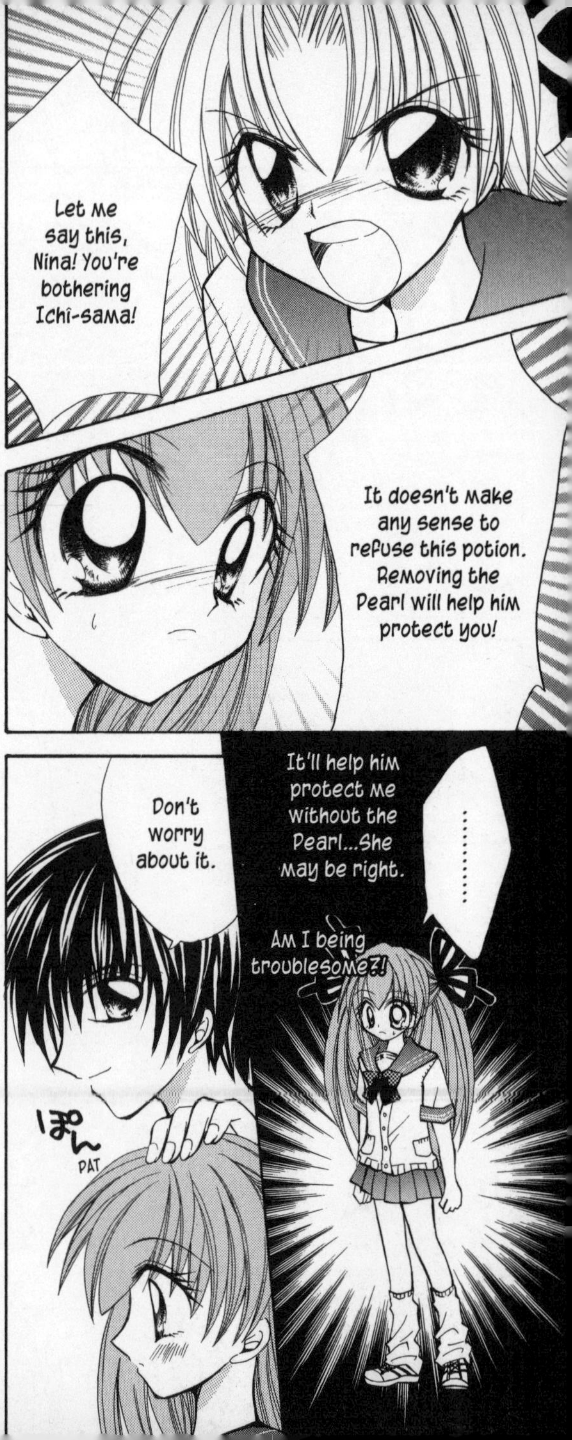

Let me say this, Nina! You're bothering Ichî-sama!
It doesn't make any sense to refuse this potion. Removing the Pearl will help him protect you!
It'll help him protect me without the Pearl...She may be right.
......
Am I being troublesome?!
Don't worry about it.
ぽん
PAT

Hello!

Hello to those I'm meeting for the first time and to those I'm not!! This is Michiyo Kikuta.

Mamotte! Lollipop volume 4 is out! I put out three manga books in 2004! That's great!

Once again, I'm including new inserts, free talks, four-frame manga, requested illustrations and character profiles. There are many bonus stories in this volume! This is all due to your support. Thank you.

Now I hope you'll like this volume. Enjoy.

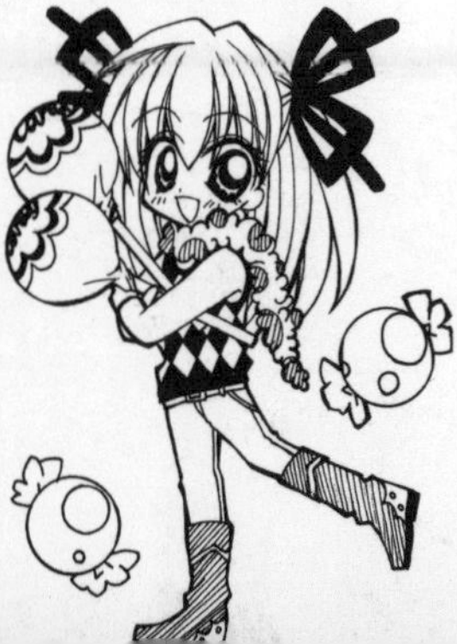

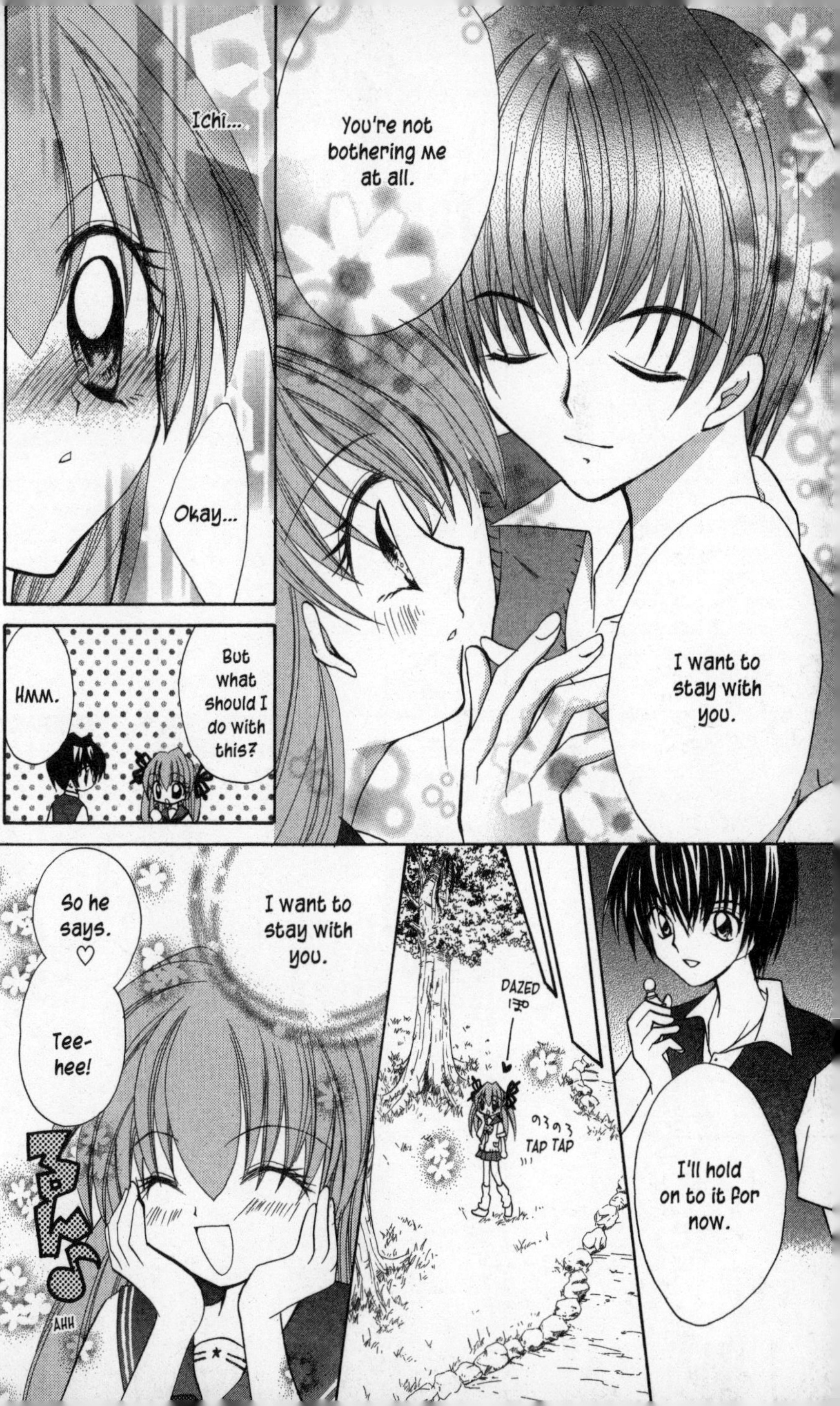
You're not bothering me at all.
I want to stay with you.
Ichi...
Okay...
But what should I do with this?
Hmm.
I'll hold on to it for now.
DAZED
TAP TAP
I want to stay with you.
So he says. ♡
Tee-hee!
AHH

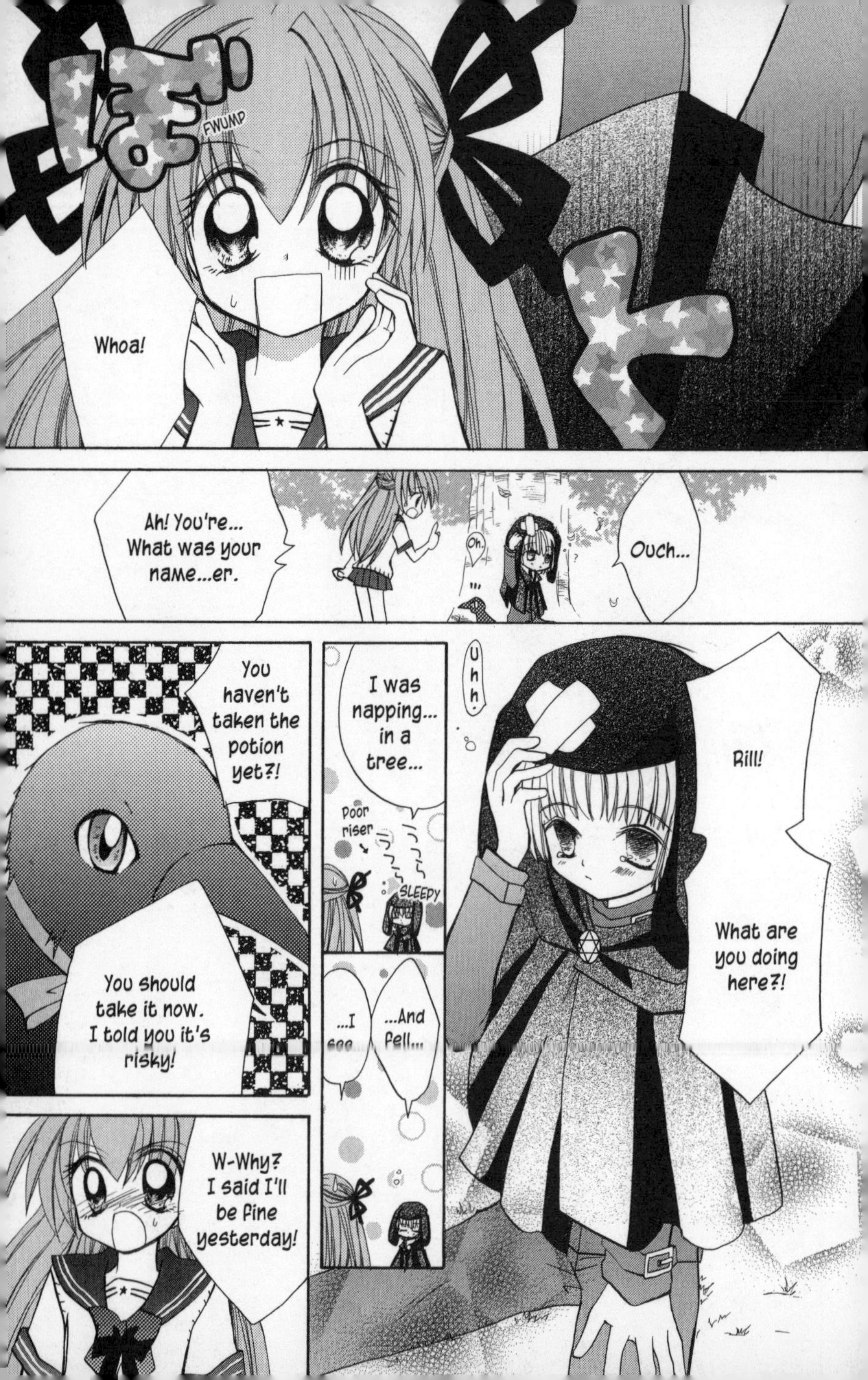
FWUMP
Whoa!
Ouch...
Oh.
...
Ah! You're... What was your name...er.
Uhh.
Rill!
What are you doing here?!
I was napping... in a tree...
Poor riser
SLEEPY
...And fell...
...I see.
You haven't taken the potion yet?!
You should take it now. I told you it's risky!
W-Why? I said I'll be fine yesterday!

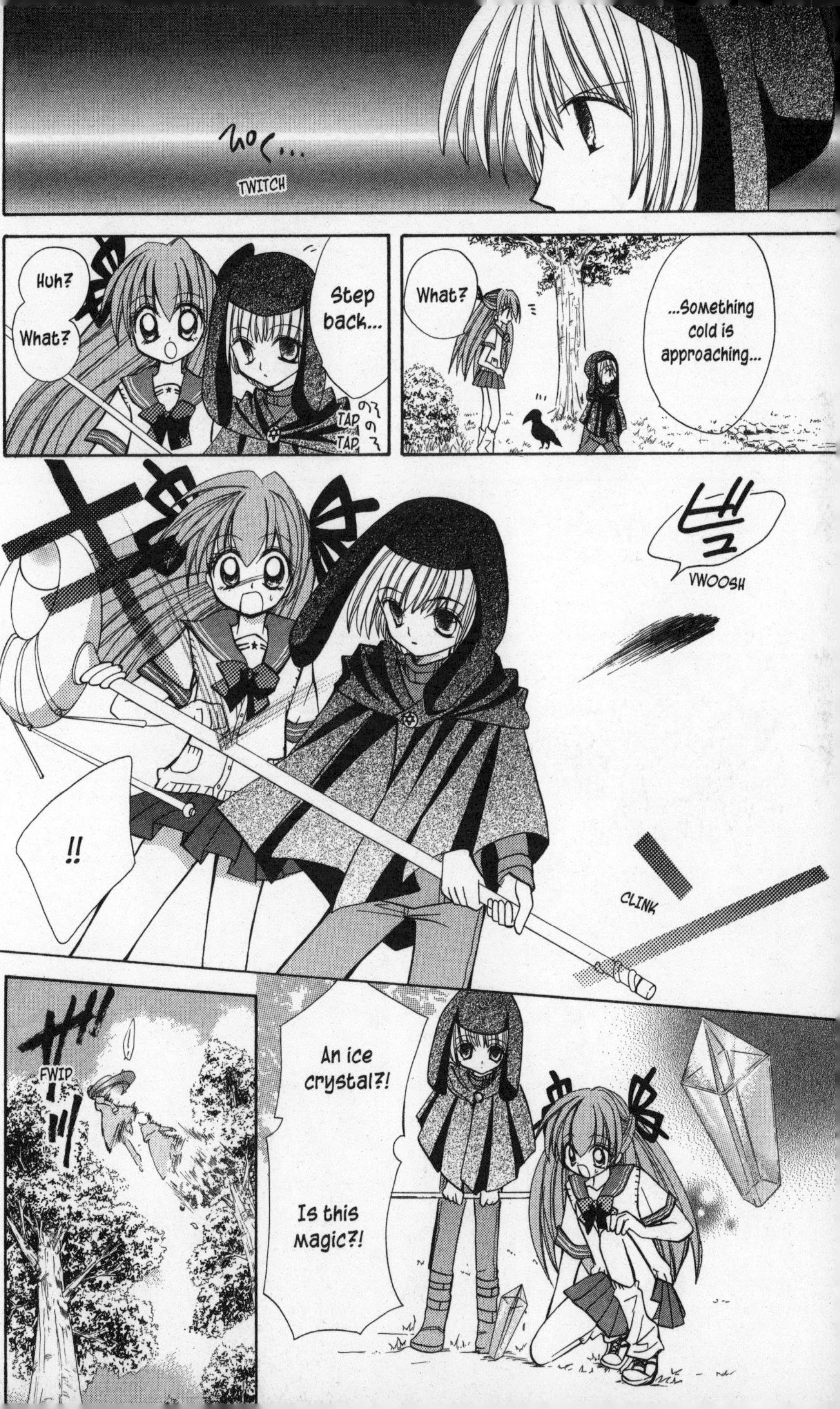
TWITCH
...Something cold is approaching...
What?
Step back...
Huh?
What?
TAP TAP
VWOOSH
!!
CLINK
An ice crystal?!
Is this magic?!
FWIP

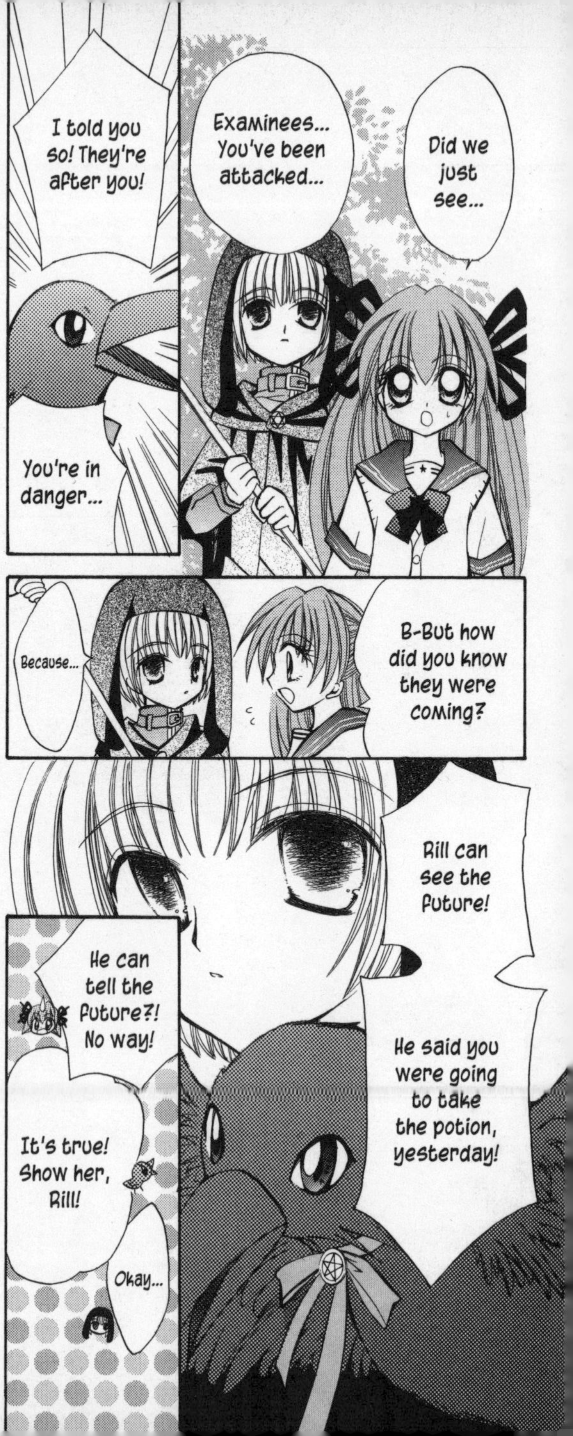
Did we just see...
Examinees... You've been attacked...
I told you so! They're after you!
You're in danger...
B-But how did you know they were coming?
Because...
Rill can see the future!
He said you were going to take the potion, yesterday!
He can tell the future?! No way!
It's true! Show her, Rill!
Okay...

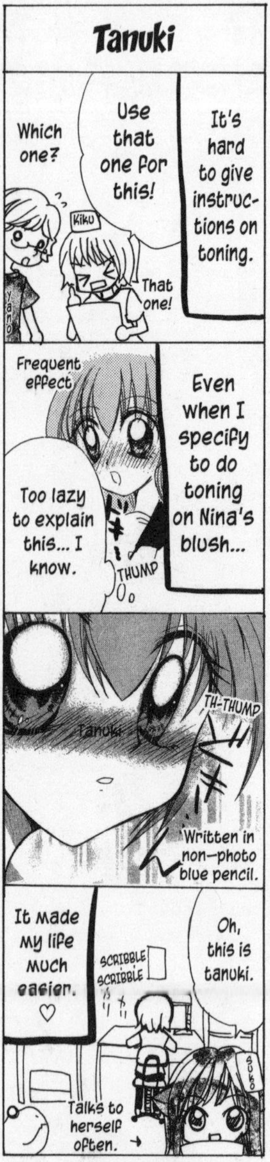
Tanuki
It's hard to give instructions on toning.
Use that one for this!
Which one?
Kiku
Yano
That one!
Even when I specify to do toning on Nina's blush...
Frequent effect
Too lazy to explain this... I know.
THUMP
TH-THUMP
Tanuki
Written in non-photo blue pencil.
Oh, this is tanuki.
It made my life much easier. ♡
SCRIBBLE SCRIBBLE
SUKO
Talks to herself often.

But it appeared lightly on the manga I photocopied at a convenience store.

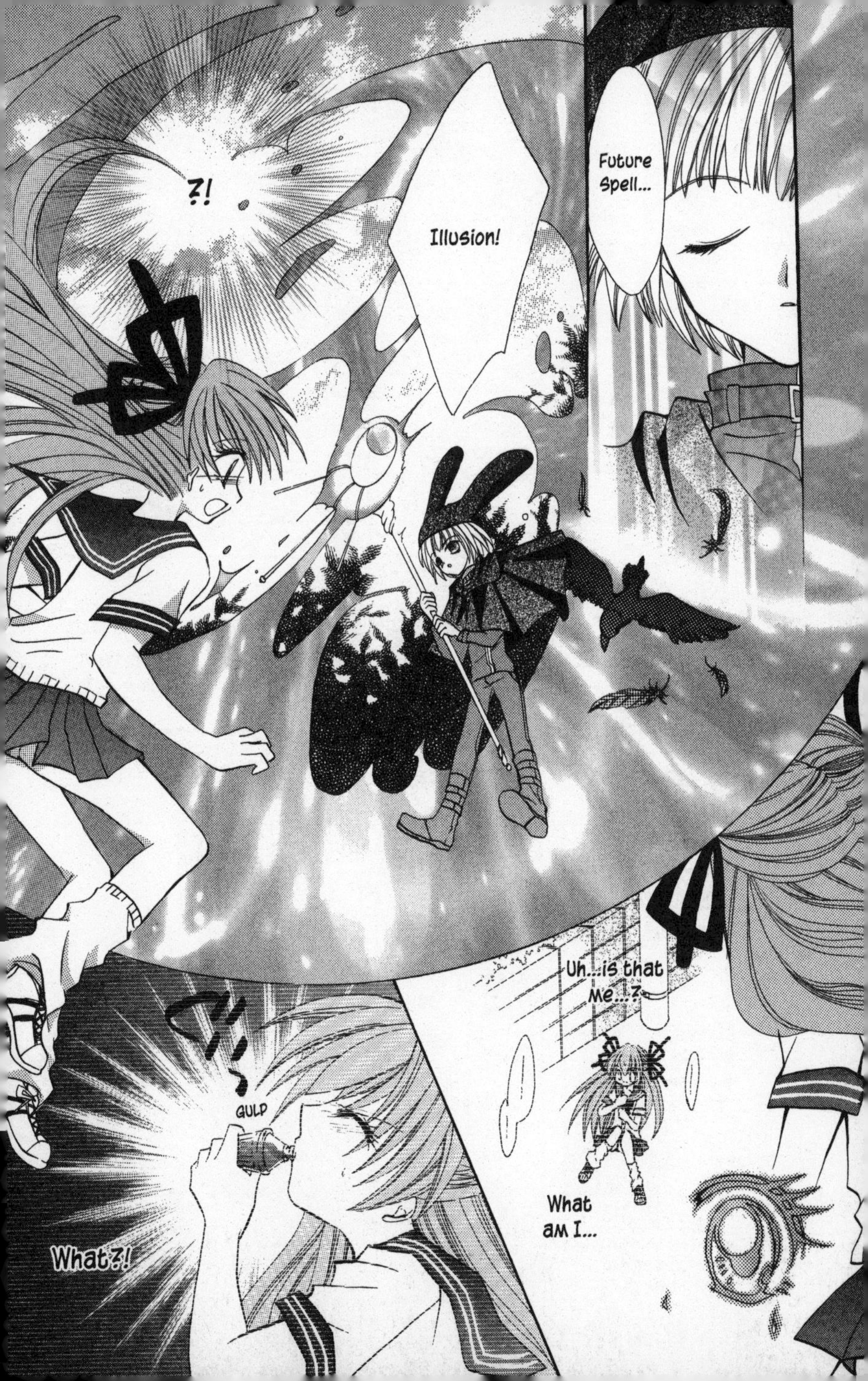
Future Spell...
Illusion!
?!
Uh...is that me...?
What am I...
GULP
What?!

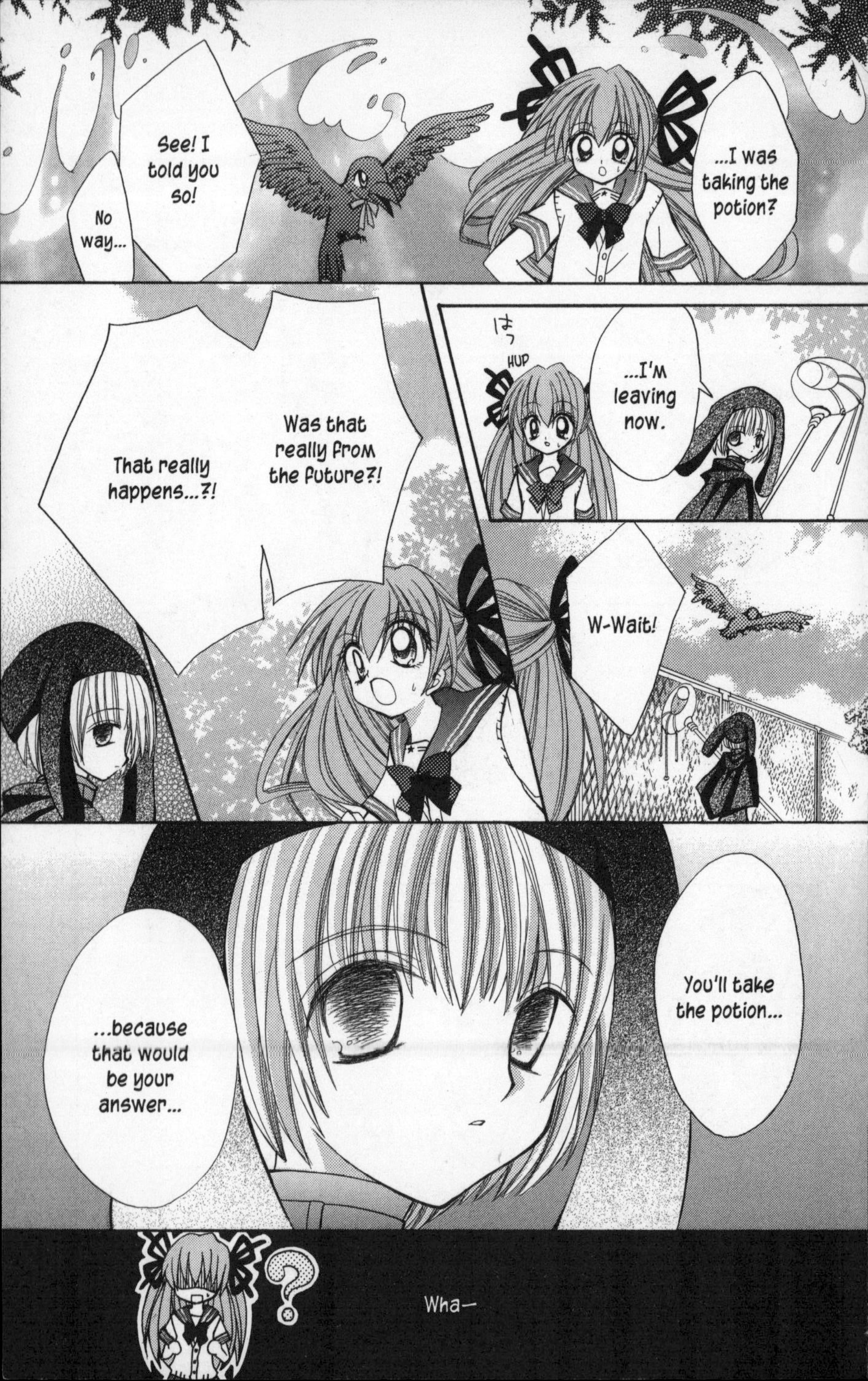
...I was taking the potion?
See! I told you so!
No way...
...I'm leaving now.
はっ
HUP
W-Wait!
Was that really from the future?!
That really happens...?!
You'll take the potion...
...because that would be your answer...
Wha—

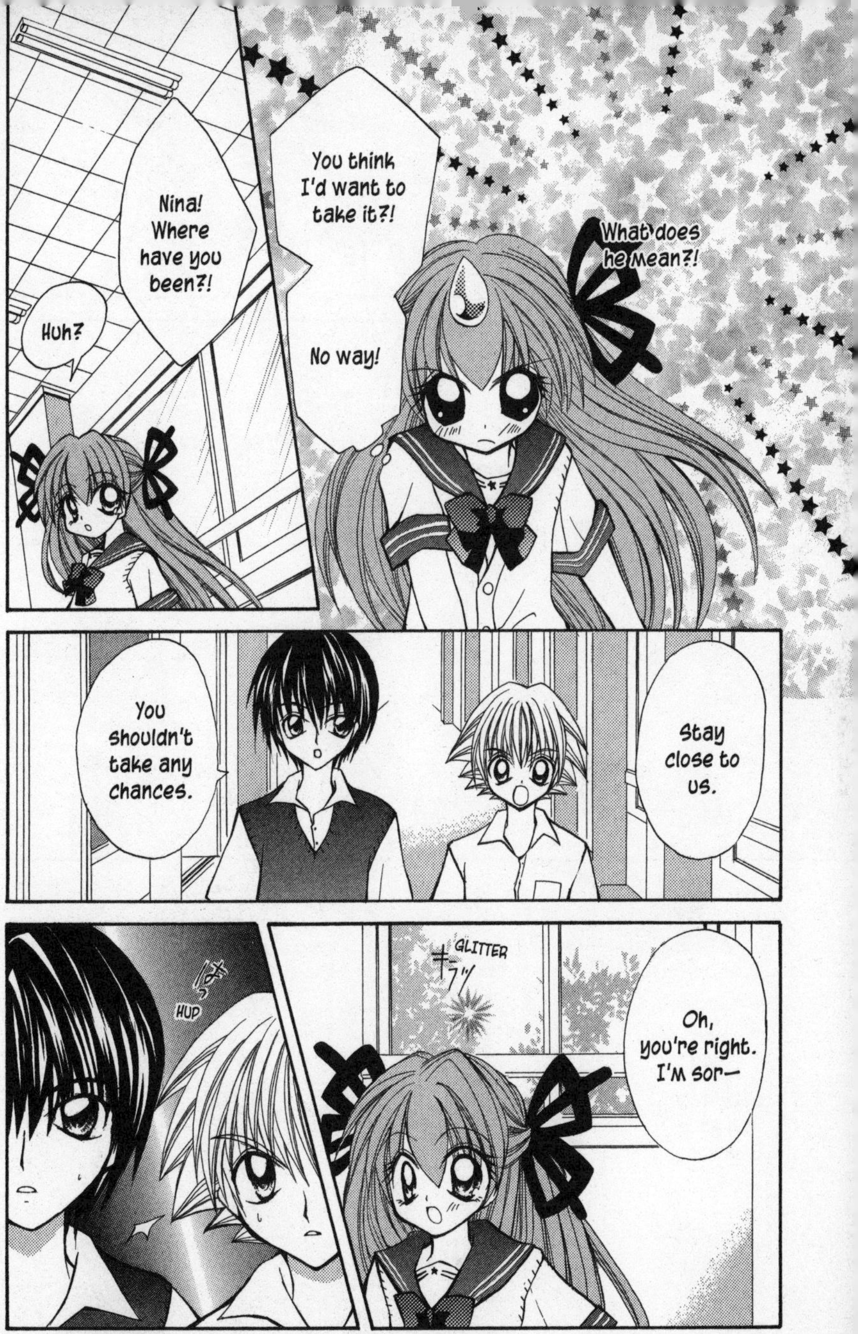
You think I'd want to take it?!
No way!
What does he mean?!
Nina! Where have you been?!
Huh?
Stay close to us.
You shouldn't take any chances.
GLITTER
Oh, you're right. I'm sor—
HUP

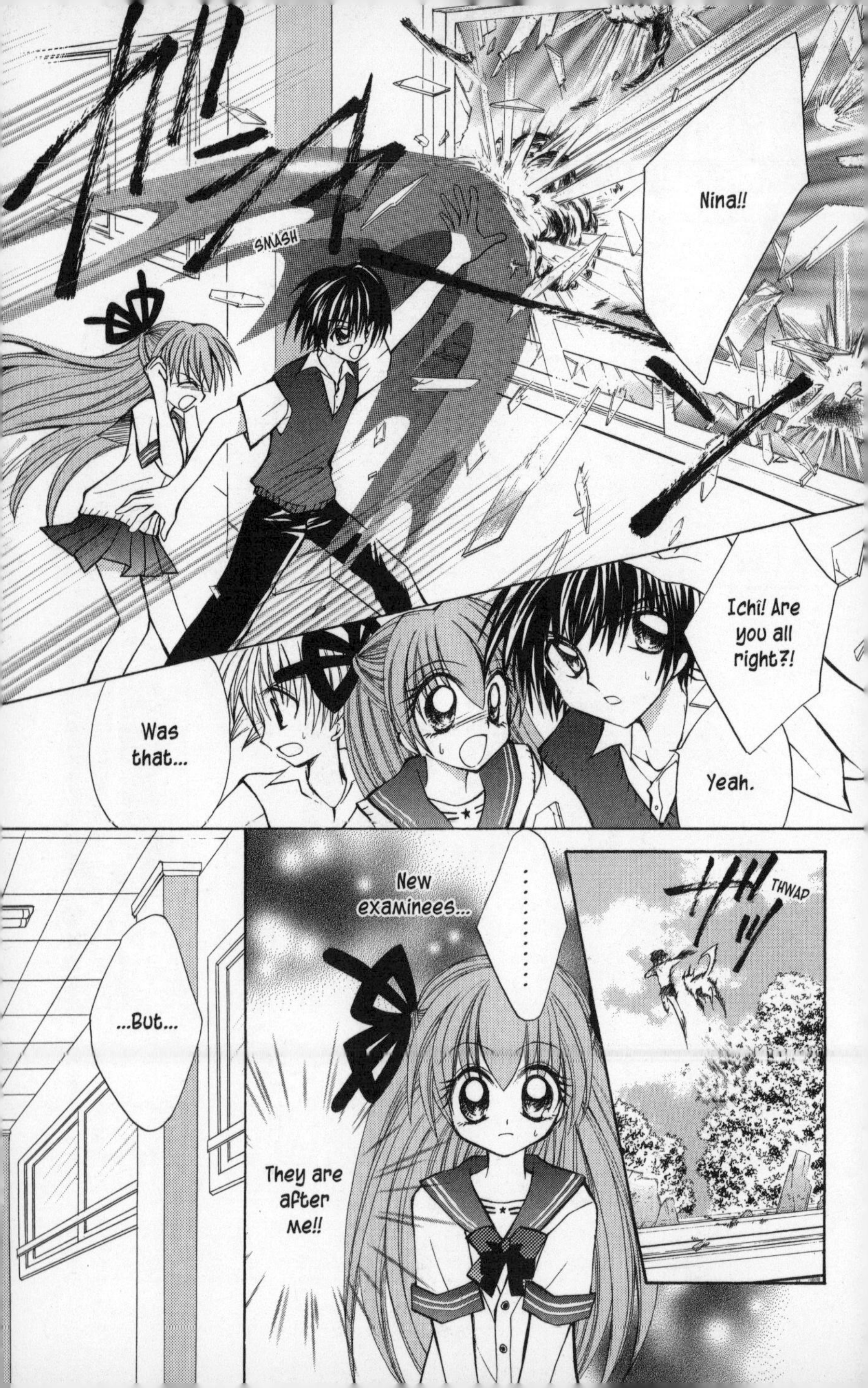

Nina!!
SMASH
Ichi! Are you all right?!
Yeah.
Was that...
THWAP
......
New examinees...
They are after me!!
...But...

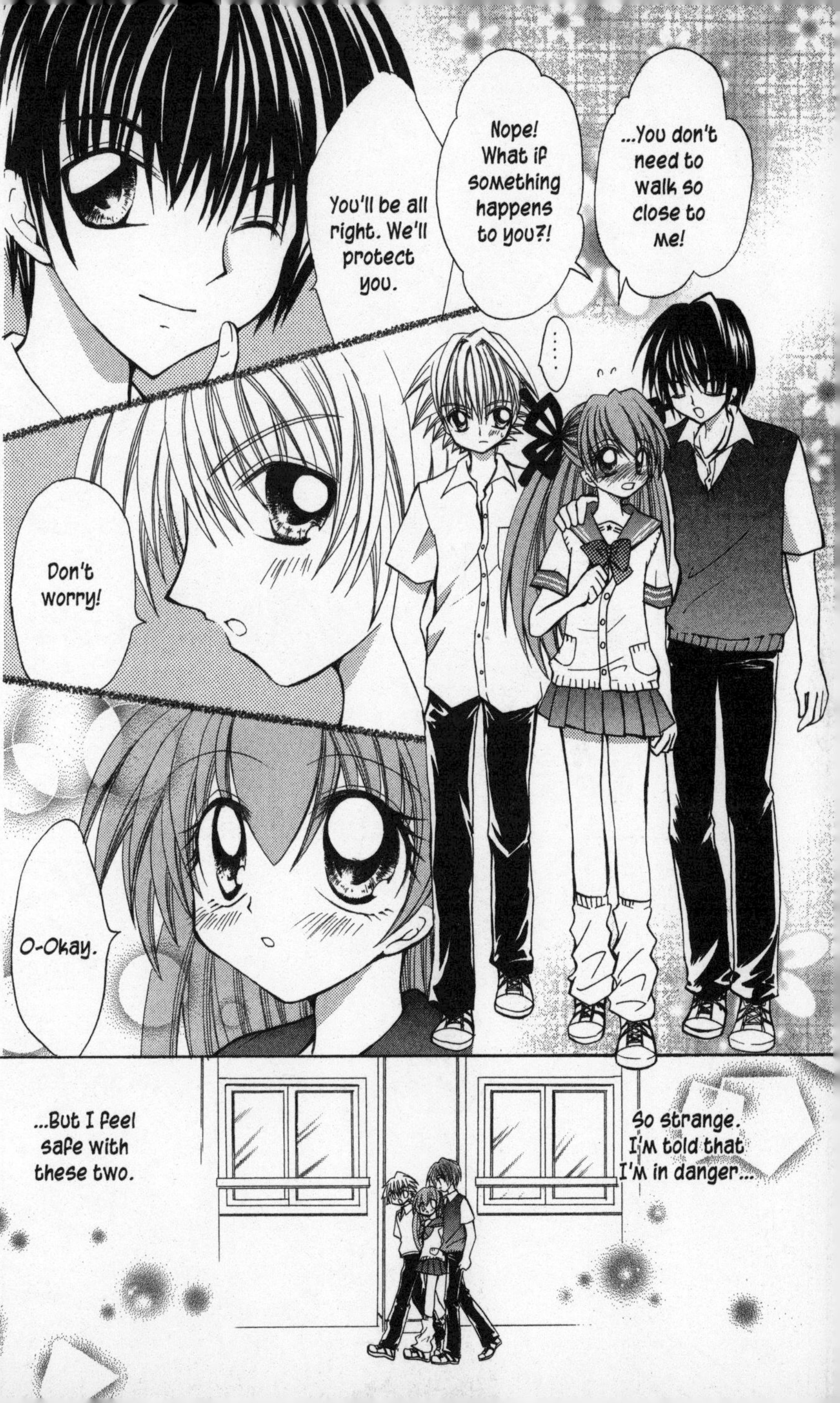
...You don't need to walk so close to me!
Nope! What if something happens to you?!
You'll be all right. We'll protect you.
.....
Don't worry!
O-Okay.
So strange. I'm told that I'm in danger...
...But I feel safe with these two.

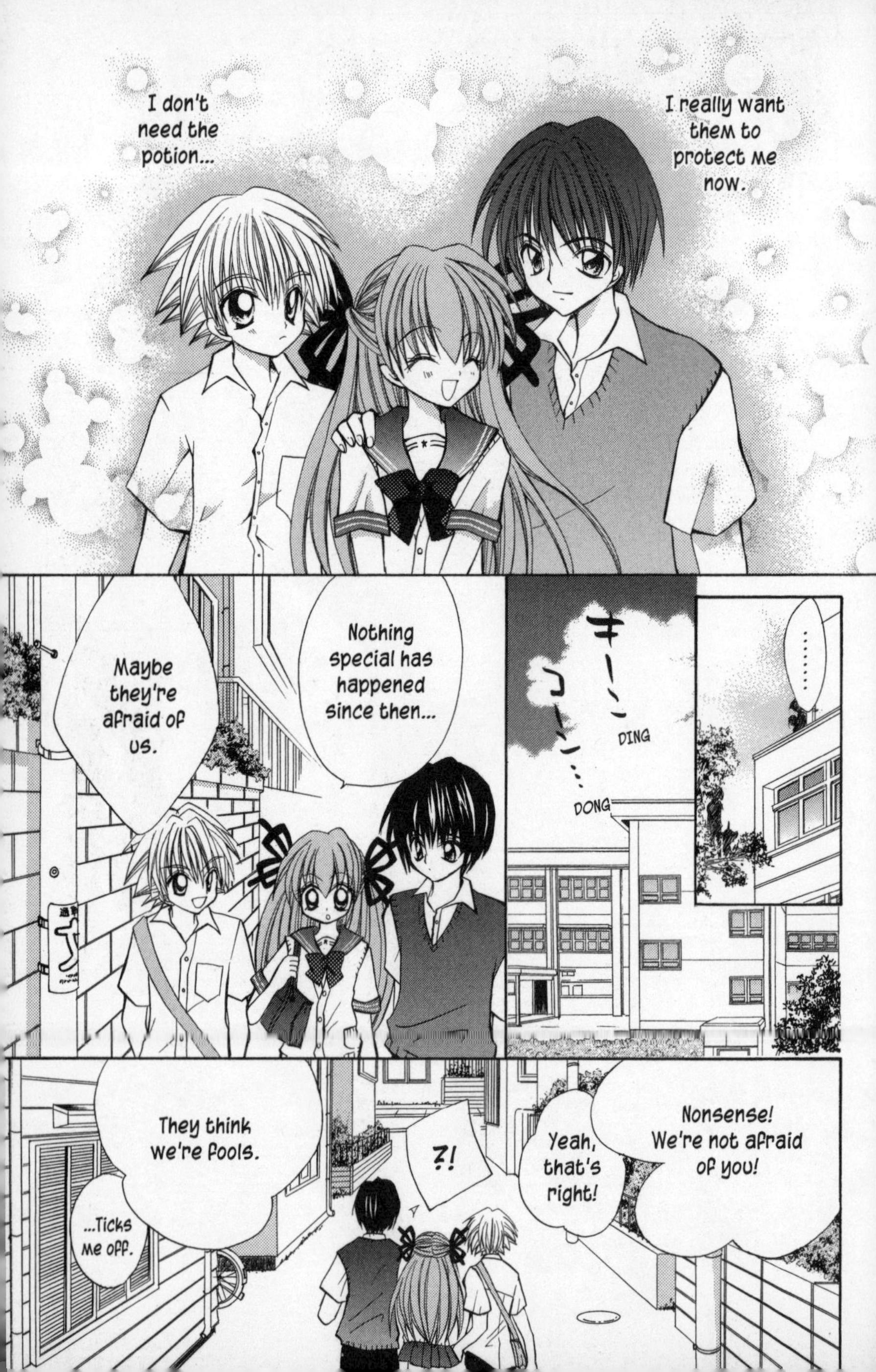
I really want them to protect me now.
I don't need the potion...
......
DING
DONG
Nothing special has happened since then...
Maybe they're afraid of us.
Nonsense! We're not afraid of you!
Yeah, that's right!
?!
They think we're fools.
...Ticks me off.

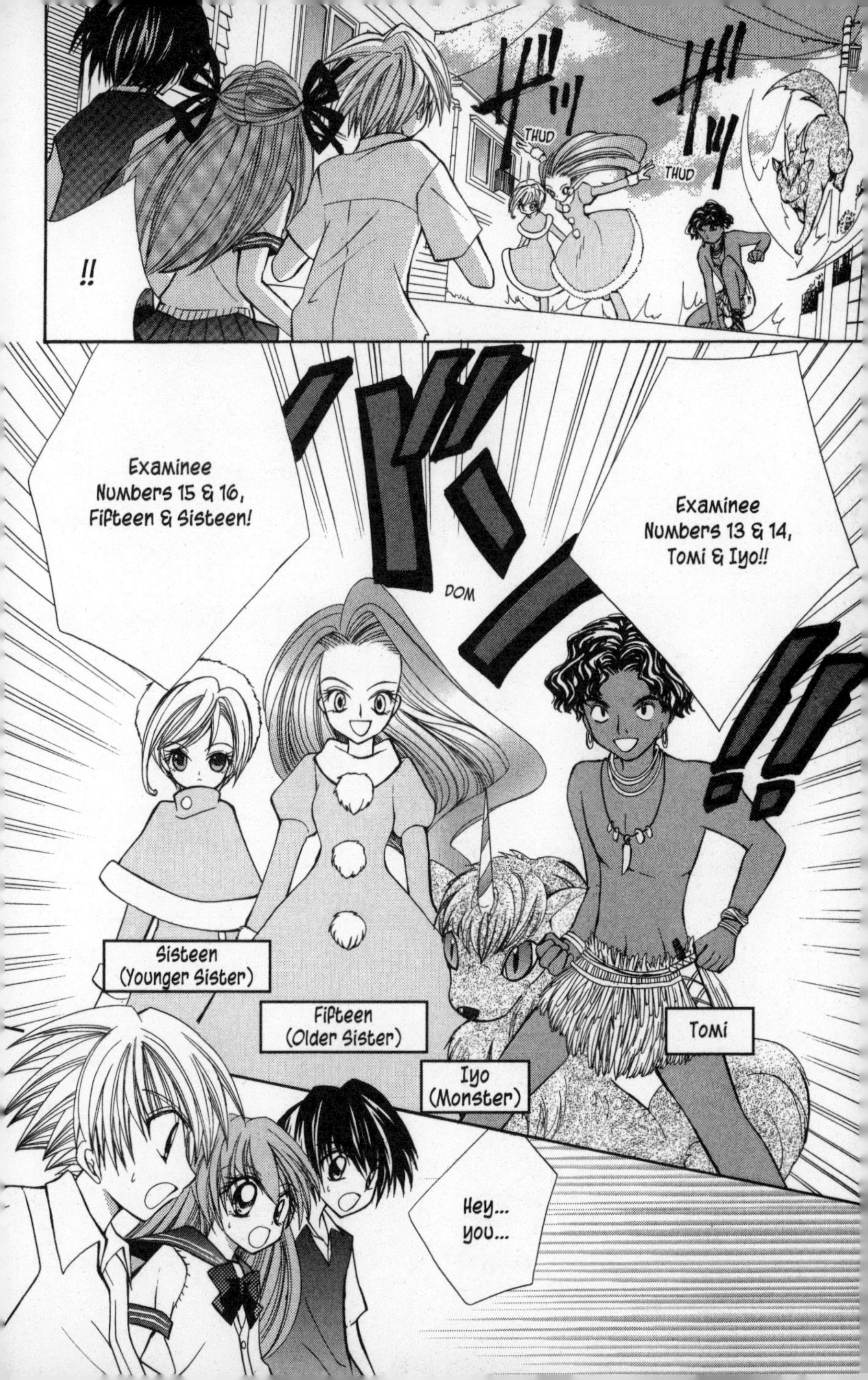
THUD
THUD
!!
Examinee Numbers 13 & 14, Tomi & Iyo!!
DOM
Examinee Numbers 15 & 16, Fifteen & Sisteen!
Tomi
Iyo (Monster)
Fifteen (Older Sister)
Sisteen (Younger Sister)
Hey... you...

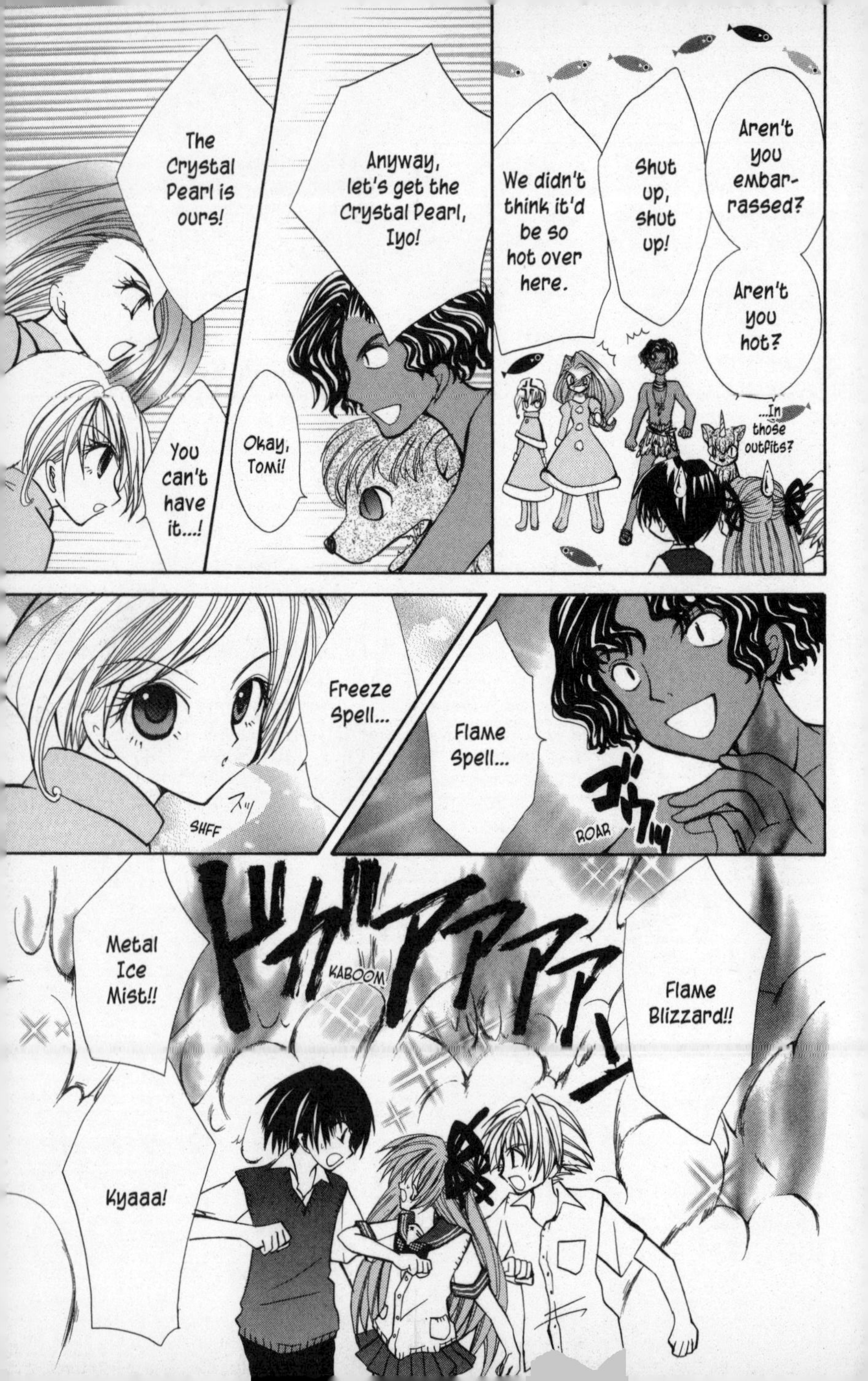

Aren't you embarrassed?
Aren't you hot?
...In those outfits?
Shut up, shut up!
We didn't think it'd be so hot over here.
Anyway, let's get the Crystal Pearl, Iyo!
Okay, Tomi!
The Crystal Pearl is ours!
You can't have it...!
Flame Spell...
ROAR
Freeze Spell...
SHFF
Flame Blizzard!!
KABOOM
Metal Ice Mist!!
Kyaaa!

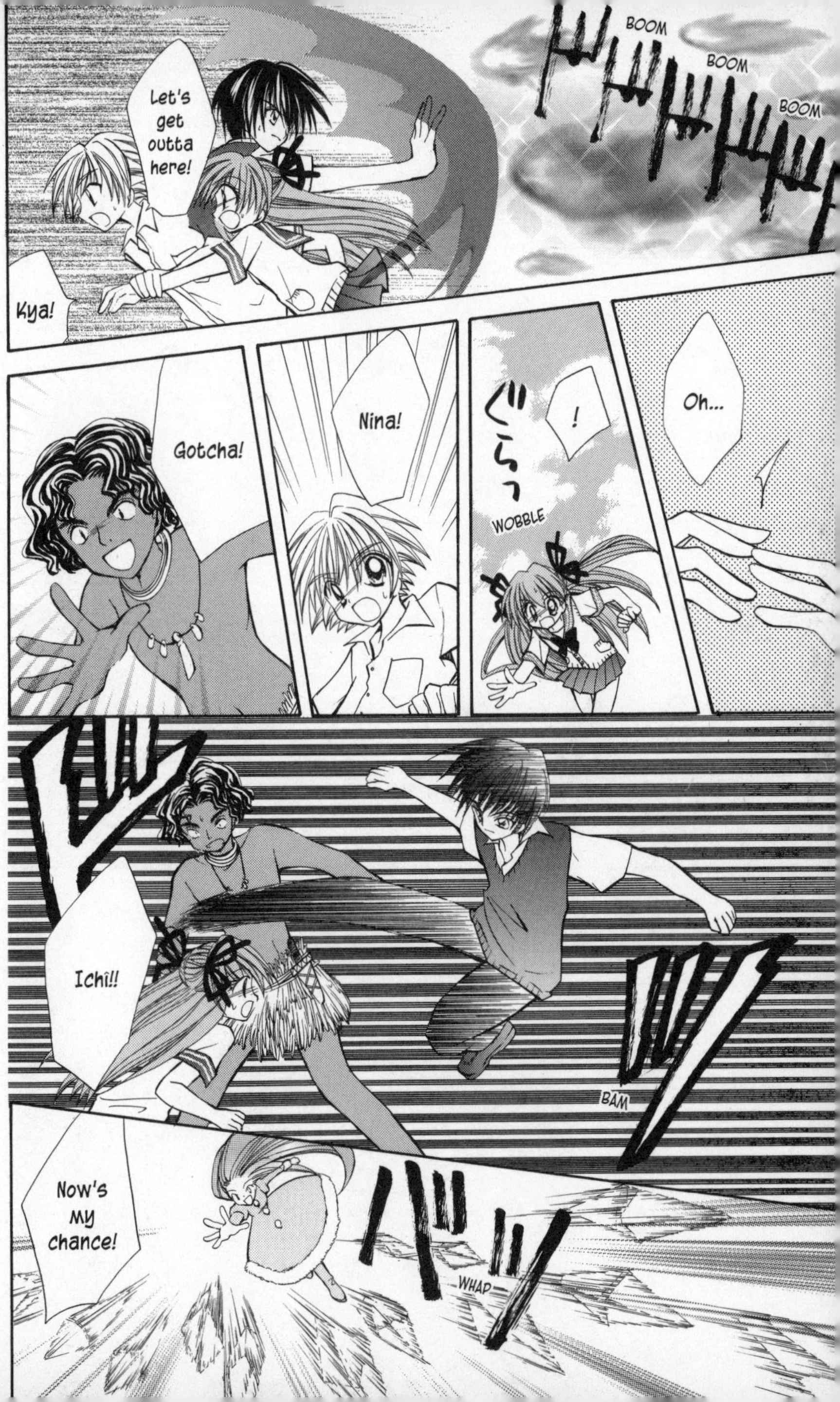
BOOM
BOOM
BOOM
Let's get outta here!
Kya!
Oh...
!
ぐらっ
WOBBLE
Nina!
Gotcha!
BAM
Ichi!!
バッ
WHAP
Now's my chance!

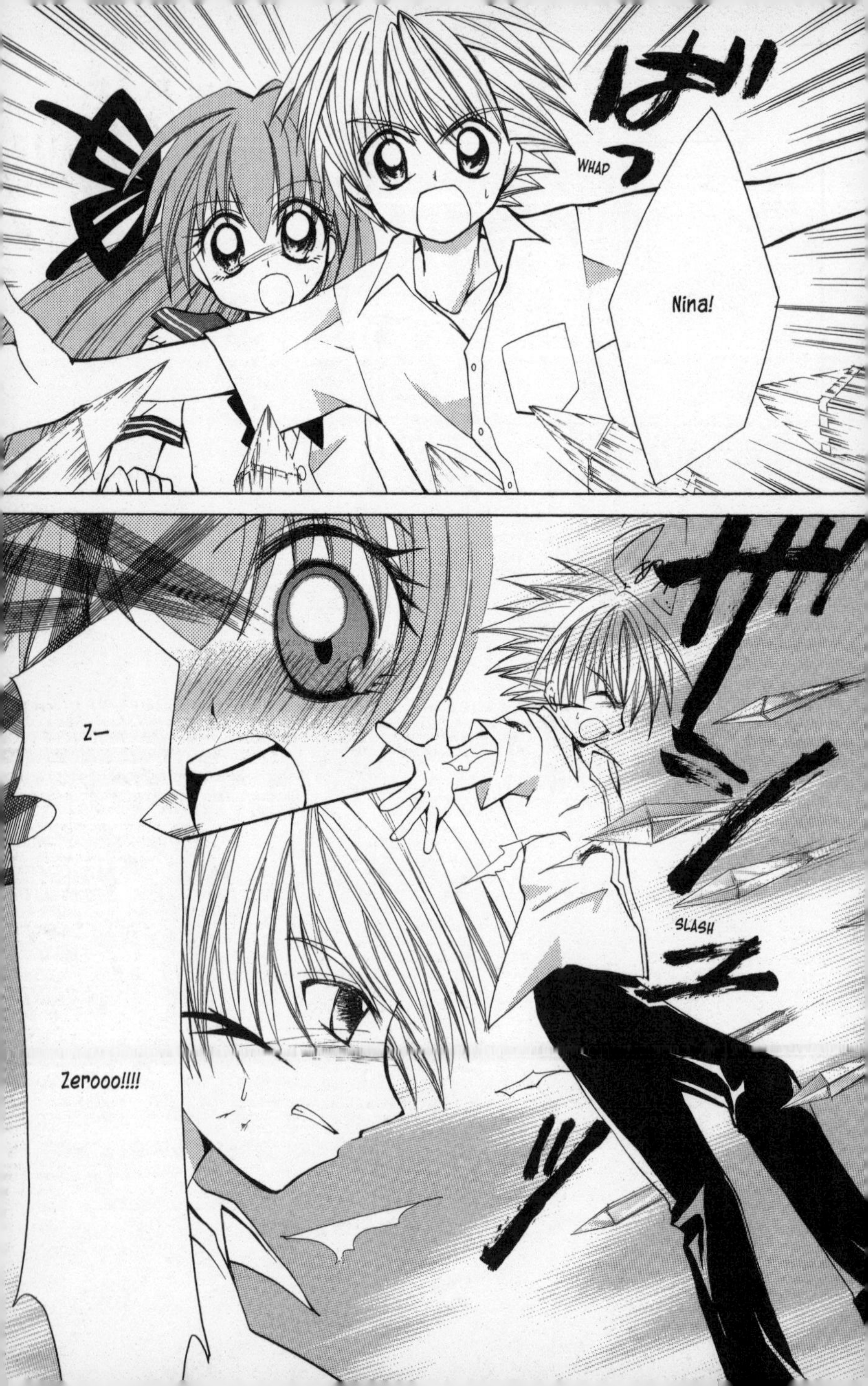
WHAP
Nina!
SLASH
Z—
Zerooo!!!!

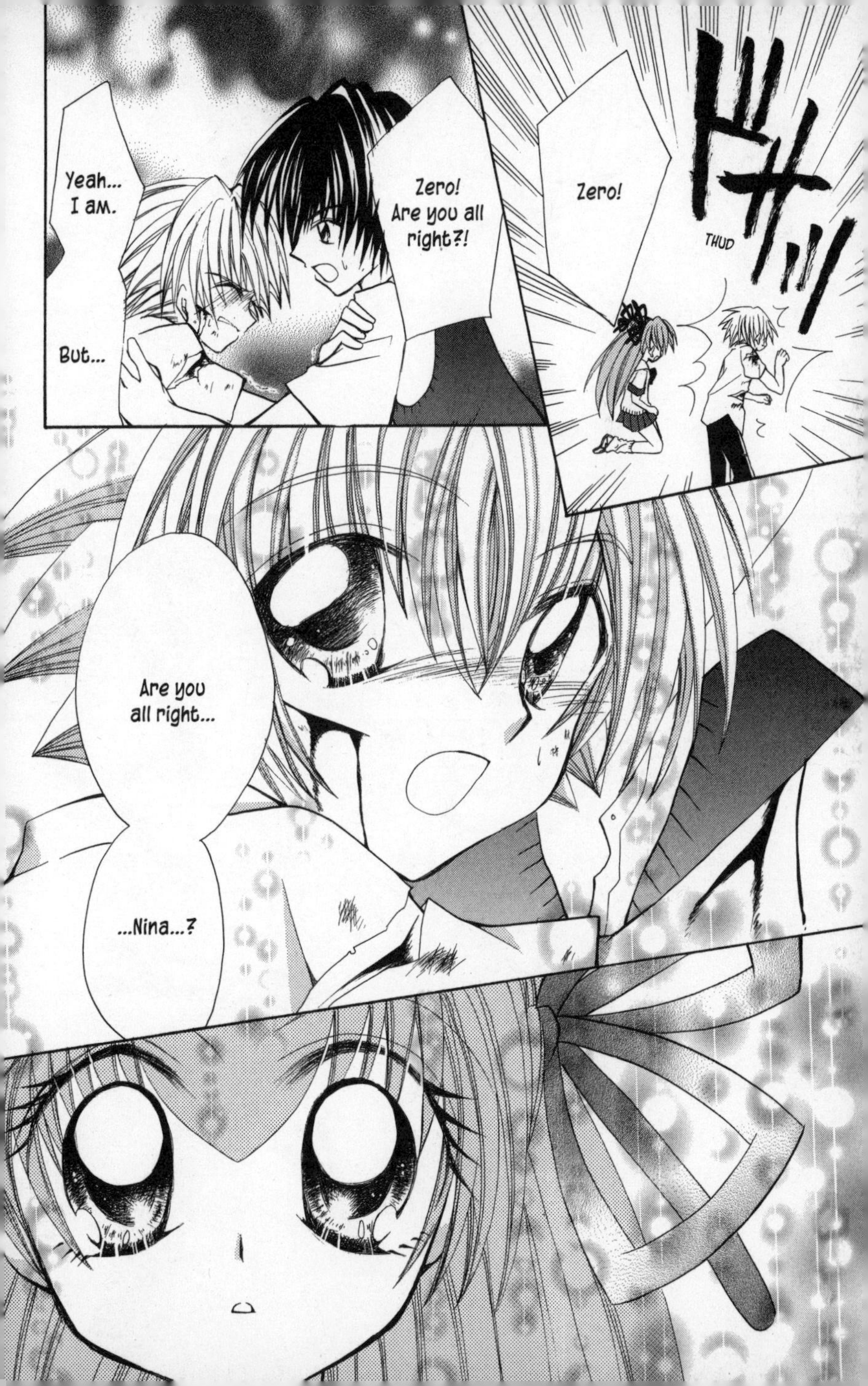
ドサッ
THUD
Zero!
Zero!
Are you all right?!
Yeah...
I am.
But...
Are you all right...
...Nina...?

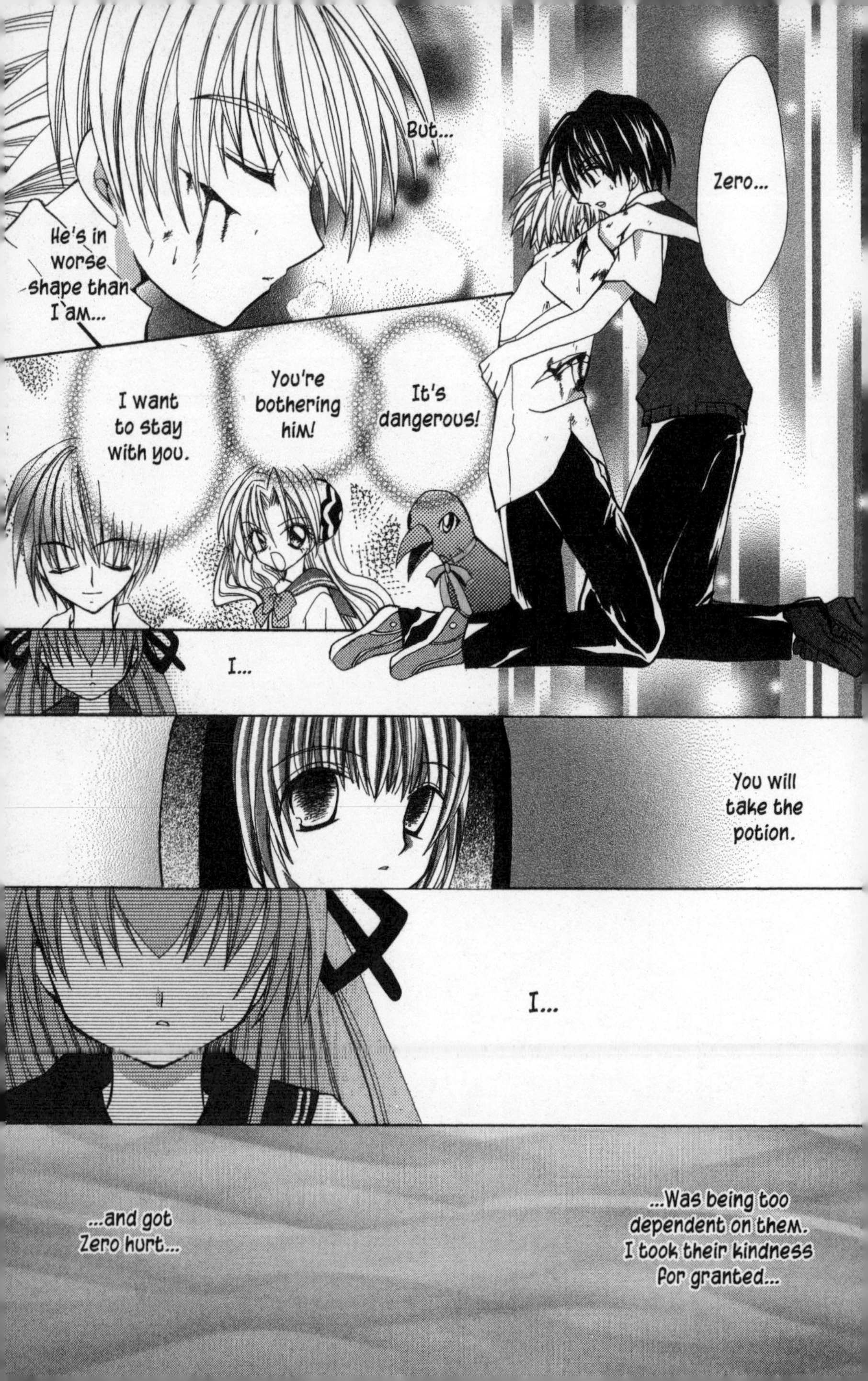
Zero...
But...
He's in worse shape than I am...
It's dangerous!
You're bothering him!
I want to stay with you.
I...
You will take the potion.
I...
...Was being too dependent on them. I took their kindness for granted...
...and got Zero hurt...

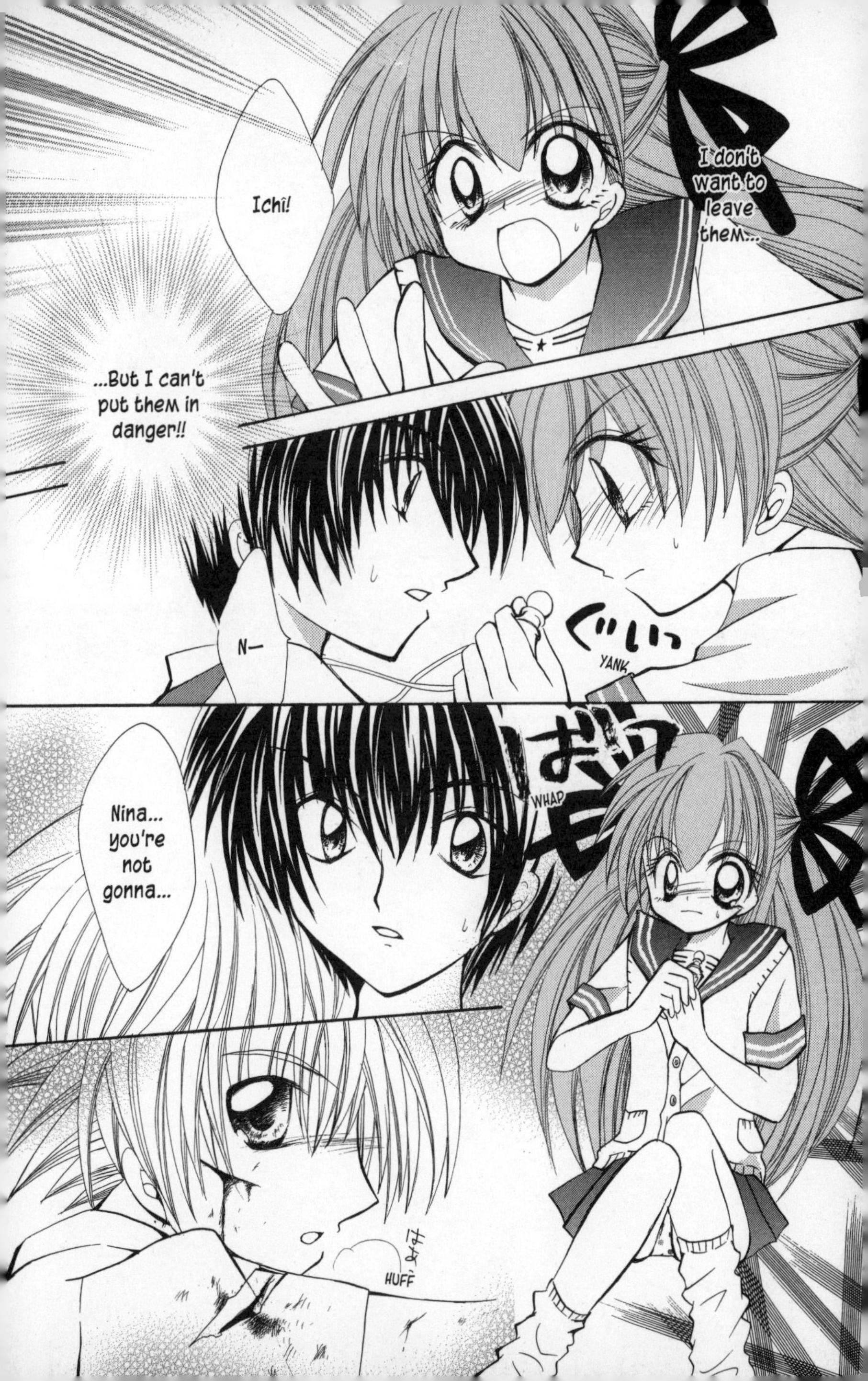
I don't want to leave them...
Ichi!
...But I can't put them in danger!!
ぐいっ
YANK
N—
WHAP
Nina... you're not gonna...
HUFF

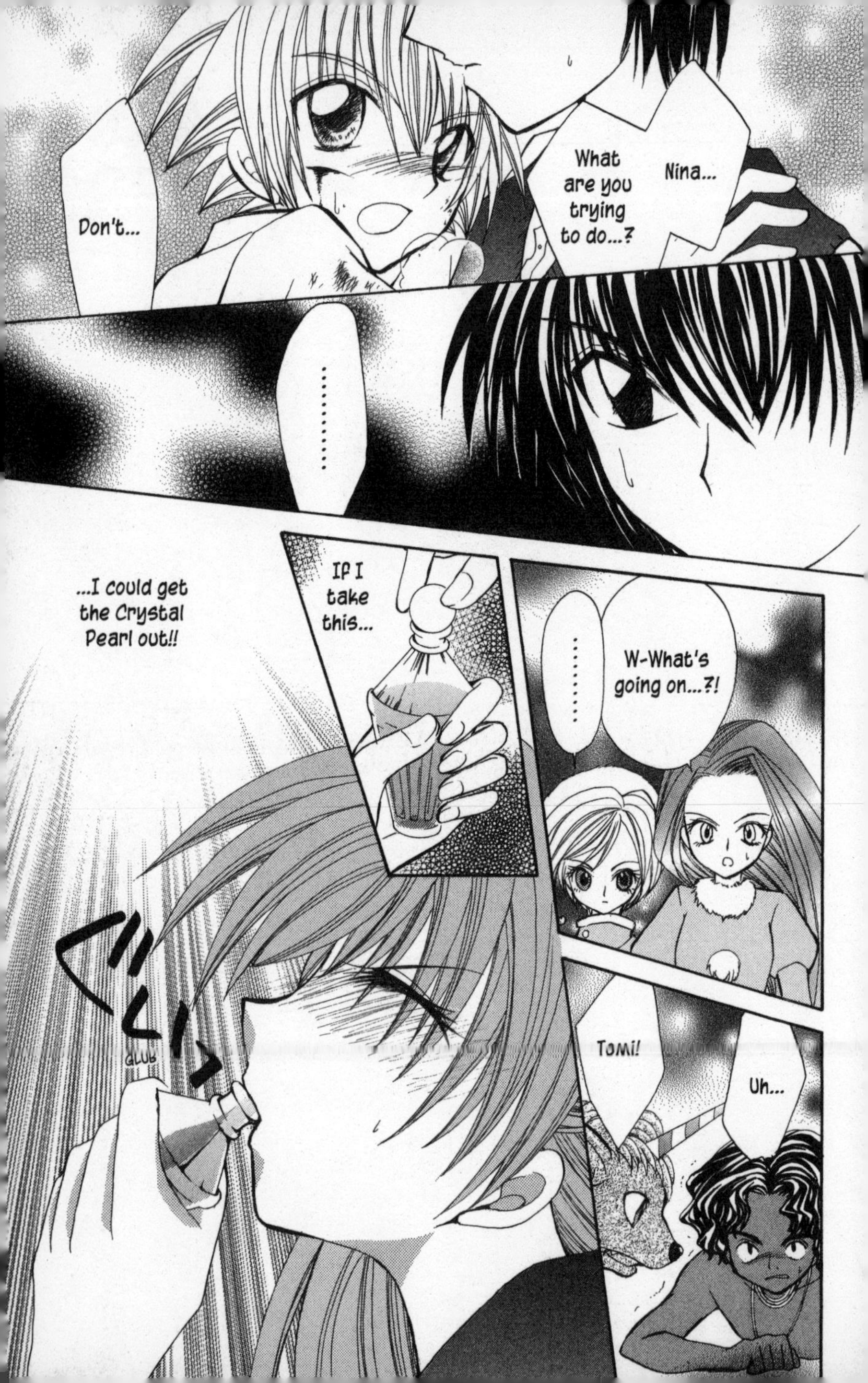
Nina...
What are you trying to do...?
Don't...
....
W-What's going on...?!
......
If I take this...
...I could get the Crystal Pearl out!!
GLUB
Tomi!
Uh...

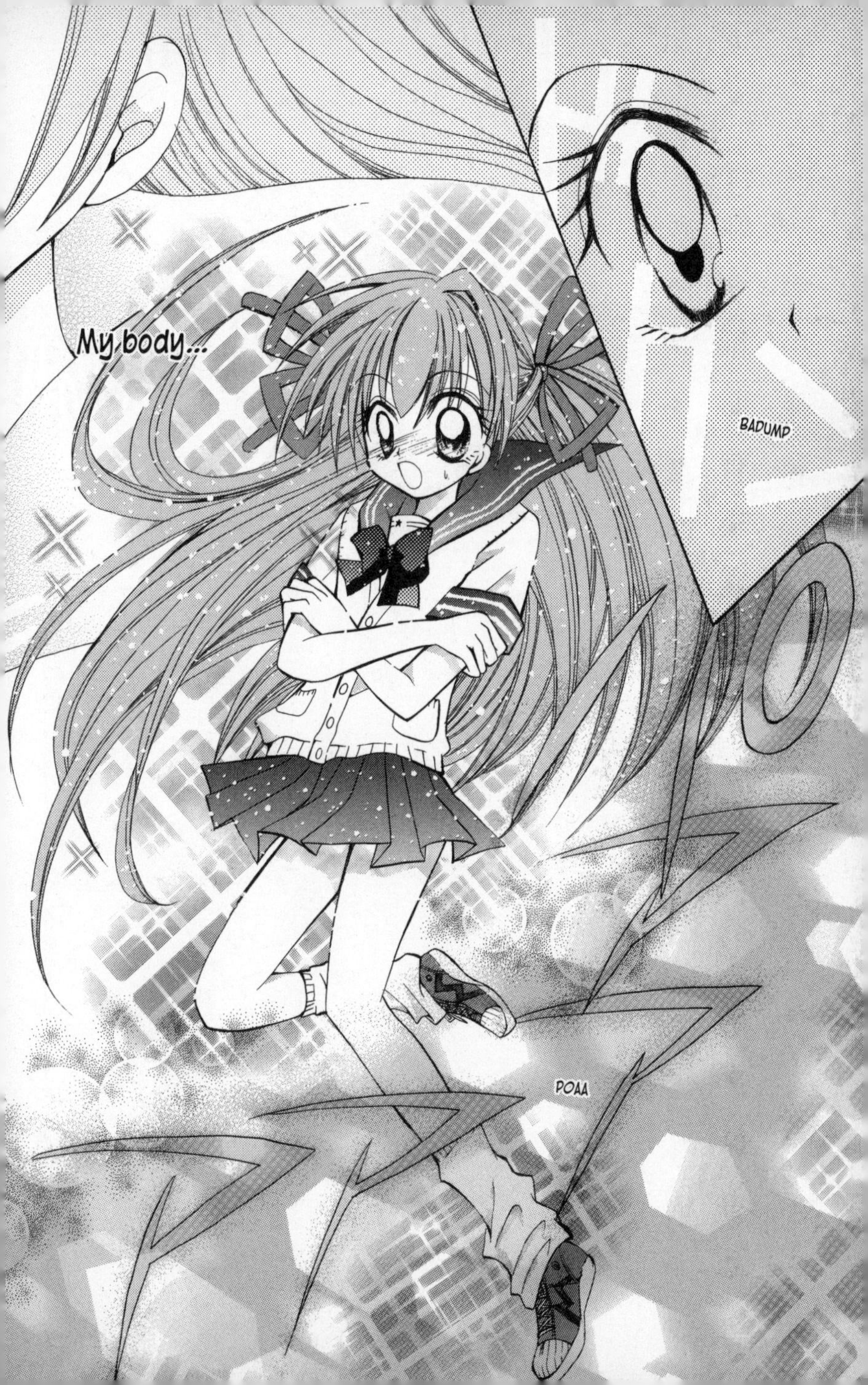
BADUMP
My body...
POAA

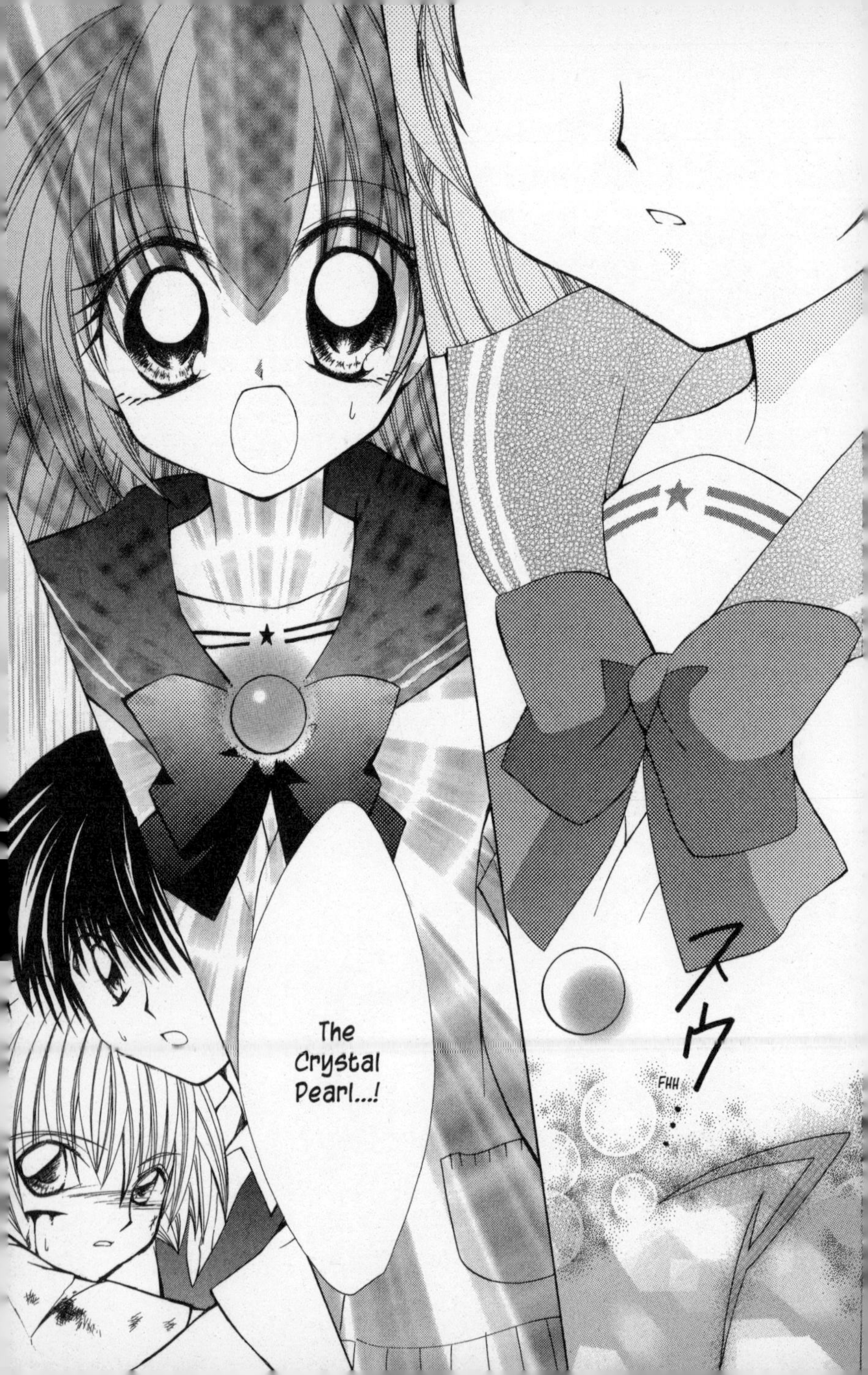
The Crystal Pearl...!
スウ
FHH...

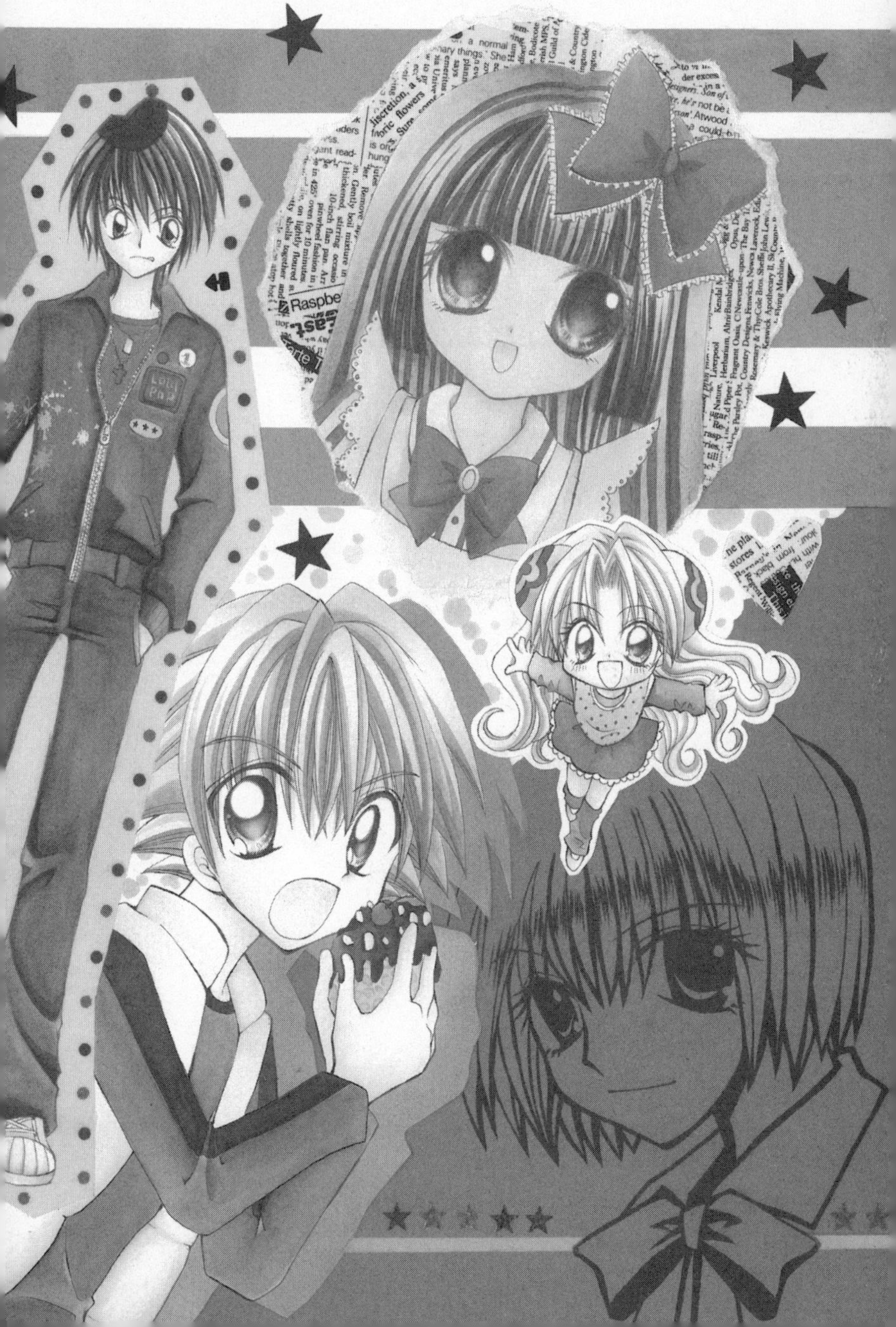

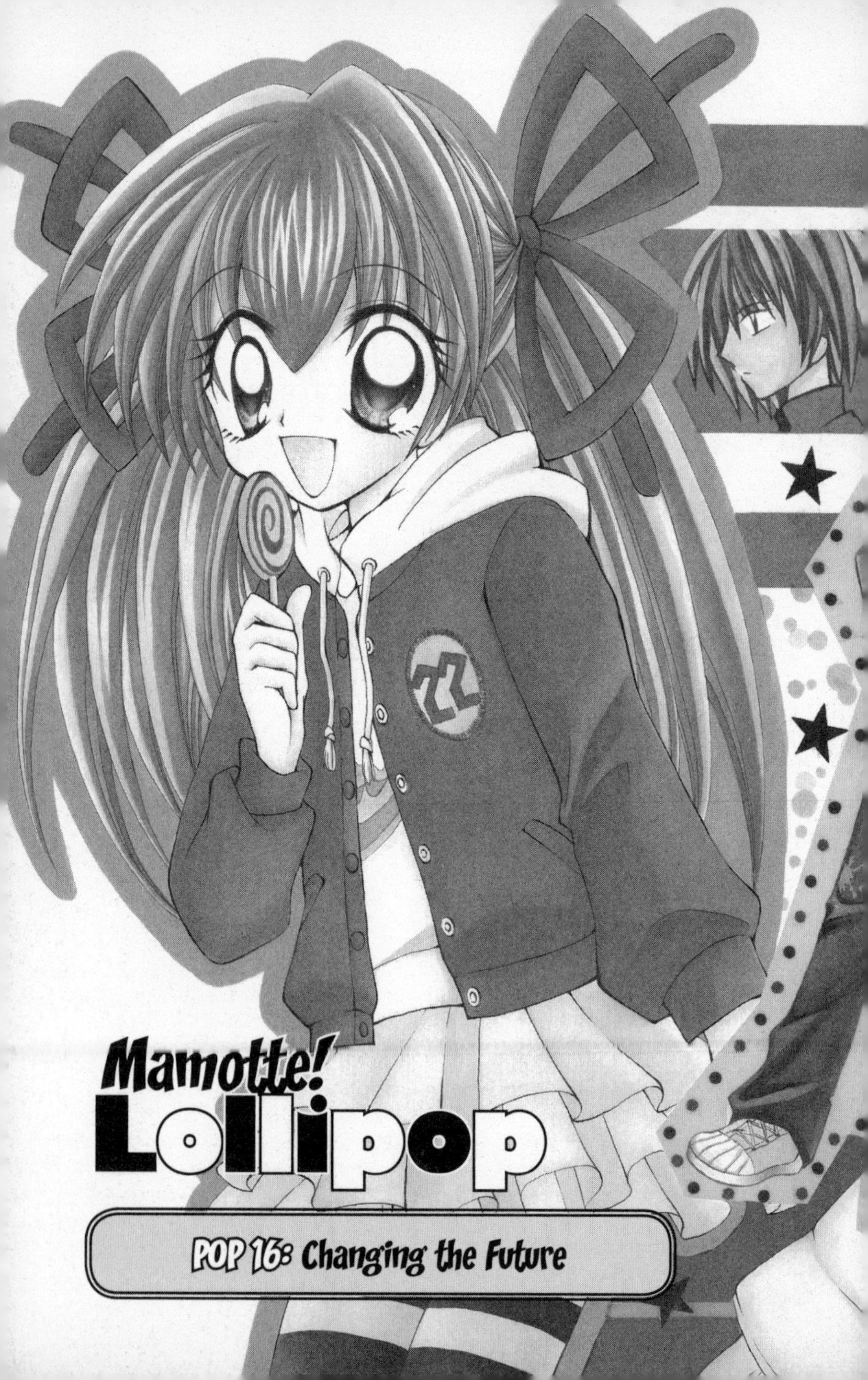

Mamotte! Lollipop
POP 16: Changing the Future

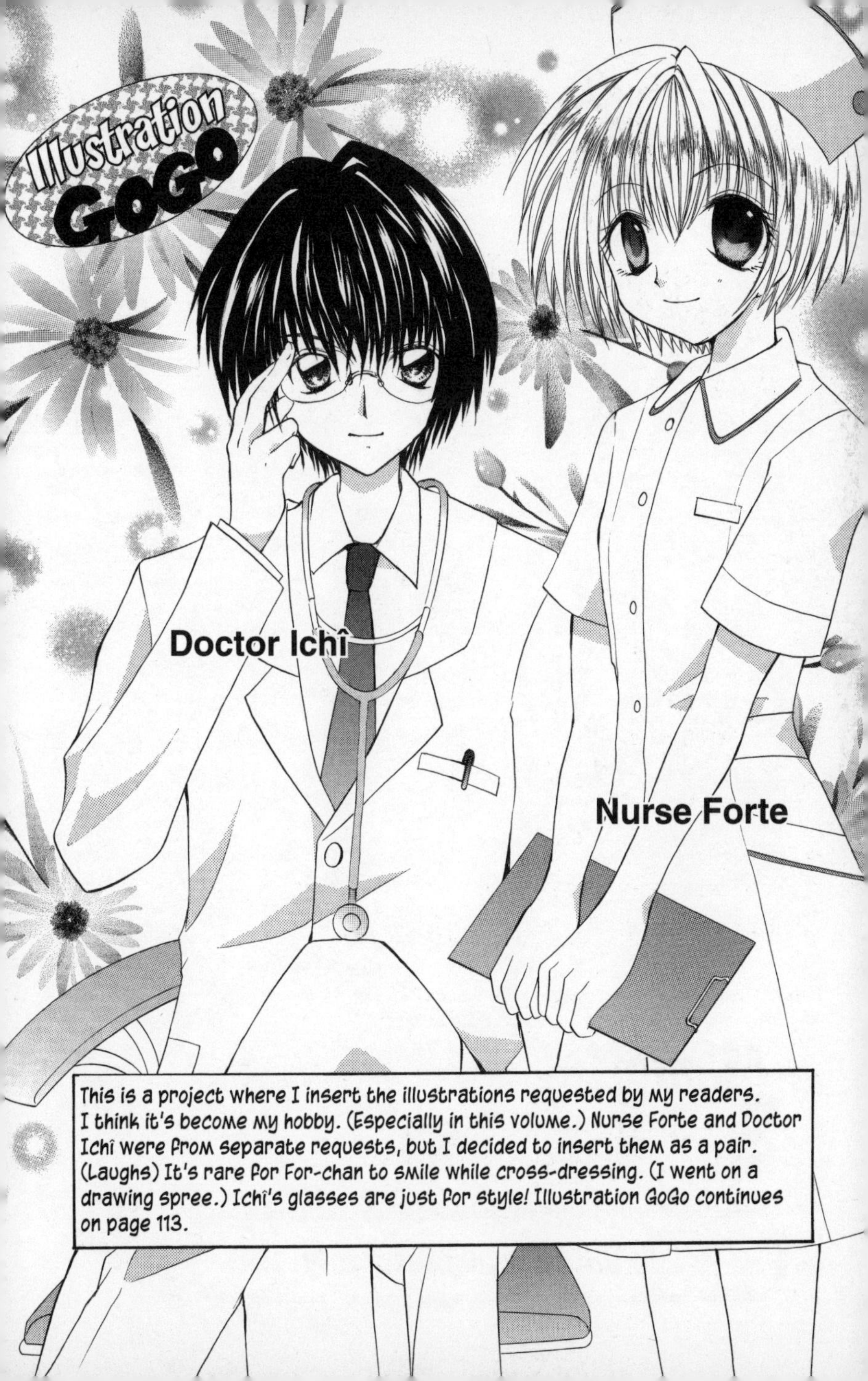
Illustration GoGo
Doctor Ichî
Nurse Forte

This is a project where I insert the illustrations requested by my readers. I think it's become my hobby. (Especially in this volume.) Nurse Forte and Doctor Ichî were from separate requests, but I decided to insert them as a pair. (Laughs) It's rare for For-chan to smile while cross-dressing. (I went on a drawing spree.) Ichî's glasses are just for style! Illustration GoGo continues on page 113.

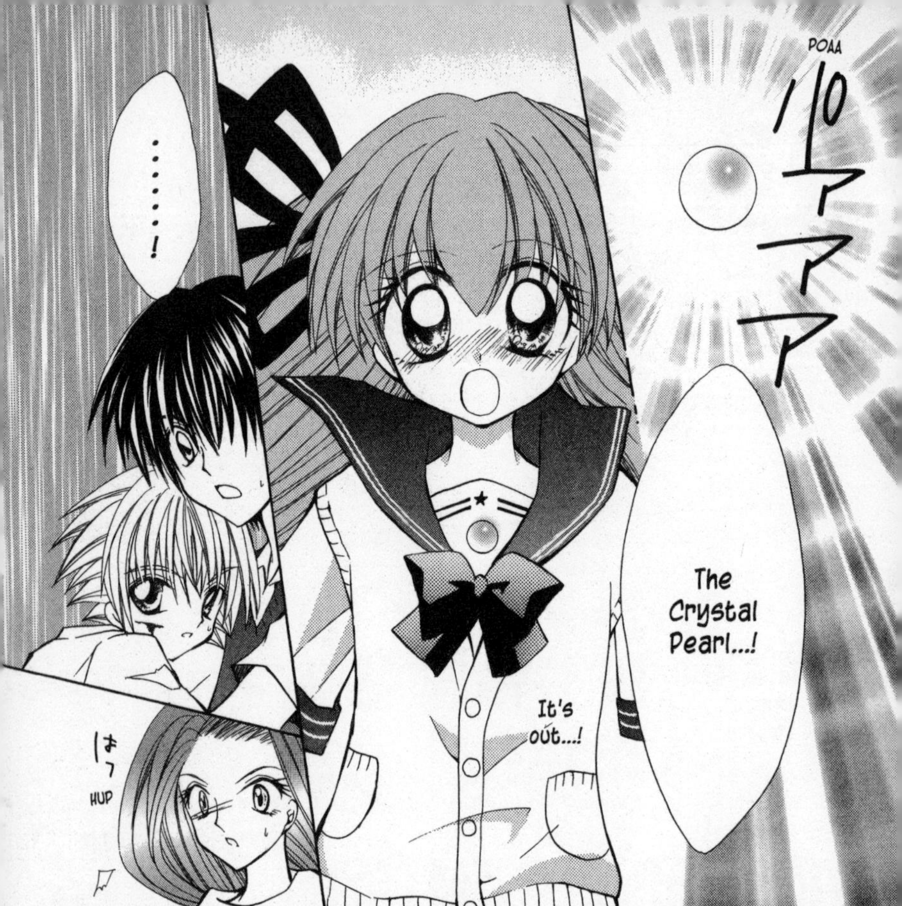

POAA
パアア
The Crystal Pearl...!
It's out...!
......!
はっ
HUP

PoP 16 Changing the Future

It was tough to draw this episode with the additional magazine cover, colored opening page and a side story, "Rokka Is All Grown Up!", but I was delighted! The cover page was something I had hoped to do for a while so I'm happy with it.

For once (?), the heroine is hanging tough in this episode. I'm glad that she's maturing since she doesn't usually do things on her own. I like both sides of the double-page layout and the way Nina smiles at Rill. I love the Zero and Ichi pairing, too.

This is when I realized this series will eventually come to an end and felt sad. It's far from over, though.

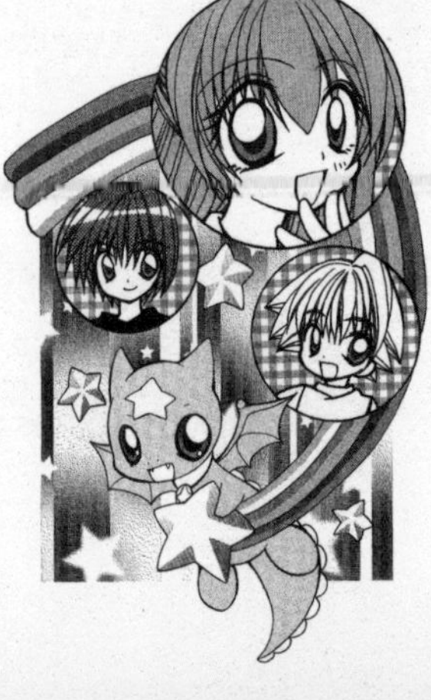

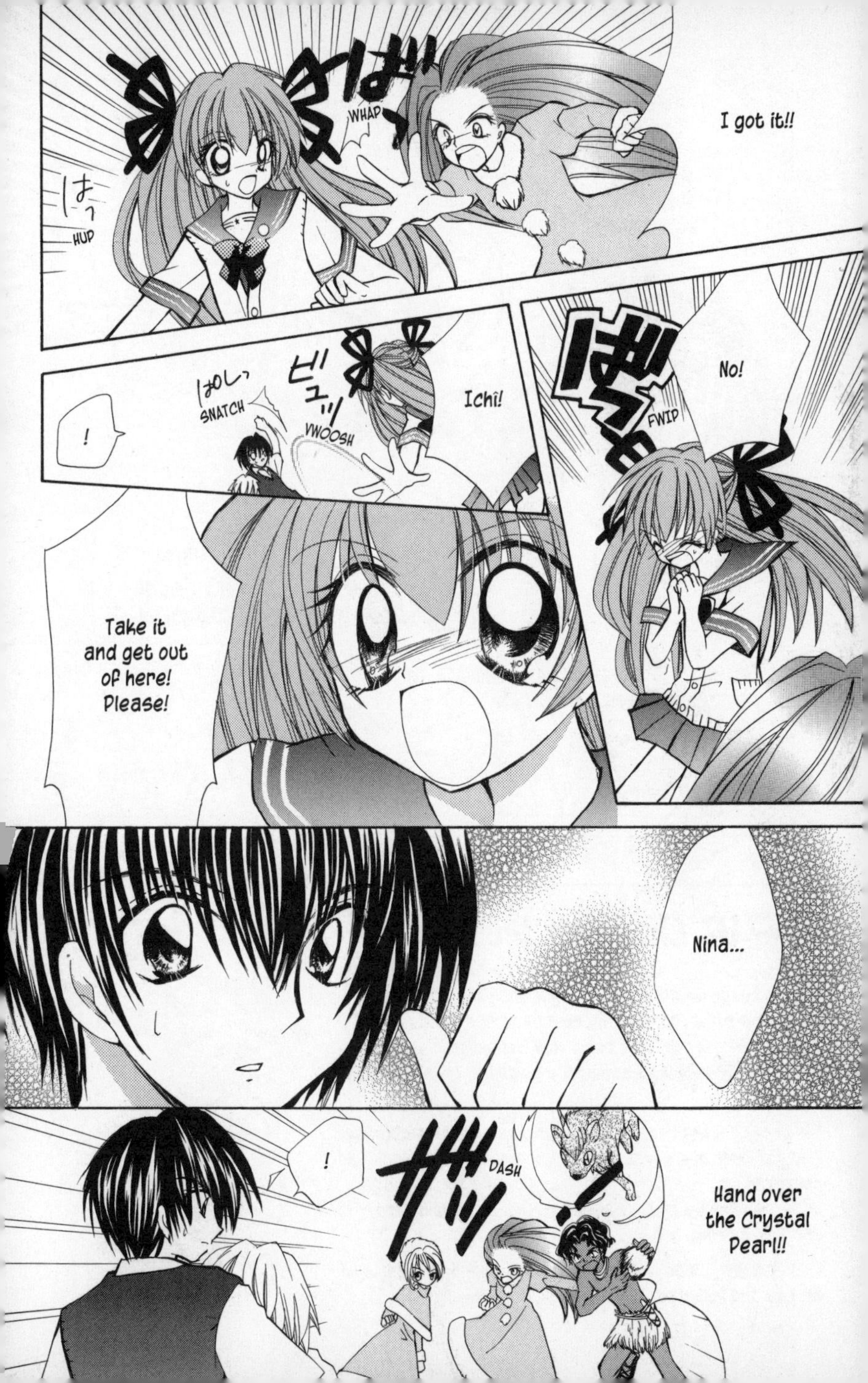

I got it!!
WHAP
はっ
HUP
No!
FWIP
Ichi!
ビュッ
VWOOSH
ぱしっ
SNATCH
!
Take it and get out of here! Please!
Nina...
Hand over the Crystal Pearl!!
DASH
!

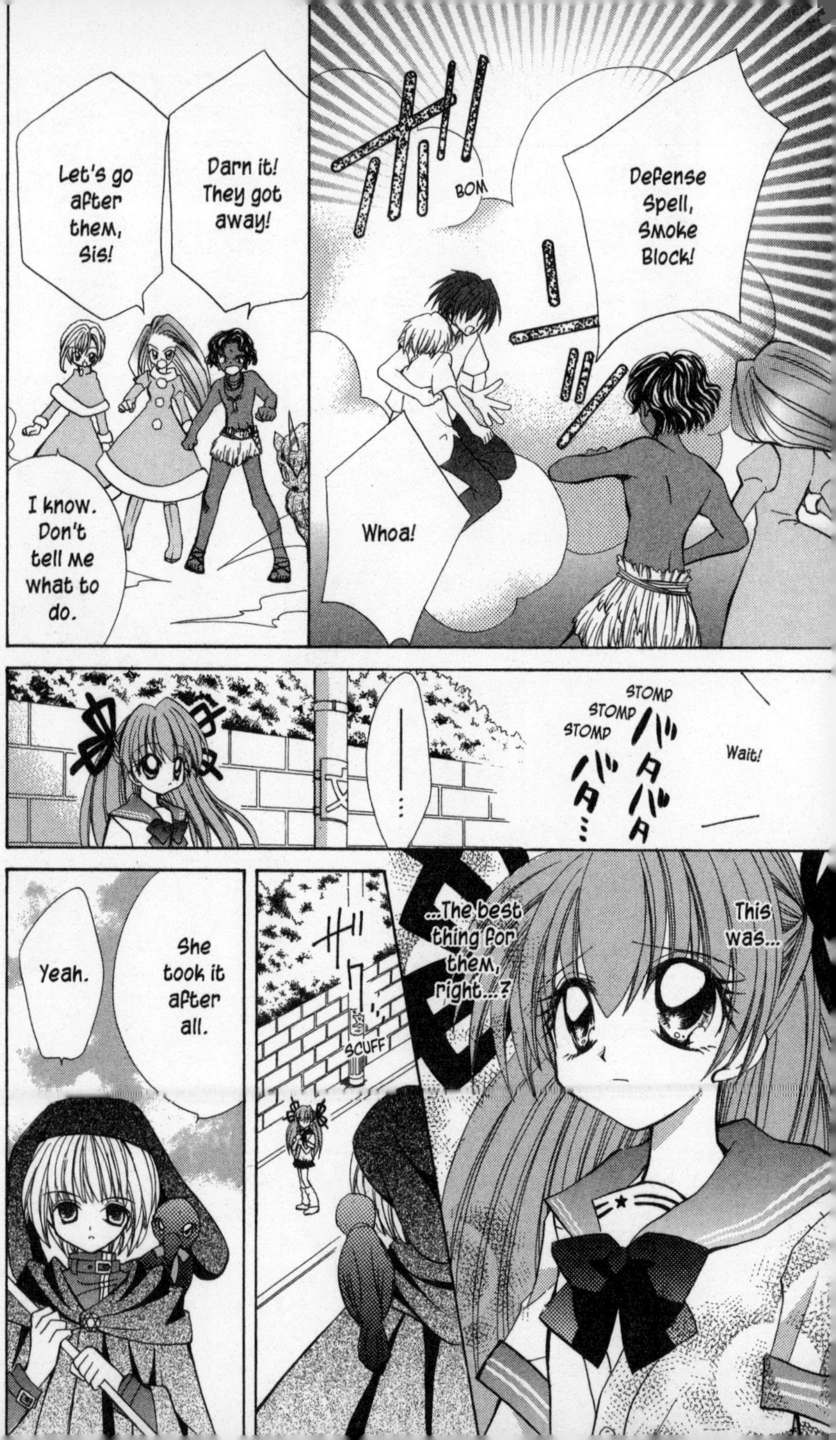

Defense Spell, Smoke Block!
BOM
Whoa!
Darn it! They got away!
Let's go after them, Sis!
I know. Don't tell me what to do.
Wait!
STOMP
STOMP
STOMP
—...
This was...
...The best thing for them, right...?
SCUFF
She took it after all.
Yeah.

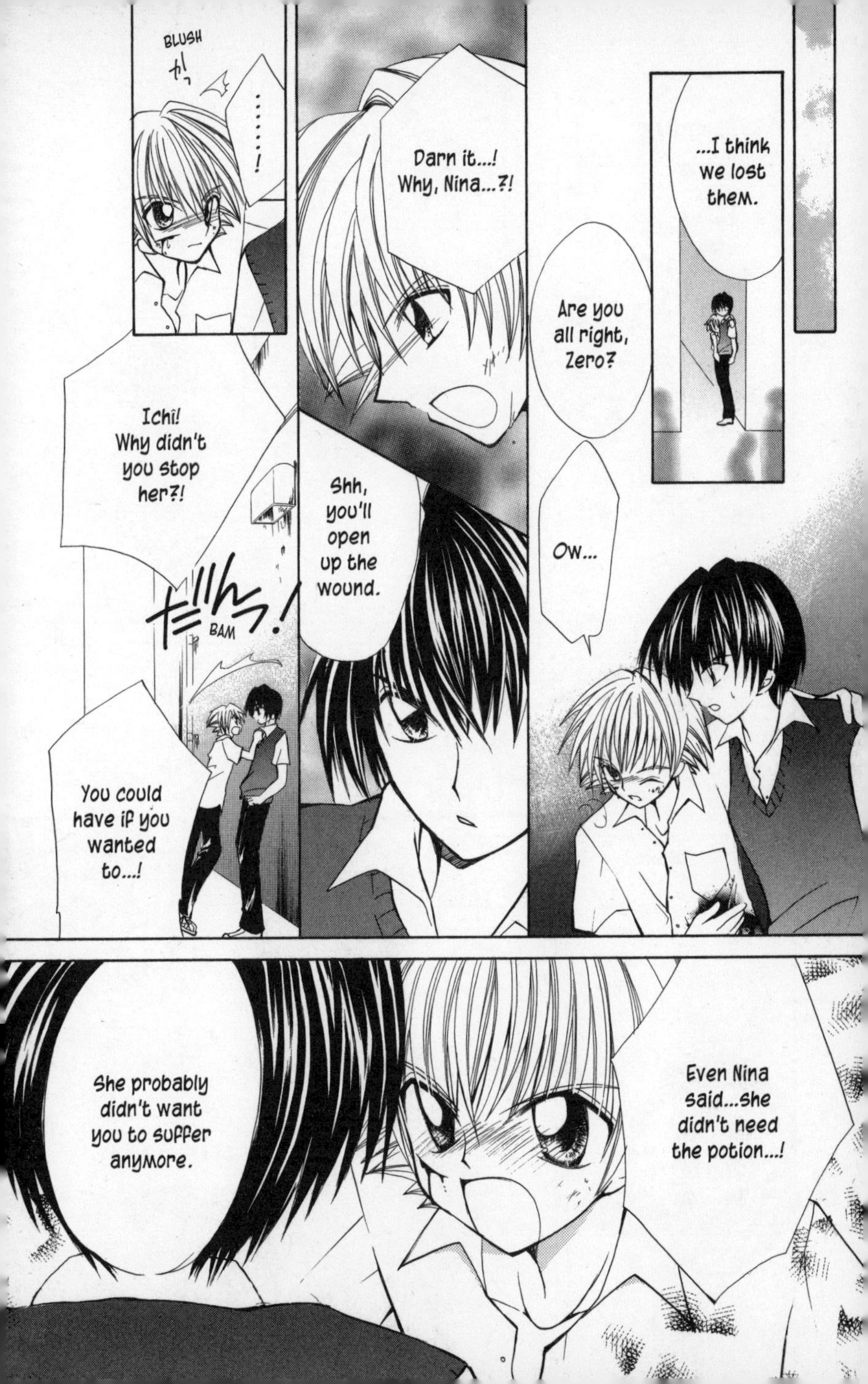
...I think we lost them.
Are you all right, Zero?
Ow...
Darn it...! Why, Nina...?!
Shh, you'll open up the wound.
BLUSH
......!
Ichi! Why didn't you stop her?!
BAM
You could have if you wanted to...!
Even Nina said...she didn't need the potion...!
She probably didn't want you to suffer anymore.

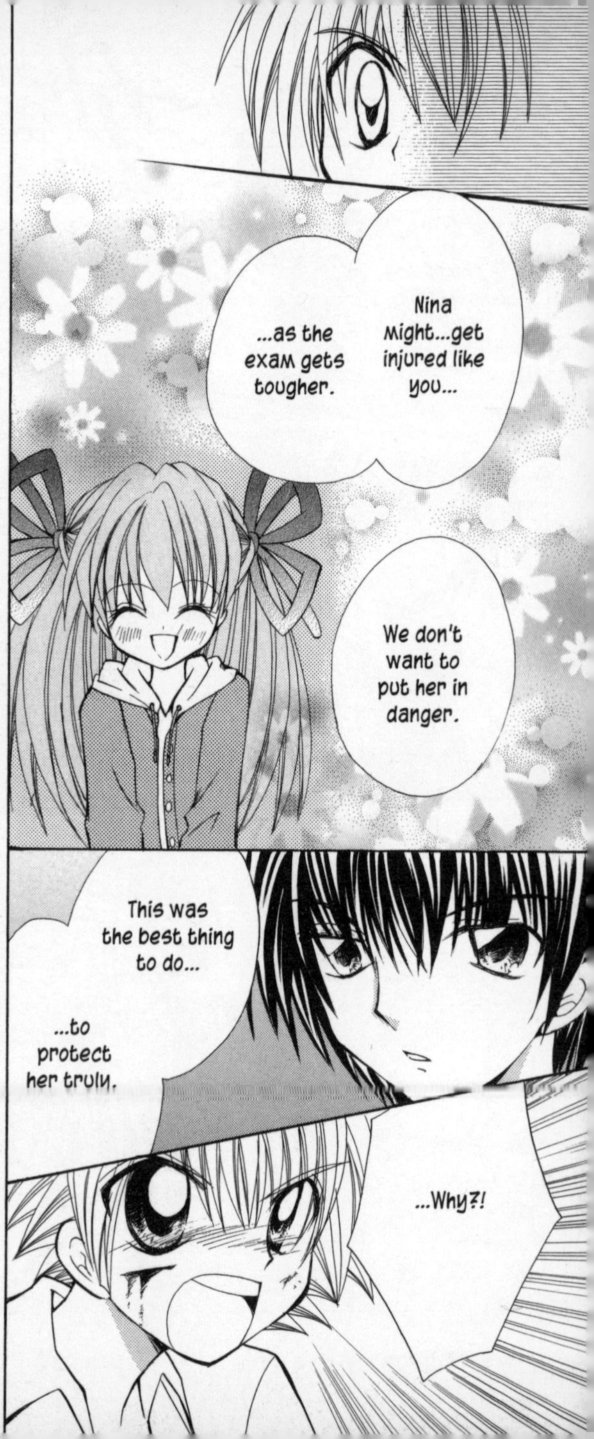
Nina might...get injured like you...
...as the exam gets tougher.
We don't want to put her in danger.
This was the best thing to do...
...to protect her truly.
...Why?!

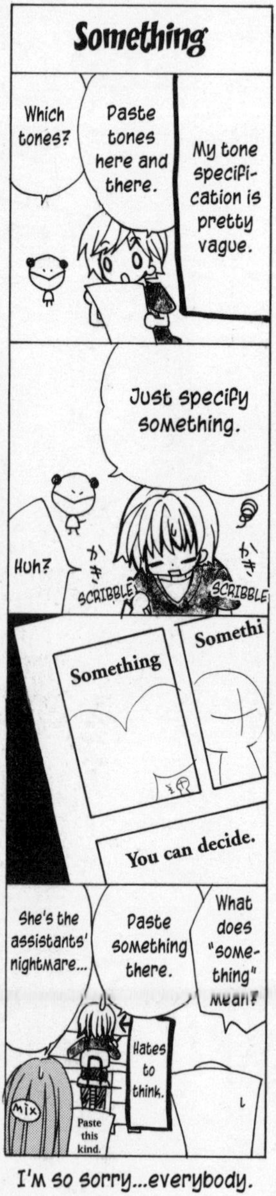
Something
My tone specification is pretty vague.
Paste tones here and there.
Which tones?
Just specify something.
かき SCRIBBLE
かき SCRIBBLE
Huh?
Somethi
Something
You can decide.
What does "something" mean?
Paste something there.
She's the assistants' nightmare...
Hates to think.
Paste this kind.
MIX

I'm so sorry...everybody.

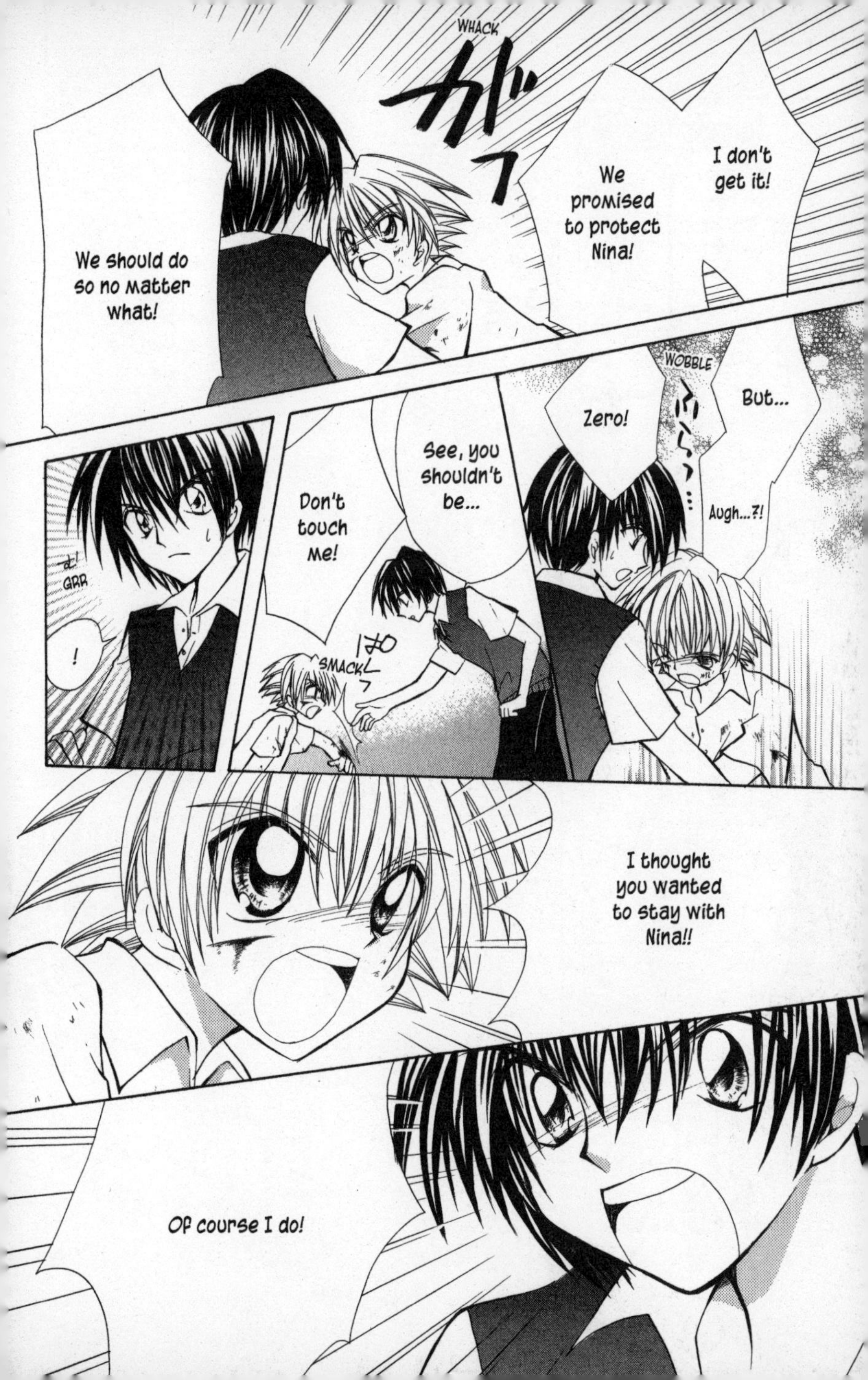
WHACK
I don't get it!
We promised to protect Nina!
We should do so no matter what!
But...
WOBBLE
Zero!
Augh...?!
See, you shouldn't be...
Don't touch me!
SMACK
GRR
!
I thought you wanted to stay with Nina!!
Of course I do!

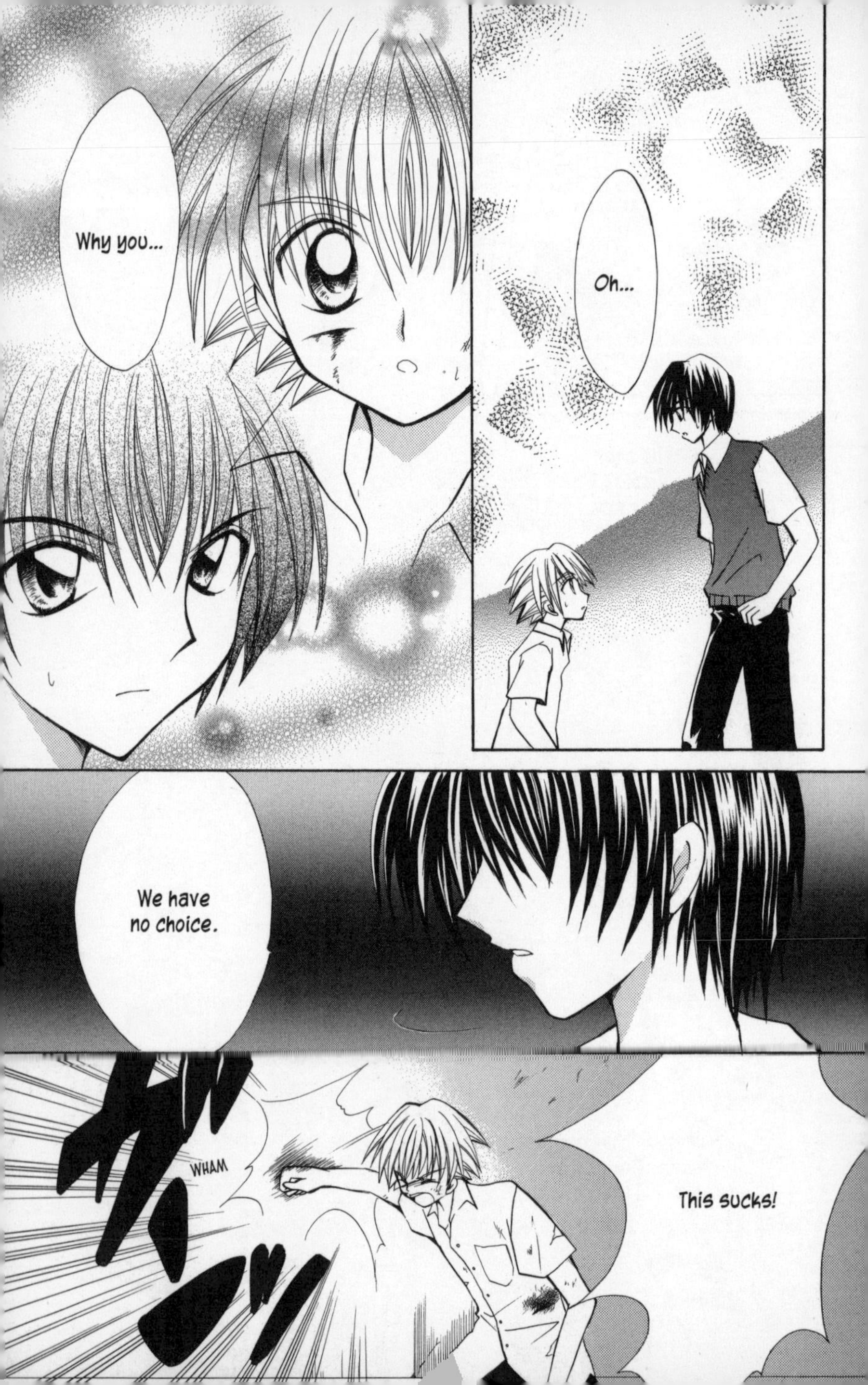
Oh...
Why you...
We have no choice.
This sucks!
WHAM

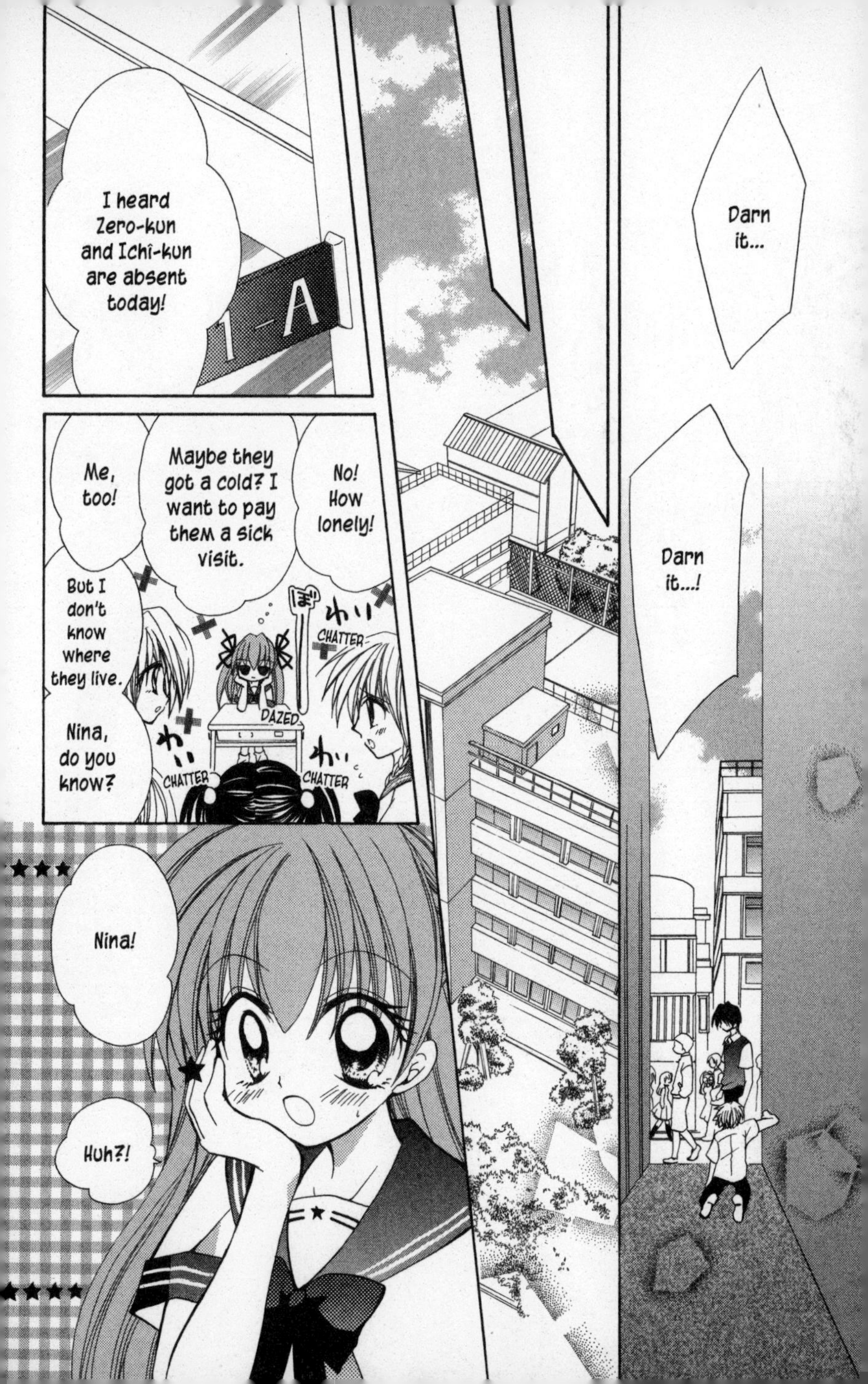
Darn it...
Darn it...!
I heard Zero-kun and Ichî-kun are absent today!
1-A
No! How lonely!
Maybe they got a cold? I want to pay them a sick visit.
Me, too!
CHATTER
DAZED
But I don't know where they live.
Nina, do you know?
CHATTER
CHATTER
Nina!
Huh?!

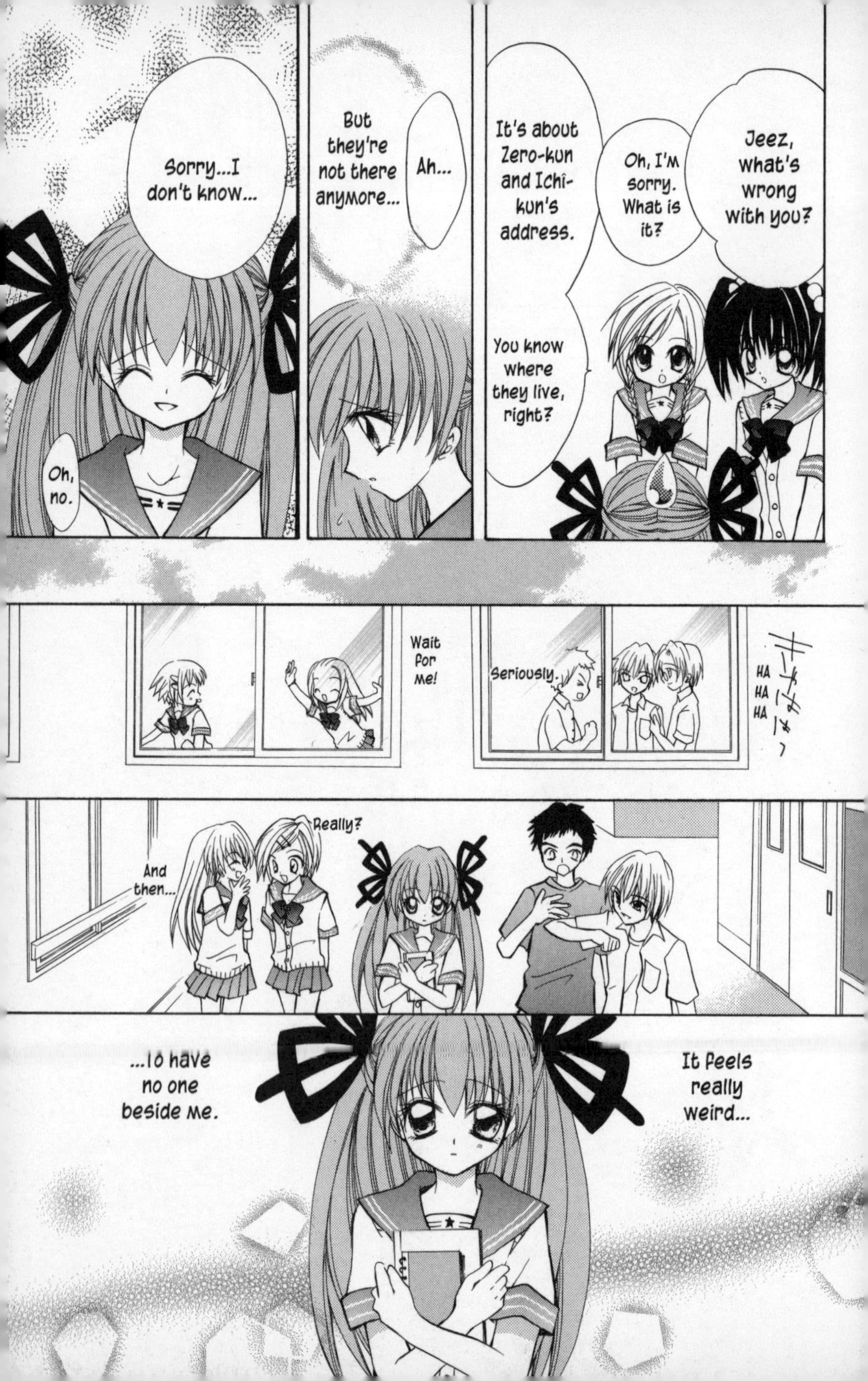
Jeez, what's wrong with you?
Oh, I'm sorry. What is it?
It's about Zero-kun and Ichi-kun's address.
You know where they live, right?
Ah...
But they're not there anymore...
Sorry...I don't know...
Oh, no.
HA HA HA
Seriously.
Wait for me!
Really?
And then...
It feels really weird...
...to have no one beside me.

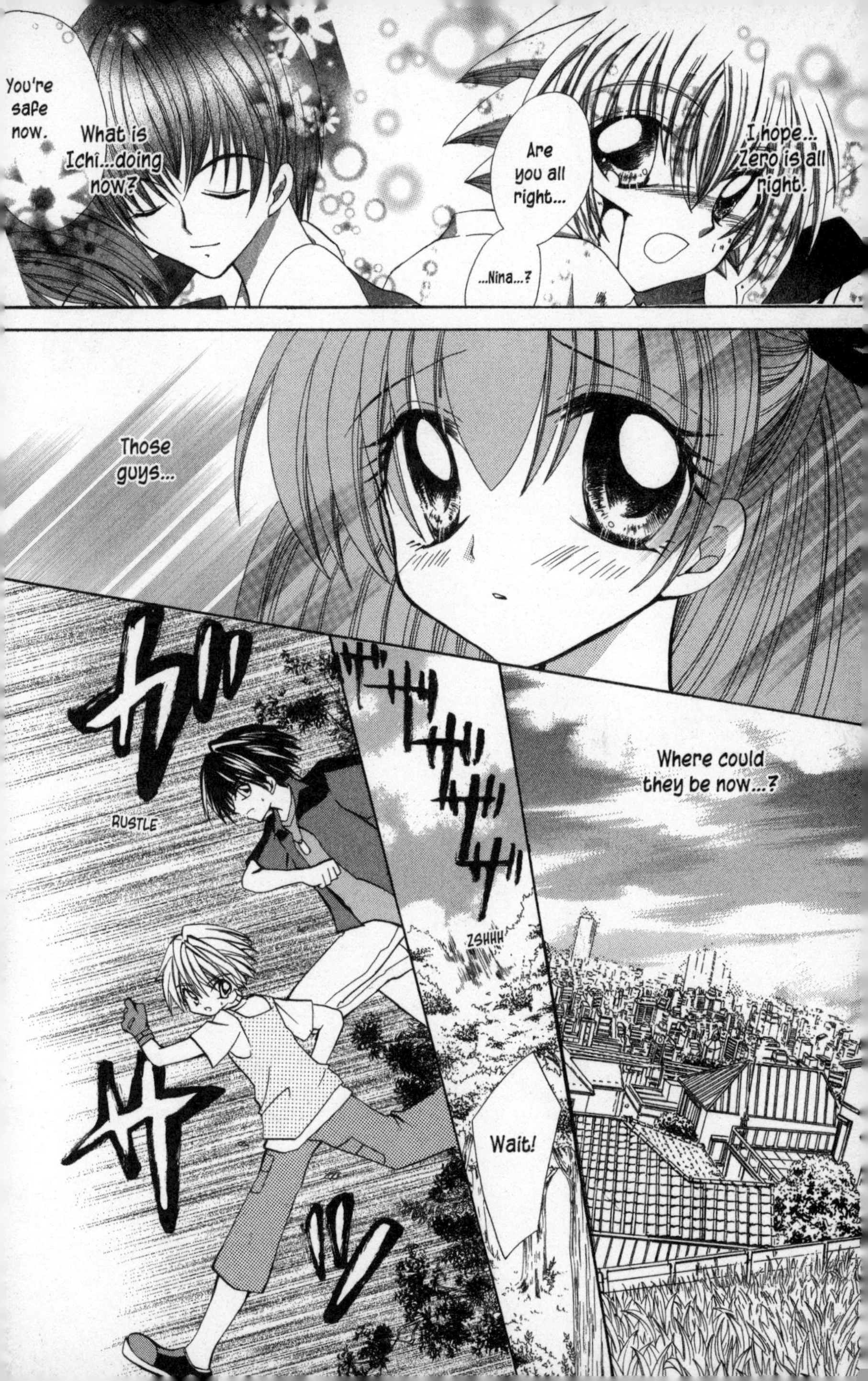
I hope... Zero is all right.
Are you all right...
...Nina...?
What is Ichi...doing now?
You're safe now.
Those guys...
Where could they be now...?
Wait!
ZSHHH
RUSTLE

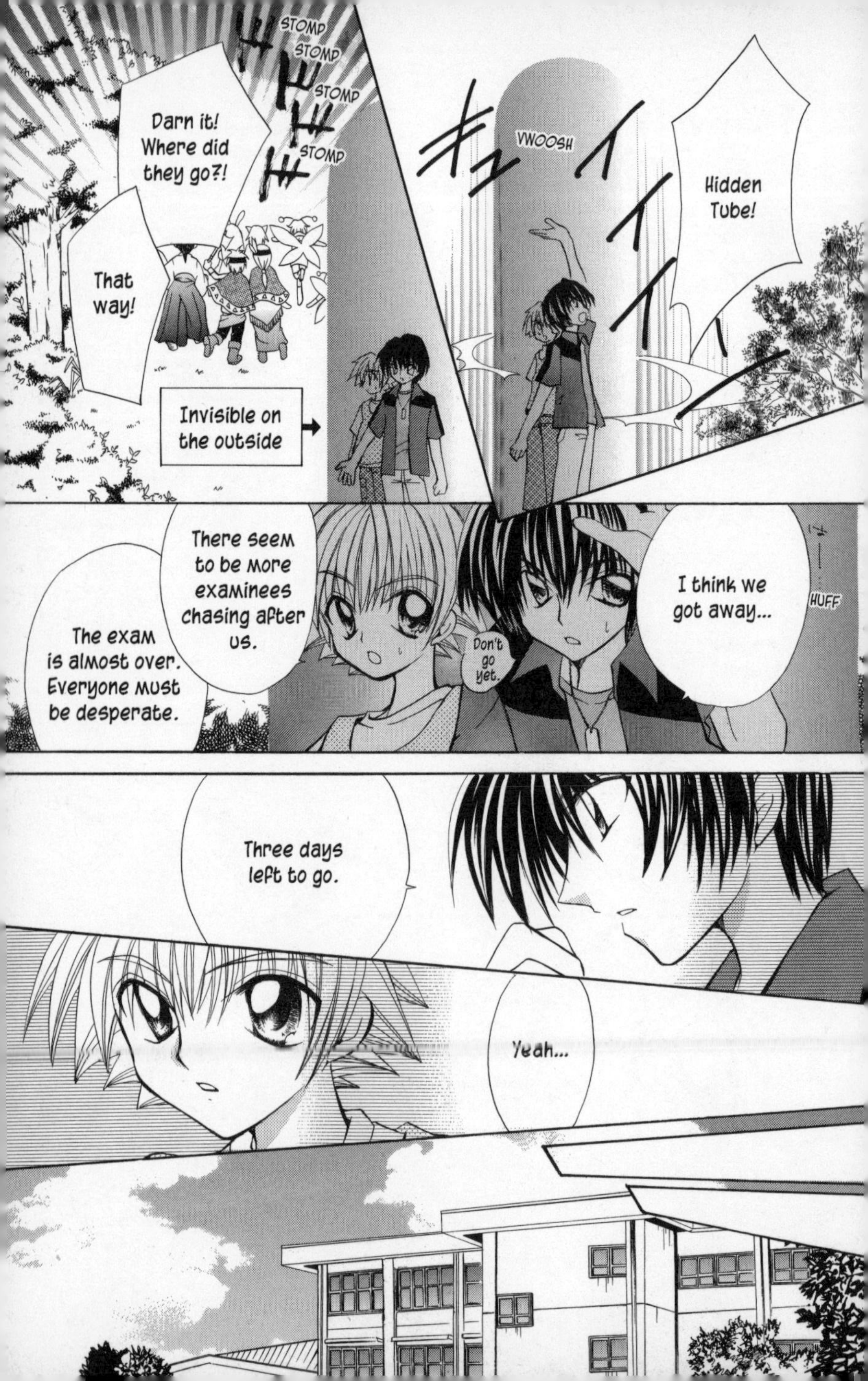
Hidden Tube!
VWOOSH
STOMP
STOMP
STOMP
STOMP
Darn it! Where did they go?!
That way!
Invisible on the outside
HUFF
I think we got away...
Don't go yet.
There seem to be more examinees chasing after us.
The exam is almost over. Everyone must be desperate.
Three days left to go.
Yeah...

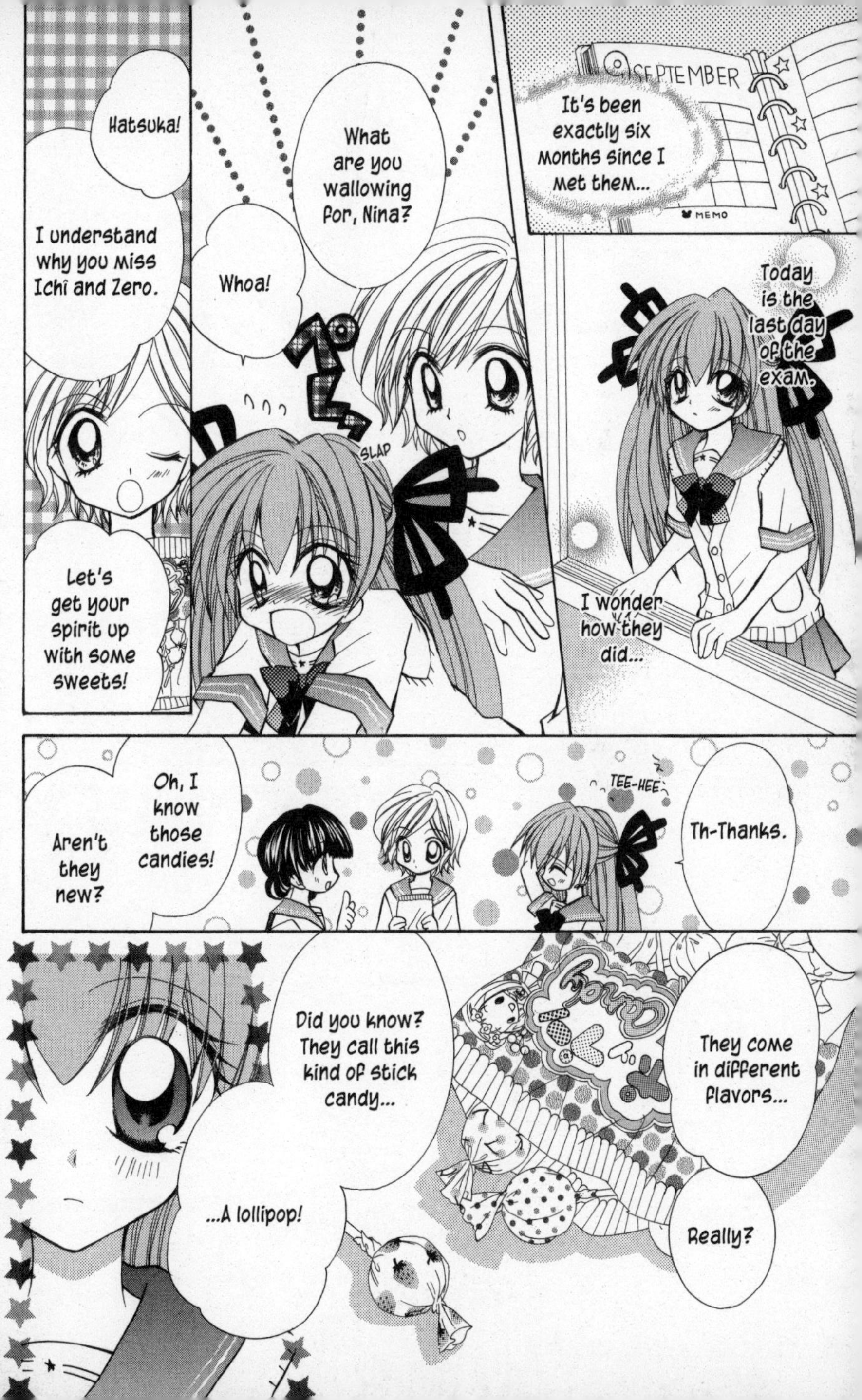
SEPTEMBER
It's been exactly six months since I met them...
MEMO
Today is the last day of the exam.
I wonder how they did...
What are you wallowing for, Nina?
Whoa!
SLAP
Hatsuka!
I understand why you miss Ichi and Zero.
Let's get your spirit up with some sweets!
Th-Thanks.
TEE-HEE
Oh, I know those candies!
Aren't they new?
They come in different flavors...
Really?
Did you know? They call this kind of stick candy...
...A lollipop!

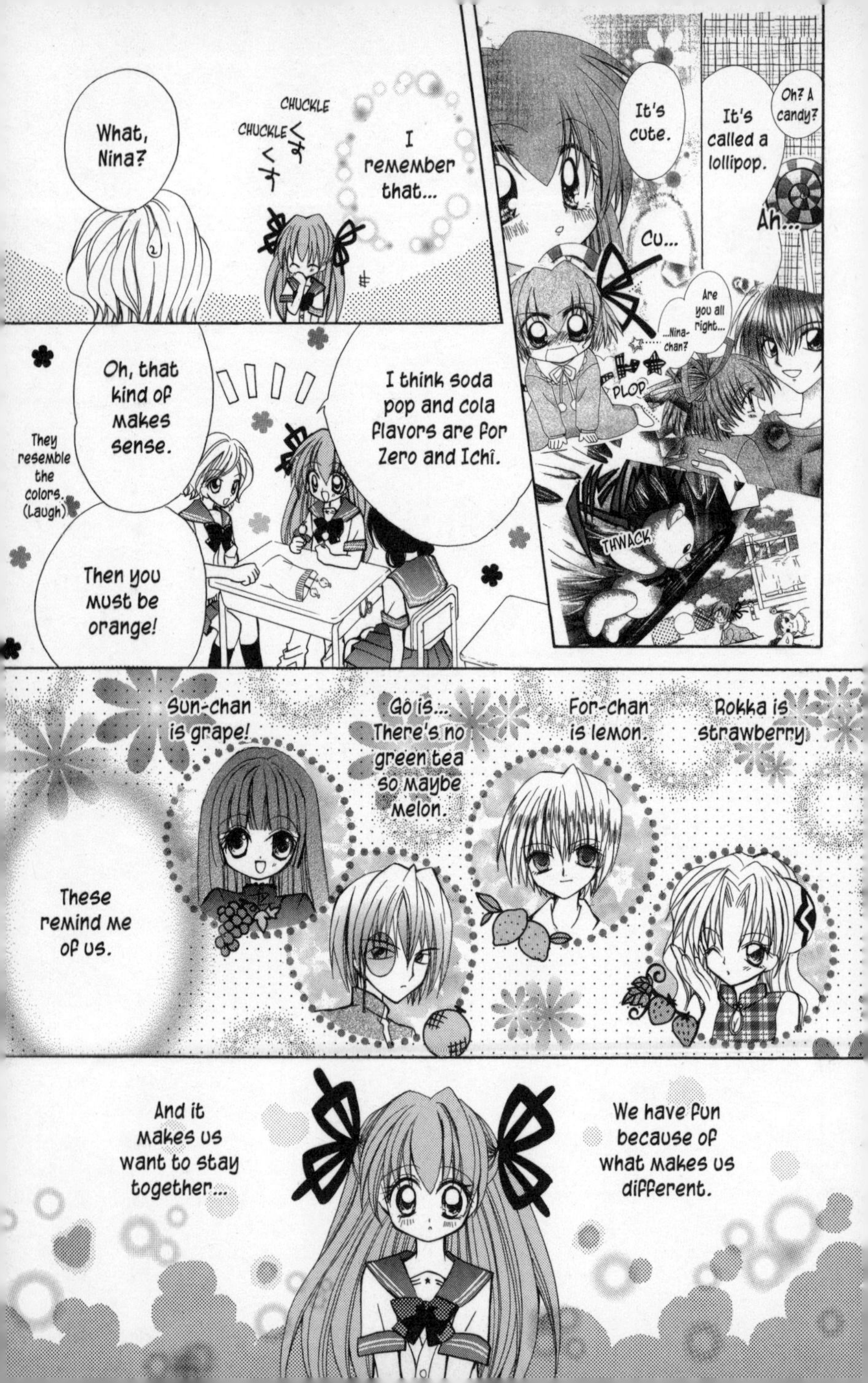
Oh? A candy?
It's called a lollipop.
Ah...
It's cute.
Cu...
Are you all right...
...Nina-chan?
PLOP
THWACK
I remember that...
CHUCKLE CHUCKLE
くす くす
What, Nina?
I think soda pop and cola flavors are for Zero and Ichî.
Oh, that kind of makes sense.
They resemble the colors. (Laugh)
Then you must be orange!
Rokka is strawberry
For-chan is lemon.
Gô is... There's no green tea so maybe melon.
Sun-chan is grape!
These remind me of us.
We have fun because of what makes us different.
And it makes us want to stay together...

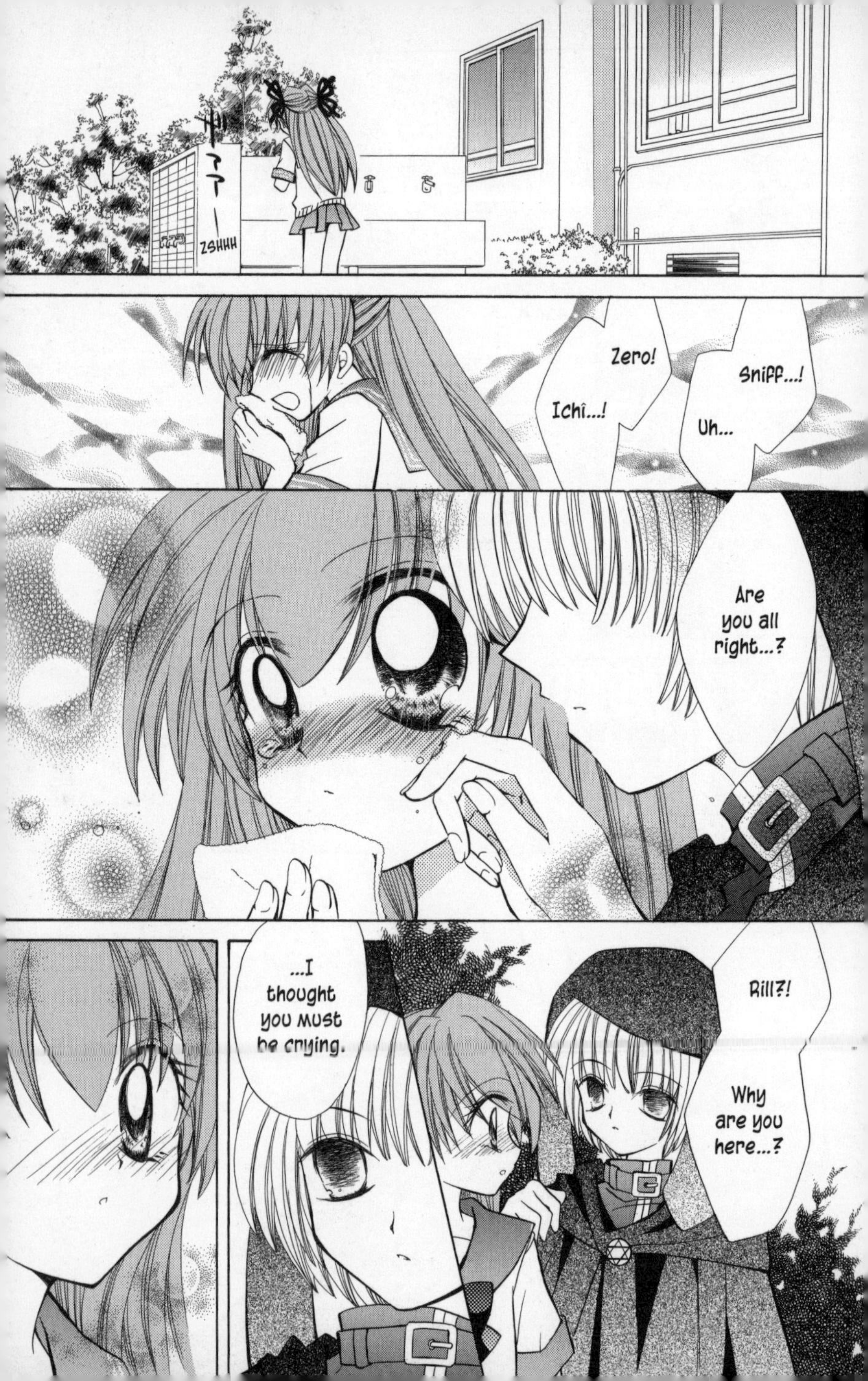
ZSHHH
Sniff...!
Uh...
Zero!
Ichî...!
Are you all right...?
Rill?!
Why are you here...?
...I thought you must be crying.

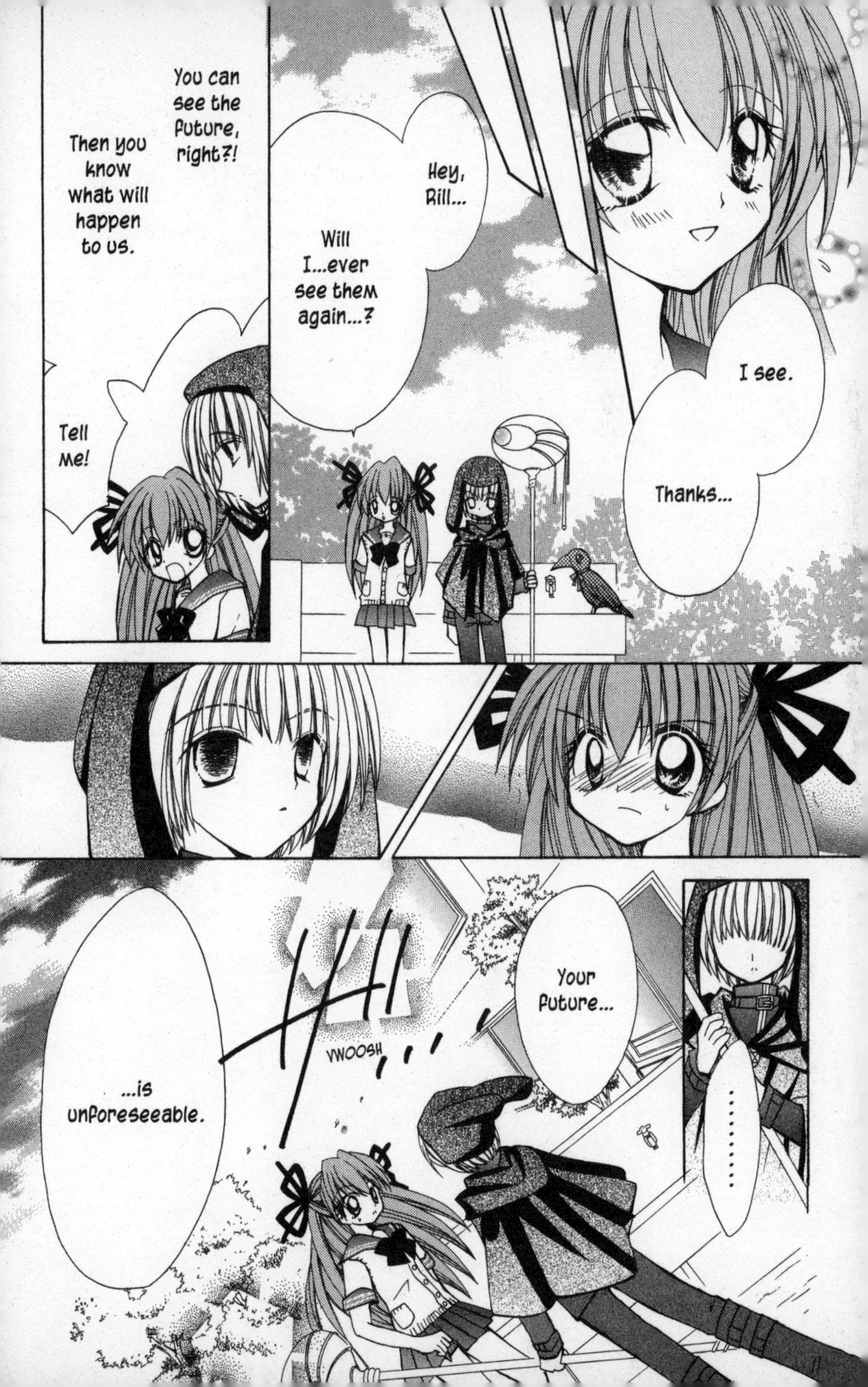
I see.
Thanks...
Hey, Rill...
Will I...ever see them again...?
You can see the future, right?!
Then you know what will happen to us.
Tell me!
......
Your future...
VWOOSH
...is unforeseeable.

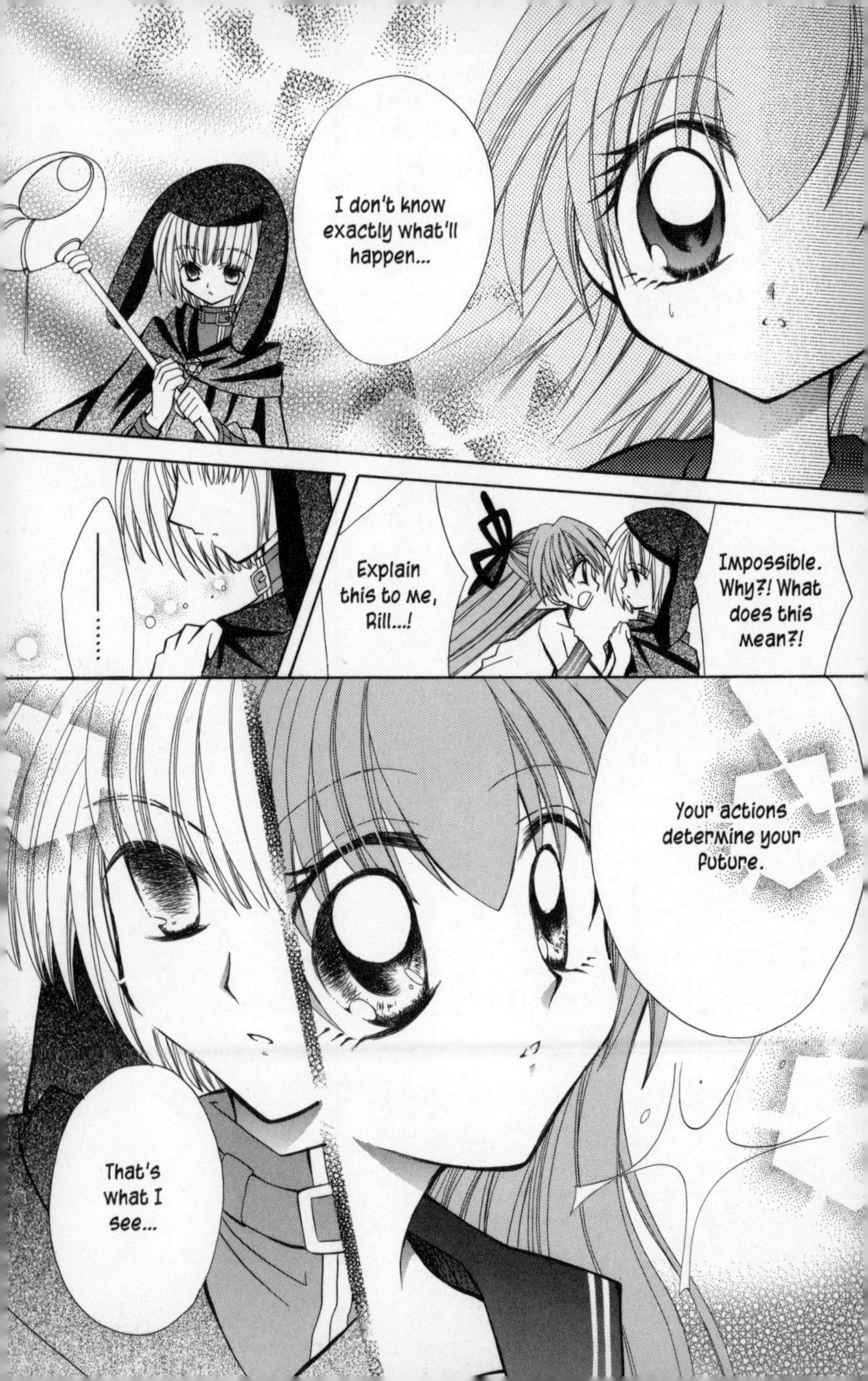
I don't know exactly what'll happen...
Impossible. Why?! What does this mean?!
Explain this to me, Rill...!
......
Your actions determine your future.
That's what I see...

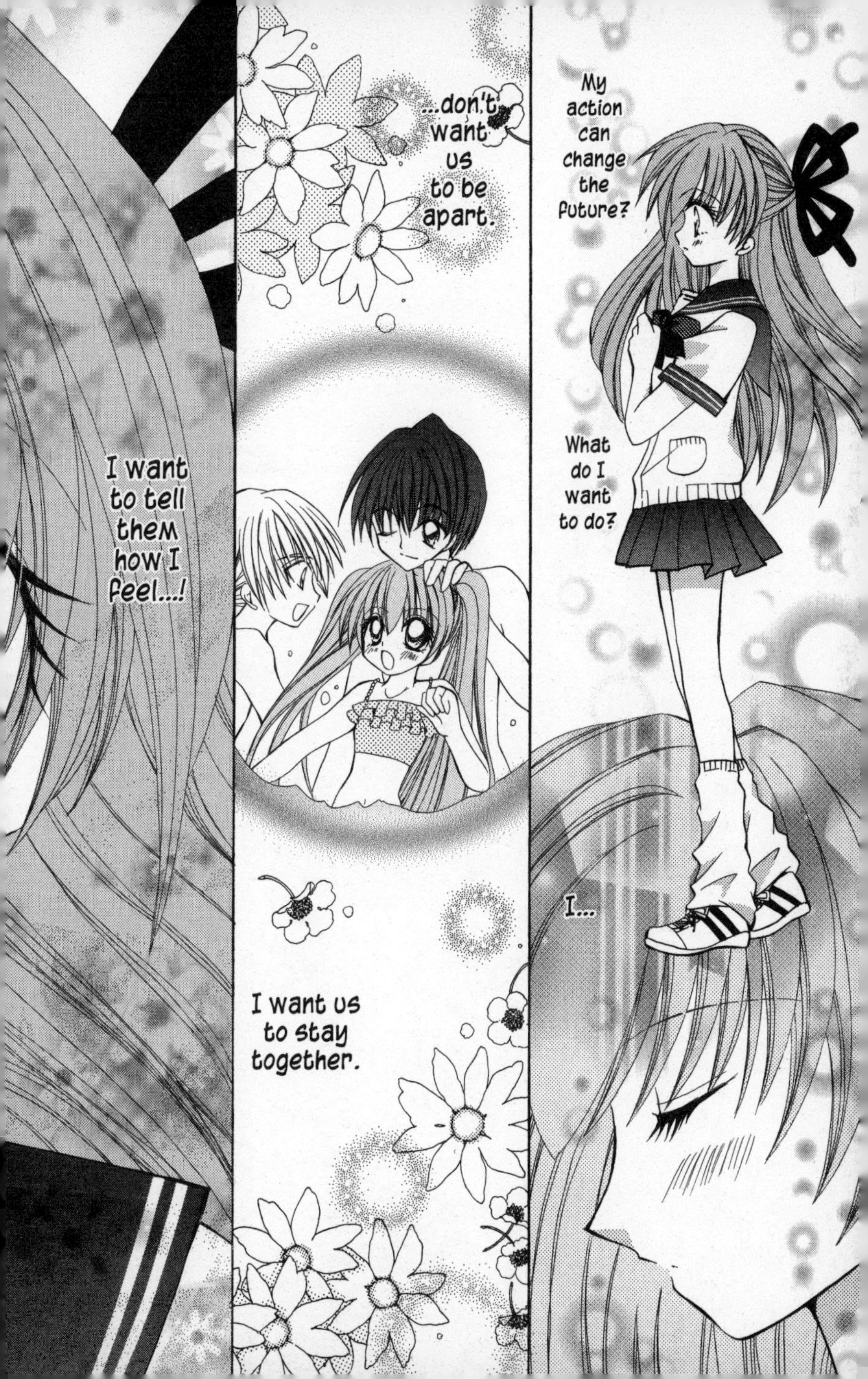
My action can change the future?
What do I want to do?
I...
...don't want us to be apart.
I want us to stay together.
I want to tell them how I feel...!

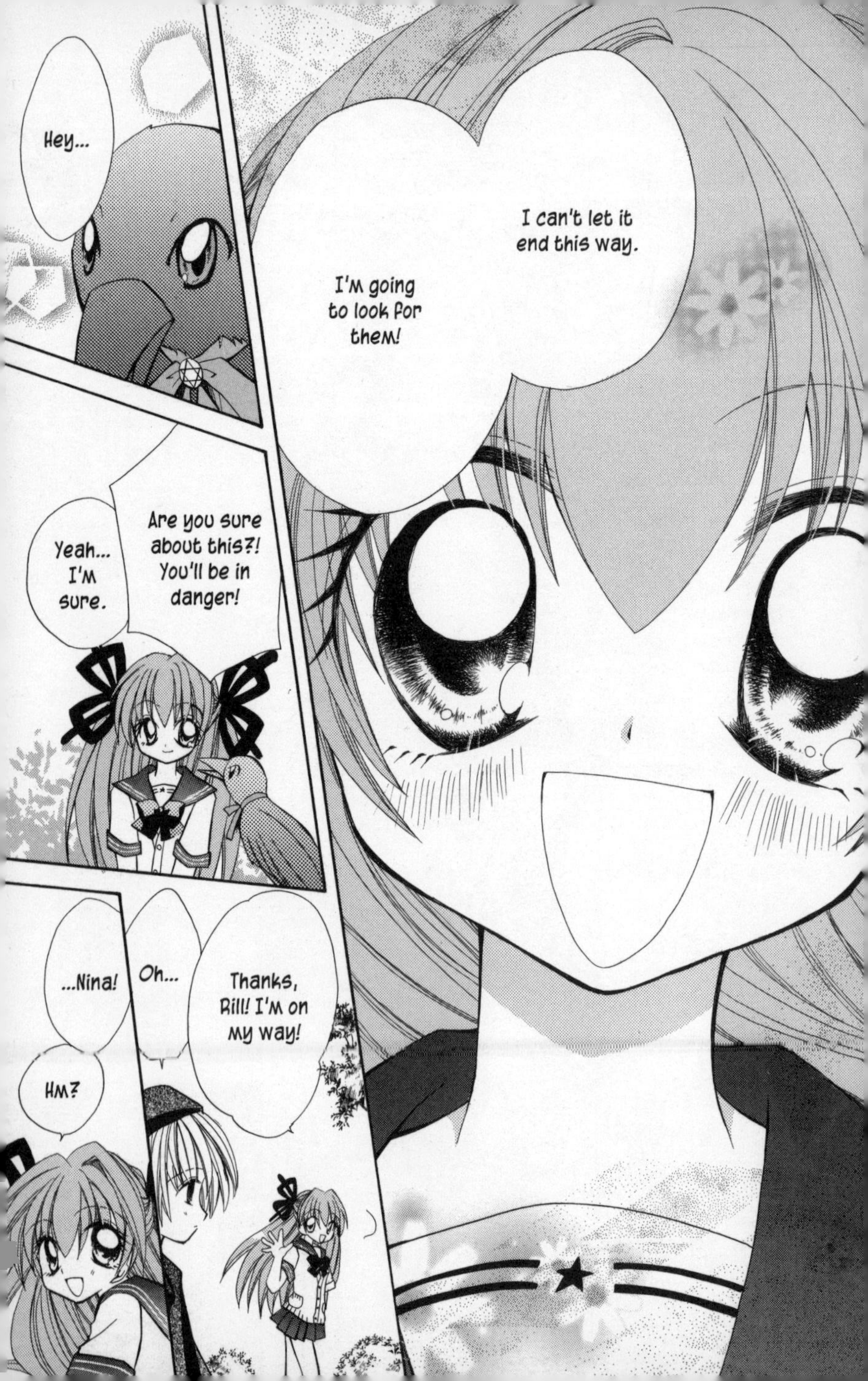
I can't let it end this way.
I'm going to look for them!
Hey...
Are you sure about this?! You'll be in danger!
Yeah... I'm sure.
Thanks, Rill! I'm on my way!
Oh...
...Nina!
Hm?

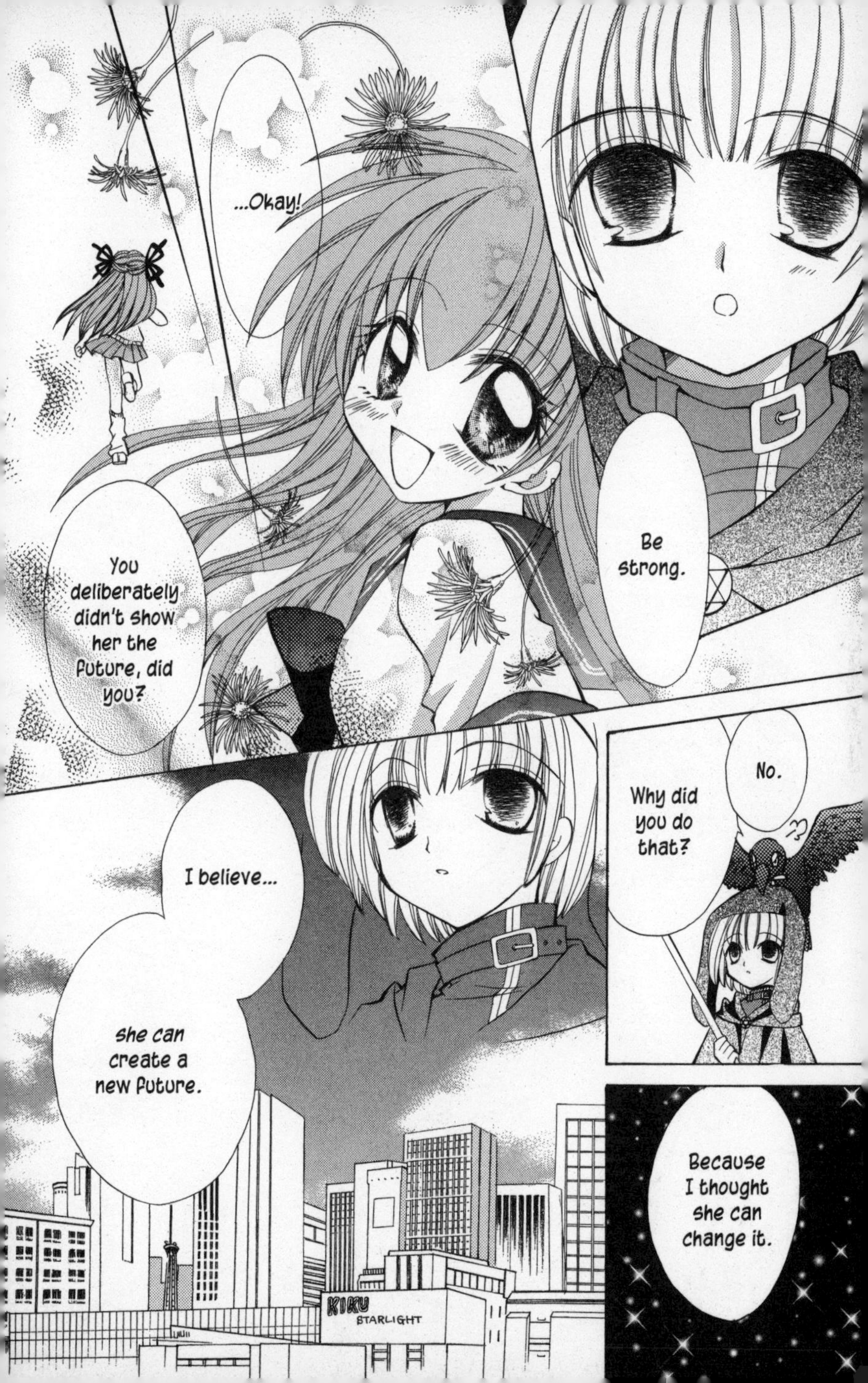
Be strong.
...Okay!
You deliberately didn't show her the future, did you?
No.
Why did you do that?
Because I thought she can change it.
I believe...
she can create a new future.
KIKU STARLIGHT

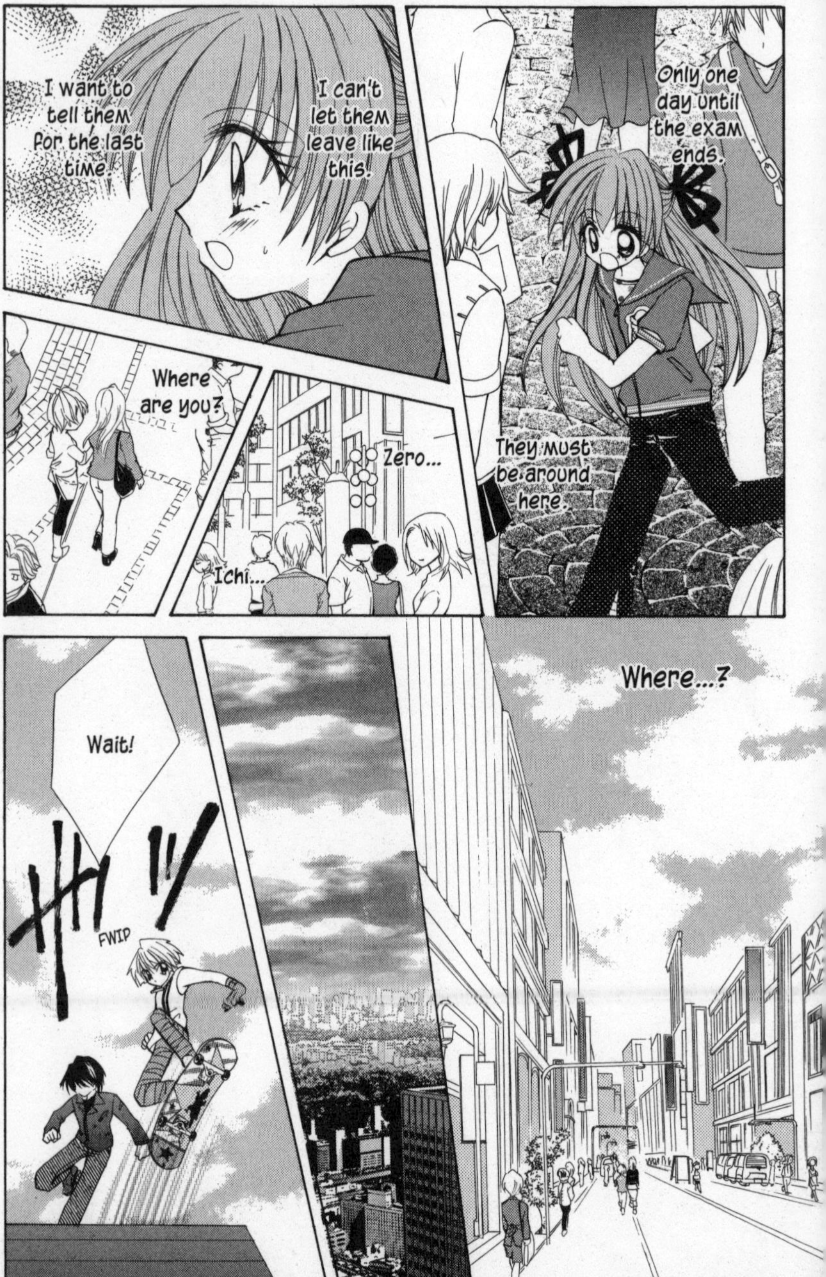
Only one day until the exam ends.
They must be around here.
I can't let them leave like this!
I want to tell them for the last time!
Zero...
Ichi...
Where are you?
Where...?
Wait!
FWIP

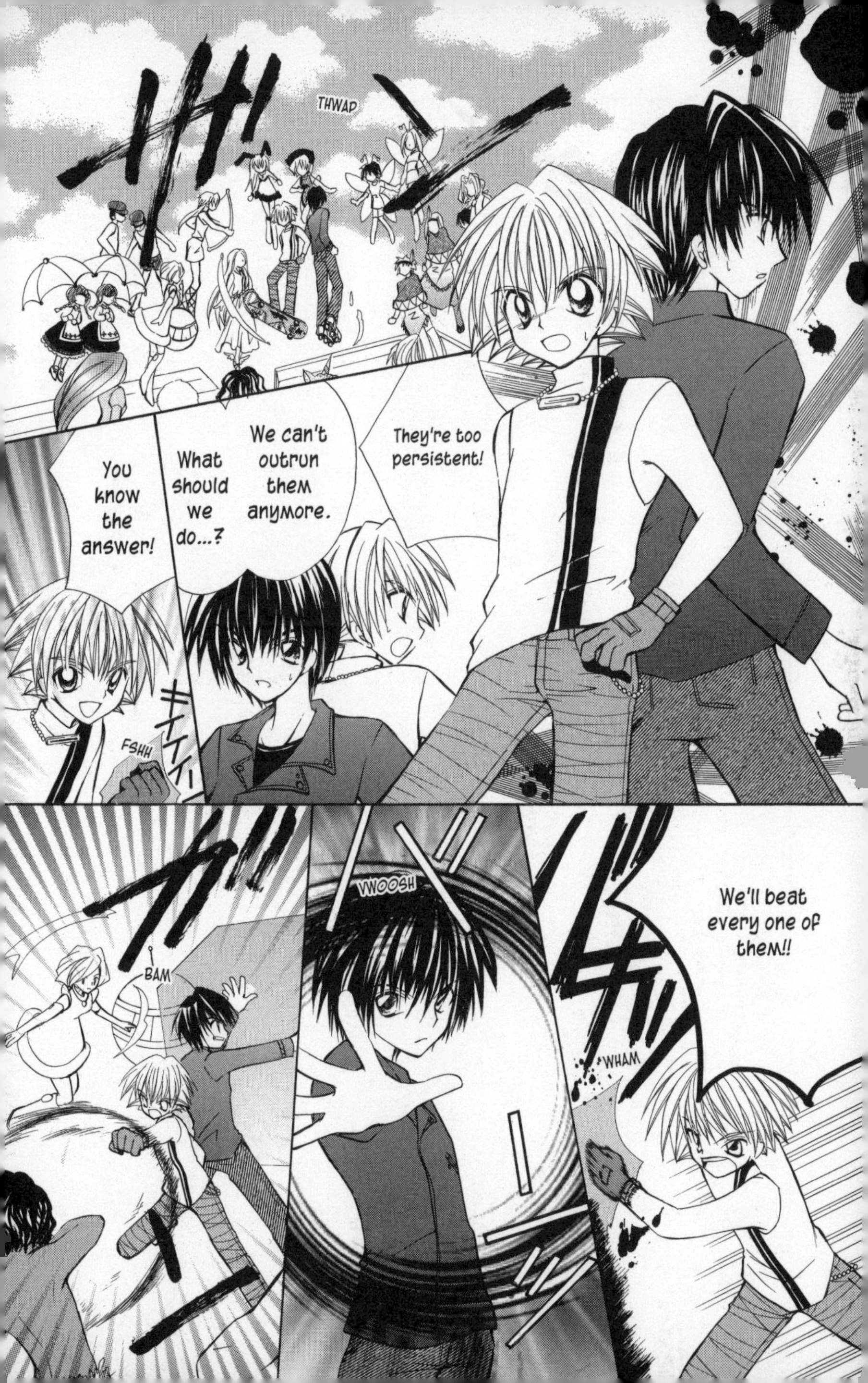
THWAP
They're too persistent!
We can't outrun them anymore.
What should we do...?
You know the answer!
FSHH
We'll beat every one of them!!
WHAM
VWOOSH
BAM

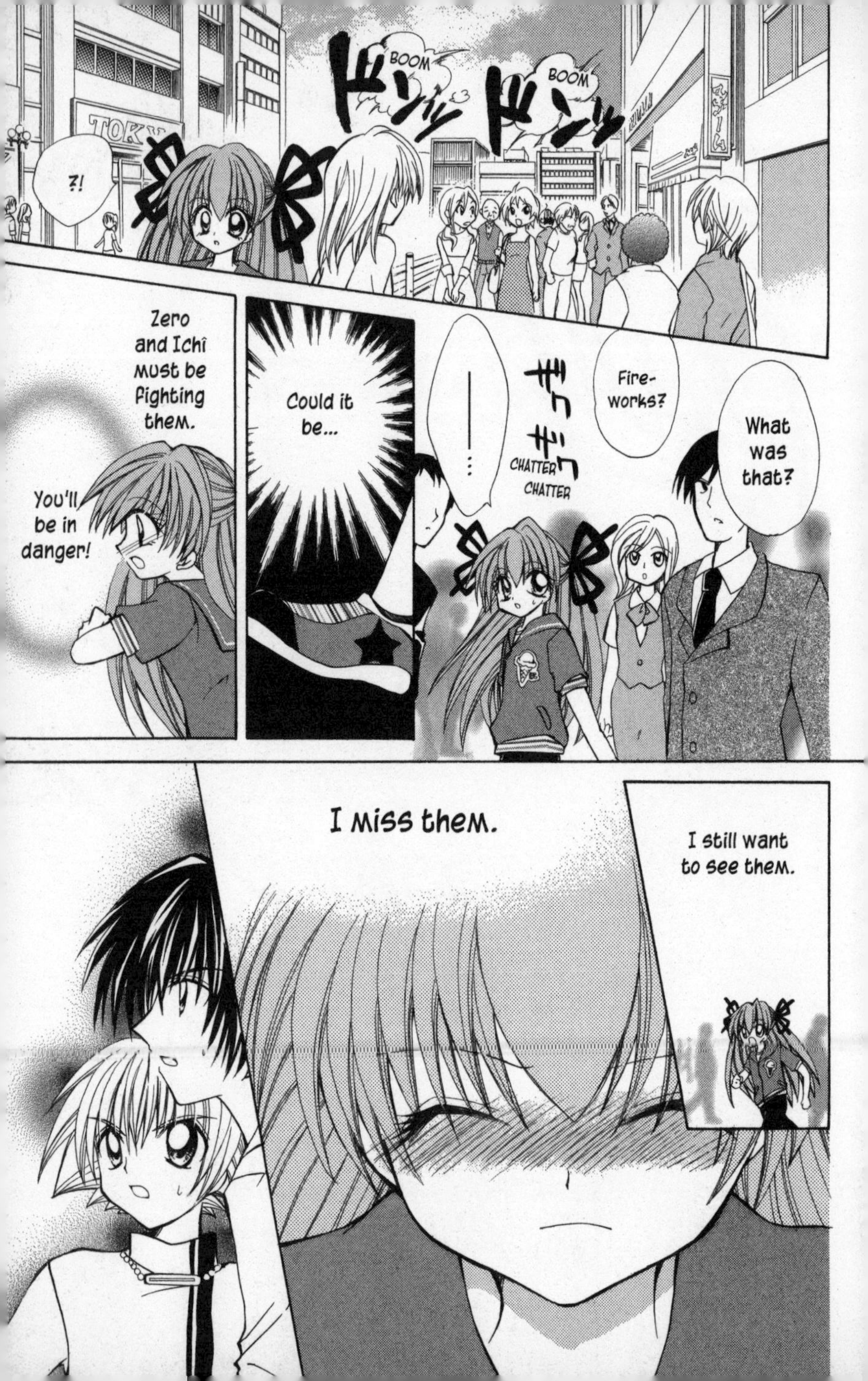
ドンッ
BOOM
ドンッ
BOOM
?!
What was that?
Fire-works?
ザワ ザワ
CHATTER CHATTER
—......
Could it be...
Zero and Ichi must be fighting them.
You'll be in danger!
I still want to see them.
I miss them.

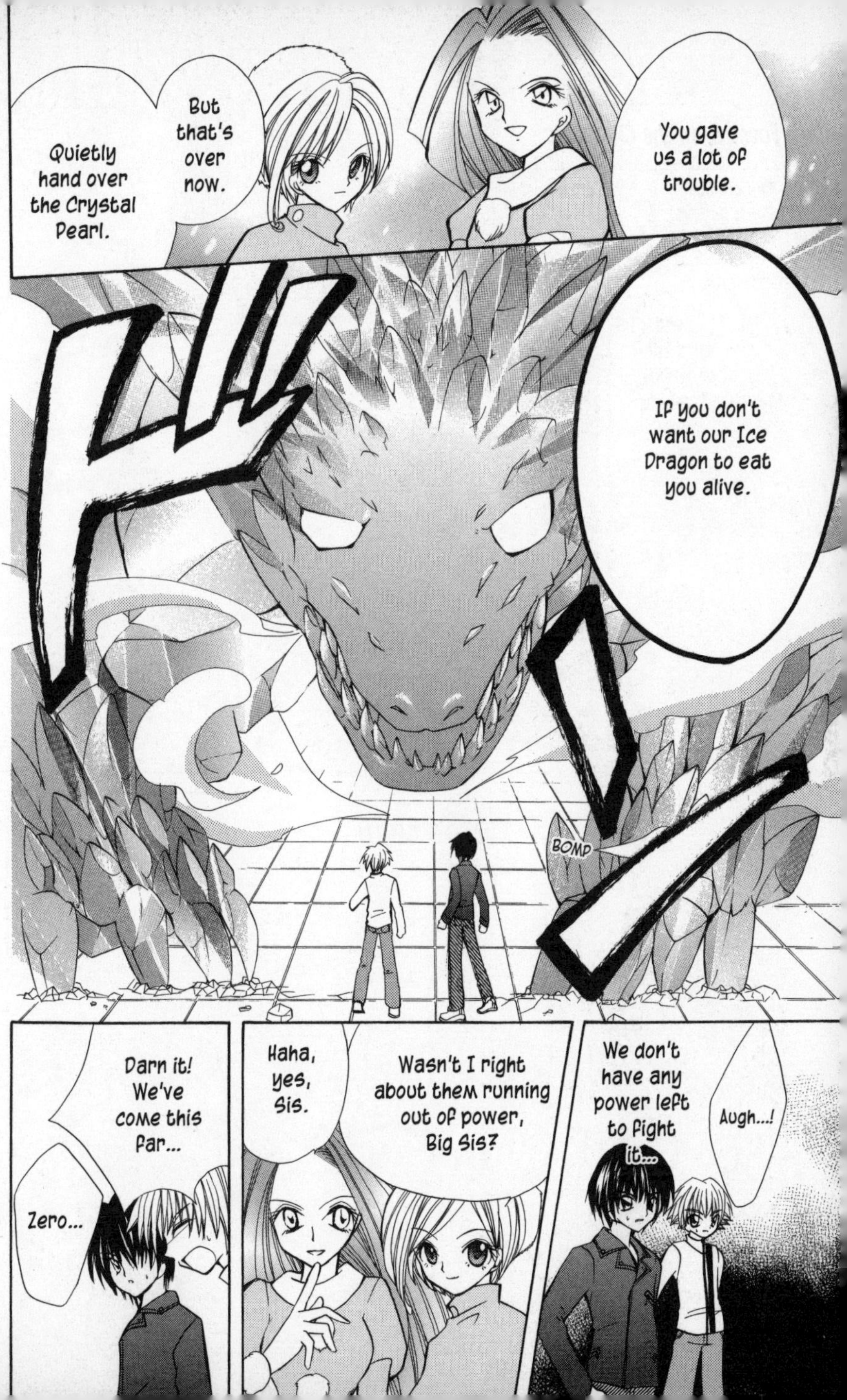
You gave us a lot of trouble.
But that's over now.
Quietly hand over the Crystal Pearl.
If you don't want our Ice Dragon to eat you alive.
BOMP
Augh...!
We don't have any power left to fight it...
Wasn't I right about them running out of power, Big Sis?
Haha, yes, Sis.
Darn it! We've come this far...
Zero...

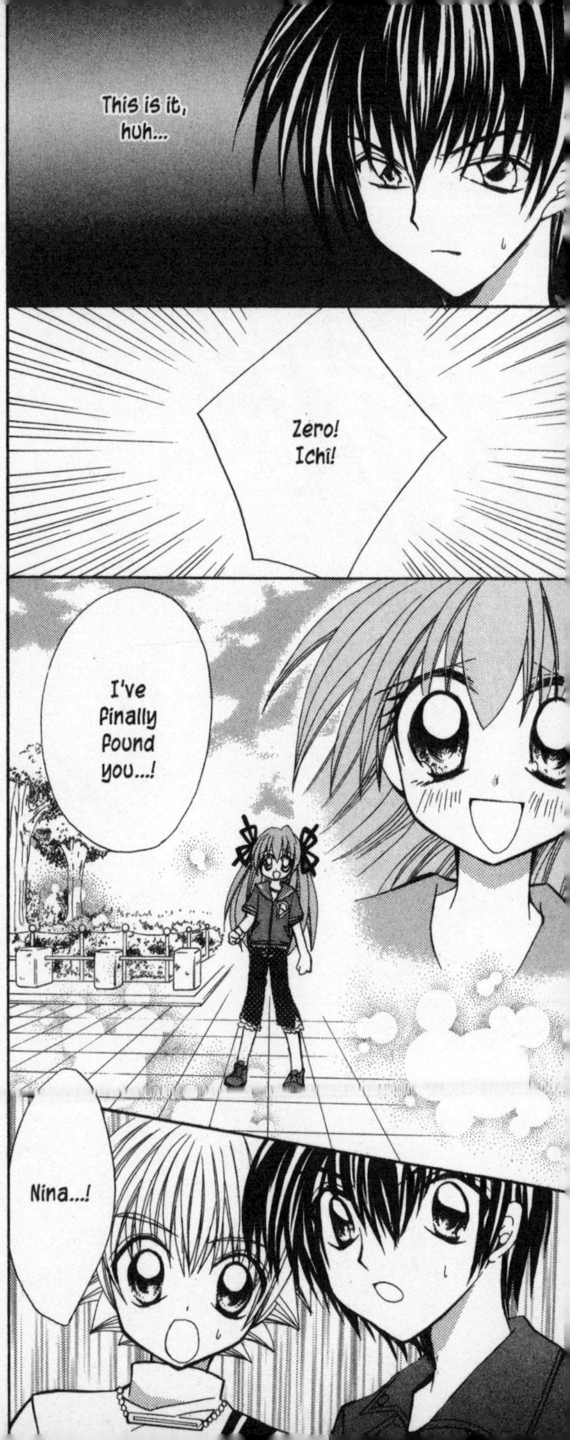
This is it, huh...
Zero! Ichi!
I've finally found you...!
Nina...!

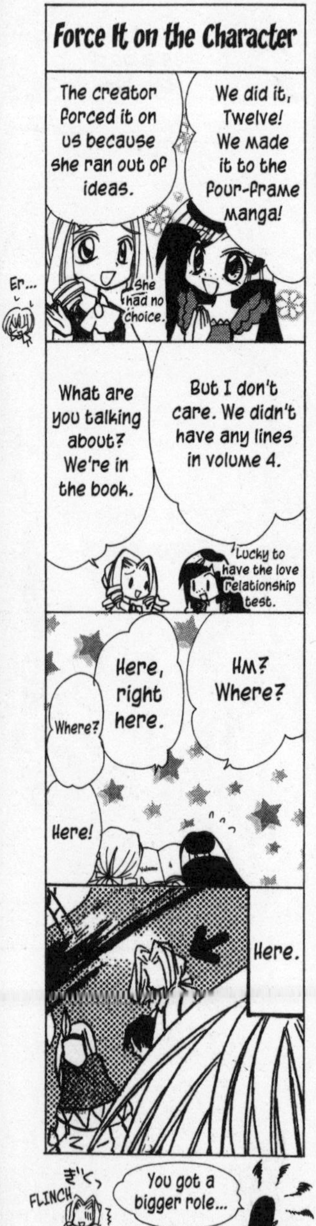
Force It on the Character
We did it, Twelve! We made it to the four-frame manga!
The creator forced it on us because she ran out of ideas.
She had no choice.
Er...
But I don't care. We didn't have any lines in volume 4.
What are you talking about? We're in the book.
Lucky to have the love relationship test.
HM? Where?
Here, right here.
Where?
Here!
Here.
You got a bigger role...
ぎくっ
FLINCH

Check out the first panel on page 60. ♡

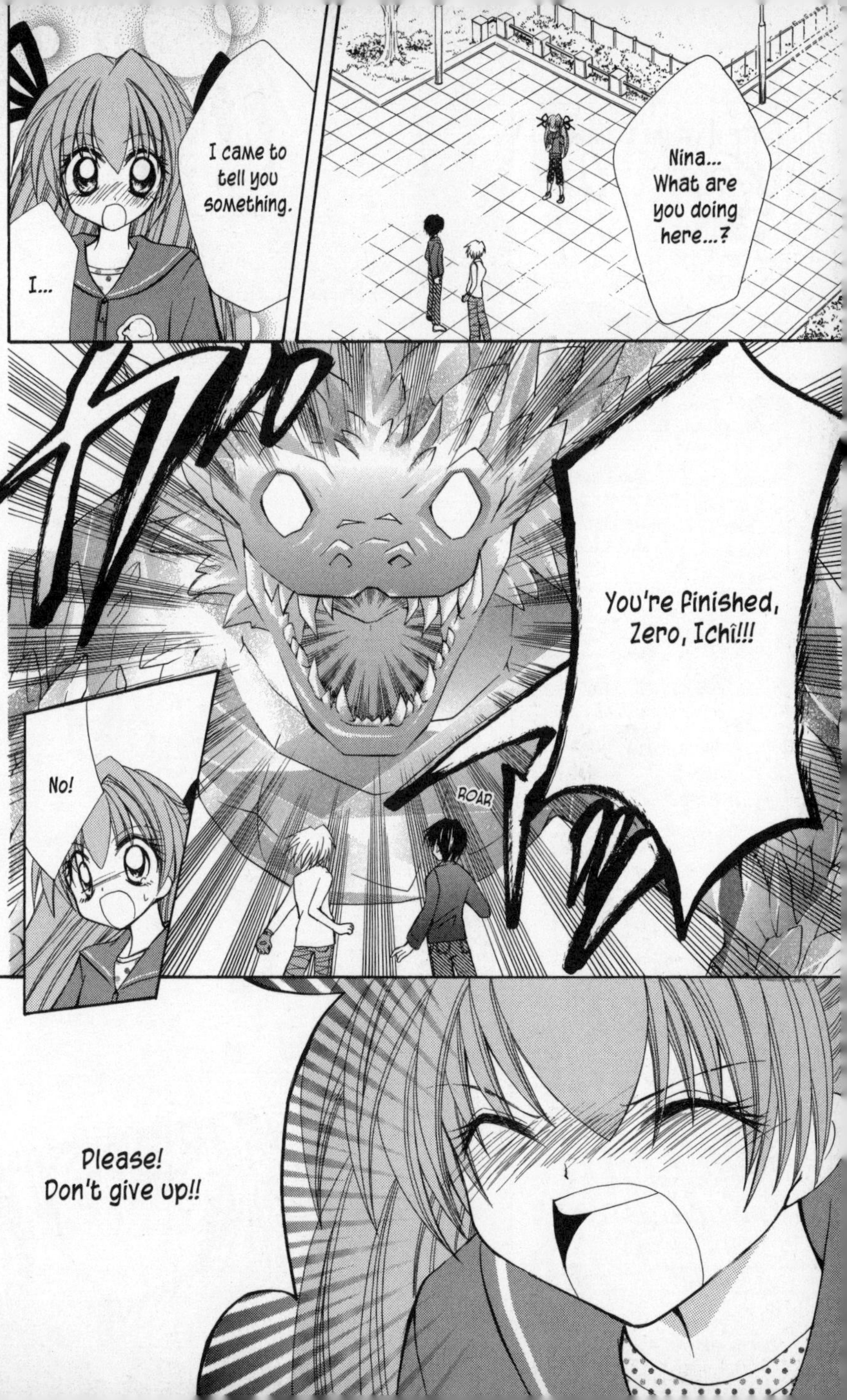
Nina... What are you doing here...?
I came to tell you something.
I...
You're finished, Zero, Ichi!!!
ROAR
No!
Please! Don't give up!!

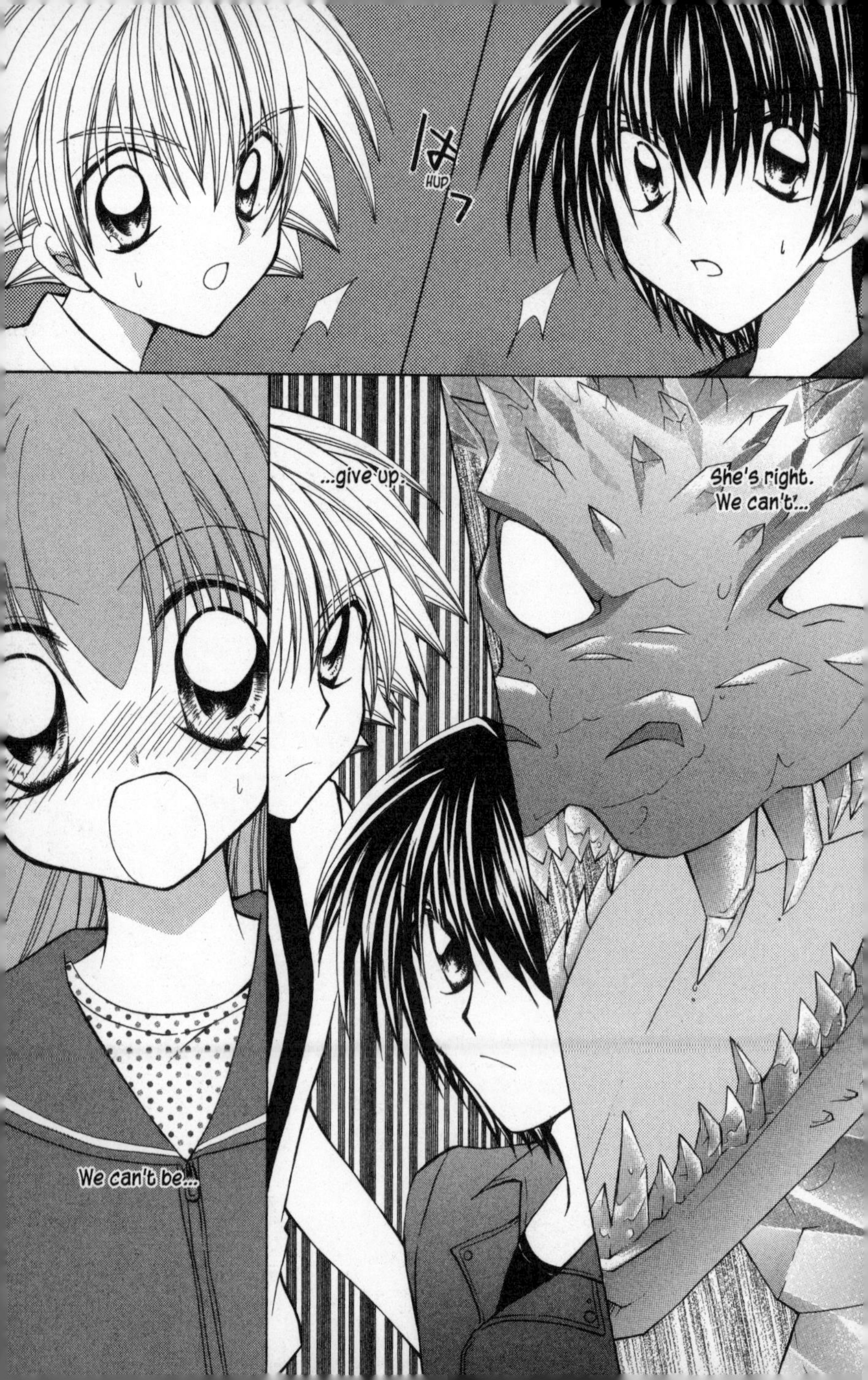
はっ
HUP
She's right. We can't...
...give up.
We can't be...

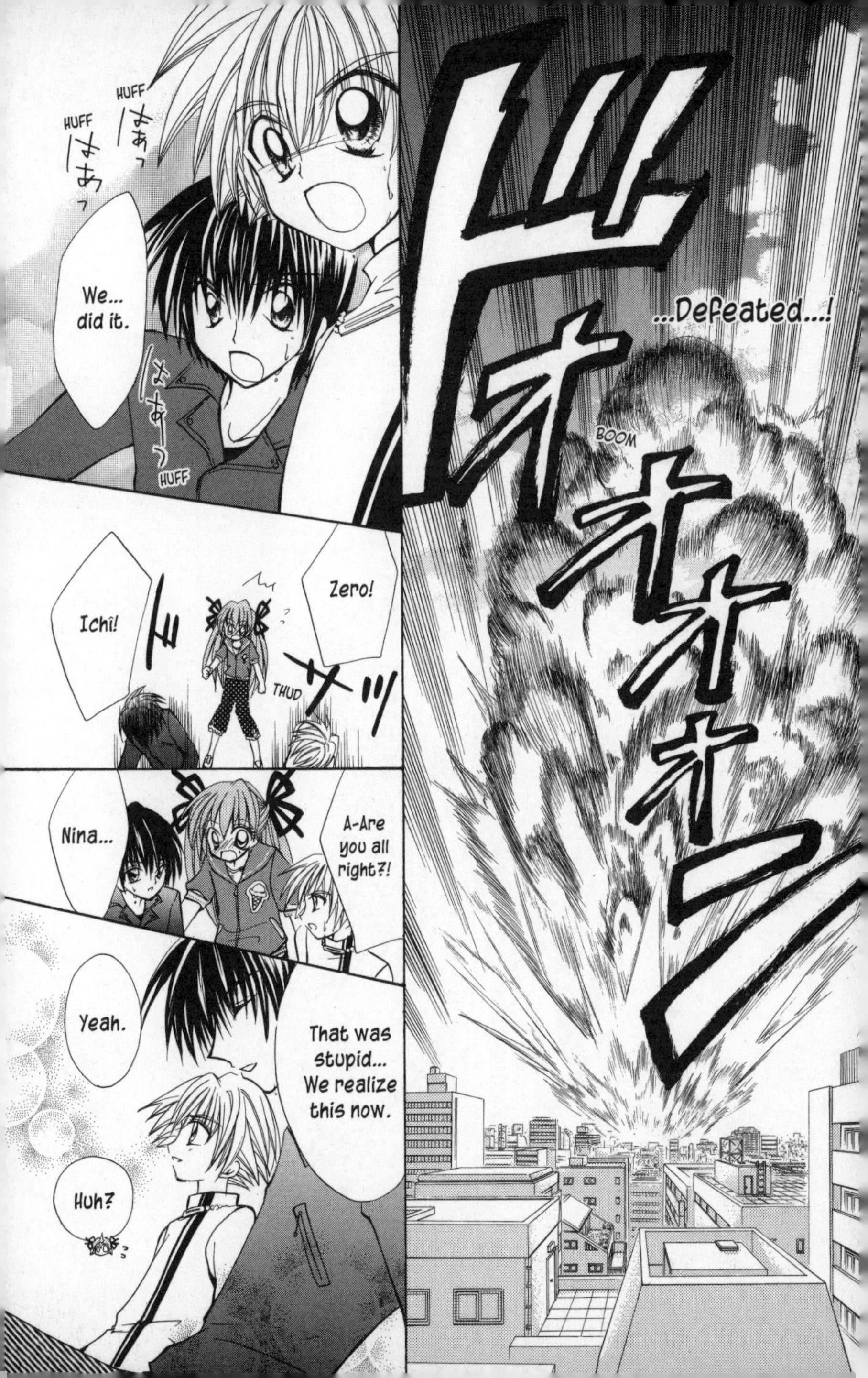
...Defeated...!
BOOM
HUFF
HUFF
We... did it.
HUFF
Zero!
THUD
Ichi!
A-Are you all right?!
Nina...
That was stupid... We realize this now.
Yeah.
Huh?

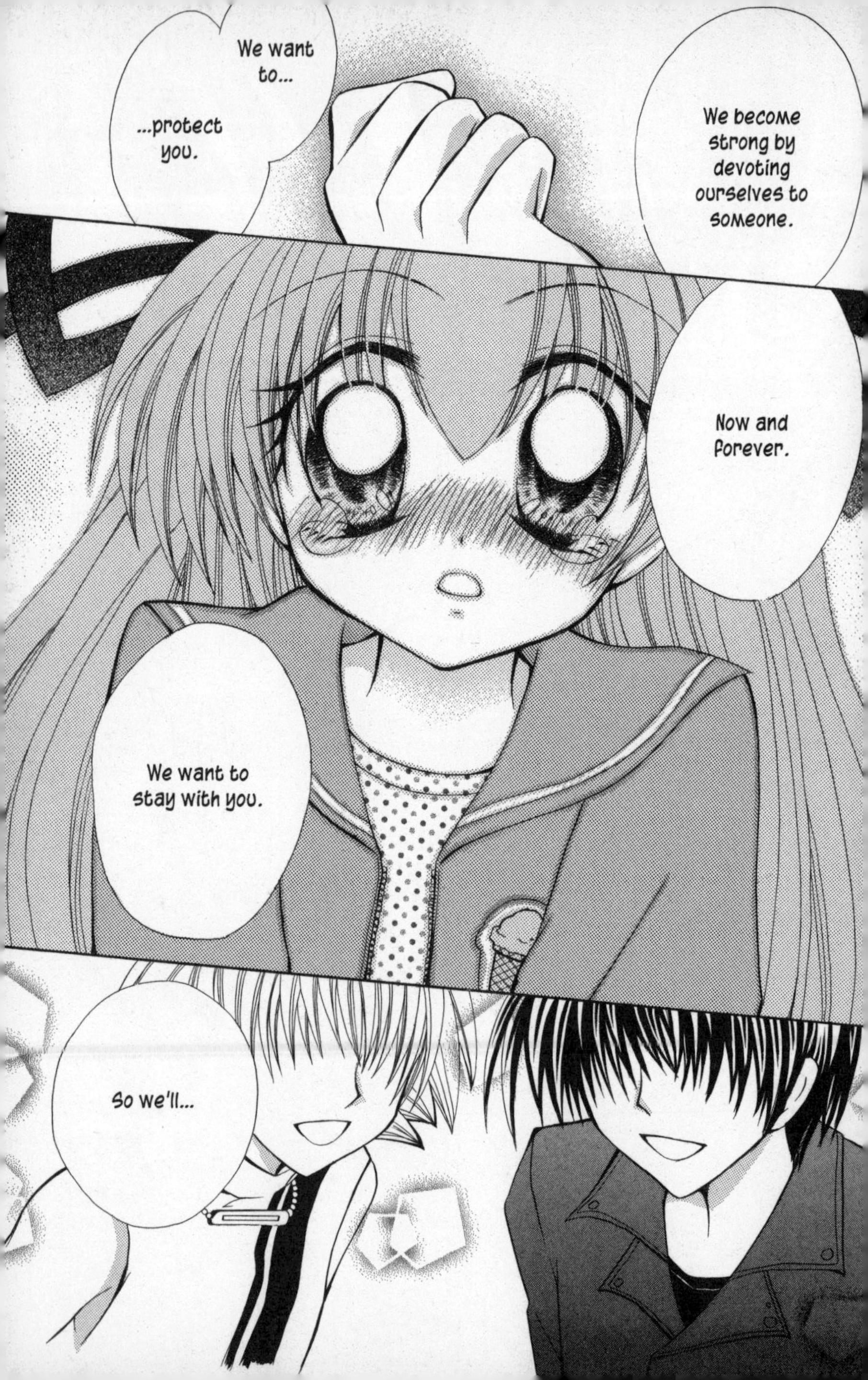

We become strong by devoting ourselves to someone.
We want to...
...protect you.
Now and forever.
We want to stay with you.
So we'll...

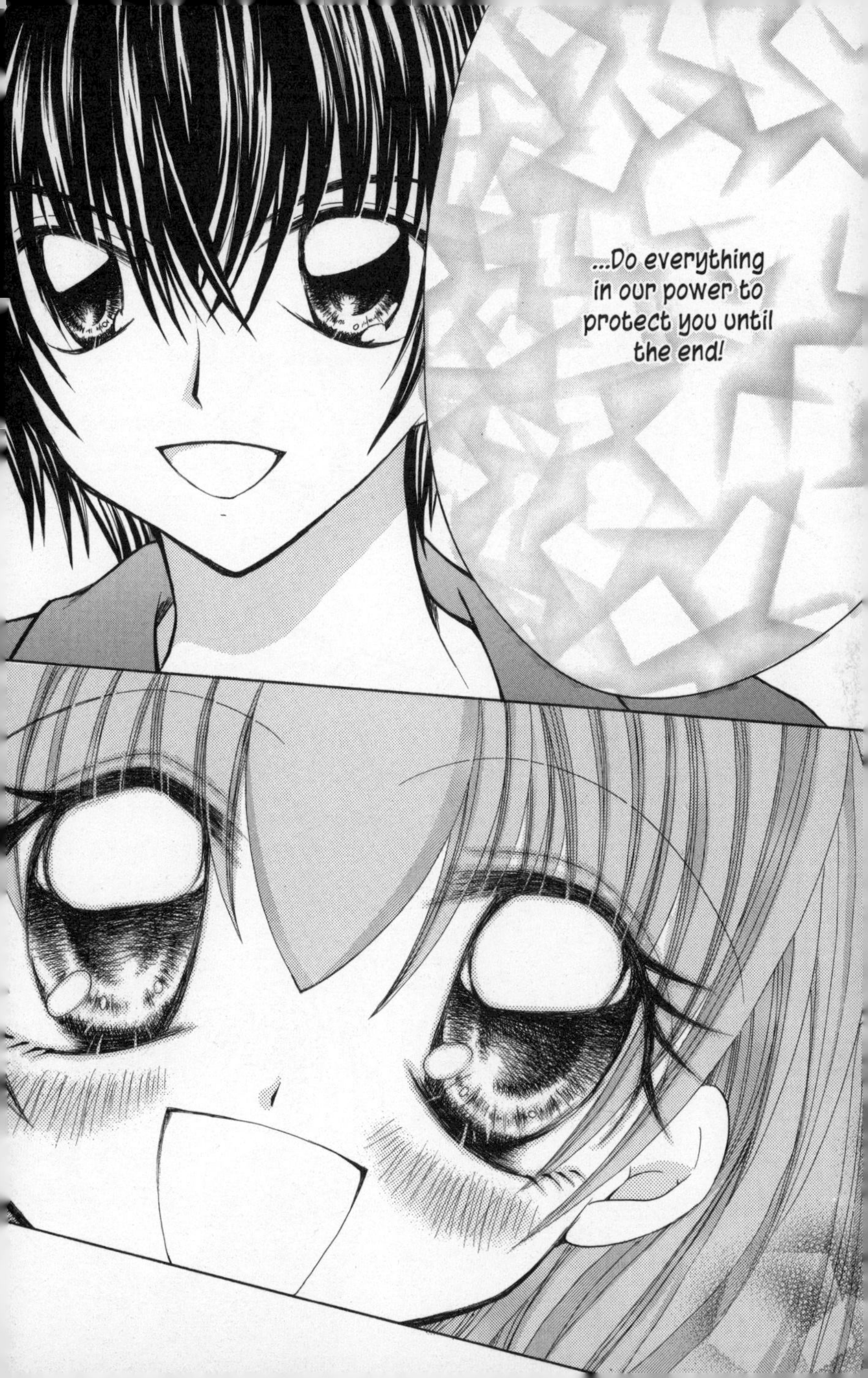
...Do everything in our power to protect you until the end!

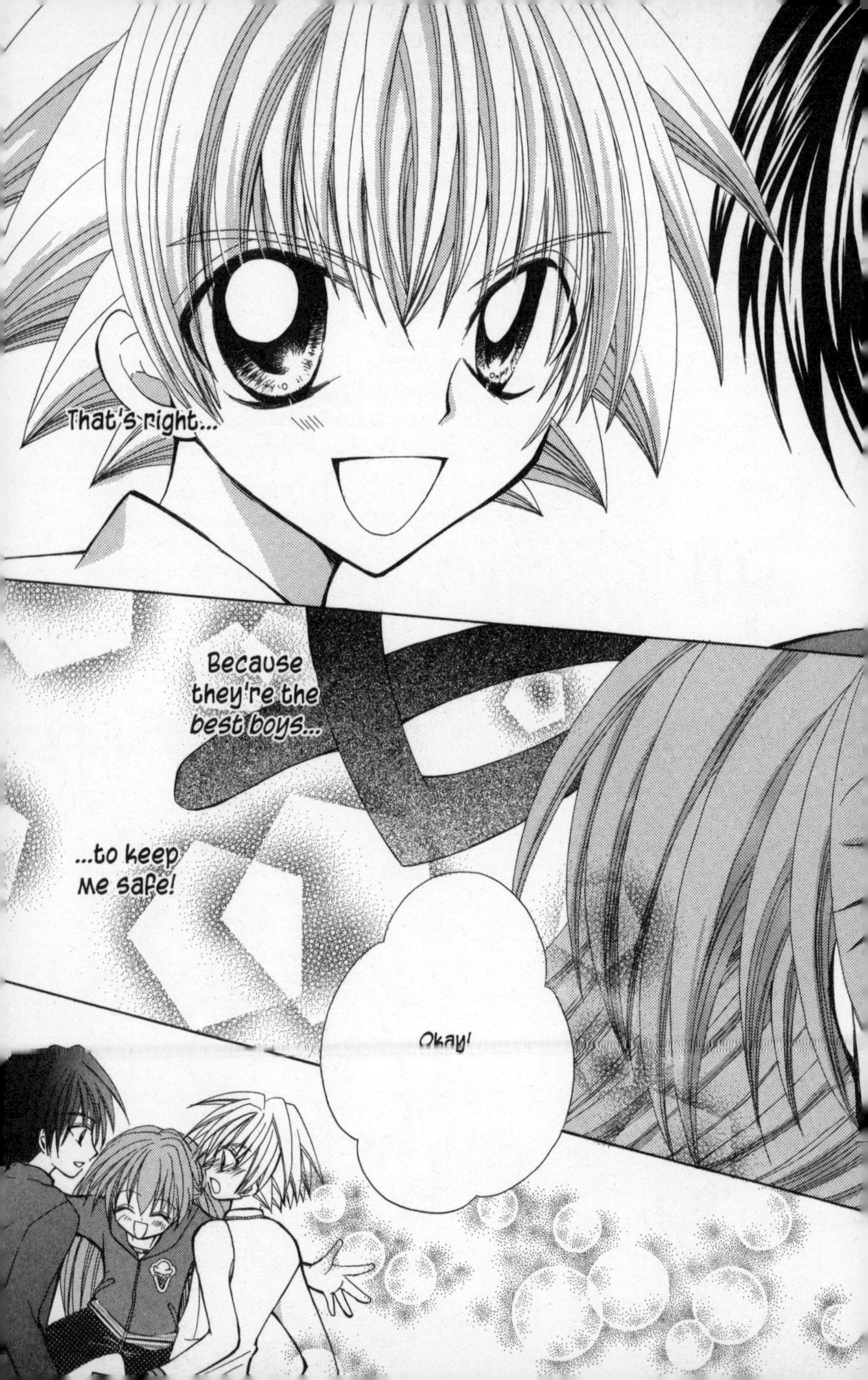
That's right...
Because they're the best boys...
...to keep me safe!
Okay!

Nina & Zero: Roommates

Mini-Theatre: TAKE 1

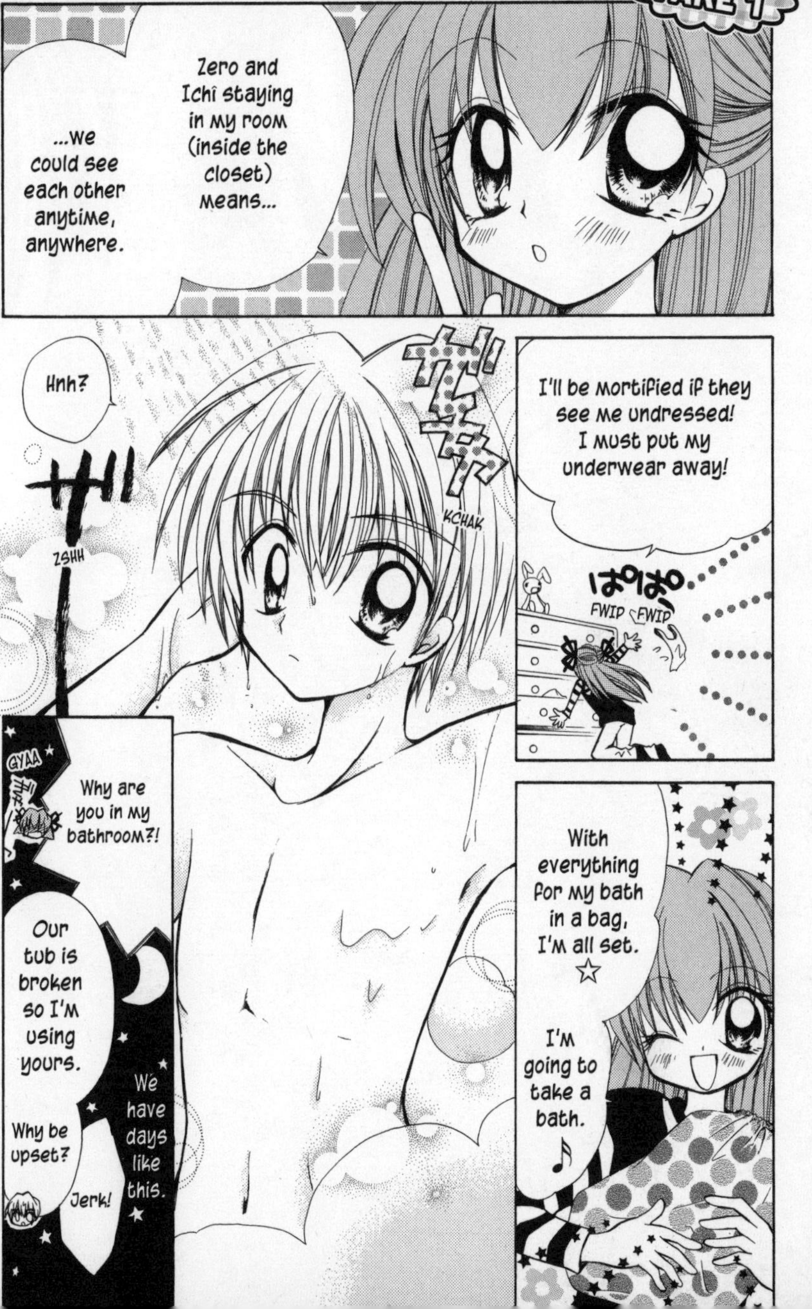
Zero and Ichî staying in my room (inside the closet) means...
...we could see each other anytime, anywhere.
I'll be mortified if they see me undressed! I must put my underwear away!
ぱぱ
FWIP FWIP
With everything for my bath in a bag, I'm all set. ☆
I'm going to take a bath. ♪
KCHAK
ZSHH
Hnh?
GYAA
Why are you in my bathroom?!
Our tub is broken so I'm using yours.
We have days like this.
Why be upset?
Jerk!

Zero & Ichî: Special Cooking

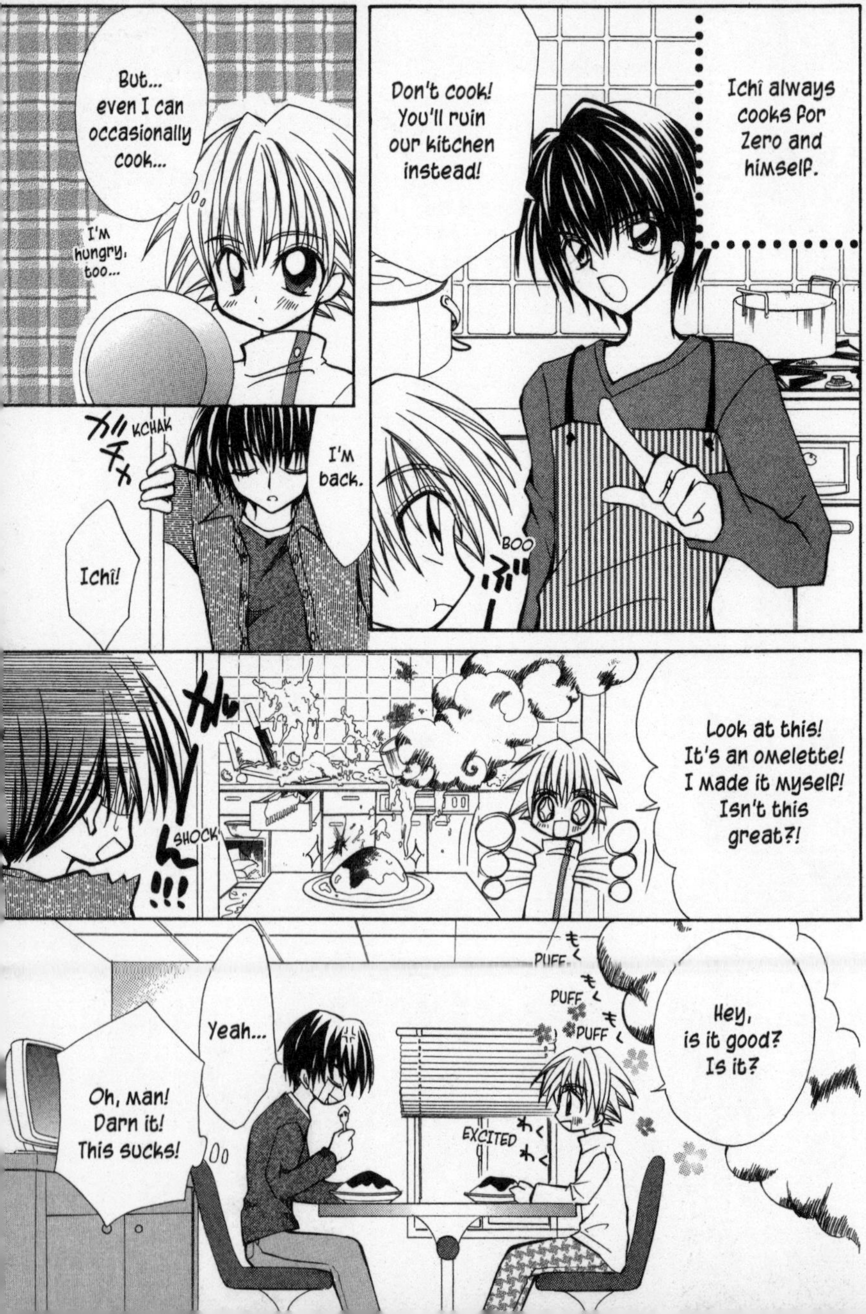
Ichî always cooks for Zero and himself.
Don't cook! You'll ruin our kitchen instead!
BOO
But... even I can occasionally cook...
I'm hungry, too...
I'm back.
KCHAK
Ichî!
Look at this! It's an omelette! I made it myself! Isn't this great?!
SHOCK
Hey, is it good? Is it?
PUFF
PUFF
PUFF
EXCITED
Yeah...
Oh, man! Darn it! This sucks!

Sun & For: Sun's Plead

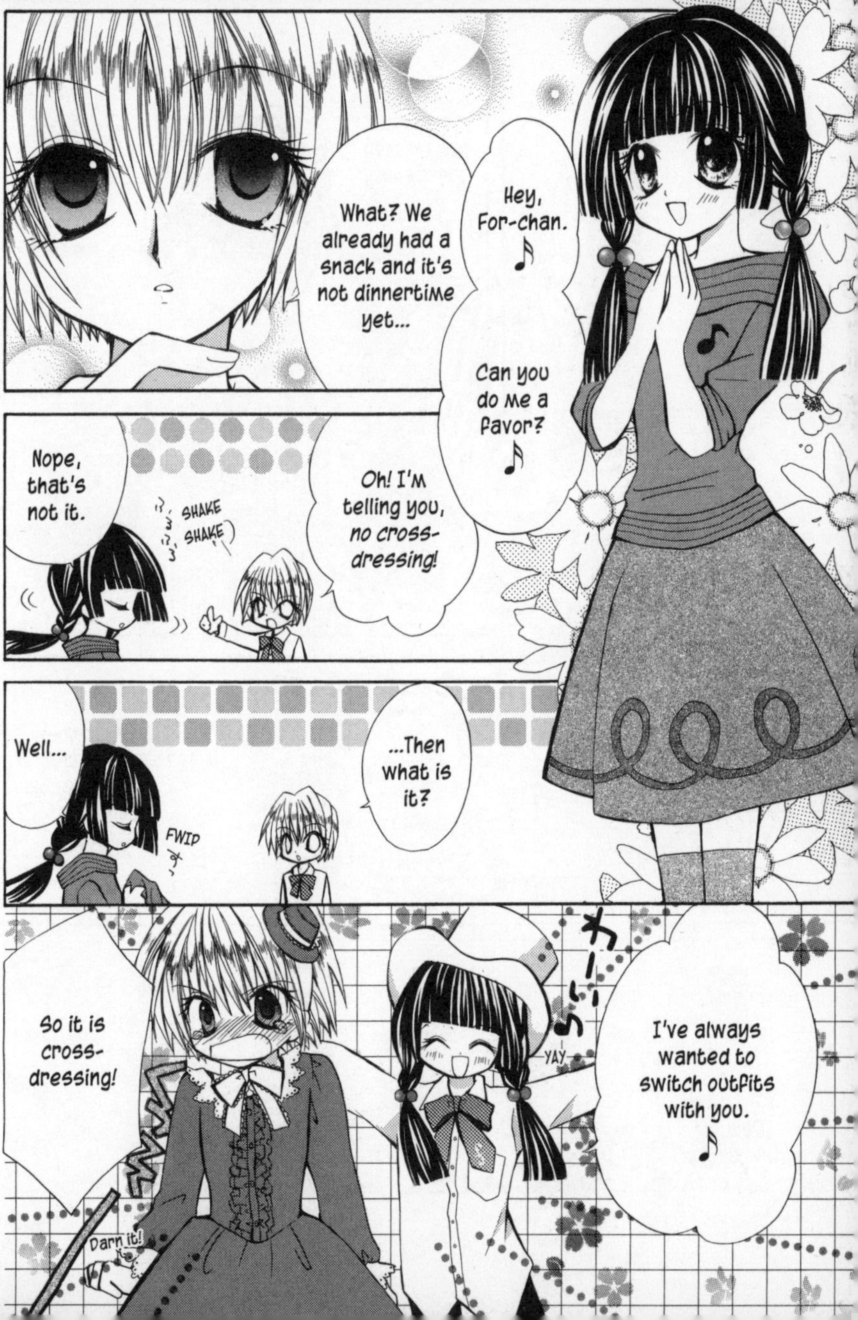
Hey, For-chan. ♪
Can you do me a favor? ♪
What? We already had a snack and it's not dinnertime yet...
Oh! I'm telling you, no cross-dressing!
SHAKE SHAKE
Nope, that's not it.
...Then what is it?
FWIP
Well...
I've always wanted to switch outfits with you. ♪
YAY
So it is cross-dressing!
Darn it!

Rokka & Gô: Only If You Do That...

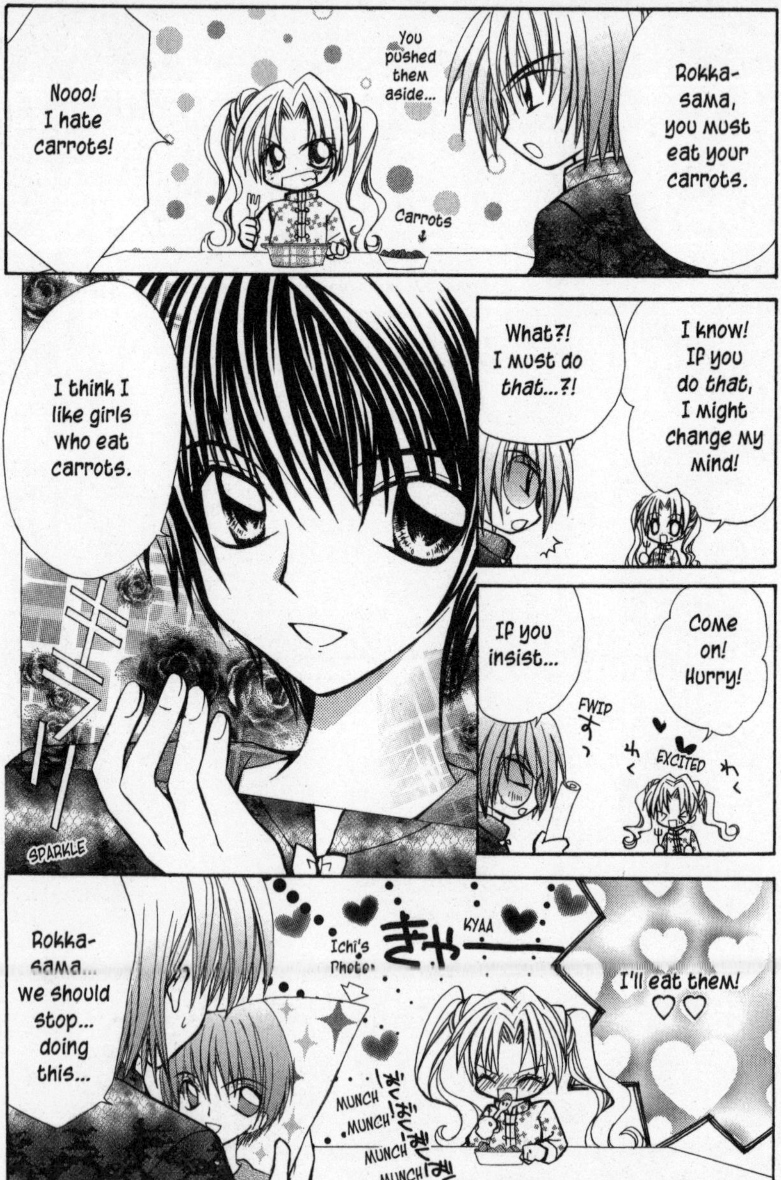
Rokka-sama, you must eat your carrots.
You pushed them aside...
Nooo! I hate carrots!
Carrots
I know! If you do that, I might change my mind!
What?! I must do that...?!
Come on! Hurry!
If you insist...
FWIP
EXCITED
I think I like girls who eat carrots.
SPARKLE
I'll eat them! ♡♡
きゃー
KYAA
Ichi's Photo
MUNCH MUNCH MUNCH MUNCH
Rokka-sama... we should stop... doing this...

Continues on page 108!

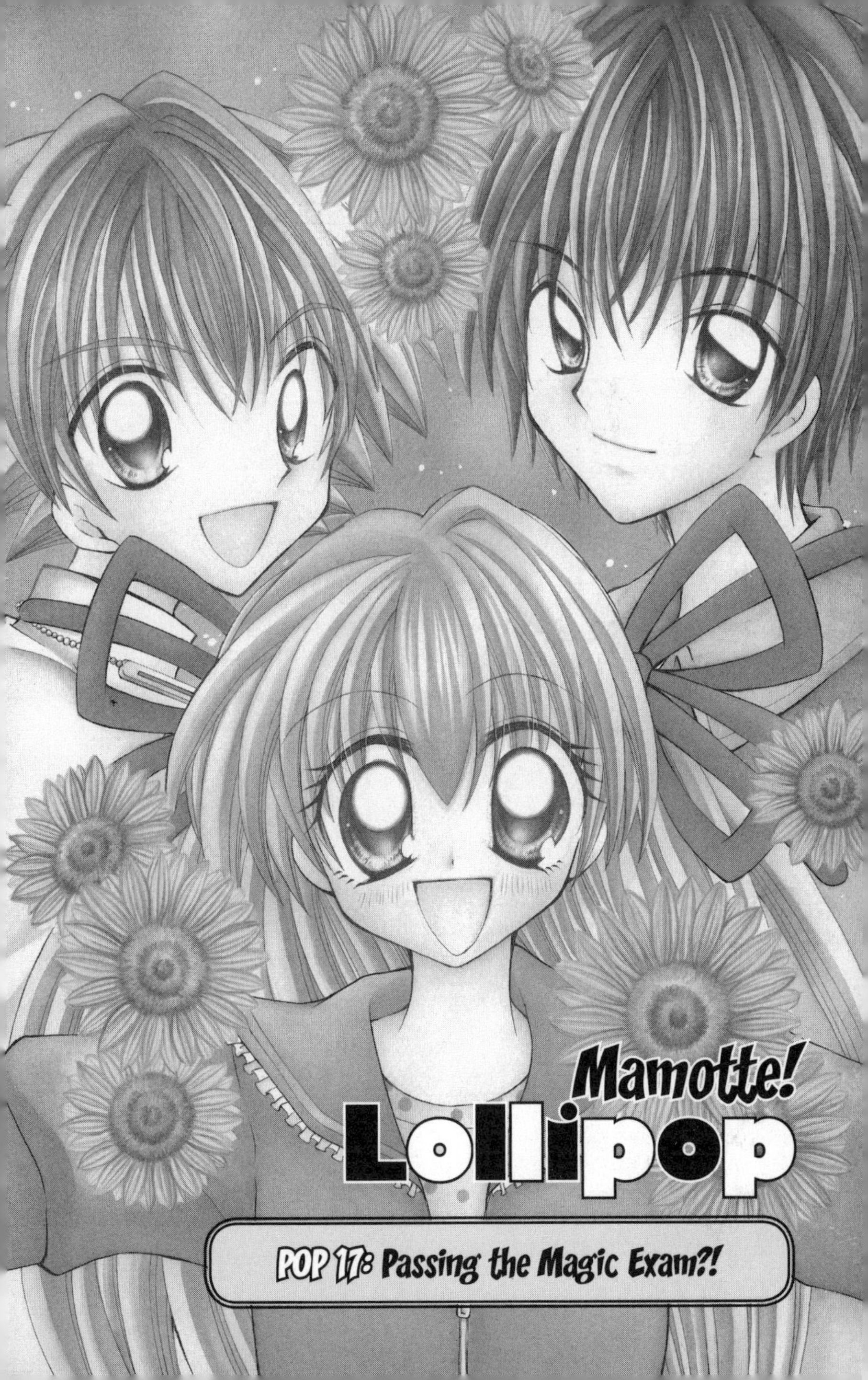
Mamotte!
Lollipop
POP 17: Passing the Magic Exam?!

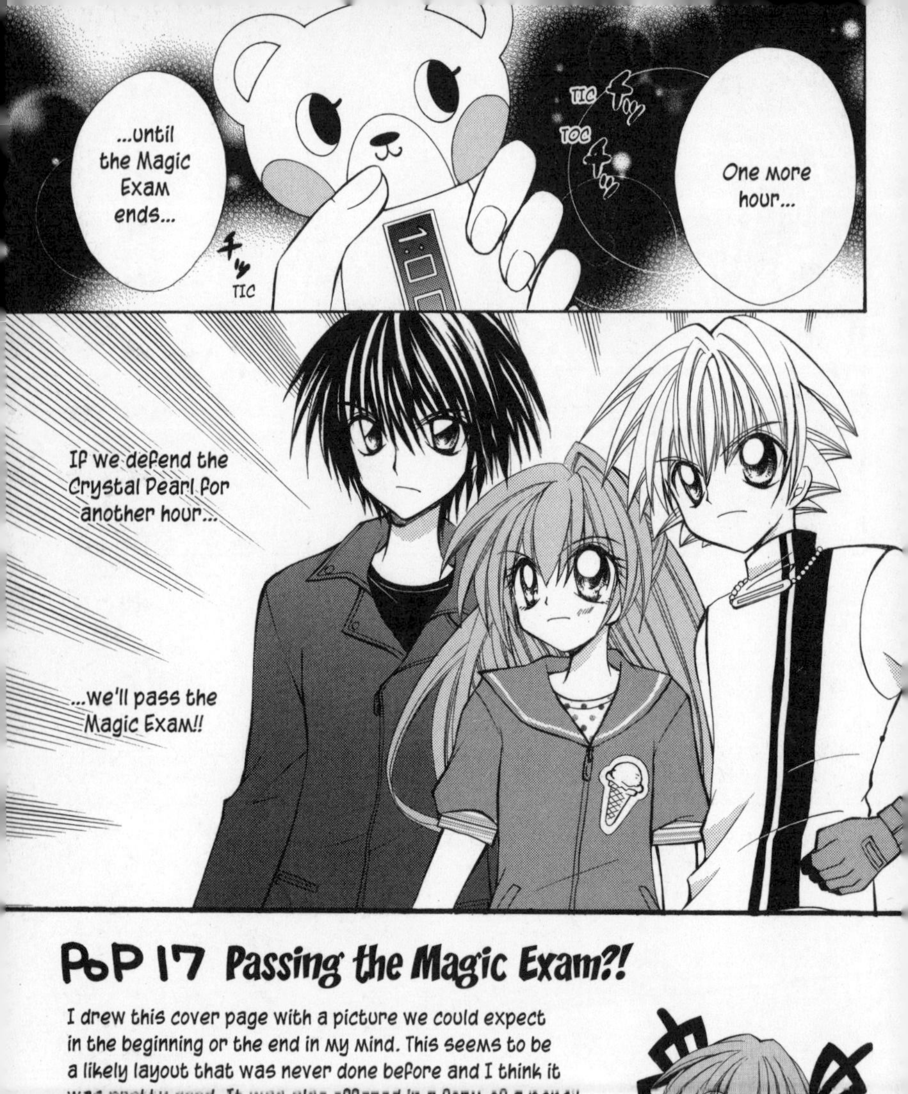
One more hour...
TIC
TOC
...until the Magic Exam ends...
TIC
If we defend the Crystal Pearl for another hour...
...we'll pass the Magic Exam!!

PoP 17 Passing the Magic Exam?!

I drew this cover page with a picture we could expect in the beginning or the end in my mind. This seems to be a likely layout that was never done before and I think it was pretty good. It was also offered in a form of a pencil board at the K Fest in 2004. There was a bunch of other merchandise, too!

In this episode, the way everyone romps around with the characters that reappear fits the image of *Mamotte! Lollipop*. And now we have a new character and new developments. I hope everyone will enjoy the new story as well.

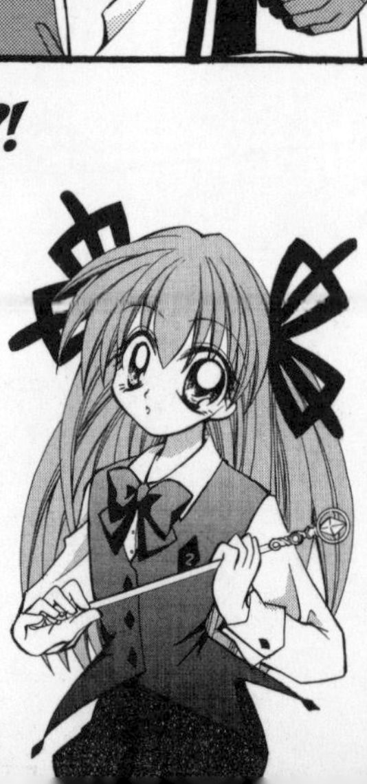

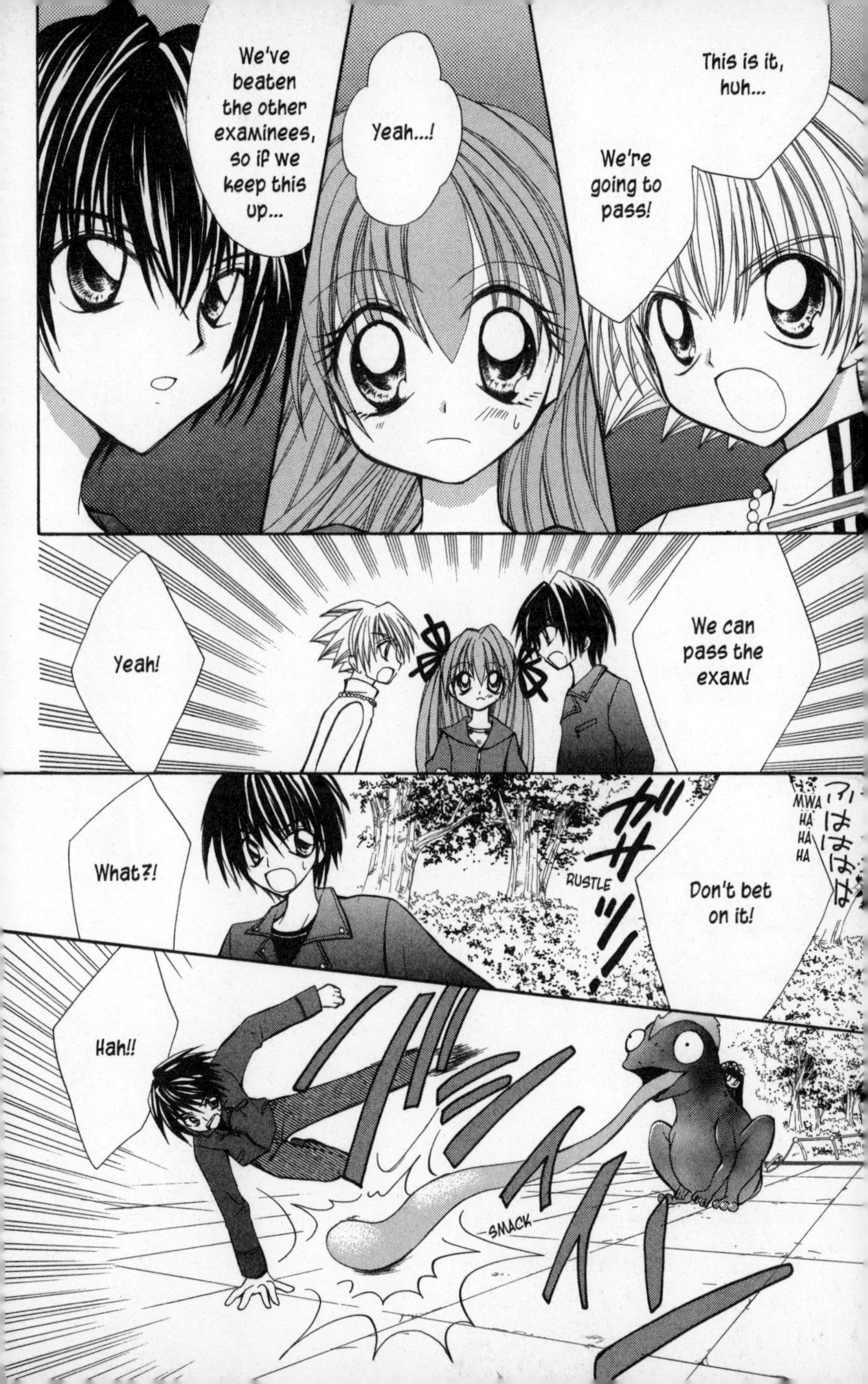
This is it, huh...
We've beaten the other examinees, so if we keep this up...
We're going to pass!
Yeah...!
We can pass the exam!
Yeah!
MWA HA HA HA
Don't bet on it!
RUSTLE
What?!
Hah!!
SMACK

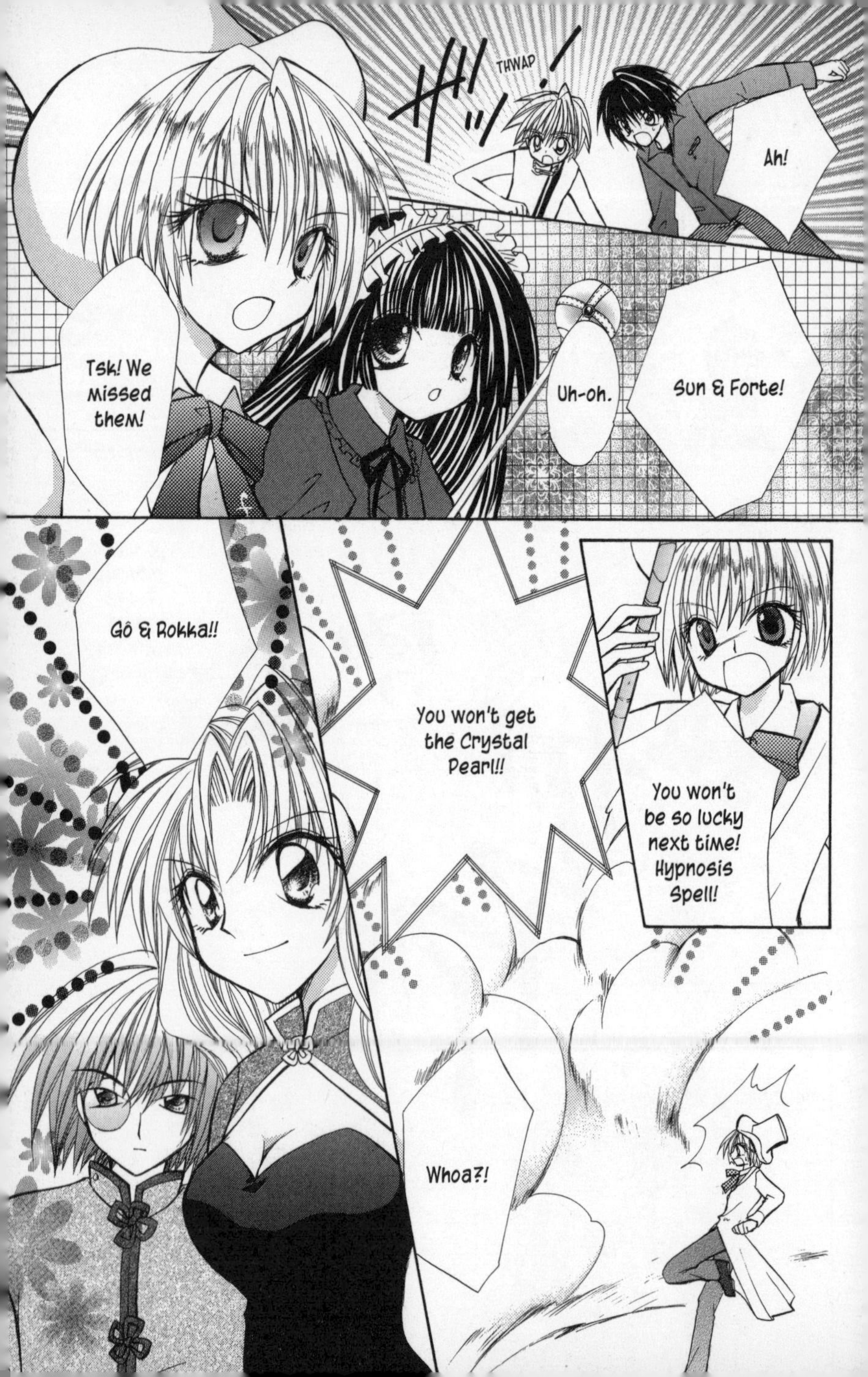
THWAP
Ah!
Sun & Forte!
Uh-oh.
Tsk! We missed them!
You won't be so lucky next time! Hypnosis Spell!
Whoa?!
Gô & Rokka!!
You won't get the Crystal Pearl!!

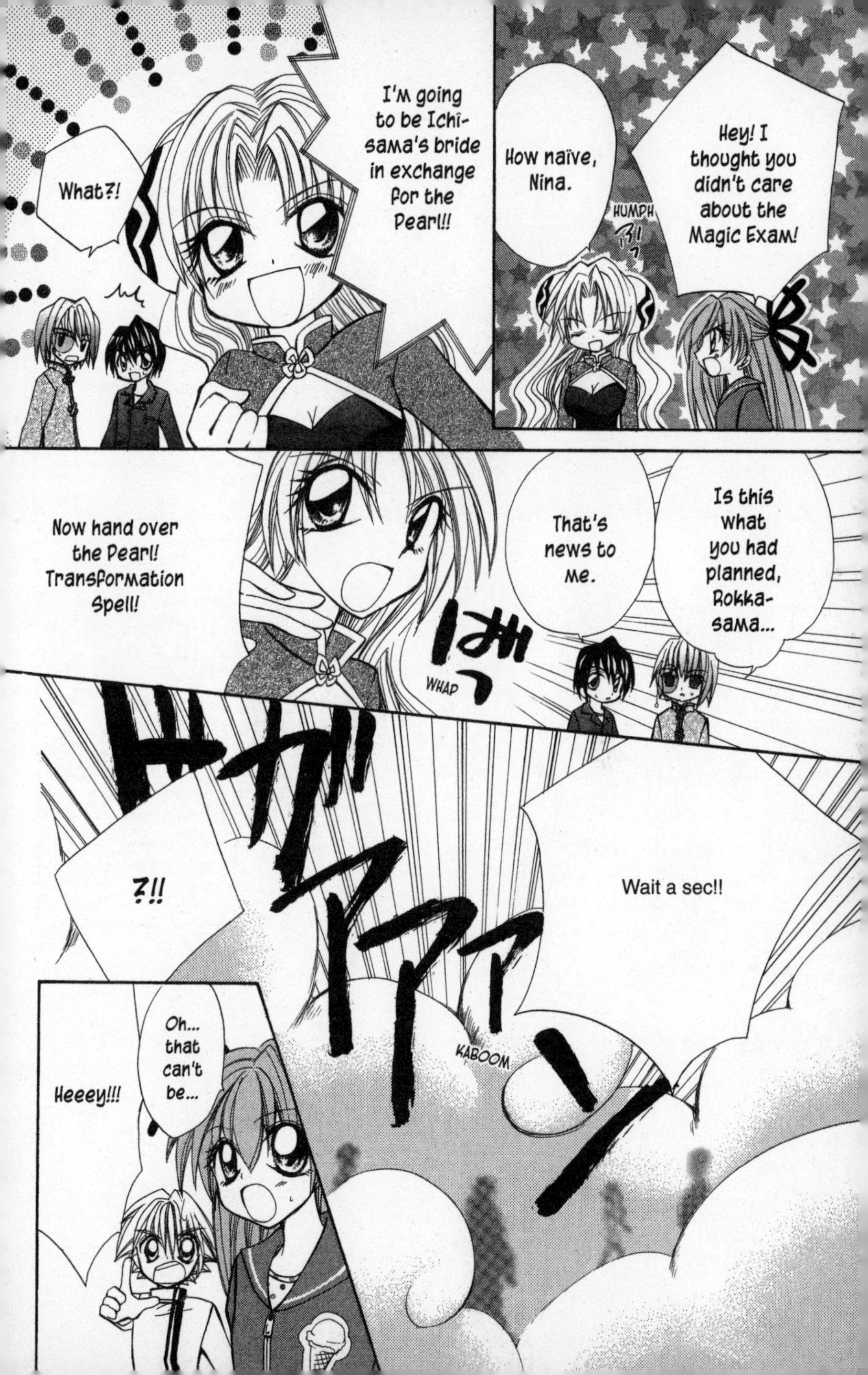
Hey! I thought you didn't care about the Magic Exam!
How naïve, Nina.
HUMPH
I'm going to be Ichi-sama's bride in exchange for the Pearl!!
What?!
Is this what you had planned, Rokka-sama...
That's news to me.
Now hand over the Pearl! Transformation Spell!
WHAP
Wait a sec!!
KABOOM
?!!
Oh... that can't be...
Heeey!!!

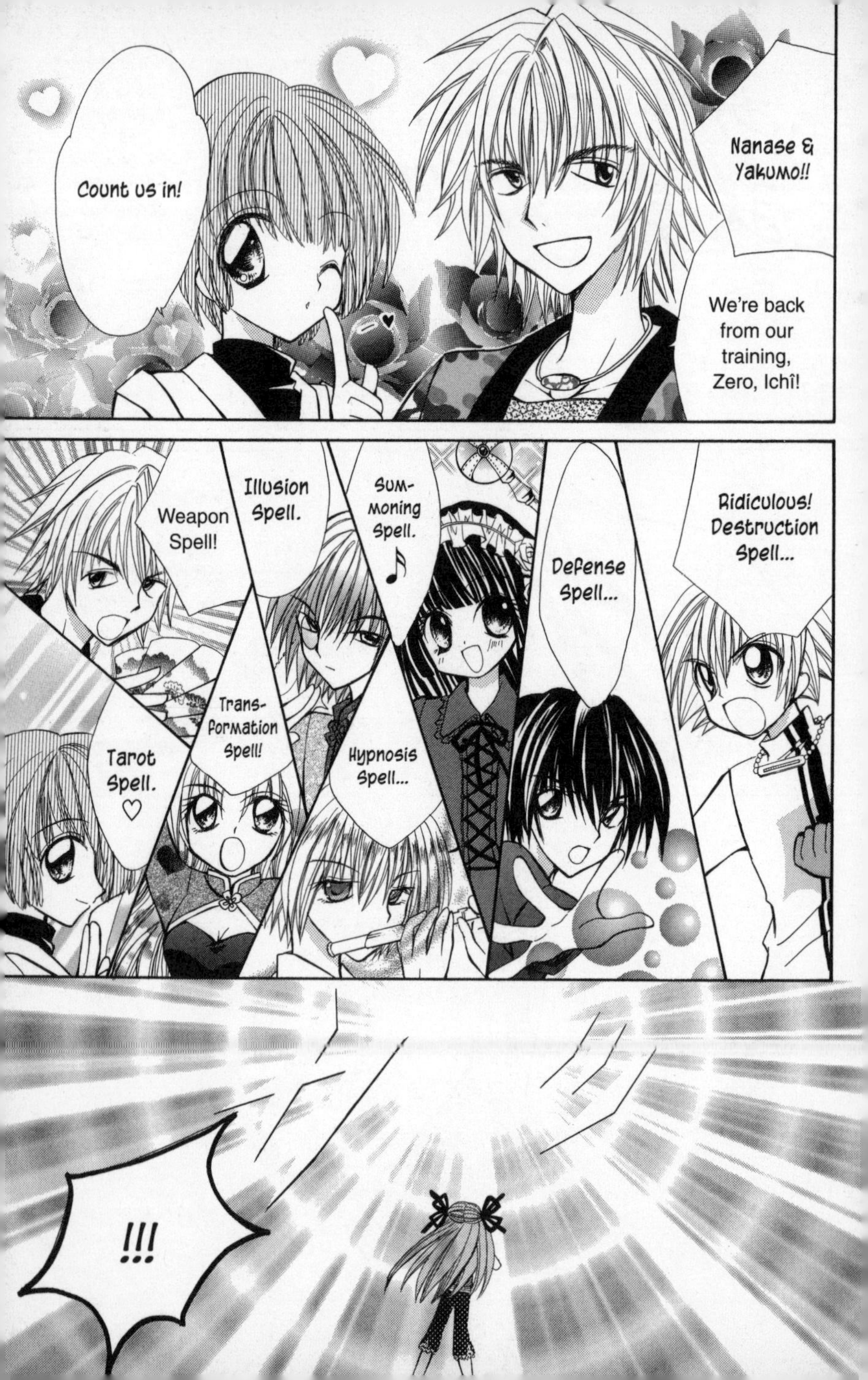
Nanase & Yakumo!!
We're back from our training, Zero, Ichî!
Count us in!
Ridiculous! Destruction Spell...
Defense Spell...
Sum-moning Spell. ♪
Hypnosis Spell...
Illusion Spell.
Trans-formation Spell!
Weapon Spell!
Tarot Spell. ♡
!!!

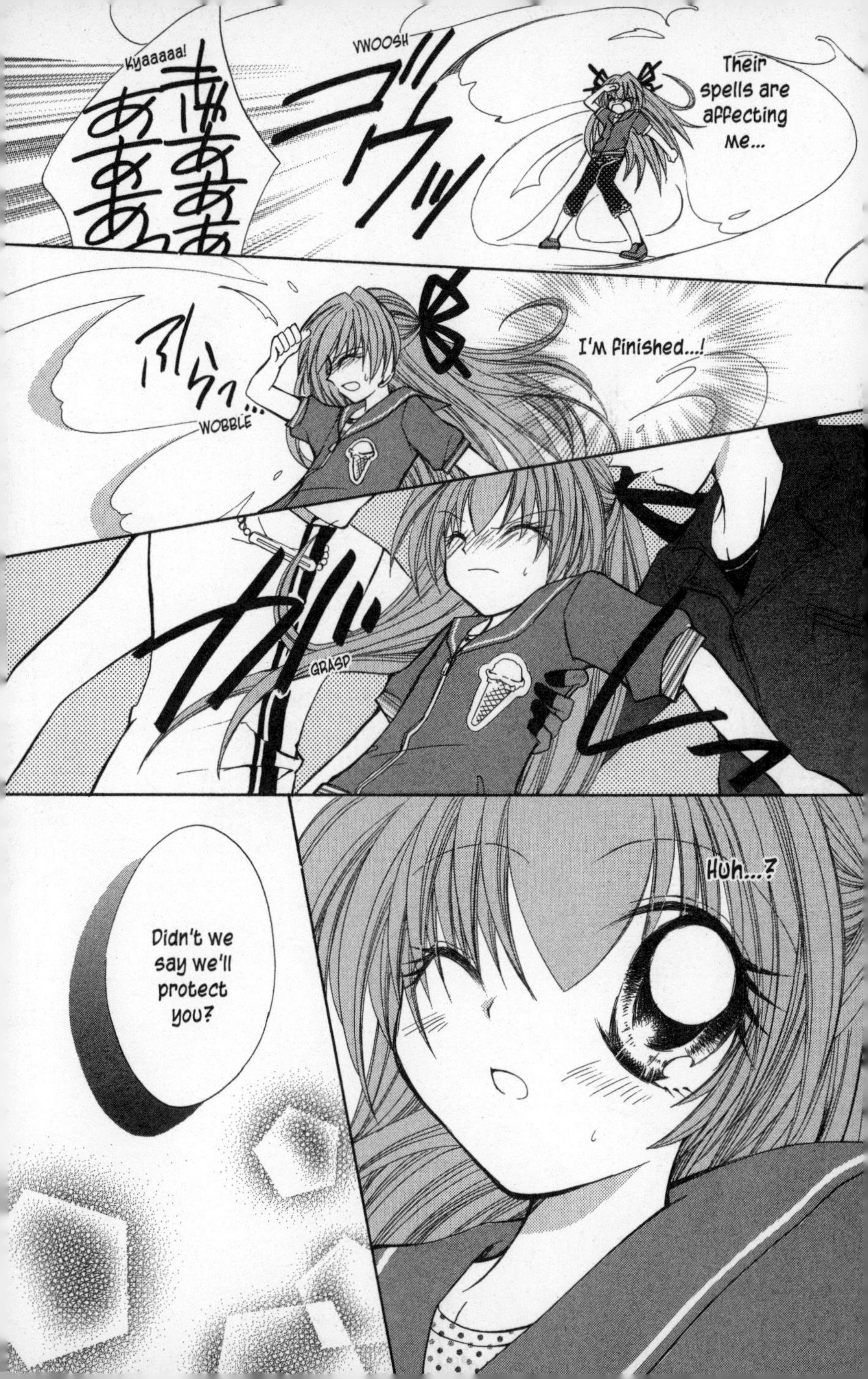

Their spells are affecting me...
VWOOSH
Kyaaaaa!
I'm finished...!
WOBBLE
GRASP
Huh...?
Didn't we say we'll protect you?

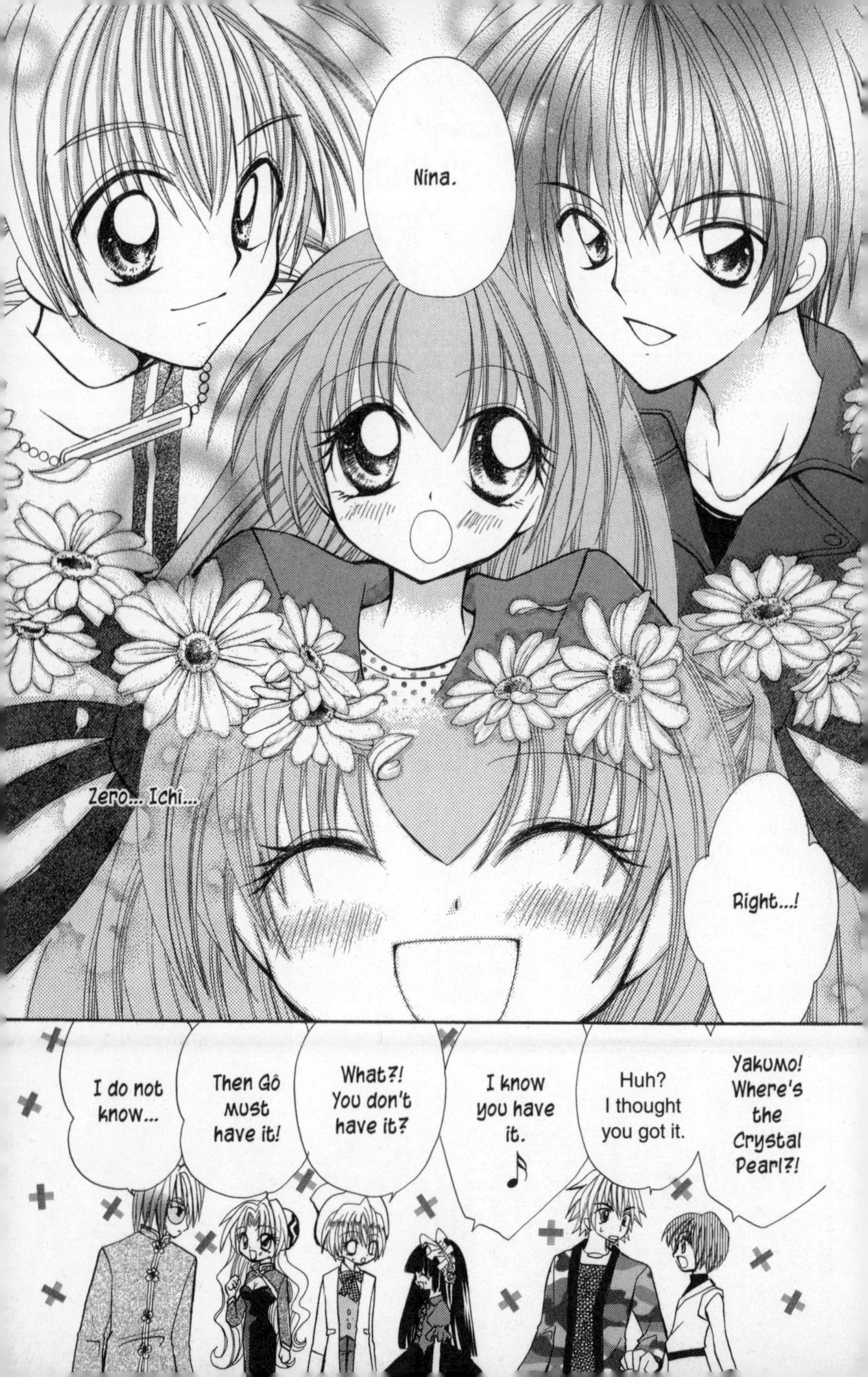
Nina.
Zero... Ichi...
Right...!
Yakumo! Where's the Crystal Pearl?!
Huh? I thought you got it.
I know you have it. ♪
What?! You don't have it?
Then Gô must have it!
I do not know...

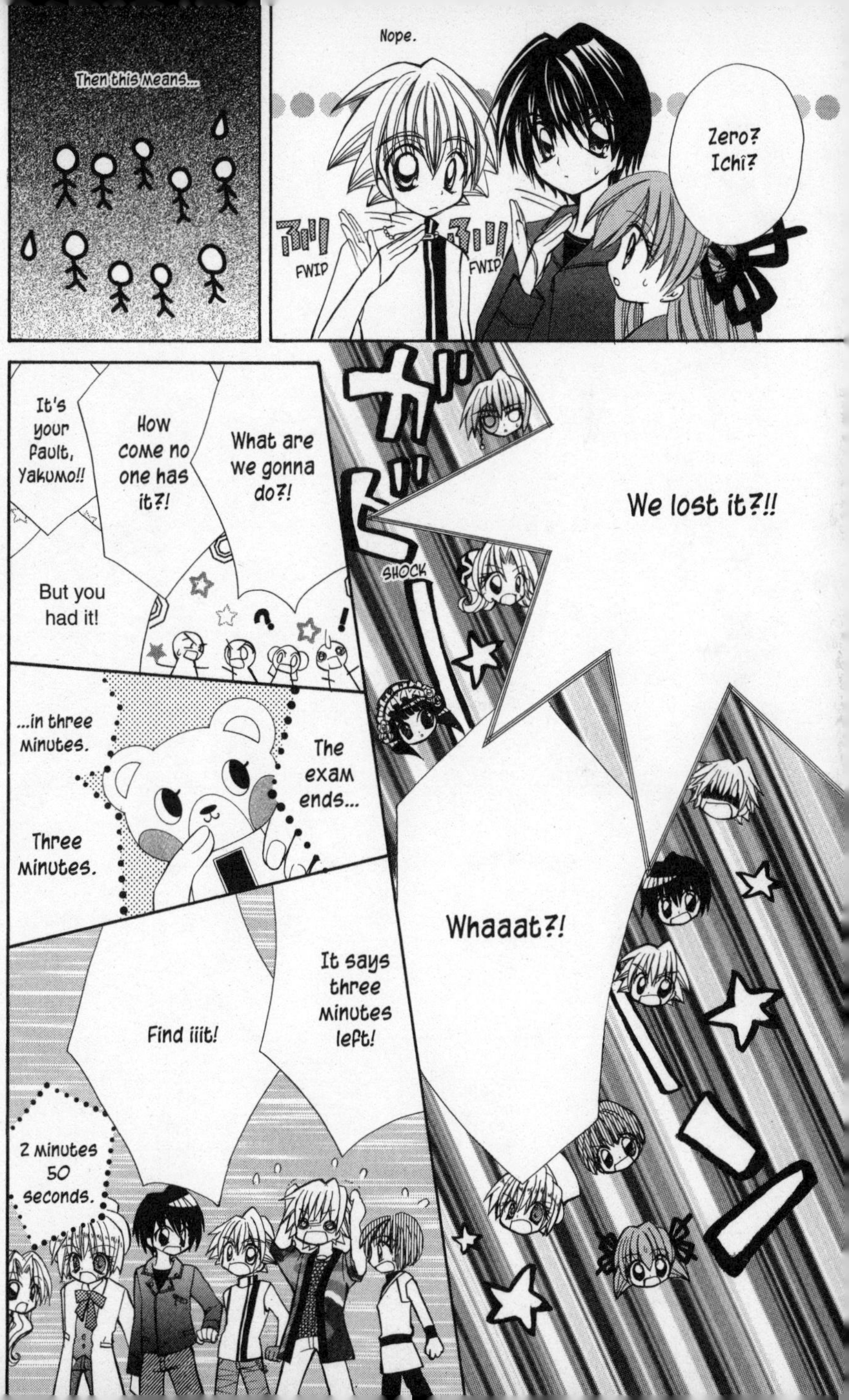
Zero? Ichi?
Nope.
ふり FWIP
ふり FWIP
Then this means...
We lost it?!!
ガーン
SHOCK
Whaaat?!
What are we gonna do?!
How come no one has it?!
It's your fault, Yakumo!!
But you had it!
The exam ends...
...in three minutes.
Three minutes.
It says three minutes left!
Find iiit!
2 minutes 50 seconds.

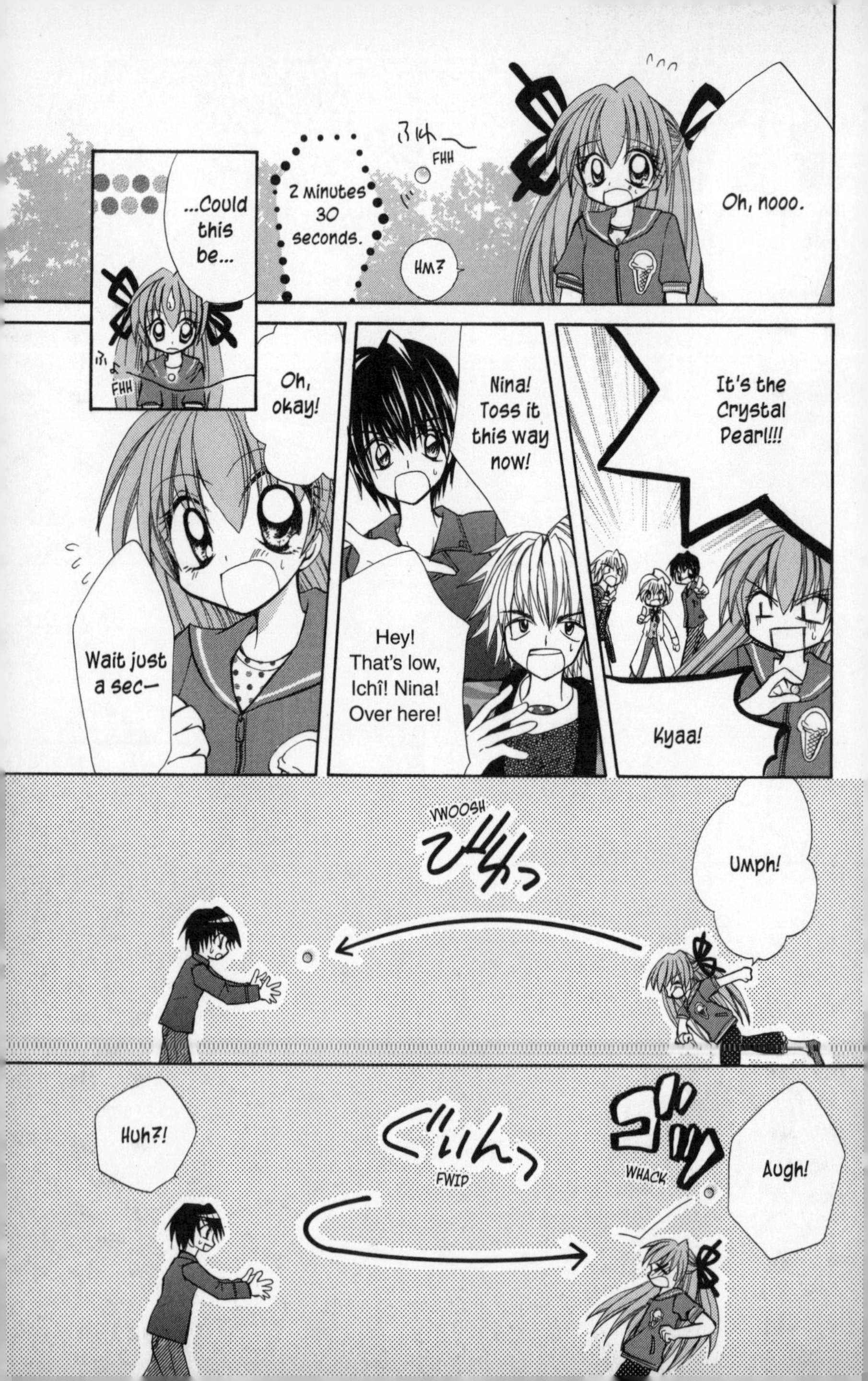
Oh, nooo.
FHH
HM?
2 minutes 30 seconds.
...Could this be...
FHH
It's the Crystal Pearl!!!
Kyaa!
Nina! Toss it this way now!
Hey! That's low, Ichî! Nina! Over here!
Oh, okay!
Wait just a sec—
Umph!
VWOOSH
Augh!
WHACK
FWIP
Huh?!

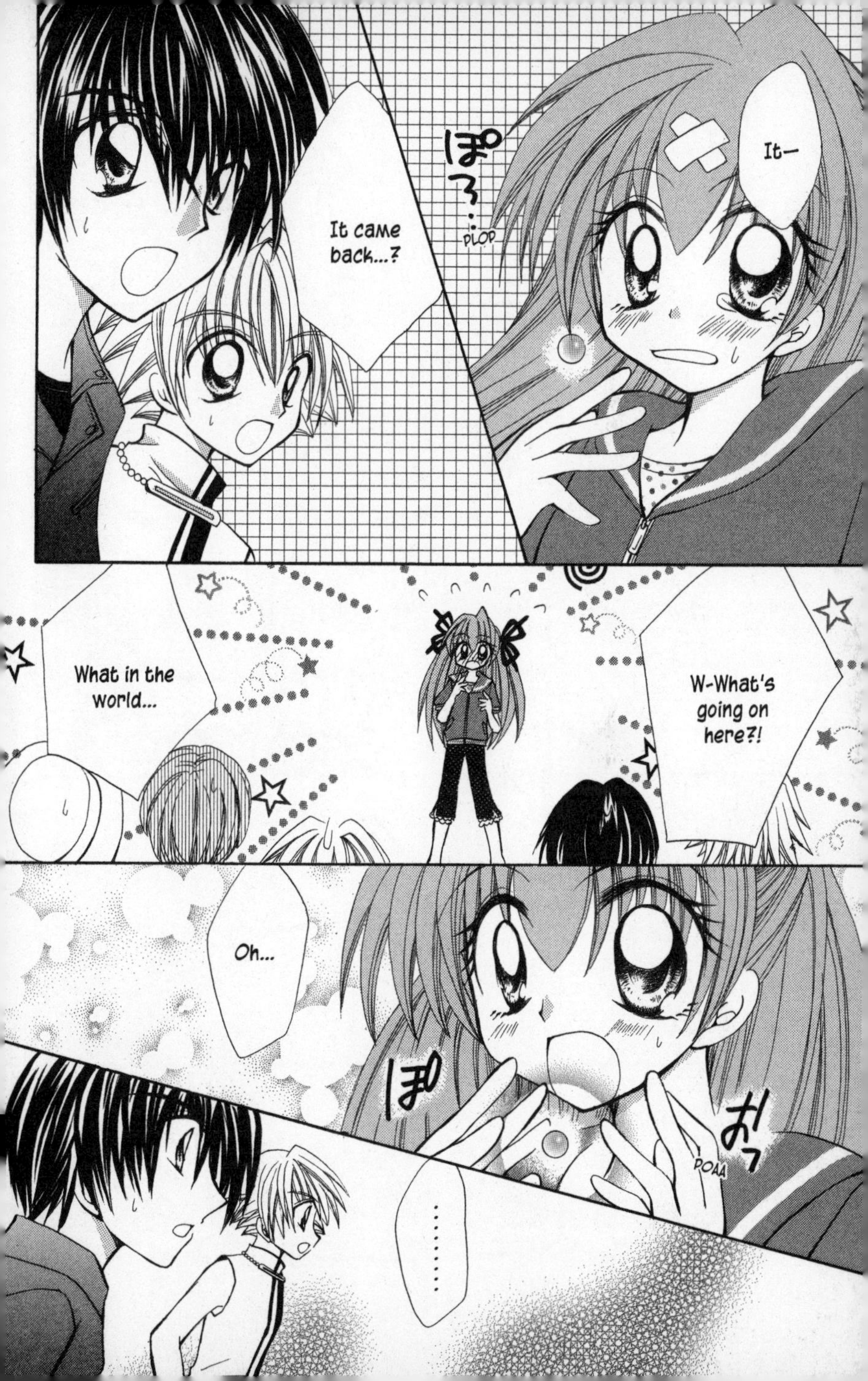
It—
ぽろ…
PLOP
It came back...?
W-What's going on here?!
What in the world...
Oh...
ぽ
おっ
POAA
....

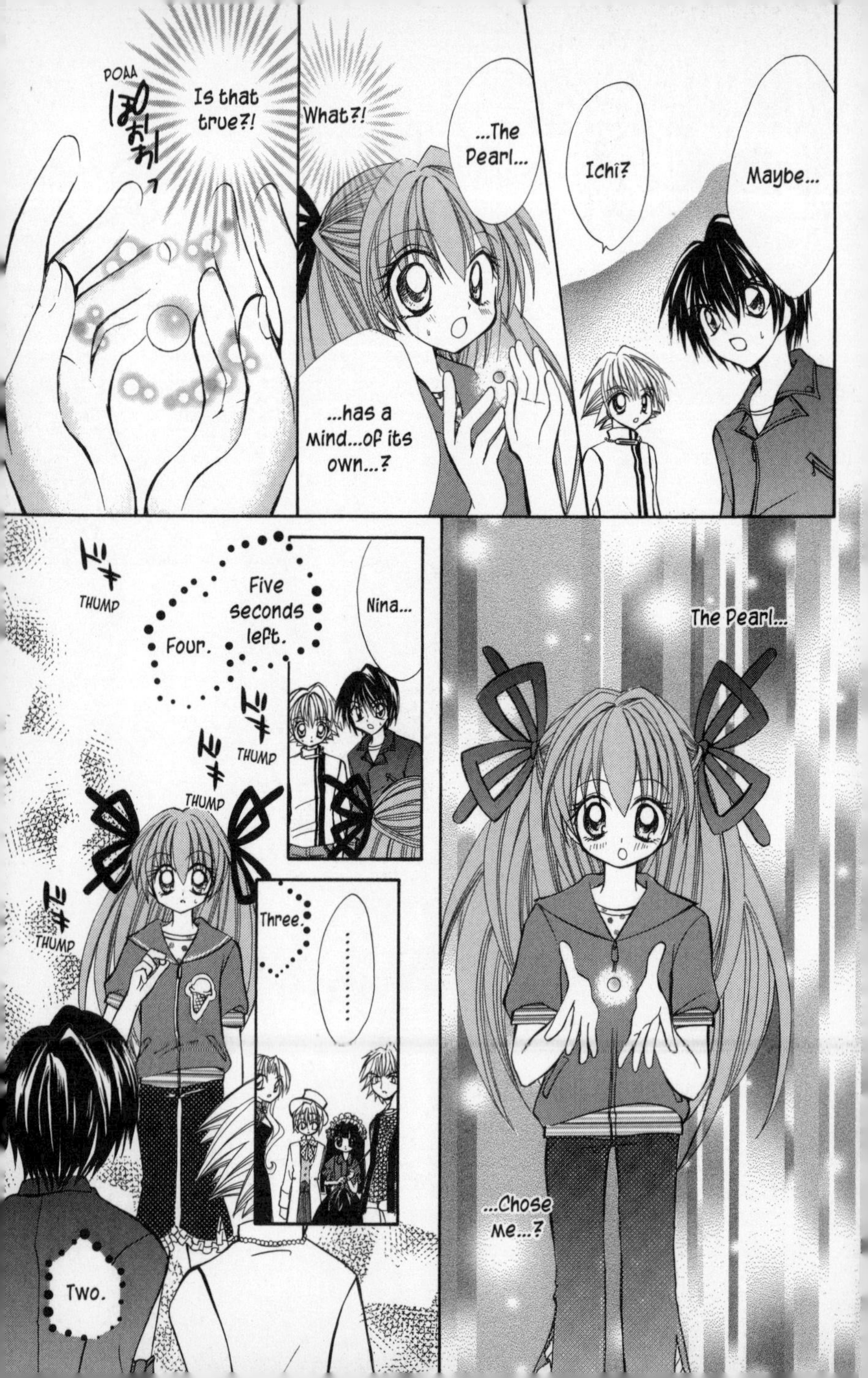

Maybe...
Ichi?
...The Pearl...
What?!
...has a mind...of its own...?
Is that true?!
POAA
The Pearl...
...Chose me...?
Nina...
Five seconds left.
ドキ THUMP
Four.
ドキ THUMP
ドキ THUMP
ドキ THUMP
Three.
......
Two.

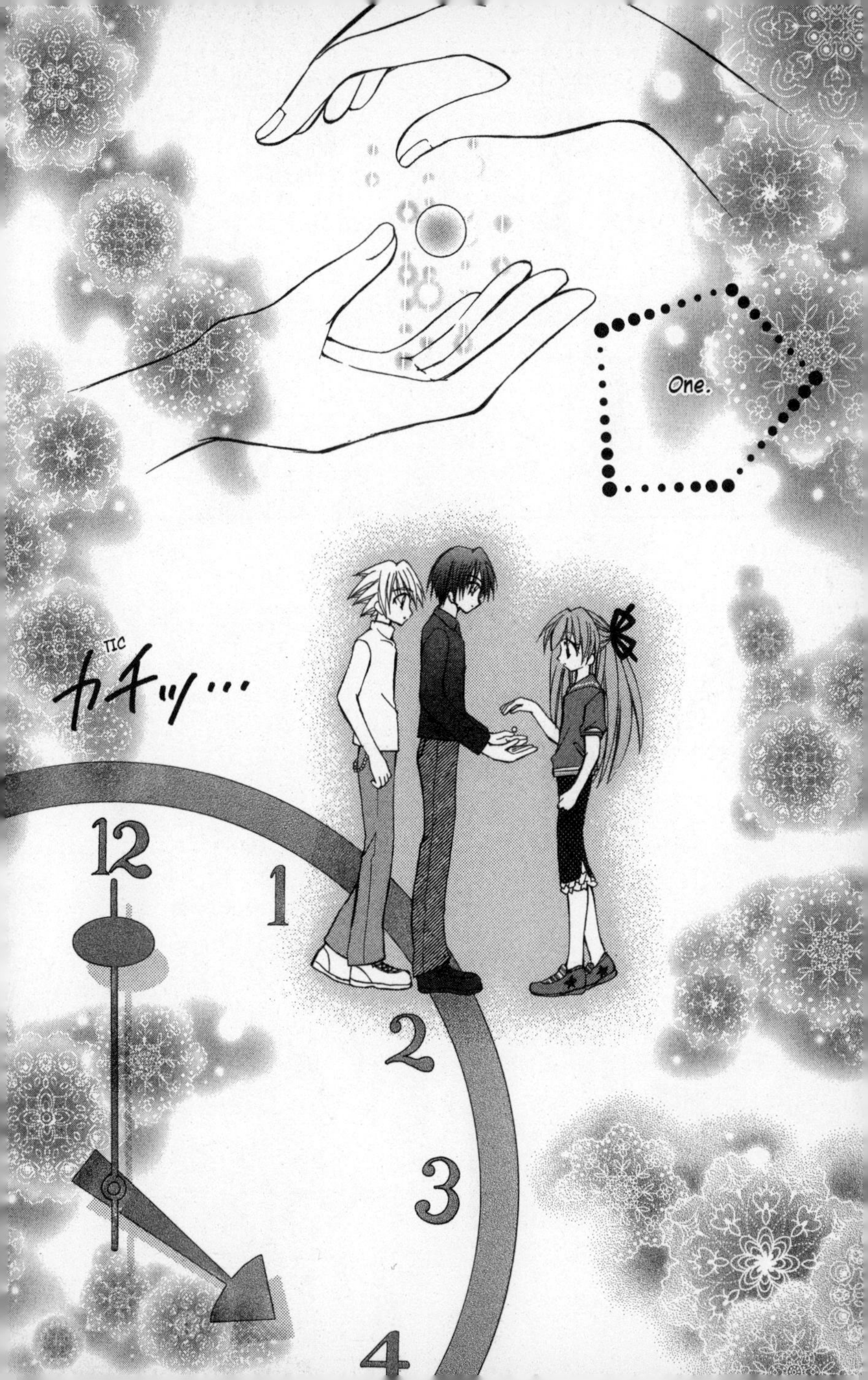
One.
TIC
カチッ…

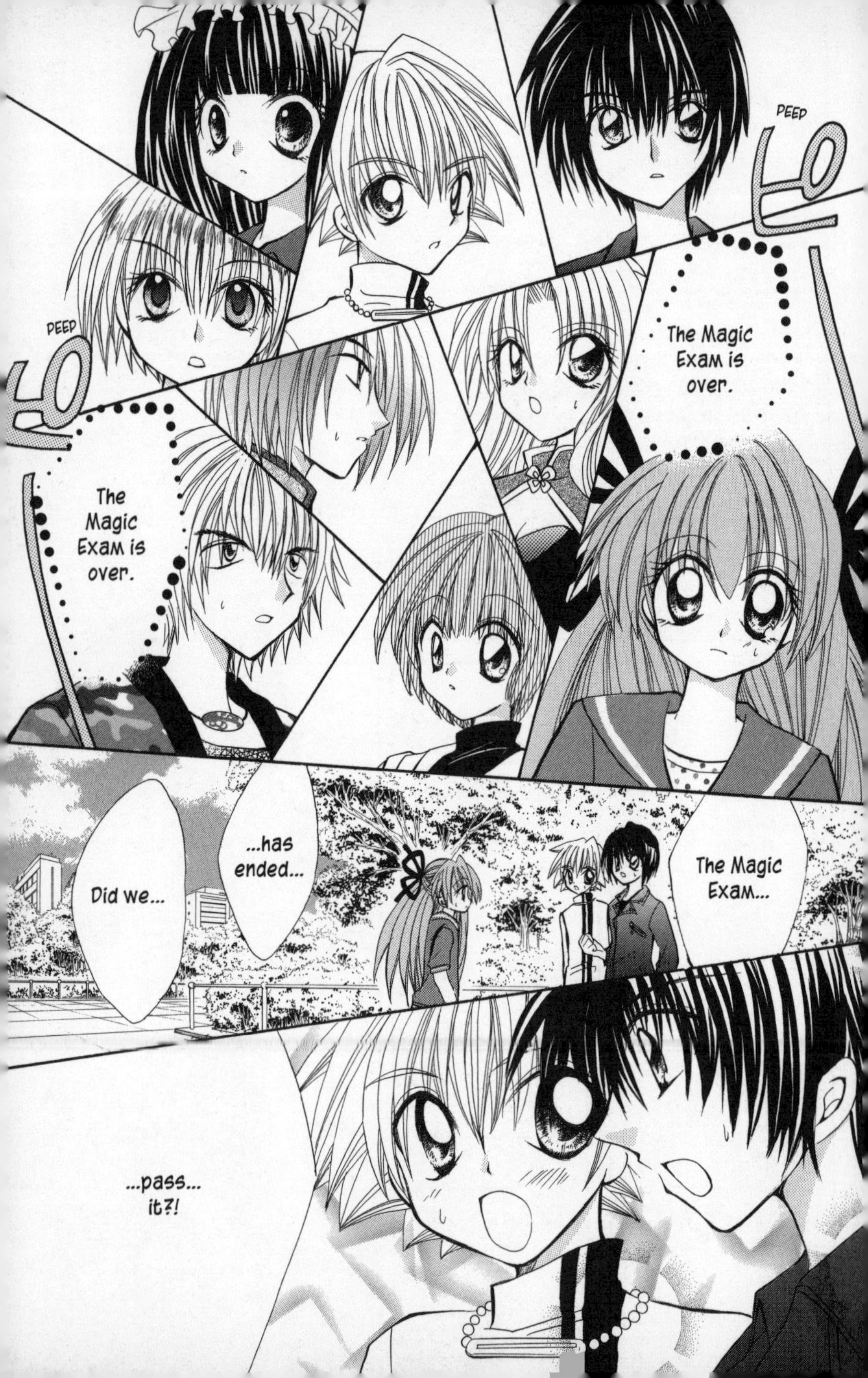
PEEP
The Magic Exam is over.
PEEP
The Magic Exam is over.
The Magic Exam...
...has ended...
Did we...
...pass... it?!

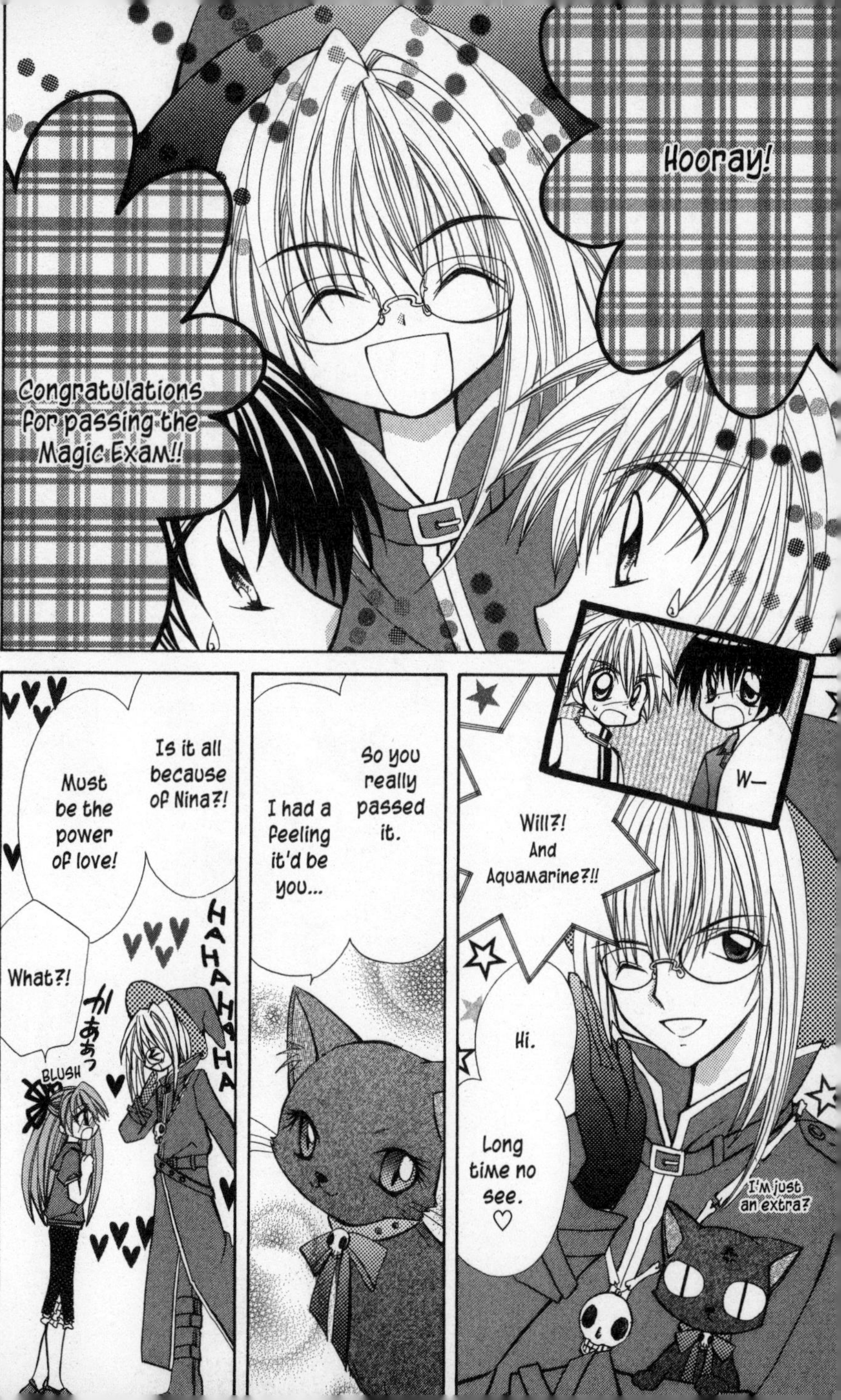
Hooray!
Congratulations for passing the Magic Exam!!
W—
Will?! And Aquamarine?!!
Hi.
Long time no see. ♡
I'm just an extra?
So you really passed it.
I had a feeling it'd be you...
Is it all because of Nina?!
Must be the power of love!
HAHAHAHA
What?!
かあぁっ
BLUSH

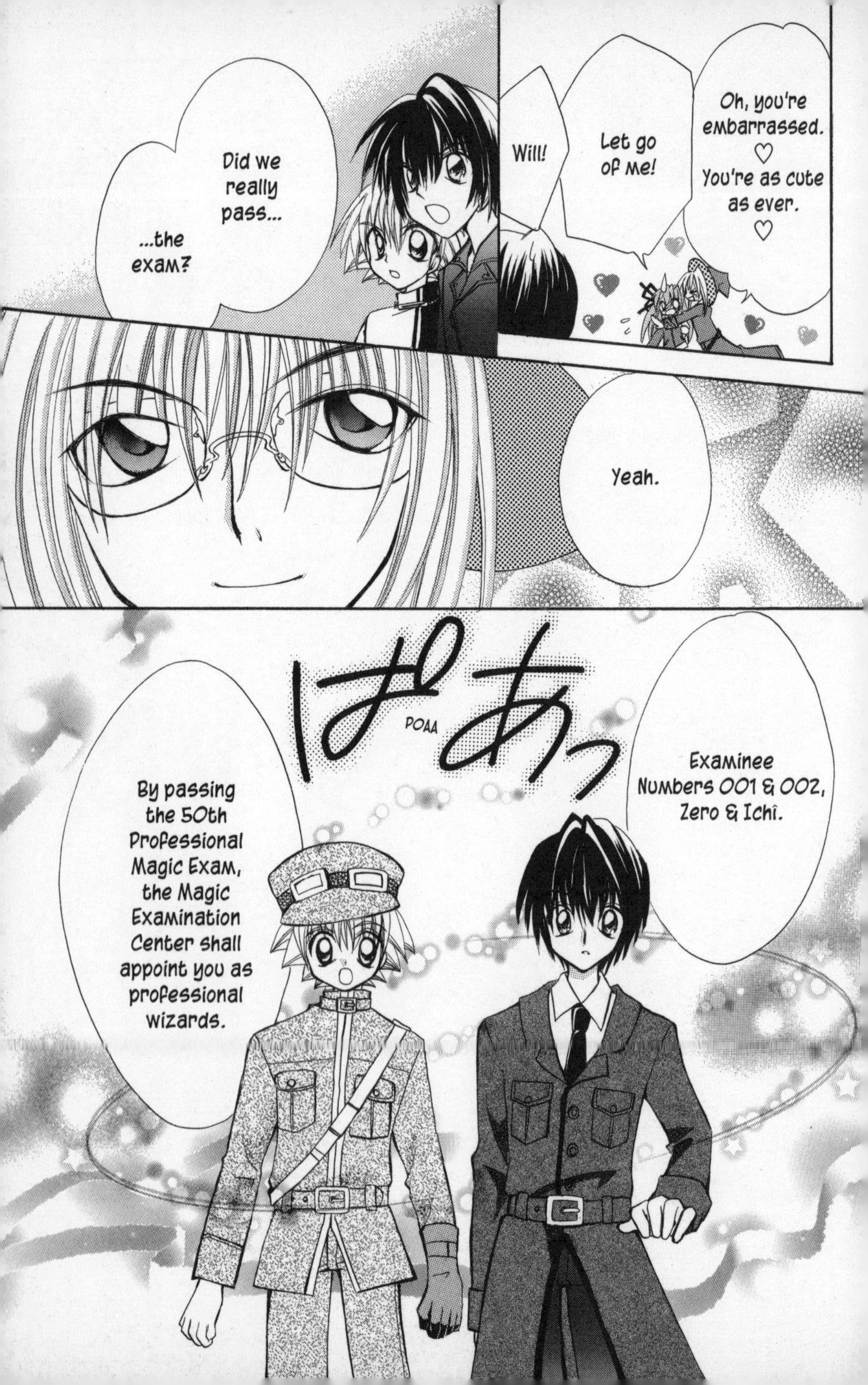

Oh, you're embarrassed. ♡ You're as cute as ever. ♡
Let go of me!
Will!
Did we really pass...
...the exam?
Yeah.
ぱあっ
POAA
Examinee Numbers 001 & 002, Zero & Ichî.
By passing the 50th Professional Magic Exam, the Magic Examination Center shall appoint you as professional wizards.

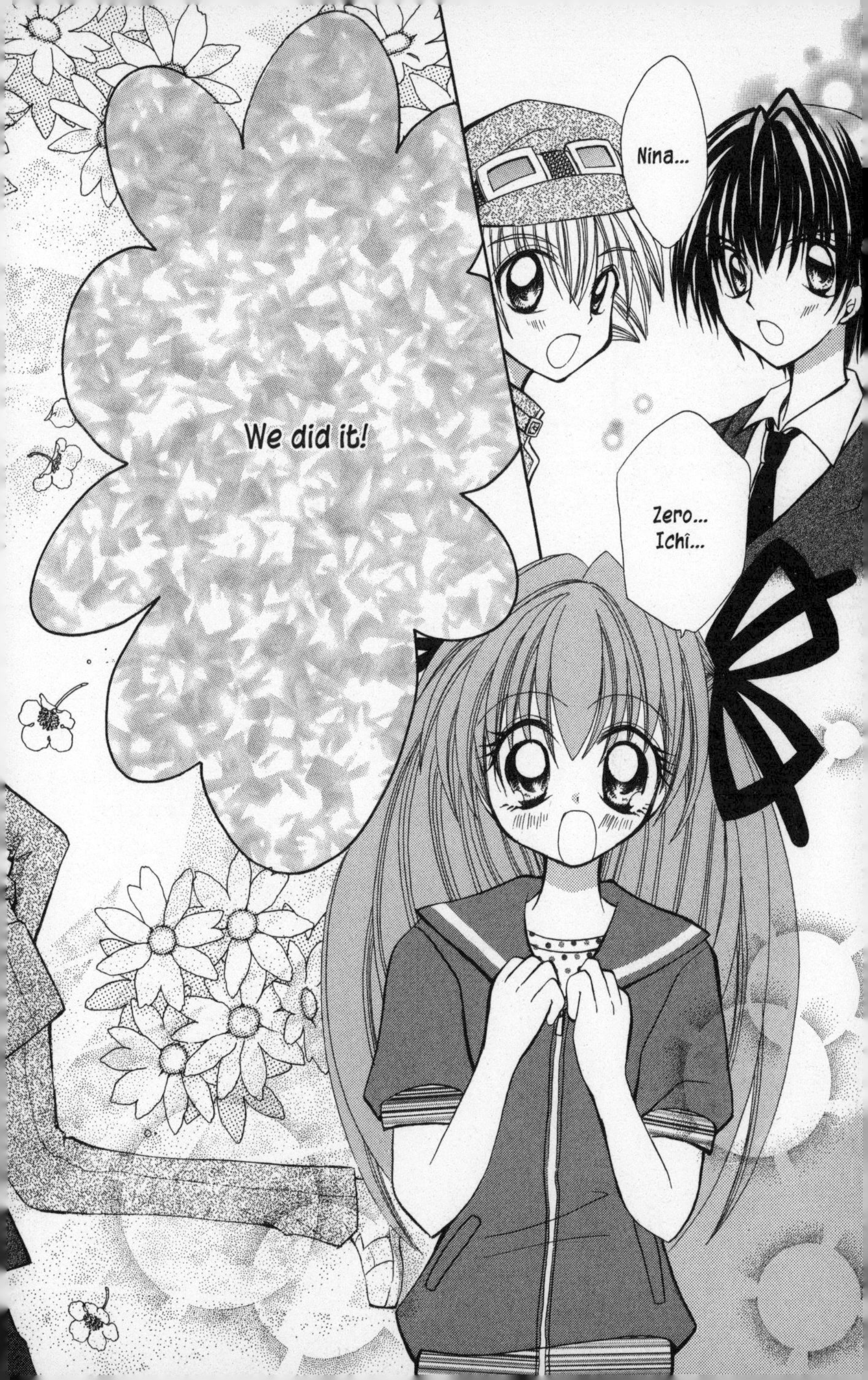
Nina...
Zero...
Ichî...
We did it!

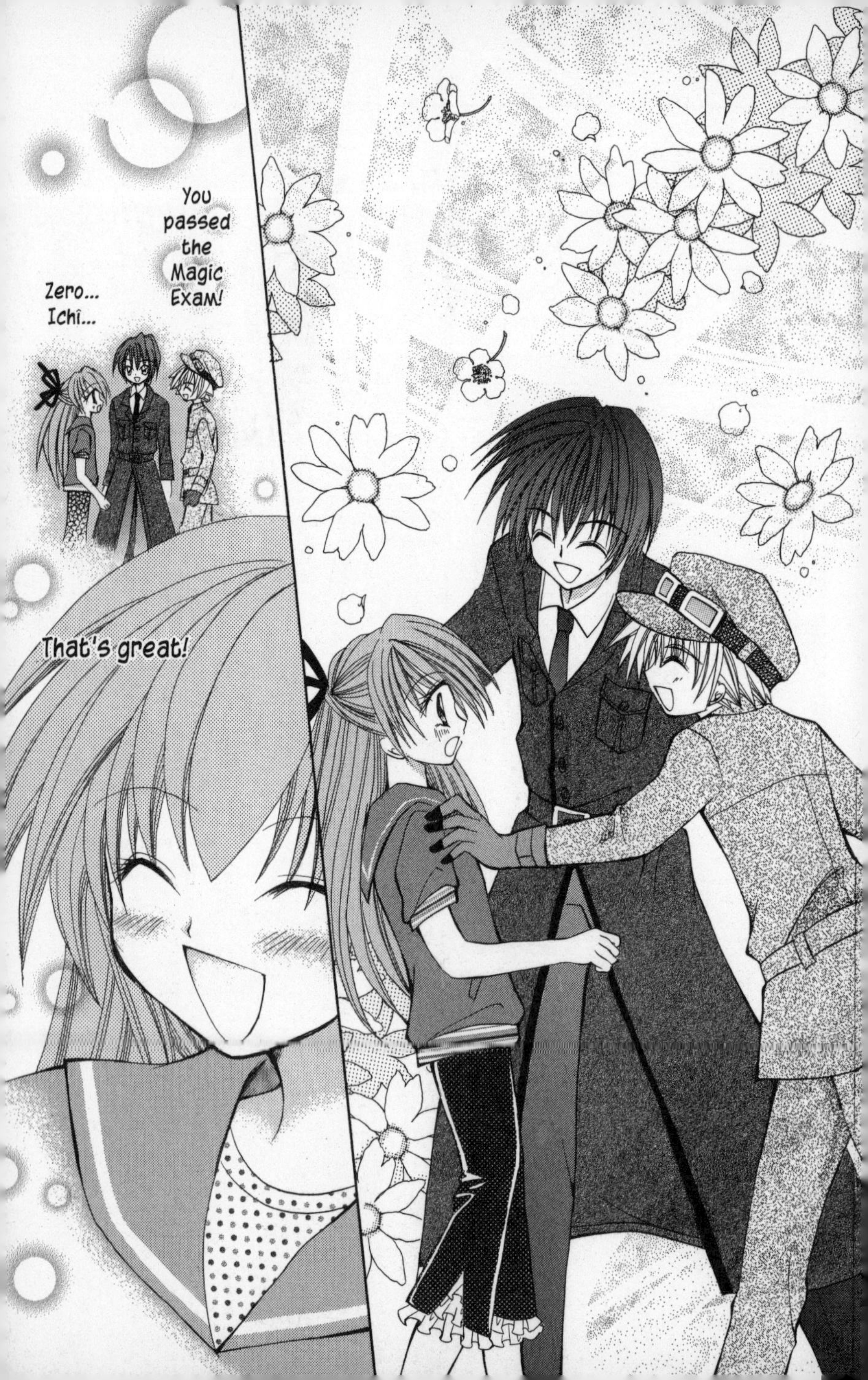
You passed the Magic Exam!
Zero... Ichi...
That's great!

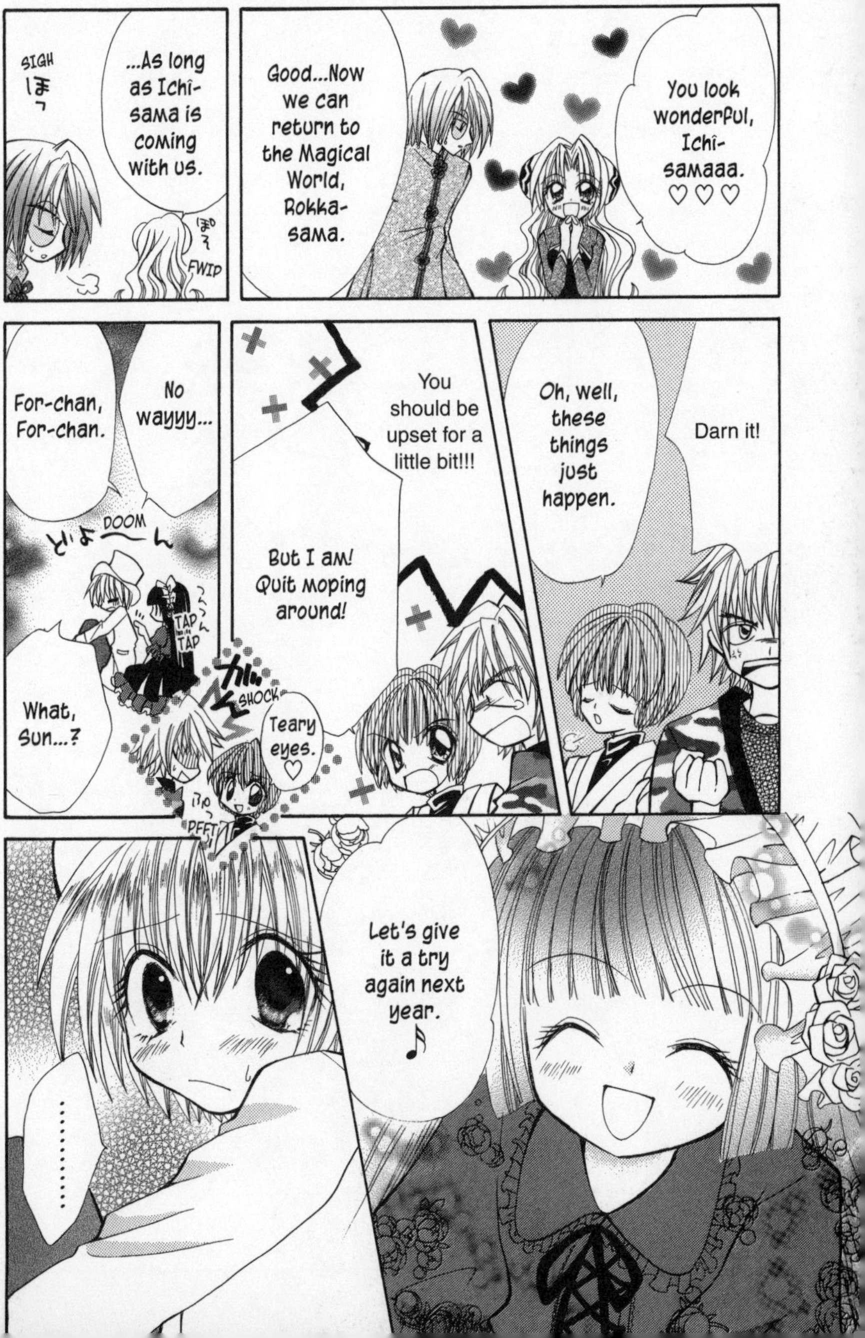

You look wonderful, Ichî-samaaa. ♡ ♡ ♡
Good...Now we can return to the Magical World, Rokka-sama.
SIGH
ほっ
...As long as Ichî-sama is coming with us.
ぽそ
FWIP
Darn it!
Oh, well, these things just happen.
You should be upset for a little bit!!!
But I am! Quit moping around!
No wayyy...
For-chan, For-chan.
どよ〜ん
DOOM
TAP TAP
What, Sun...?
SHOCK
Teary eyes. ♡
ぷっ
PFFT
Let's give it a try again next year. ♪
....

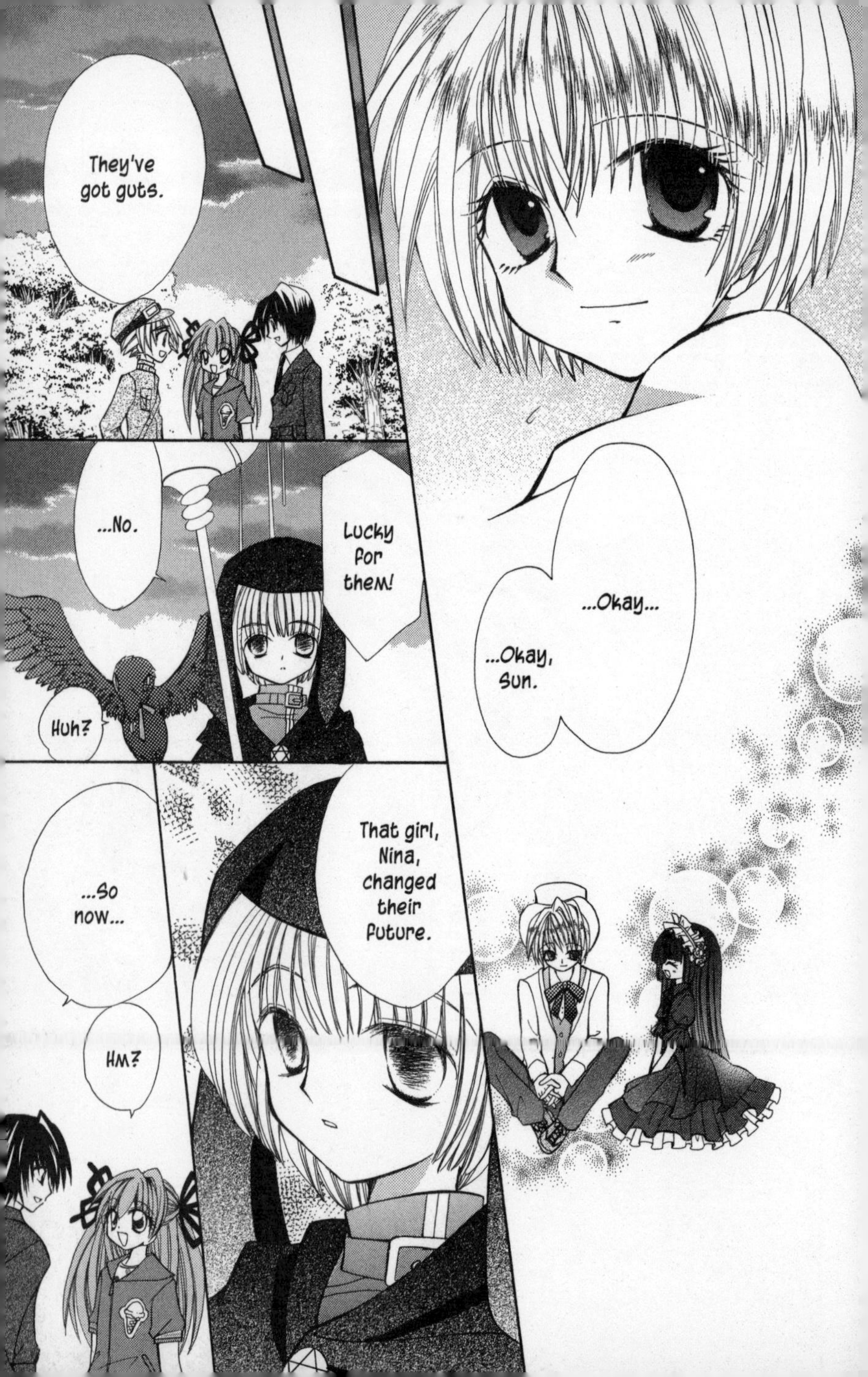
...Okay...
...Okay, Sun.
They've got guts.
Lucky for them!
...No.
Huh?
That girl, Nina, changed their future.
...So now...
Hm?

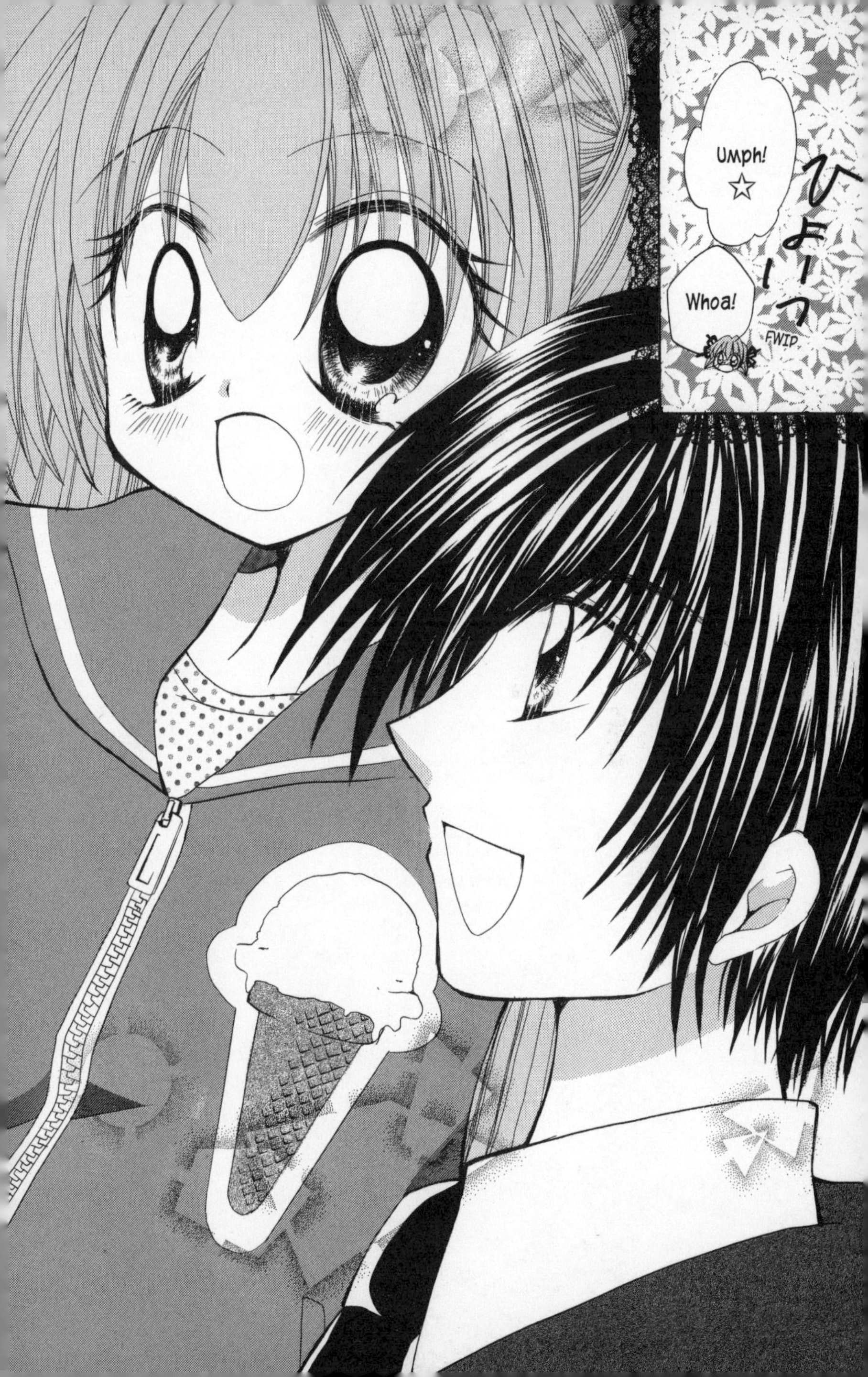
ひよーっ
FWIP
Umph! ☆
Whoa!

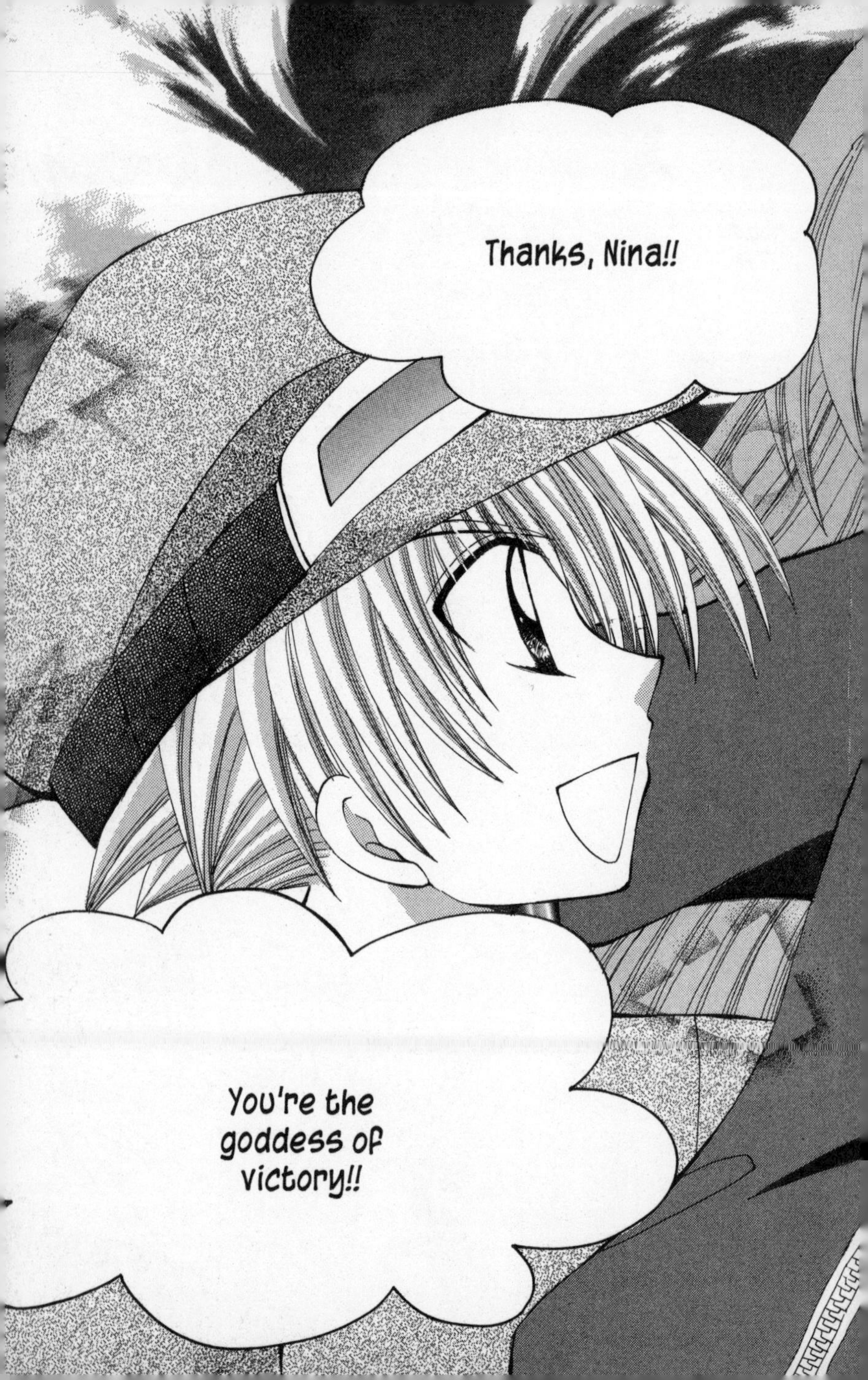
Thanks, Nina!!
You're the goddess of victory!!

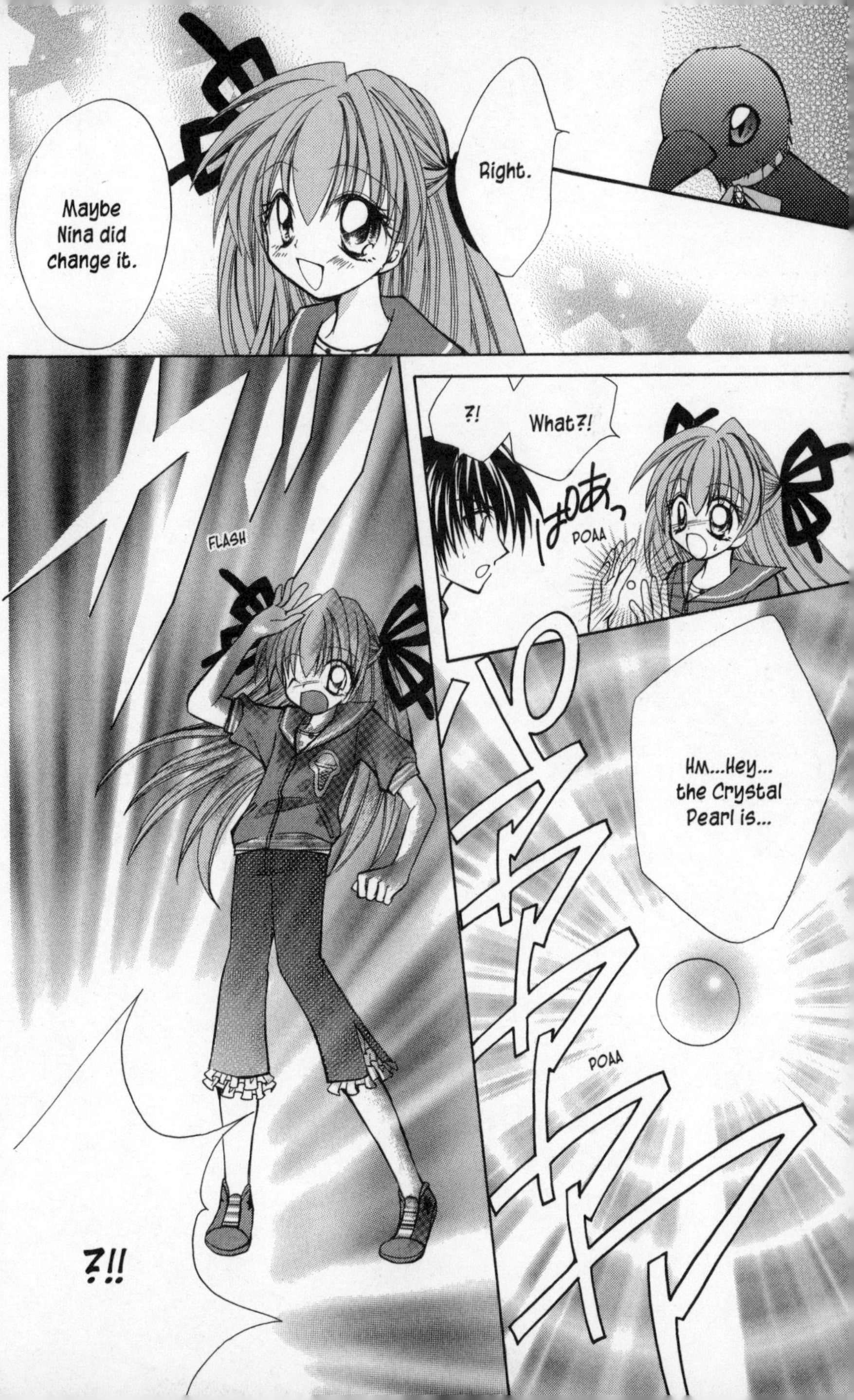
Right.
Maybe Nina did change it.
What?!
?!
ぱぁあっ
POAA
Hm...Hey... the Crystal Pearl is...
POAA
FLASH
?!!

Data 6
* Gô *

Name:	Gô
Birthday:	May 5th
Blood Type:	AB
Height:	178 cm*
Favorite Food:	Green tea, sweet red bean jelly
Least Favorite Food:	None
Weak Point:	Rokka-sama's demands
Treasure:	Pine bonsai tree
Hobby:	Bonsai trees
Special Talent:	Illusion Spell
Favorite Type of Girl:	......?
Remarks:	Actually his age is unknown.

*5'10"

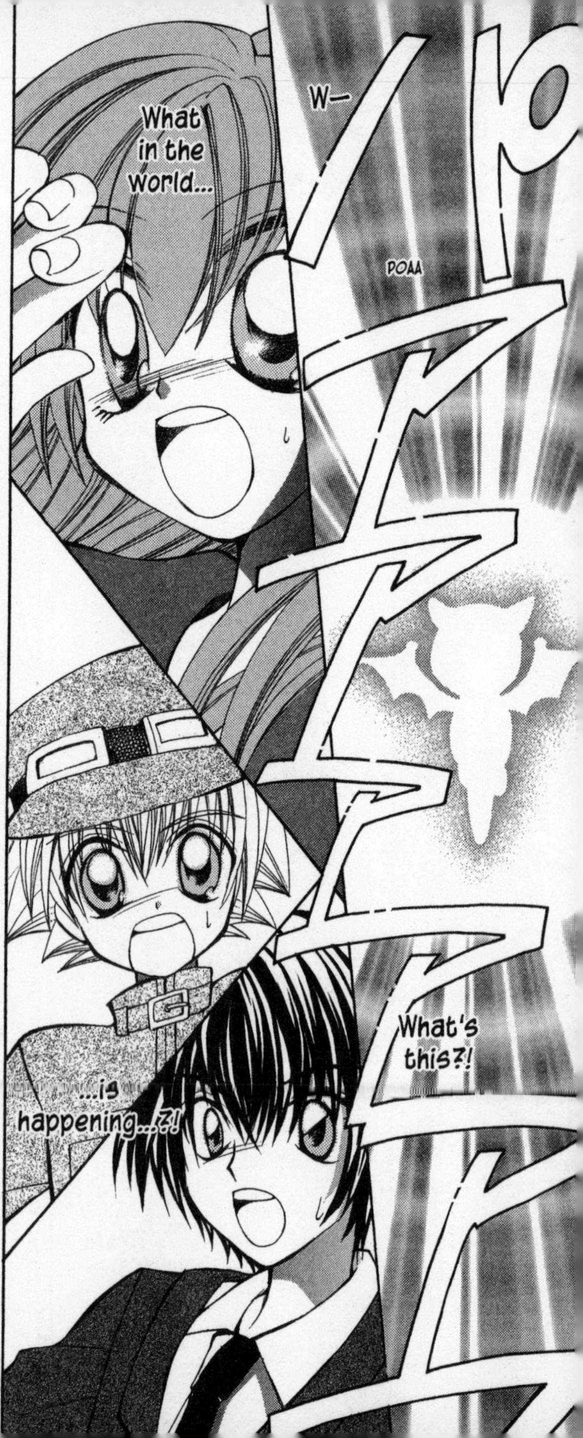
W—
What in the world...
POAA
What's this?!
...is happening...?!

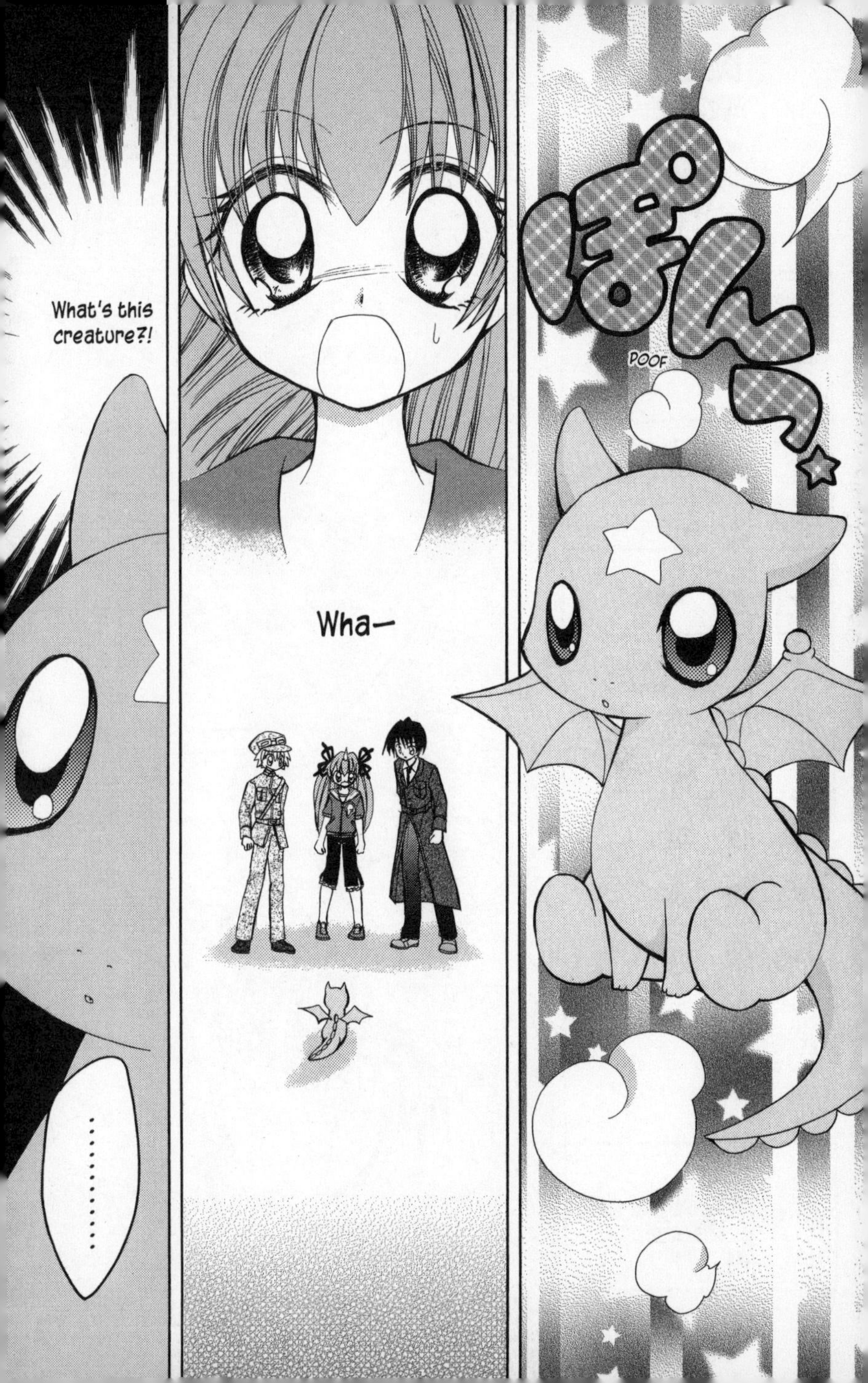
ぽんっ☆
POOF
Wha-
What's this creature?!
......

Data 7
* Rokka *

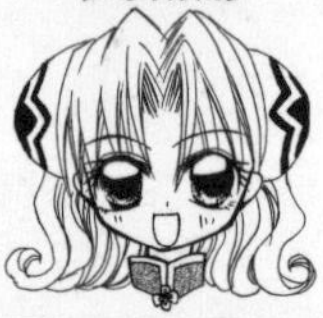

Name:	Rokka
Birthday:	September 6th
Blood Type:	B
Height:	120 cm* (as a child), 161 cm* (as an adult)
Favorite Food:	Cream stew, strawberries
Least Favorite Food:	Carrots
Weak Point:	Gô's punishment
Treasure:	A stuffed panda bear Ichi gave her
Hobby:	Visiting Ichi-sama ♡
Special Talent:	Illusion Spell
Favorite Type of Boy:	Of course, Ichi-sama. ♡ ♡
Remarks:	Can't stay up later than nine o'clock.

*4'0", 5'3"

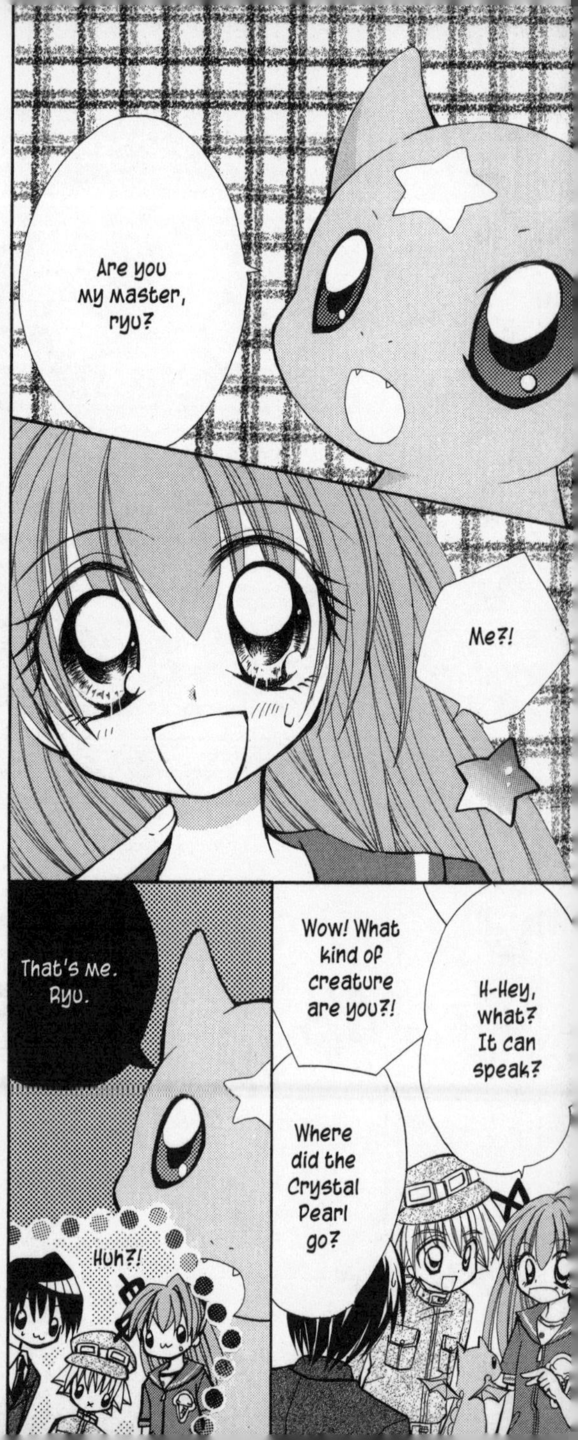
Are you my master, ryu?
Me?!
H-Hey, what? It can speak?
Wow! What kind of creature are you?!
Where did the Crystal Pearl go?
That's me. Ryu.
Huh?!

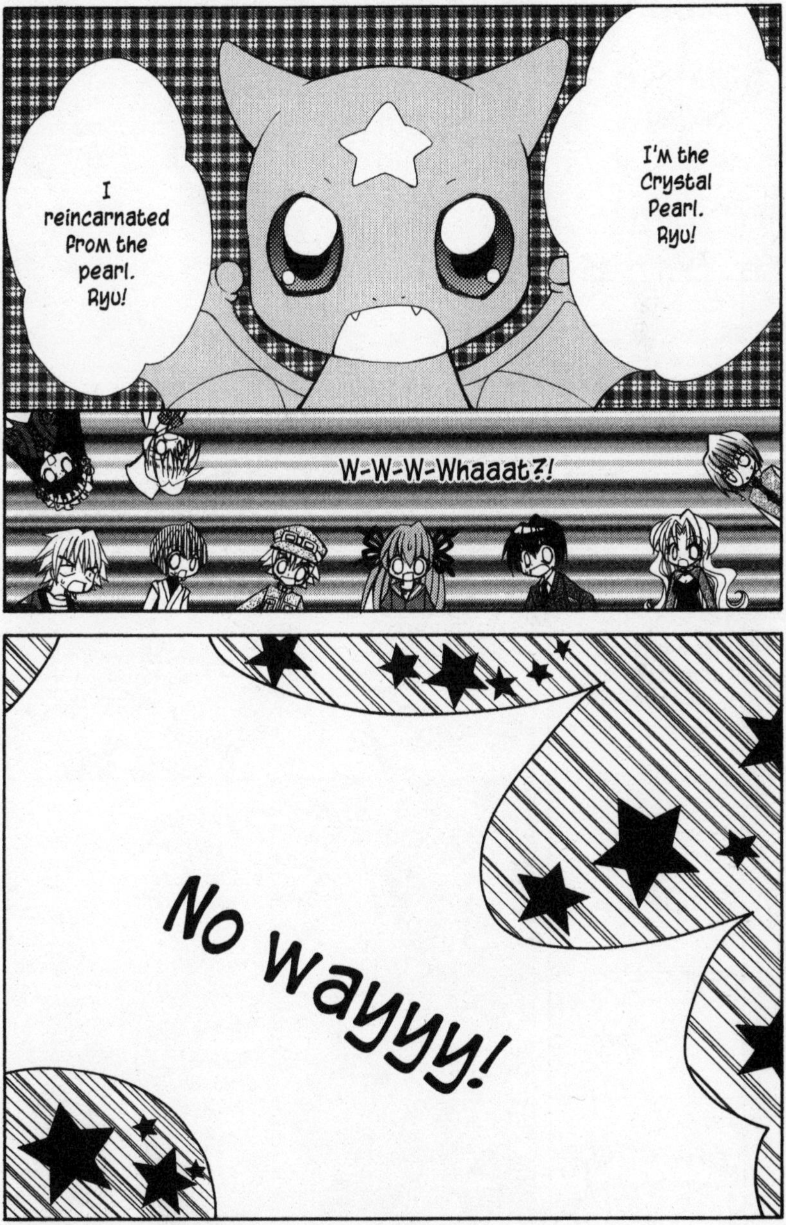
I'm the Crystal Pearl. Ryu!
I reincarnated from the pearl. Ryu!
W-W-W-Whaaat?!
No wayyy!

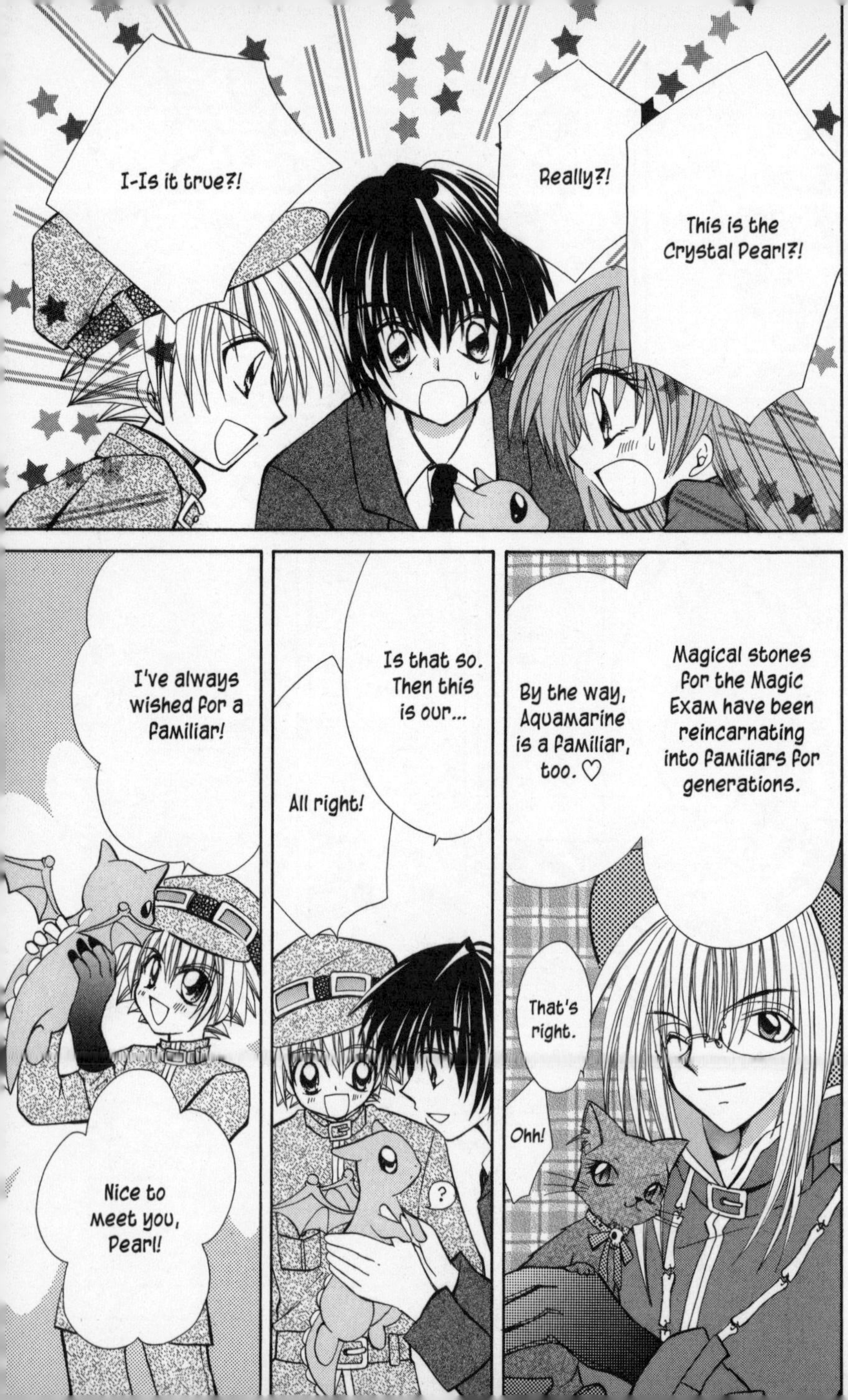
This is the Crystal Pearl!?!
Really?!
I-Is it true?!
Magical stones for the Magic Exam have been reincarnating into familiars for generations.
By the way, Aquamarine is a familiar, too. ♡
That's right.
Ohh!
Is that so. Then this is our...
All right!
?
I've always wished for a familiar!
Nice to meet you, Pearl!

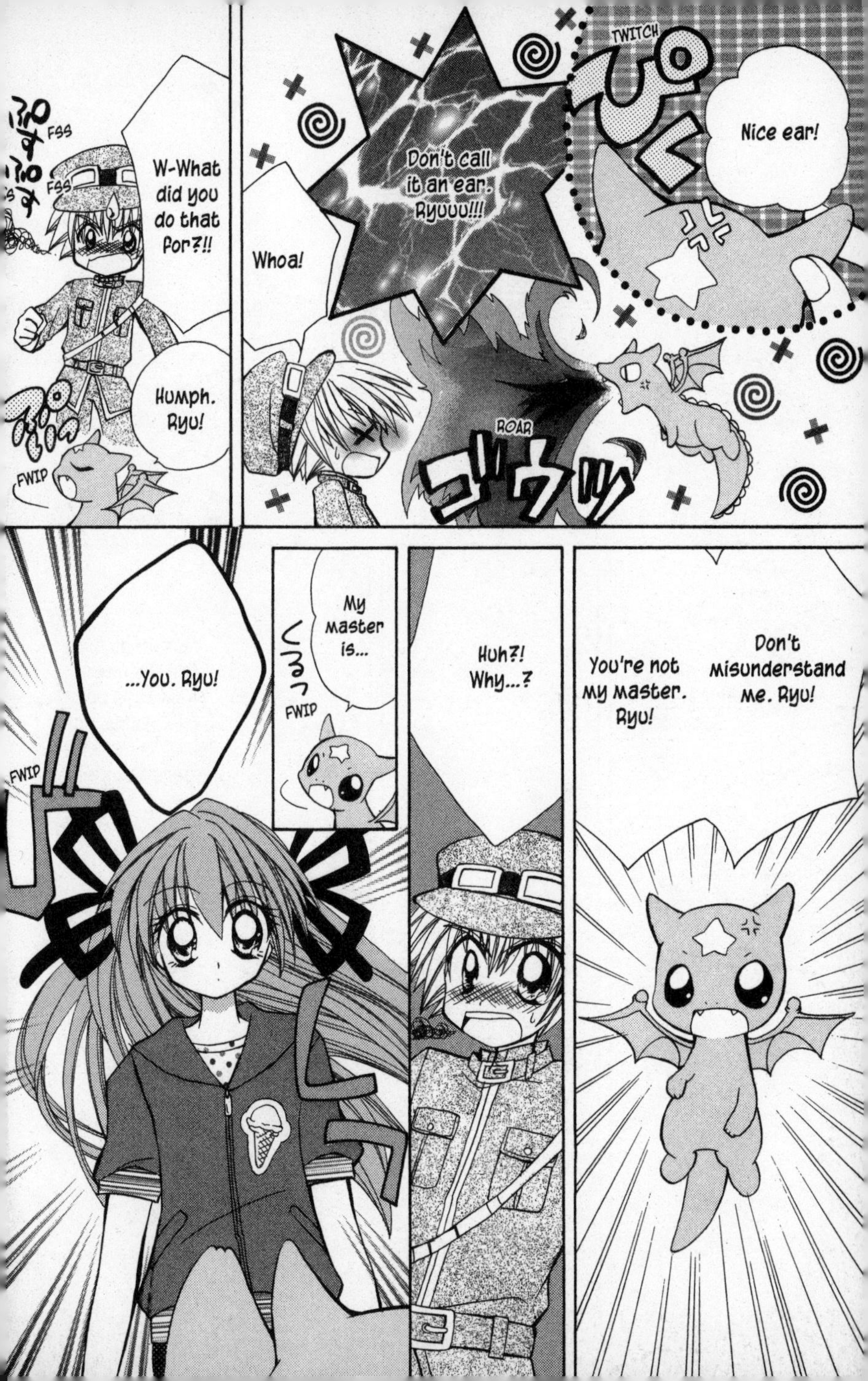
TWITCH
Nice ear!
Don't call it an ear. Ryuuu!!!
Whoa!
ROAR
FSS
FSS
W-What did you do that for?!!
Humph. Ryu!
FWIP
Don't misunderstand me. Ryu!
You're not my master. Ryu!
Huh?! Why...?
My master is...
FWIP
...You. Ryu!
FWIP

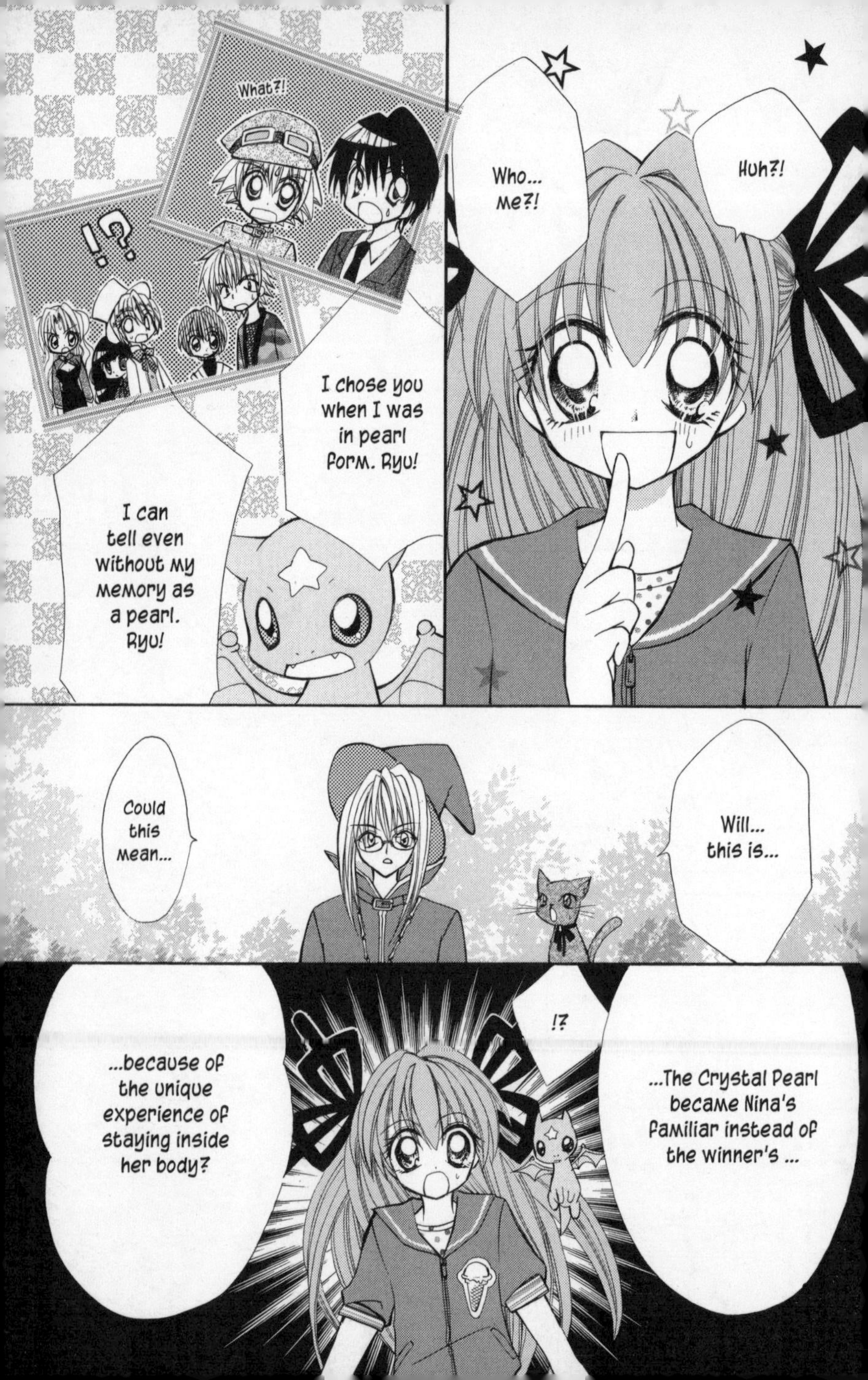
Huh?!
Who... me?!
What?!
!?
I chose you when I was in pearl form. Ryu!
I can tell even without my memory as a pearl. Ryu!
Will... this is...
Could this mean...
!?
...The Crystal Pearl became Nina's familiar instead of the winner's ...
...because of the unique experience of staying inside her body?

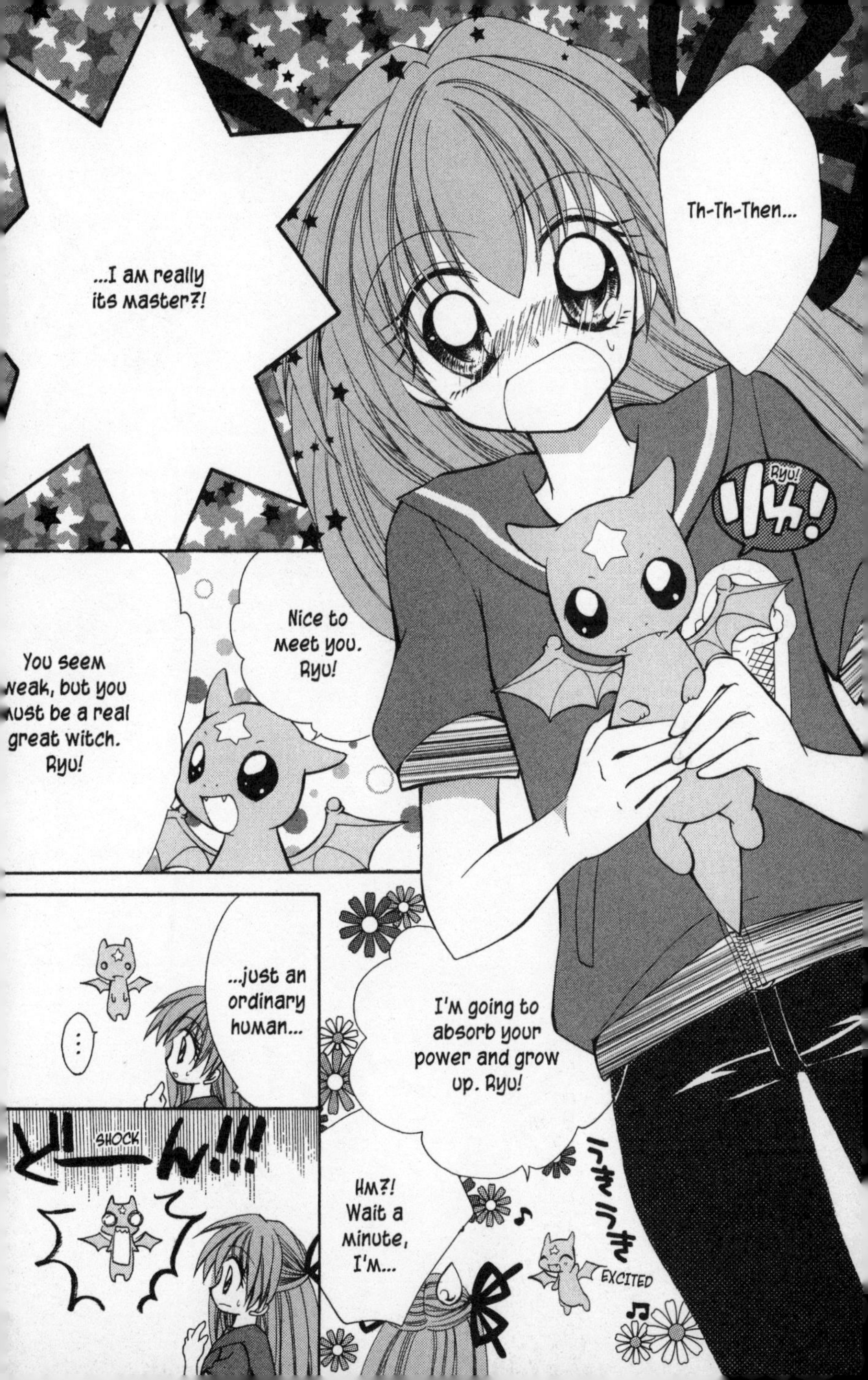

Th-Th-Then...
...I am really its master?!
りゅ! Ryu!
Nice to meet you. Ryu!
You seem weak, but you must be a real great witch. Ryu!
I'm going to absorb your power and grow up. Ryu!
うきうき EXCITED
Hm?! Wait a minute, I'm...
...just an ordinary human...
...
どーん!!! SHOCK

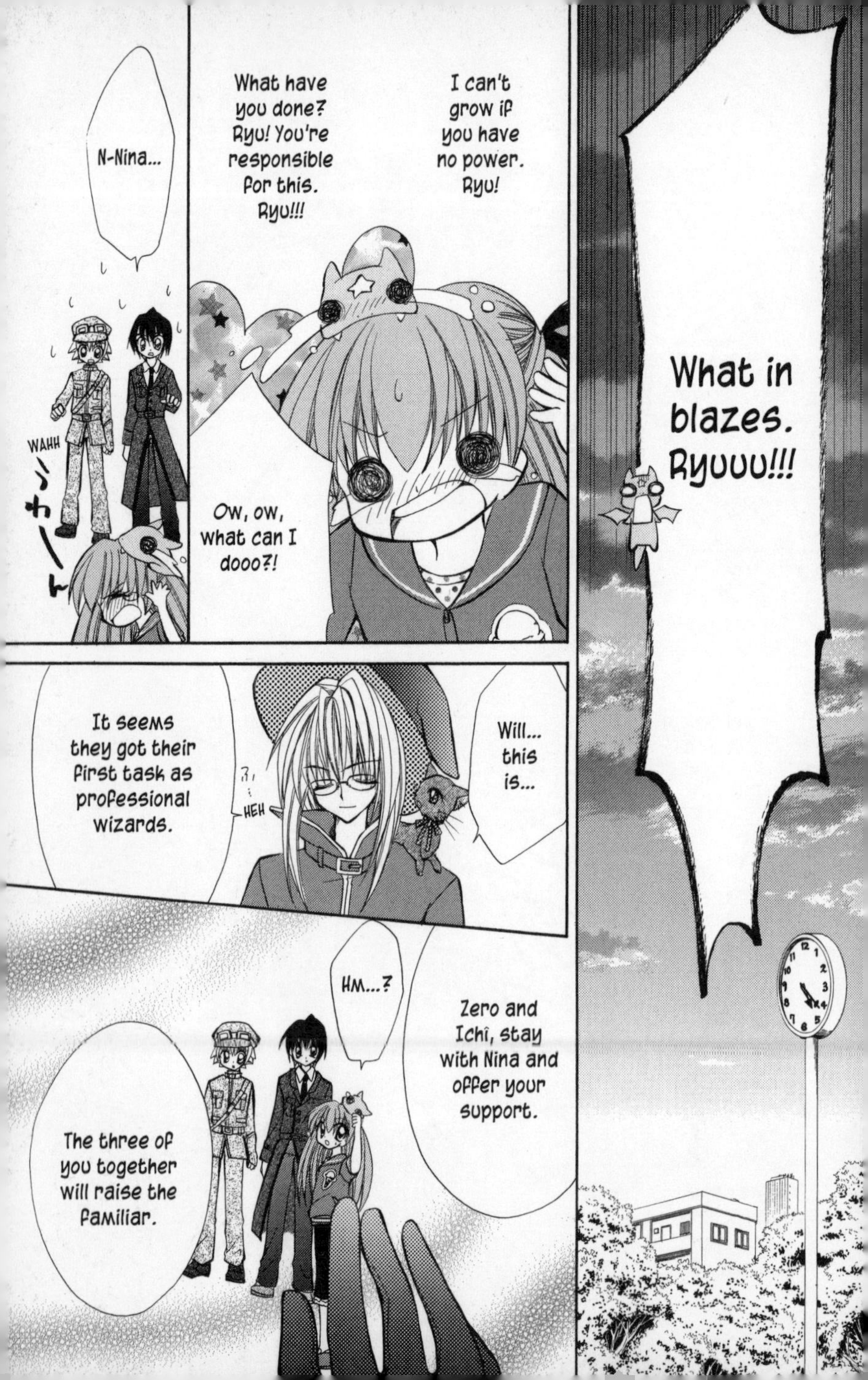
What in blazes. Ryuuu!!!
I can't grow if you have no power. Ryu!
What have you done? Ryu! You're responsible for this. Ryu!!!
Ow, ow, what can I dooo?!
N-Nina...
WAHH
Will... this is...
HEH
It seems they got their first task as professional wizards.
Zero and Ichi, stay with Nina and offer your support.
Hm...?
The three of you together will raise the familiar.

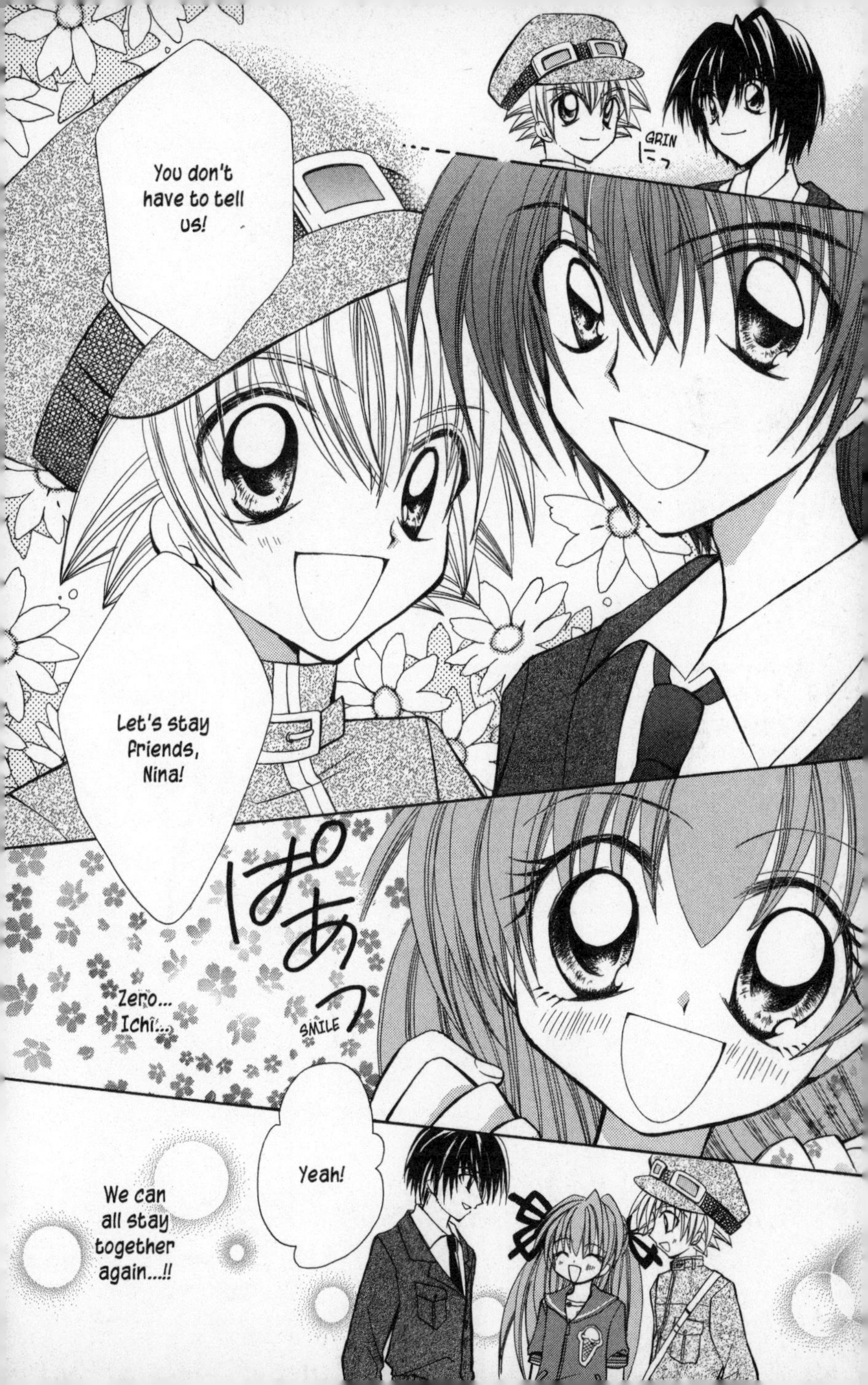
GRIN
にっ
You don't have to tell us!
Let's stay friends, Nina!
ぱあっ
SMILE
Zero... Ichi...
Yeah!
We can all stay together again...!!

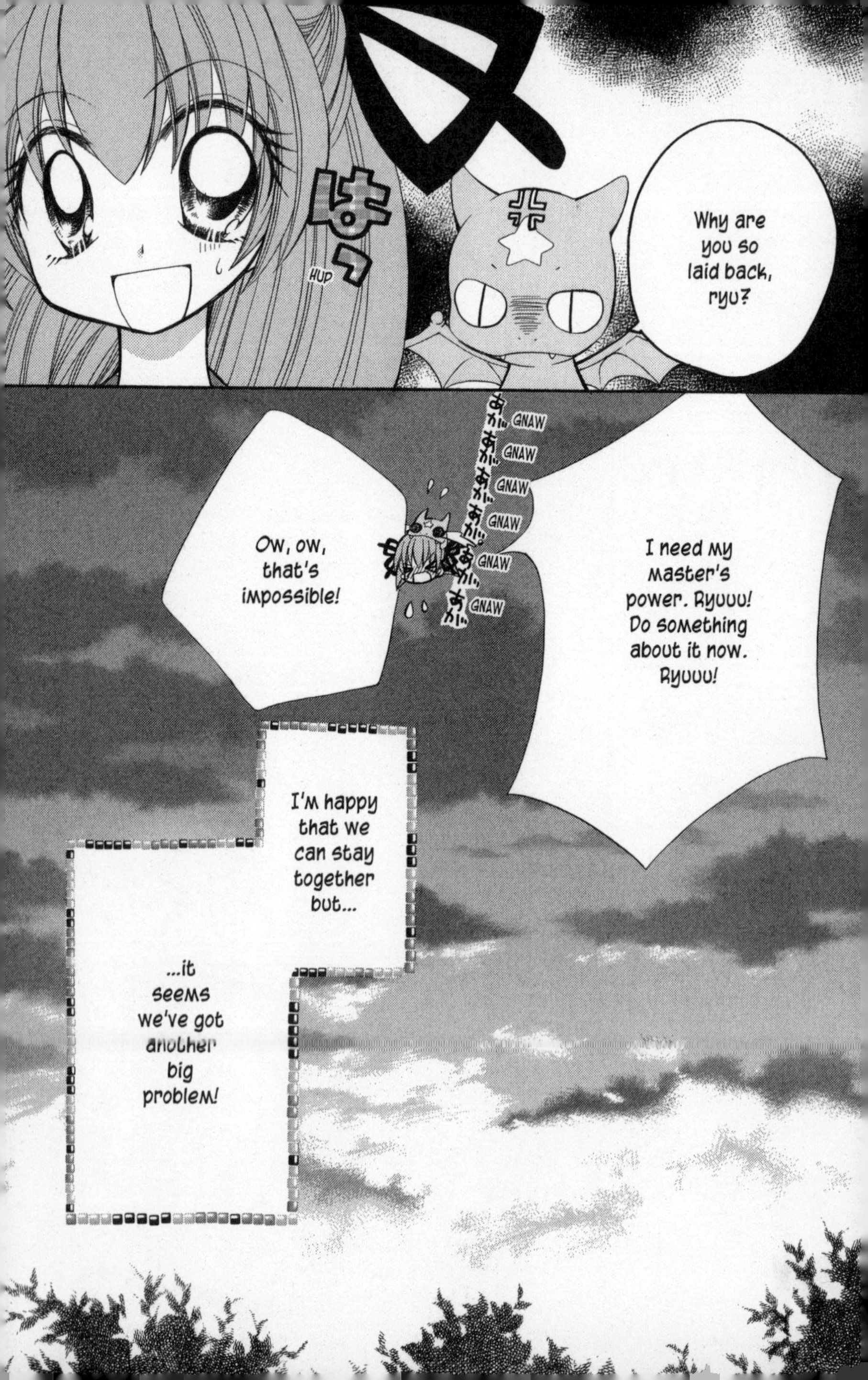
Why are you so laid back, ryu?
はっ
HUP
I need my master's power. Ryuuu! Do something about it now. Ryuuu!
GNAW GNAW GNAW GNAW GNAW GNAW
Ow, ow, that's impossible!
I'm happy that we can stay together but...
...it seems we've got another big problem!

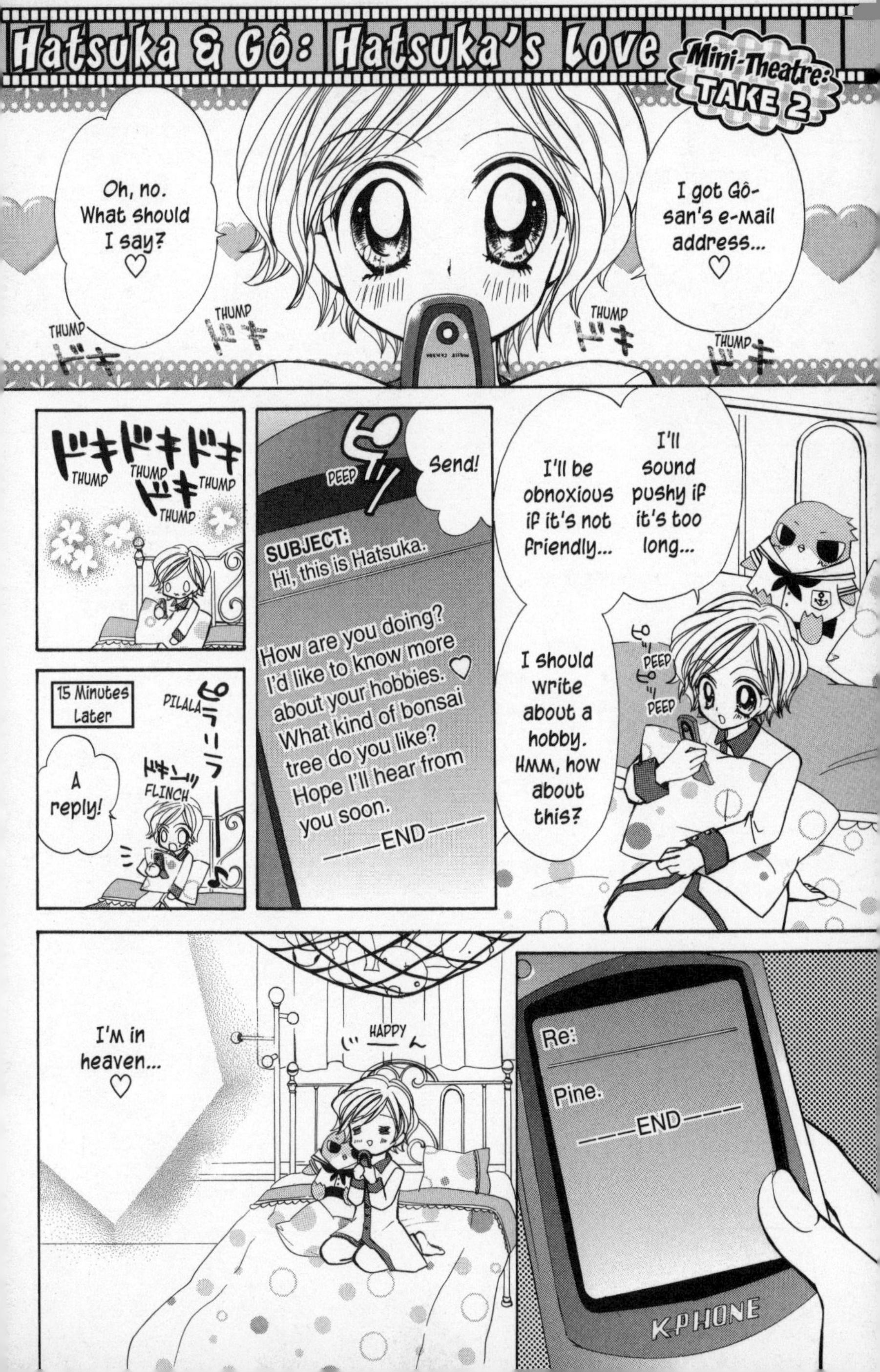
Hatsuka & Gô: Hatsuka's Love
Mini-Theatre: TAKE 2
I got Gô-san's e-mail address... ♡
THUMP
THUMP
Oh, no. What should I say? ♡
THUMP
THUMP
I'll sound pushy if it's too long...
I'll be obnoxious if it's not friendly...
I should write about a hobby. Hmm, how about this?
PEEP
PEEP
PEEP
Send!
SUBJECT:
Hi, this is Hatsuka.
How are you doing? I'd like to know more about your hobbies. ♡ What kind of bonsai tree do you like? Hope I'll hear from you soon.
———END———
THUMP THUMP THUMP THUMP
15 Minutes Later
PILALA
FLINCH
A reply!
Re:
Pine.
———END———
K-PHONE
HAPPY
I'm in heaven... ♡

Kuku & Toto: The Flame of Love

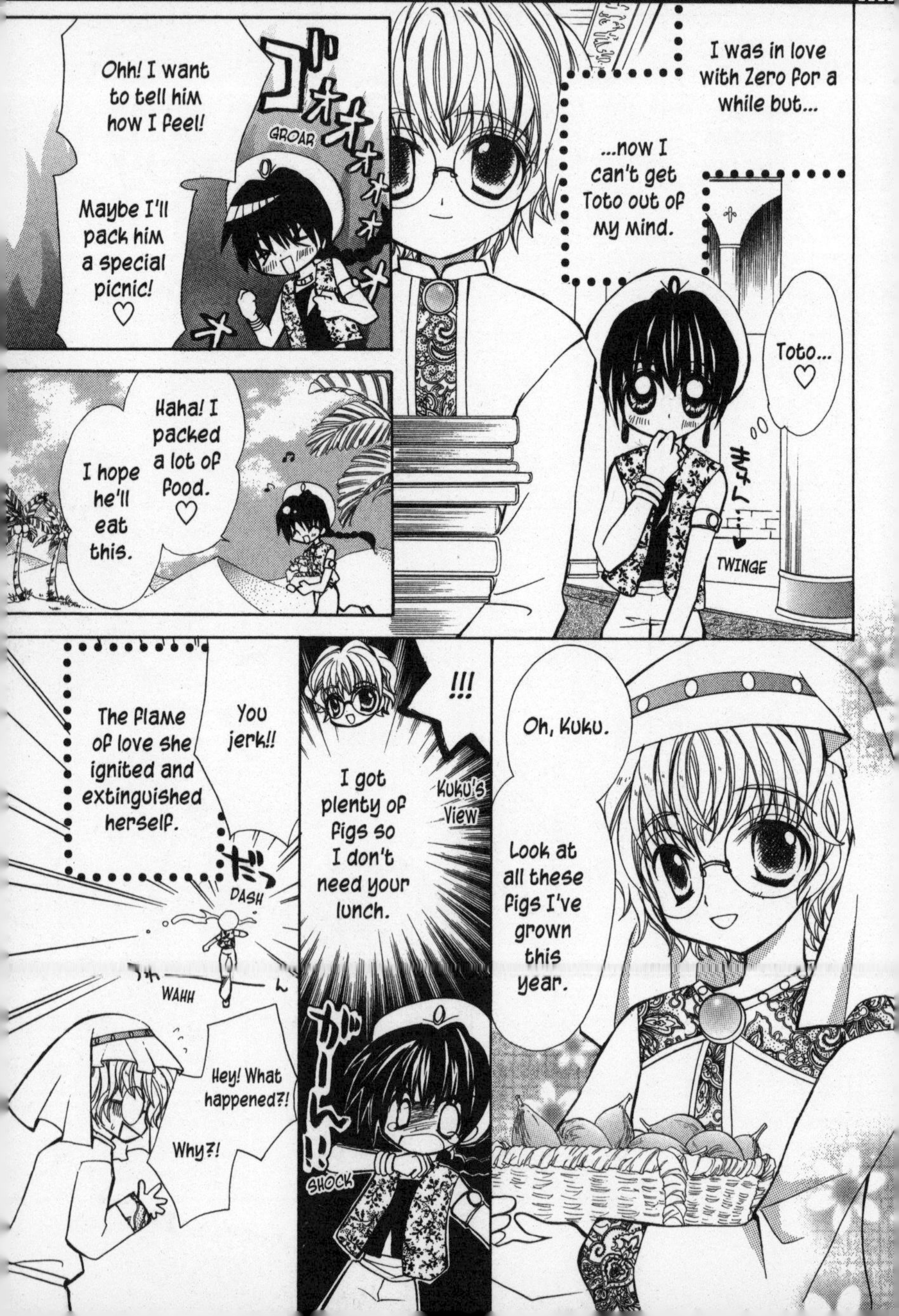
I was in love with Zero for a while but...
...now I can't get Toto out of my mind.
Toto... ♡
TWINGE
Ohh! I want to tell him how I feel!
GROAR
Maybe I'll pack him a special picnic! ♡
Haha! I packed a lot of food. ♡
I hope he'll eat this.
Oh, Kuku.
Look at all these figs I've grown this year.
!!!
I got plenty of figs so I don't need your lunch.
Kuku's View
SHOCK
You jerk!!
The flame of love she ignited and extinguished herself.
DASH
WAHH
Hey! What happened?!
Why?!

Kuku & Toto: The Figs of Love

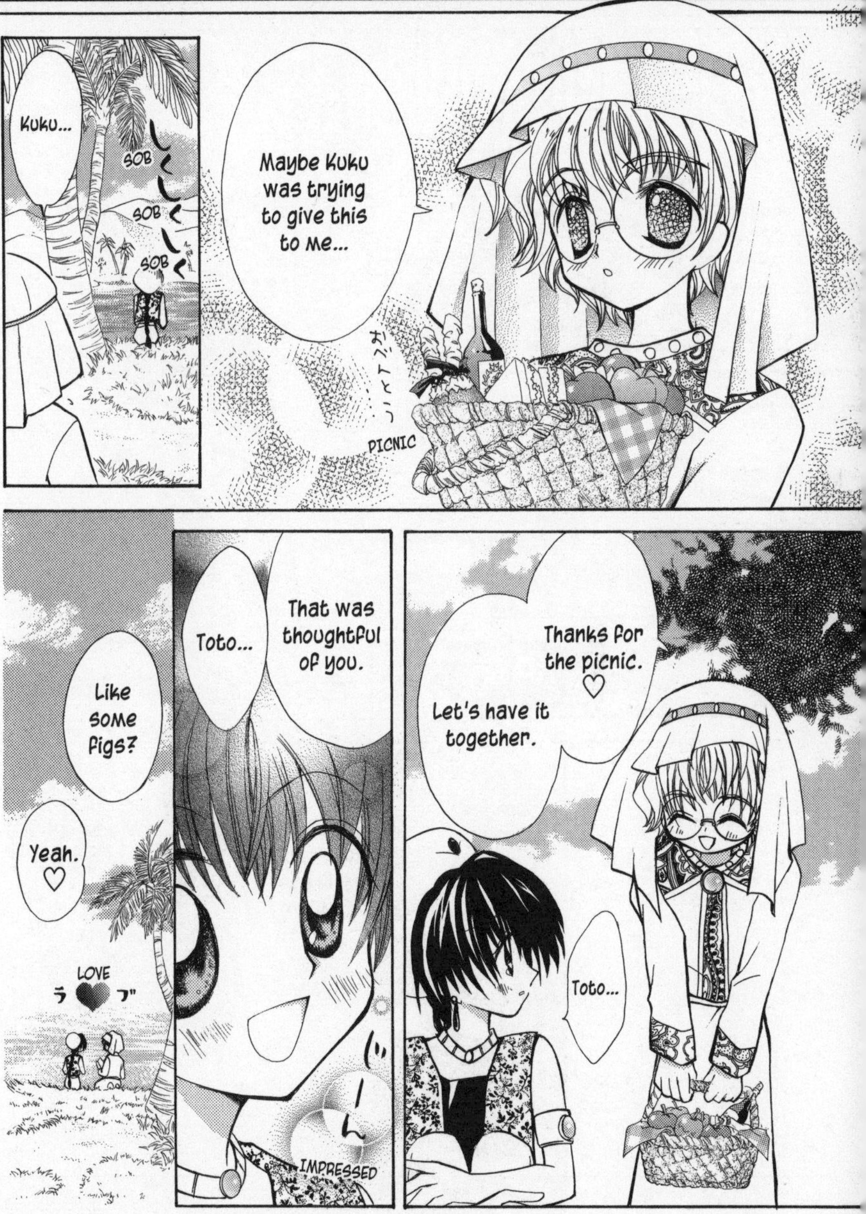

Maybe Kuku was trying to give this to me...
おべんとう
PICNIC
Kuku...
しくしくしく
SOB
SOB
SOB
Thanks for the picnic. ♡
Let's have it together.
Toto...
That was thoughtful of you.
Toto...
じーん
IMPRESSED
Like some figs?
Yeah. ♡
ラブ
LOVE

Sarasa & Jeff: Love for Their Brothers

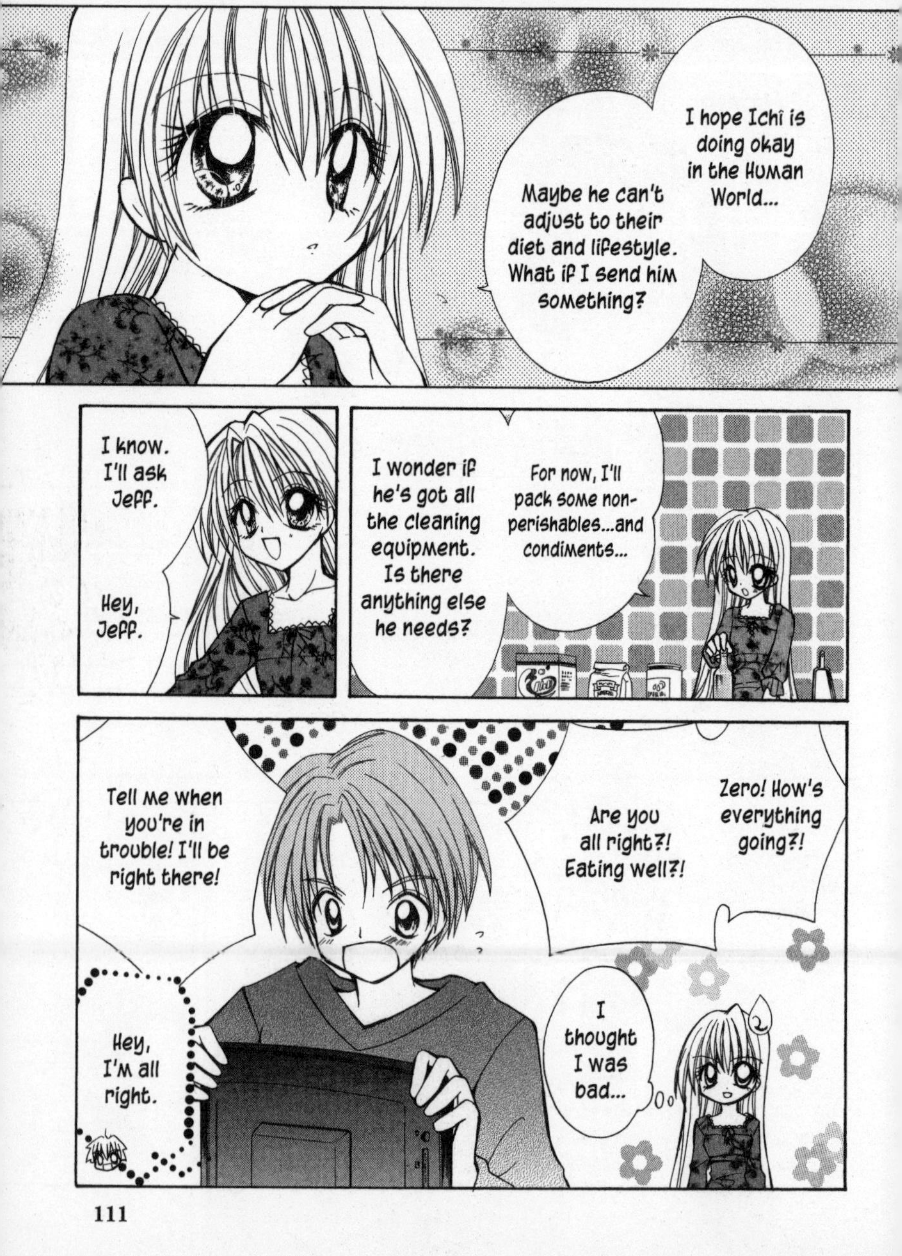
I hope Ichi is doing okay in the Human World...
Maybe he can't adjust to their diet and lifestyle. What if I send him something?
For now, I'll pack some non-perishables...and condiments...
I wonder if he's got all the cleaning equipment. Is there anything else he needs?
I know. I'll ask Jeff.
Hey, Jeff.
Zero! How's everything going?!
Are you all right?! Eating well?!
Tell me when you're in trouble! I'll be right there!
I thought I was bad...
Hey, I'm all right.

Ijûin & Sue: Teachers' Love

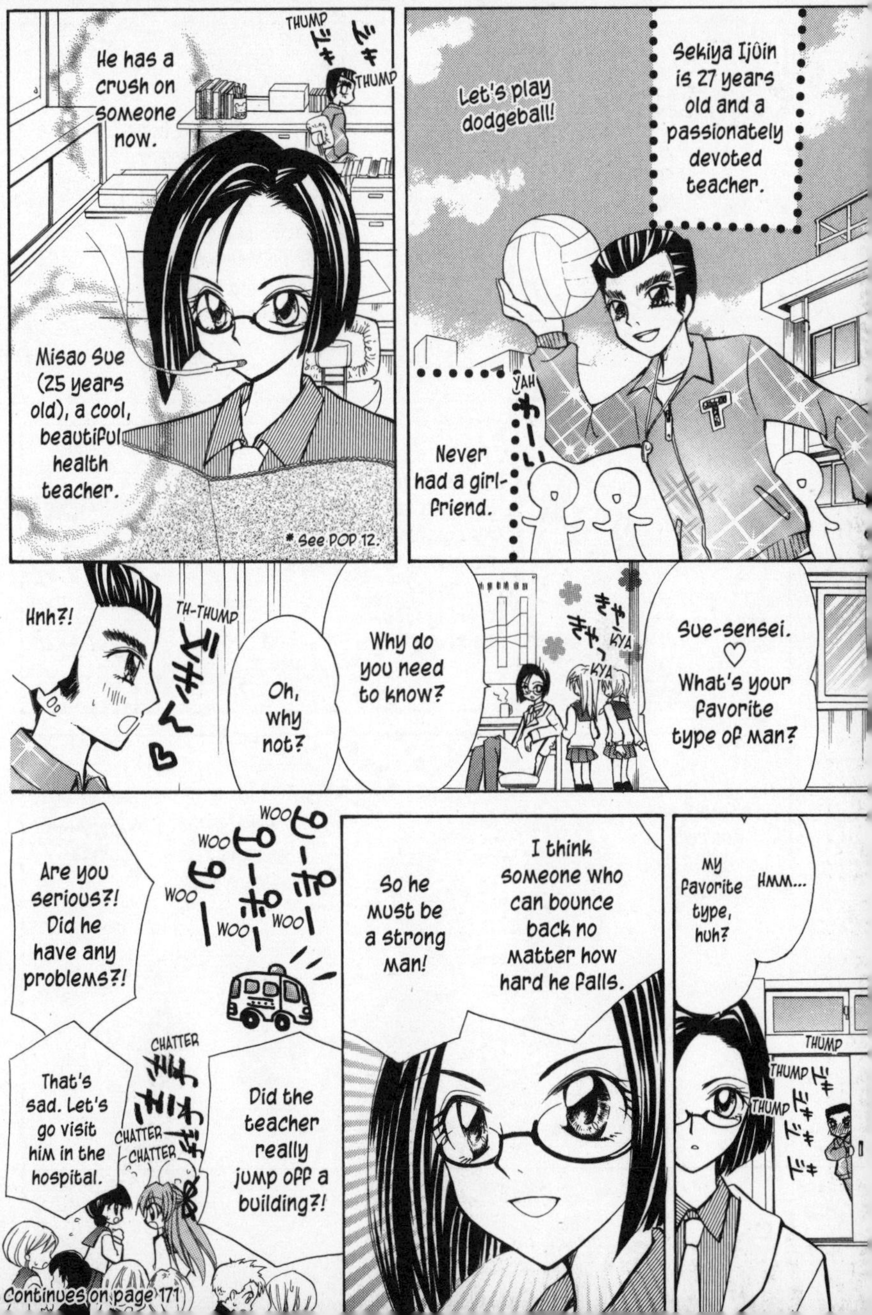

Sekiya Ijûin is 27 years old and a passionately devoted teacher.
Let's play dodgeball!
YAH
わーい
Never had a girl-friend.
THUMP
ドキ
THUMP
ドキ
He has a crush on someone now.
Misao Sue (25 years old), a cool, beautiful health teacher.
* See POP 12.
Sue-sensei. ♡ What's your favorite type of man?
KYA
きゃ
KYA
きゃっ
Why do you need to know?
Oh, why not?
TH-THUMP
Hnh?!
My favorite type, huh?
HMM...
THUMP
THUMP
THUMP
I think someone who can bounce back no matter how hard he falls.
So he must be a strong man!
WOO
WOO
WOO
WOO
WOO
Are you serious?! Did he have any problems?!
CHATTER
CHATTER
CHATTER
Did the teacher really jump off a building?!
That's sad. Let's go visit him in the hospital.

← Continues on page 171

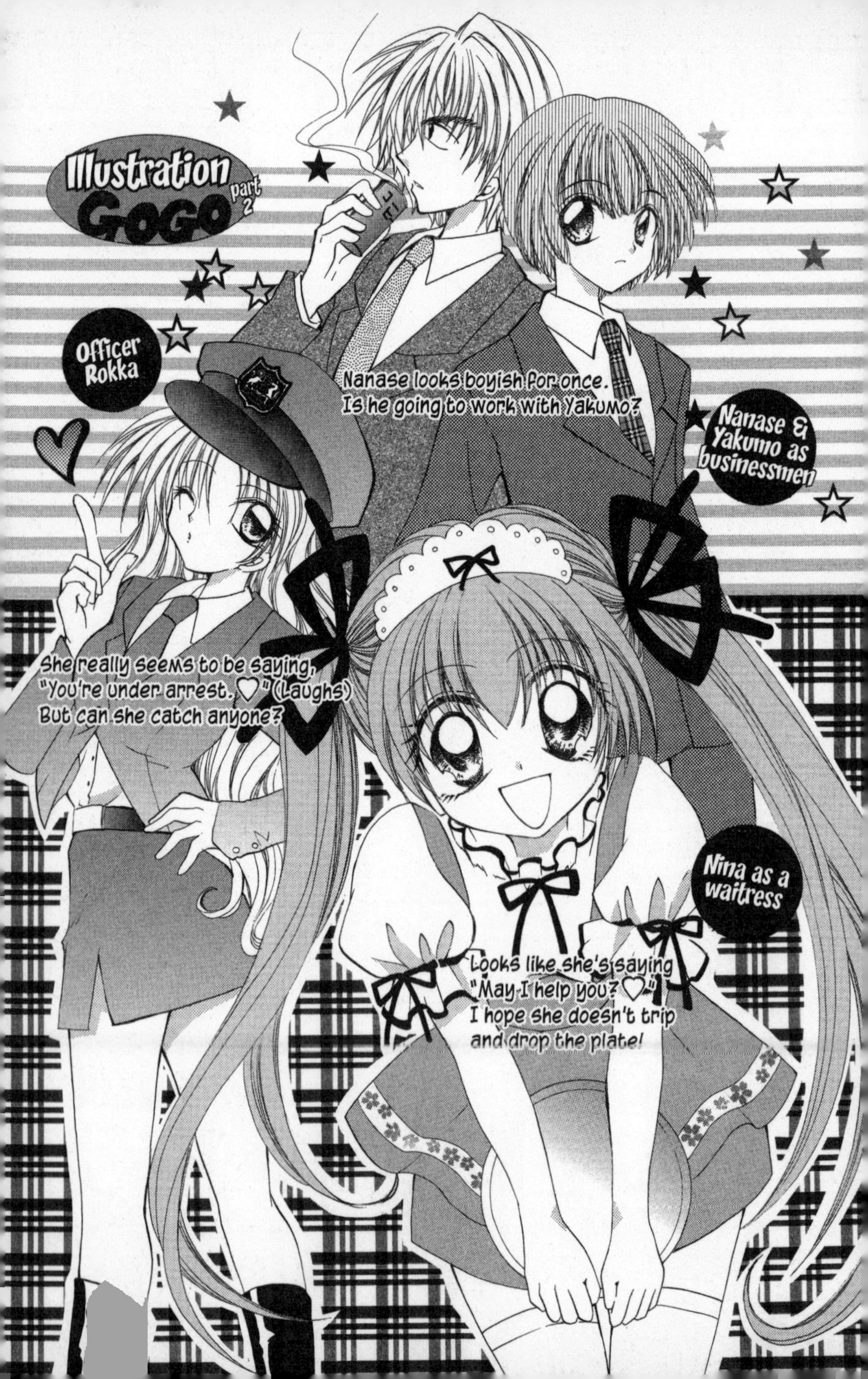
Illustration GoGo part 2
Nanase & Yakumo as businessmen
Nanase looks boyish for once. Is he going to work with Yakumo?
Officer Rokka
She really seems to be saying, "You're under arrest. ♡" (Laughs) But can she catch anyone?
Nina as a waitress
Looks like she's saying "May I help you? ♡" I hope she doesn't trip and drop the plate!

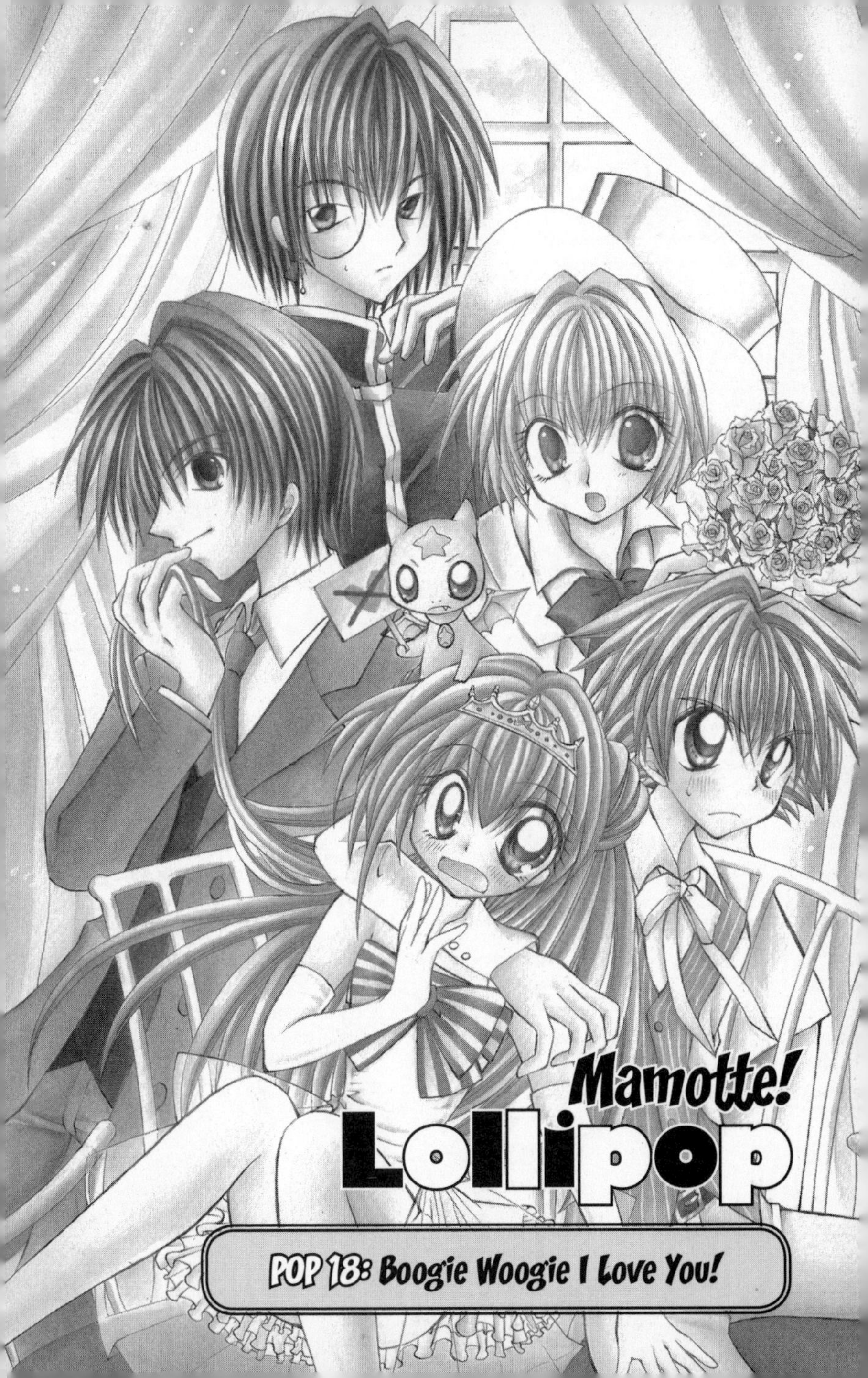
Mamotte!
Lollipop
POP 18: Boogie Woogie I Love You!

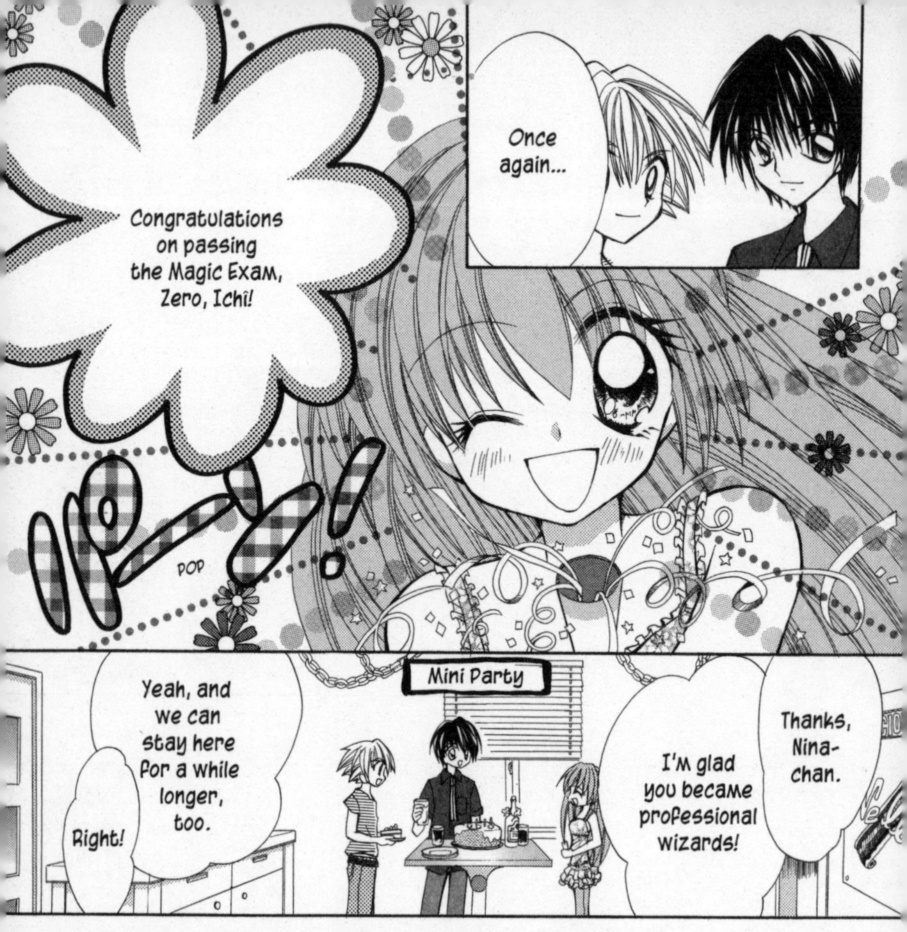
Once again...
Congratulations on passing the Magic Exam, Zero, Ichî!
POP
Thanks, Nina-chan.
I'm glad you became professional wizards!
Mini Party
Yeah, and we can stay here for a while longer, too.
Right!

PoP 18 Boogie Woogie I Love You!

Now we're really entering the new chapter of the story. I love the cover page. I've always wanted to do one mainly of boys! But I feel I could have drawn better . . . My favorite is Zero looking slightly embarrassed.

Nina hasn't changed a bit in the story . . . I like the relationship between Zero, Ichî and Pearl. Pearl turned out to be more immature than I had expected, but I think he's cute the way he is. I guess For-chan is the main focus of this episode. Haha . . .

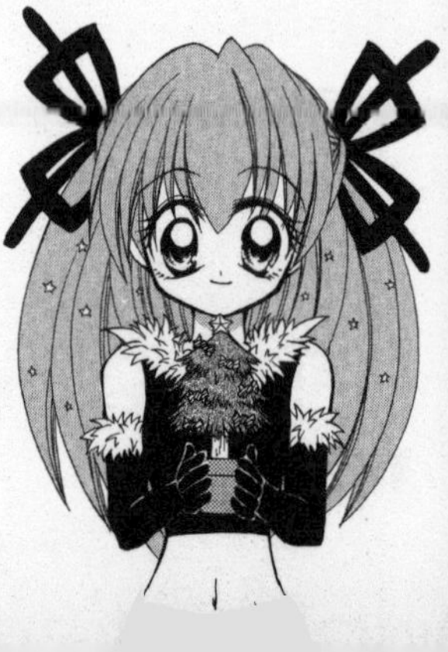

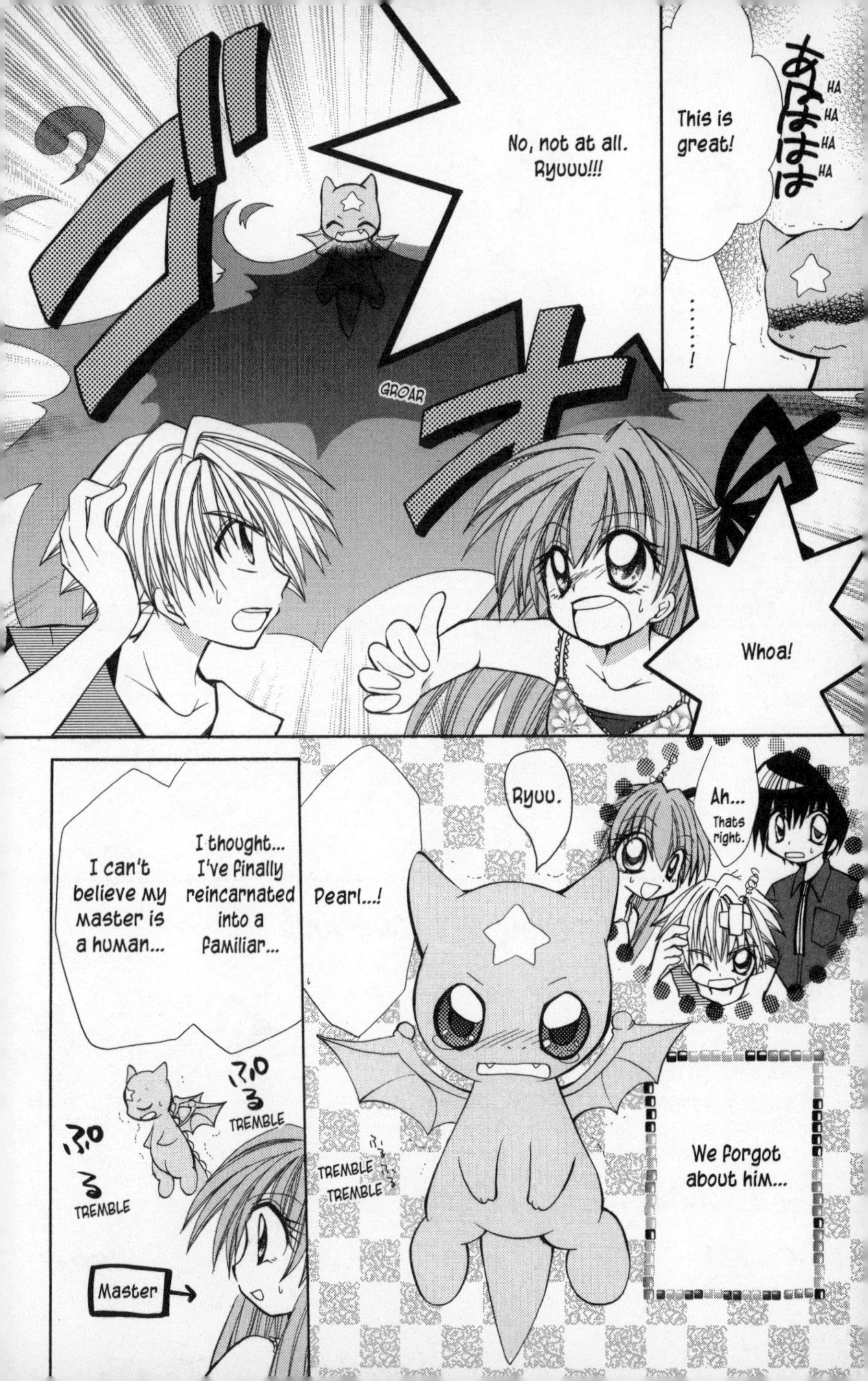

あははは
HA HA HA HA
This is great!
......!
No, not at all. Ryuuu!!!
GROAR
Whoa!
Ryuu.
Ah... Thats right.
We forgot about him...
Pearl...!
I thought... I've finally reincarnated into a familiar...
I can't believe my master is a human...
TREMBLE TREMBLE
ぷる
TREMBLE
ぷる
TREMBLE
Master

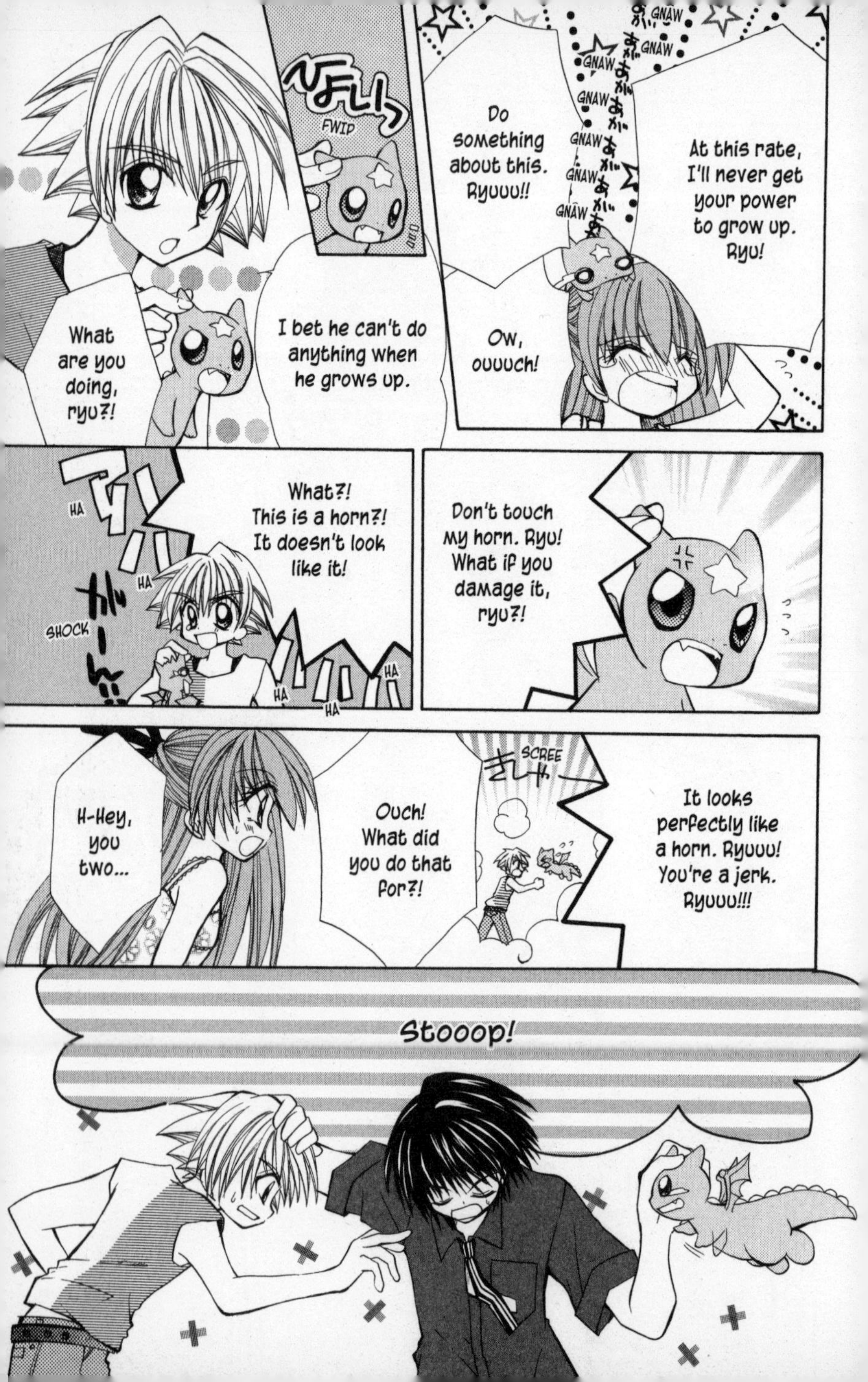
At this rate, I'll never get your power to grow up. Ryu!
GNAW
GNAW
GNAW
GNAW
GNAW
GNAW
GNAW
Do something about this. Ryuuu!!
Ow, ouuuch!
FWIP
I bet he can't do anything when he grows up.
What are you doing, ryu?!
Don't touch my horn. Ryu! What if you damage it, ryu?!
What?! This is a horn?! It doesn't look like it!
HA
HA
SHOCK
HA
HA
HA
It looks perfectly like a horn. Ryuuu! You're a jerk. Ryuuu!!!
SCREE
Ouch! What did you do that for?!
H-Hey, you two...
Stooop!

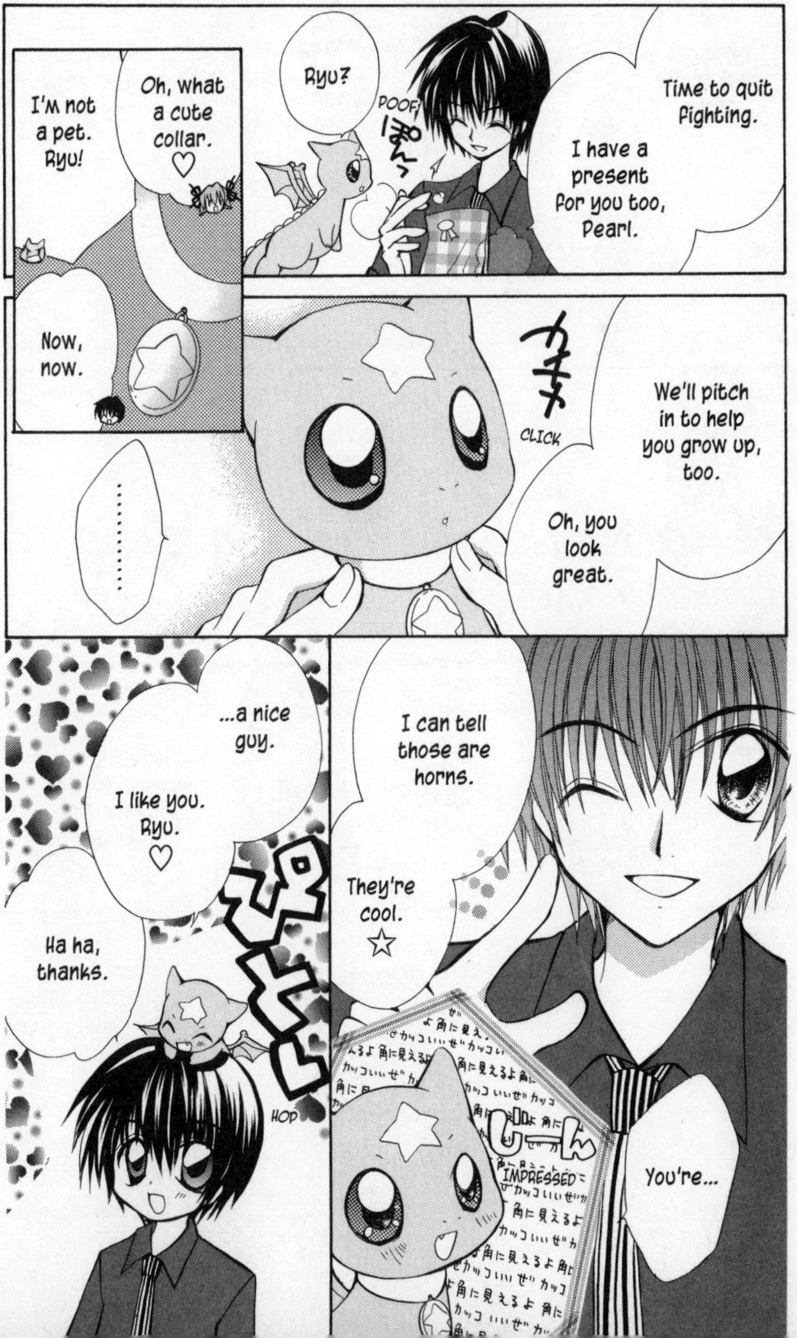
Time to quit fighting.
I have a present for you too, Pearl.
Ryu?
ぽんっ
POOF
Oh, what a cute collar. ♡
I'm not a pet. Ryu!
Now, now.
We'll pitch in to help you grow up, too.
Oh, you look great.
カチャ
CLICK
......
You're...
I can tell those are horns.
They're cool. ☆
じーん
IMPRESSED
角に見えるよ カッコいいぜ
...a nice guy.
I like you. Ryu. ♡
Ha ha, thanks.
HOP

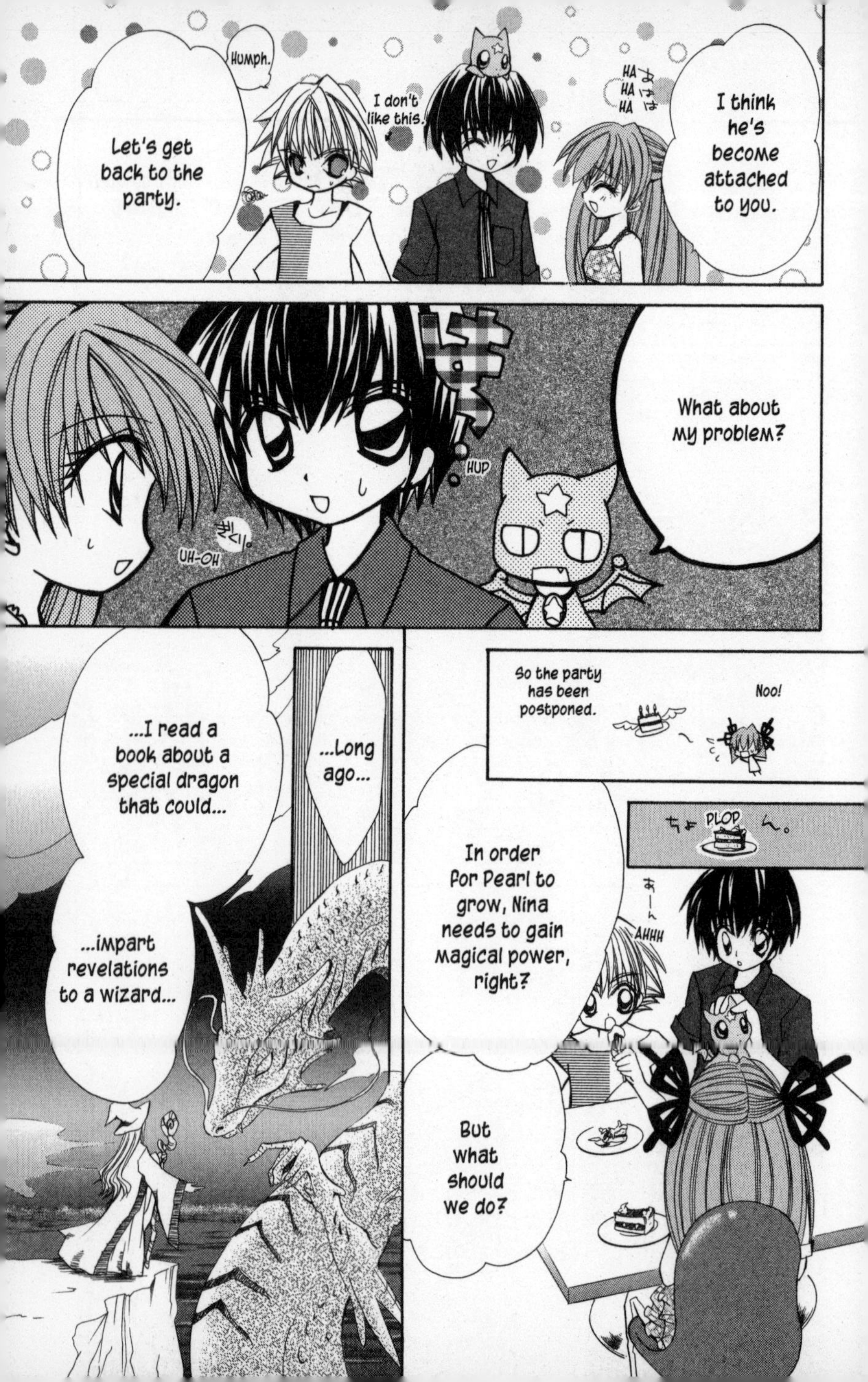
I think he's become attached to you.
HA HA HA
あはは
I don't like this.
Humph.
Let's get back to the party.
What about my problem?
HUP
UH-OH
So the party has been postponed.
Noo!
PLOP
In order for Pearl to grow, Nina needs to gain magical power, right?
あーん
AHHH
But what should we do?
...Long ago...
...I read a book about a special dragon that could...
...impart revelations to a wizard...

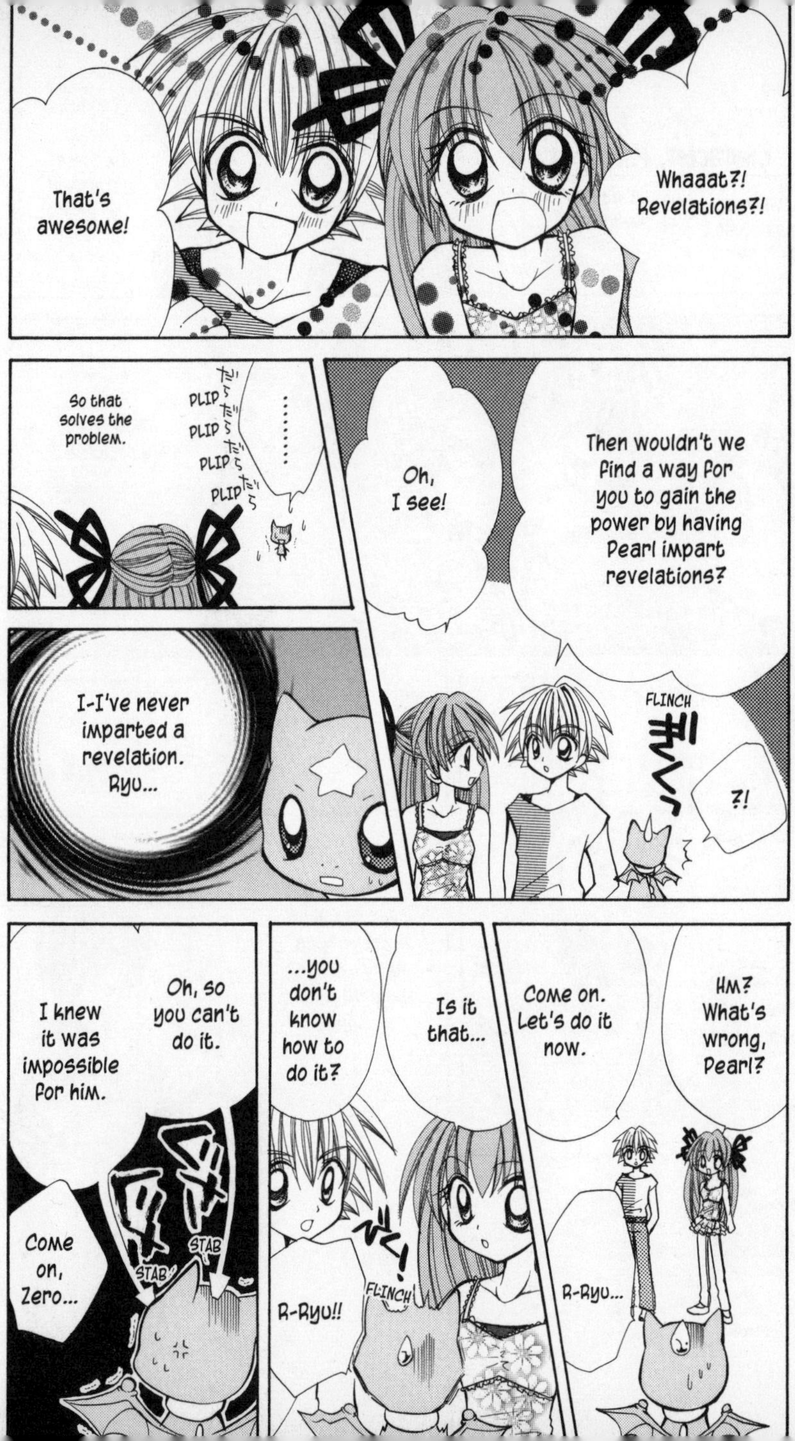
Whaaat?! Revelations?!
That's awesome!
Then wouldn't we find a way for you to gain the power by having Pearl impart revelations?
Oh, I see!
FLINCH
?!
......
PLIP
PLIP
PLIP
PLIP
So that solves the problem.
I-I've never imparted a revelation. Ryu...
Hm? What's wrong, Pearl?
Come on. Let's do it now.
R-Ryu...
Is it that...
...you don't know how to do it?
FLINCH
R-Ryu!!
Oh, so you can't do it.
I knew it was impossible for him.
STAB
STAB
Come on, Zero...

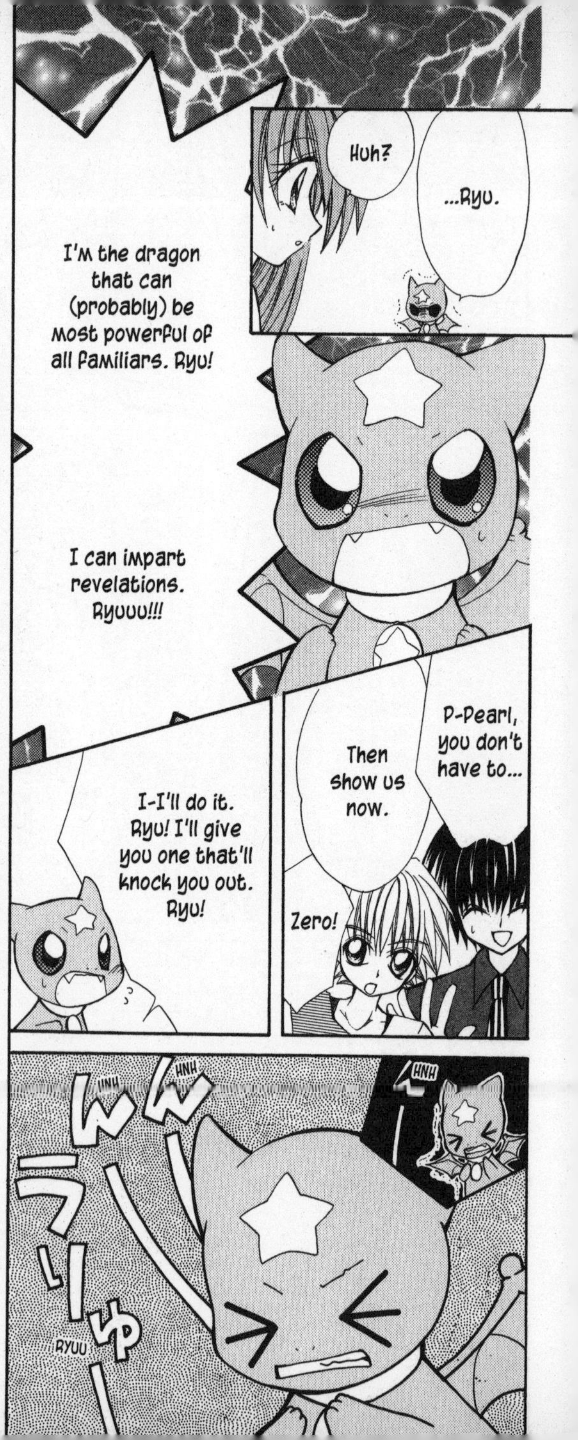
Huh?
...Ryu.
I'm the dragon that can (probably) be most powerful of all familiars. Ryu!
I can impart revelations. Ryuuu!!!
P-Pearl, you don't have to...
Then show us now.
Zero!
I-I'll do it. Ryu! I'll give you one that'll knock you out. Ryu!
HNH
HNH
HNH
RYUU

Force It on the Character, Part 2

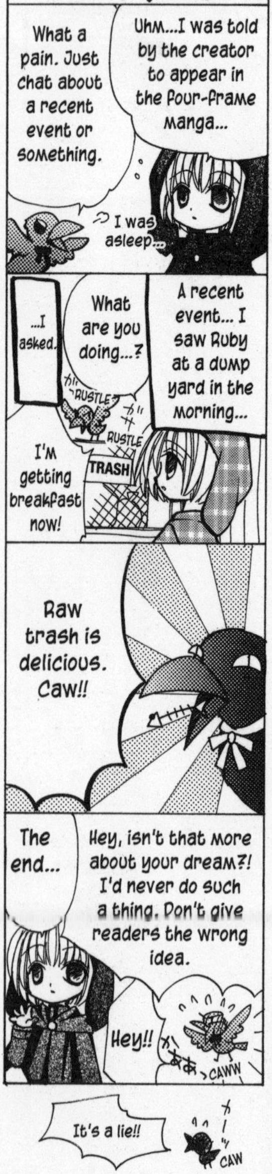
Uhm...I was told by the creator to appear in the four-frame manga...
What a pain. Just chat about a recent event or something.
I was asleep...
A recent event... I saw Ruby at a dump yard in the morning...
What are you doing...?
...I asked.
RUSTLE
RUSTLE
TRASH
I'm getting breakfast now!
Raw trash is delicious. Caw!!
Hey, isn't that more about your dream?! I'd never do such a thing. Don't give readers the wrong idea.
The end...
Hey!!
CAWW
It's a lie!!
CAW

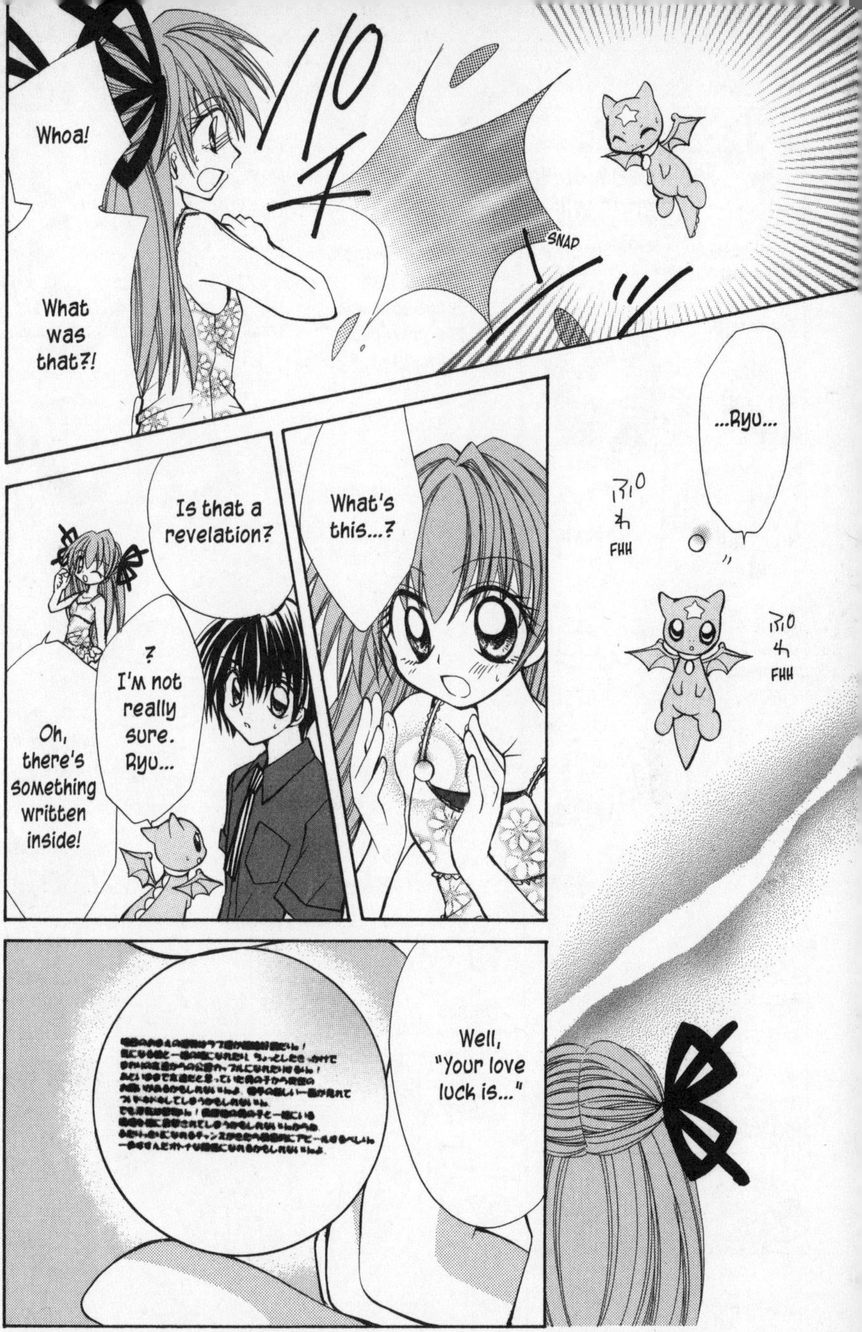
SNAP
Whoa!
What was that?!
...Ryu...
FHH
FHH
What's this...?
Is that a revelation?
? I'm not really sure. Ryu...
Oh, there's something written inside!
Well, "Your love luck is..."

Your love luck is really on your side tomorrow. Ryu! You'll team up with the boy you're interested in and friends will acknowledge you as a couple. Ryu!

Also, a boy you think is just a friend might suddenly ask you out. Ryu. You could see another side of him and feel your heart pound. Ryu.

But cheating is a big no-no. Ryu! He might accidentally catch you with another boy. Ryu. If you get a chance to be alone with him, aggressively attract him. Ryu! You might progress to a mature relationship. Ryu.

Lucky Item: Handkerchief

Lucky Number: 7

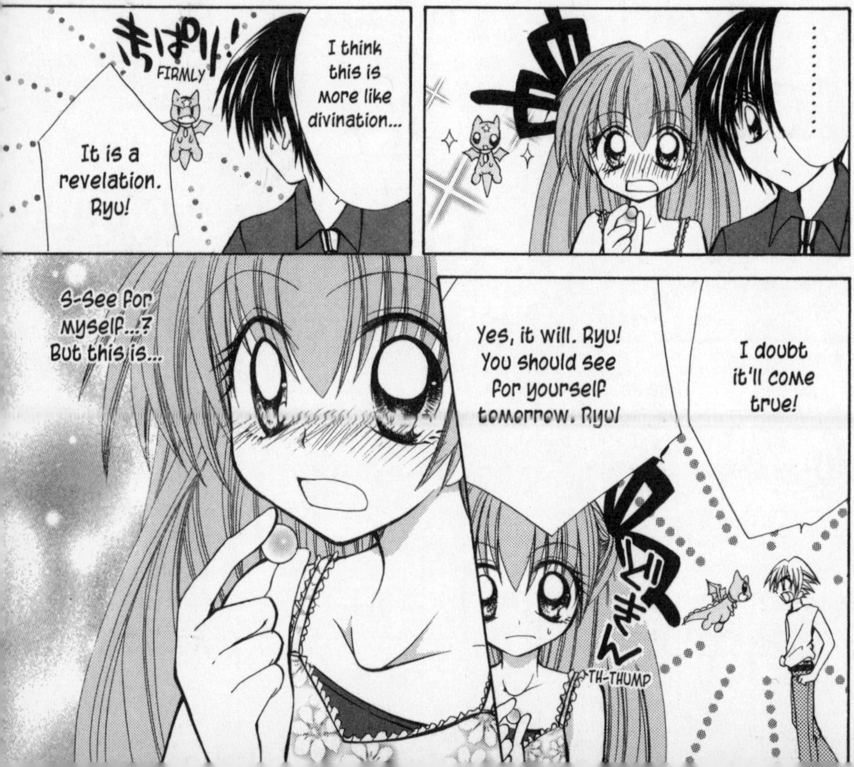
......
I think this is more like divination...
FIRMLY
It is a revelation. Ryu!
I doubt it'll come true!
Yes, it will. Ryu! You should see for yourself tomorrow. Ryu!
TH-THUMP
S-See for myself...? But this is...

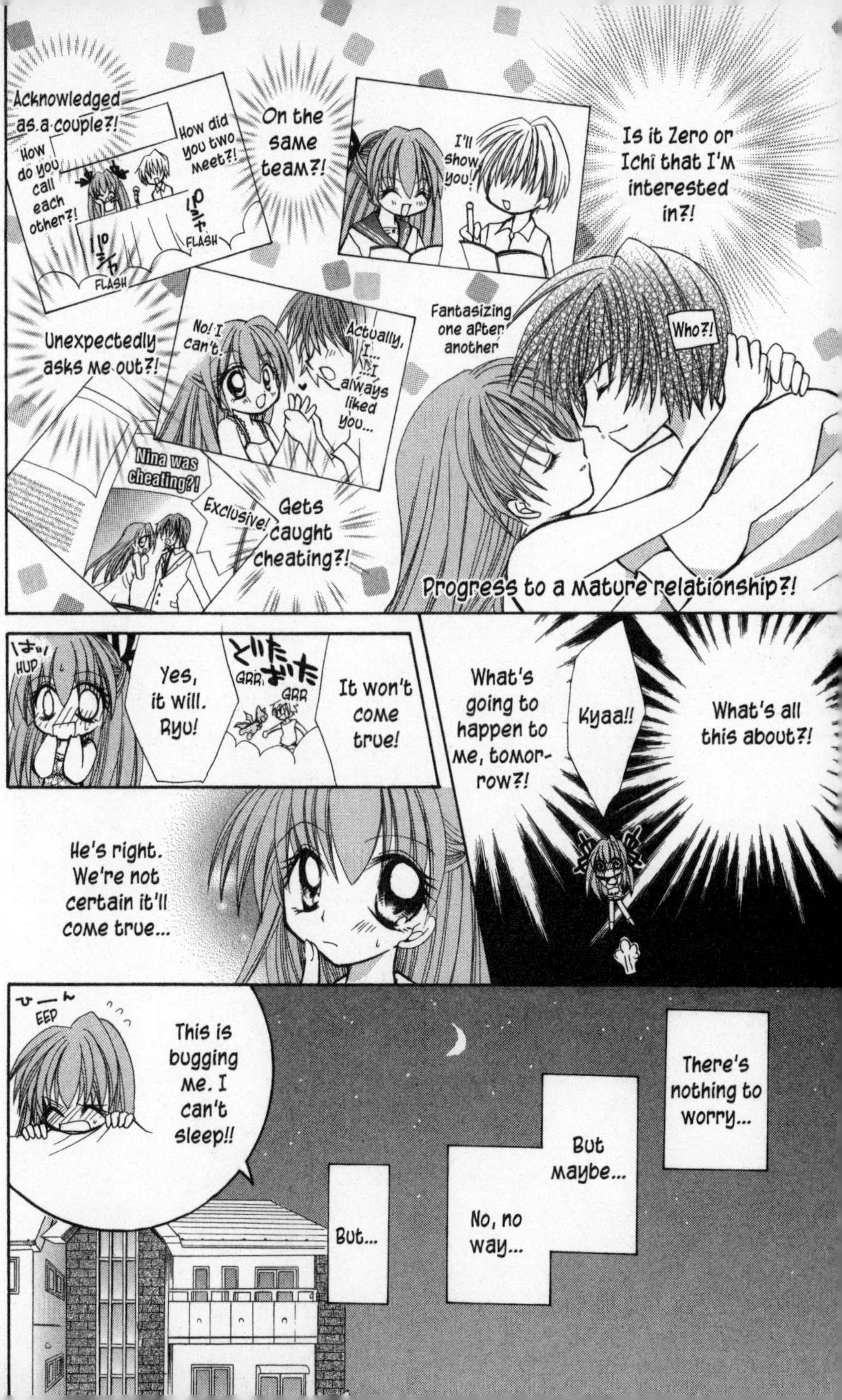
Is it Zero or Ichi that I'M interested in?!
On the same team?!
I'll show you!
Acknowledged as a couple?!
How did you two meet?!
How do you call each other?!
FLASH
FLASH
Who?!
Fantasizing one after another
Actually, I... ...I always liked you...
No! I can't.
Unexpectedly asks me out?!
Gets caught cheating?!
Exclusive!
Nina was cheating?!
Progress to a mature relationship?!
What's all this about?!
Kyaa!!
What's going to happen to me, tomorrow?!
It won't come true!
GRR
GRR
Yes, it will. Ryu!
HUP
He's right. We're not certain it'll come true...
There's nothing to worry...
But maybe...
No, no way...
But...
This is bugging me. I can't sleep!!
EEP

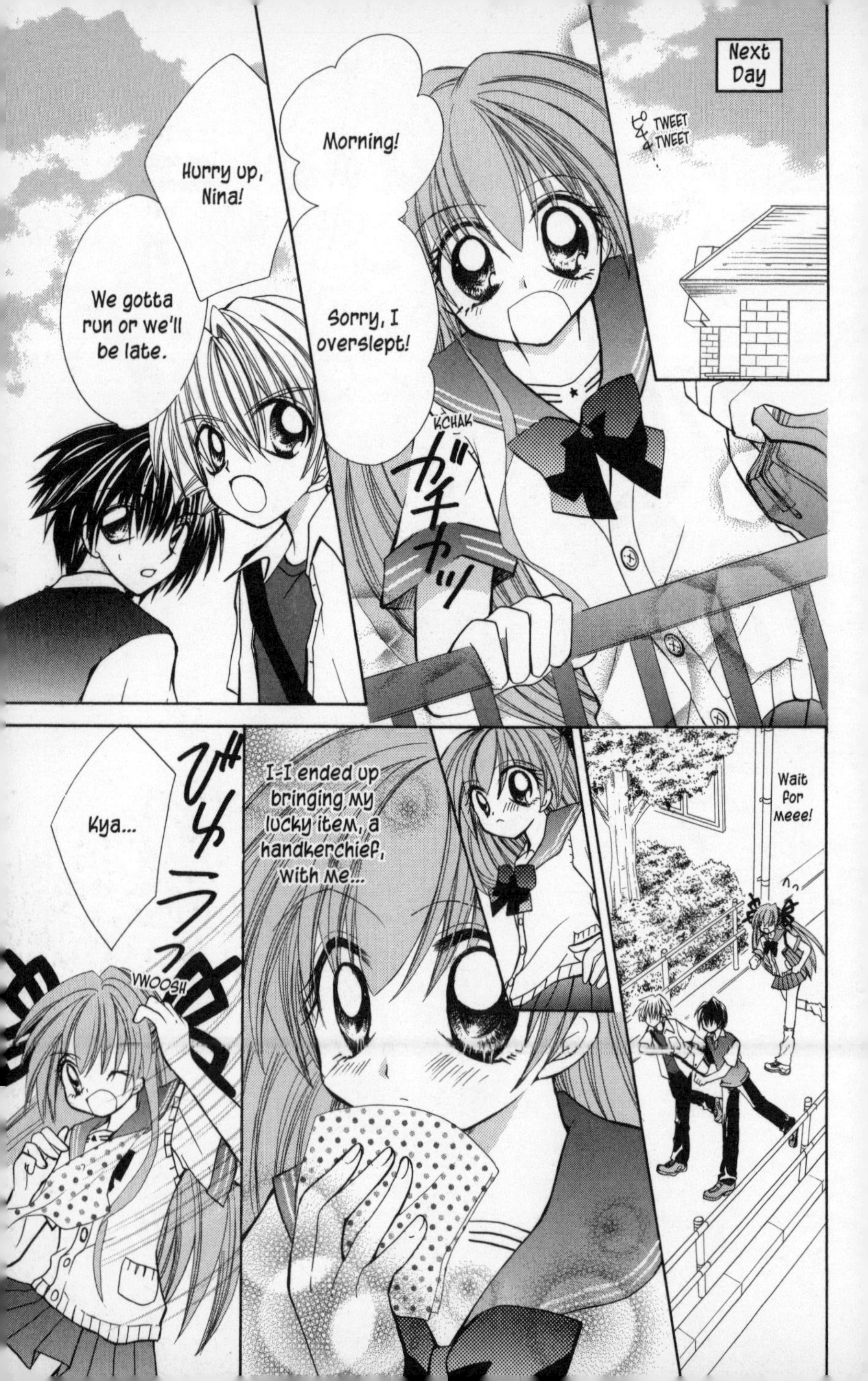
Next Day
TWEET TWEET
Morning!
Sorry, I overslept!
KCHAK
ガチャッ
Hurry up, Nina!
We gotta run or we'll be late.
Wait for meee!
I-I ended up bringing my lucky item, a handkerchief, with me...
Kya...
VWOOSH

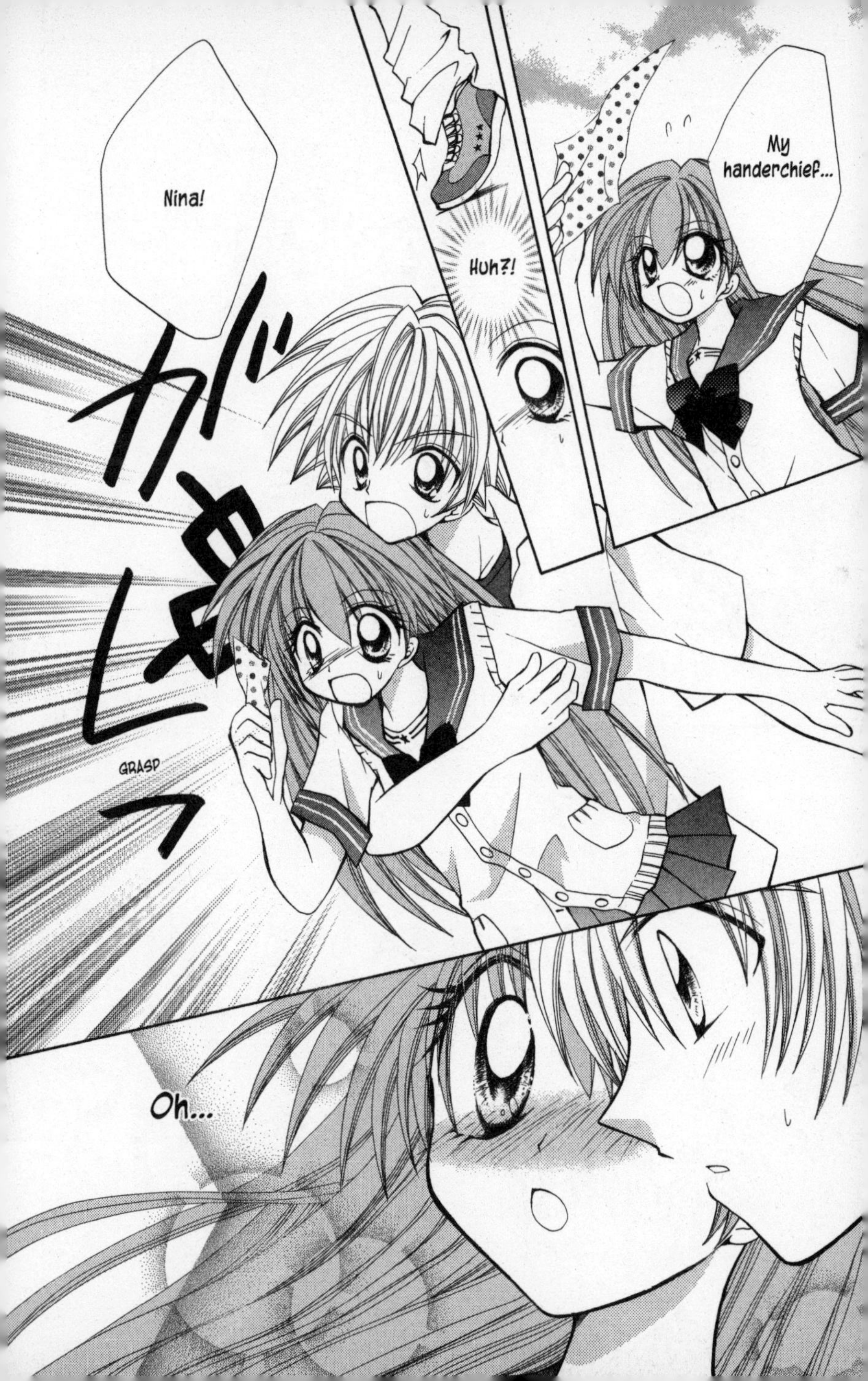
My handerchief...
Huh?!
Nina!
GRASP
Oh...

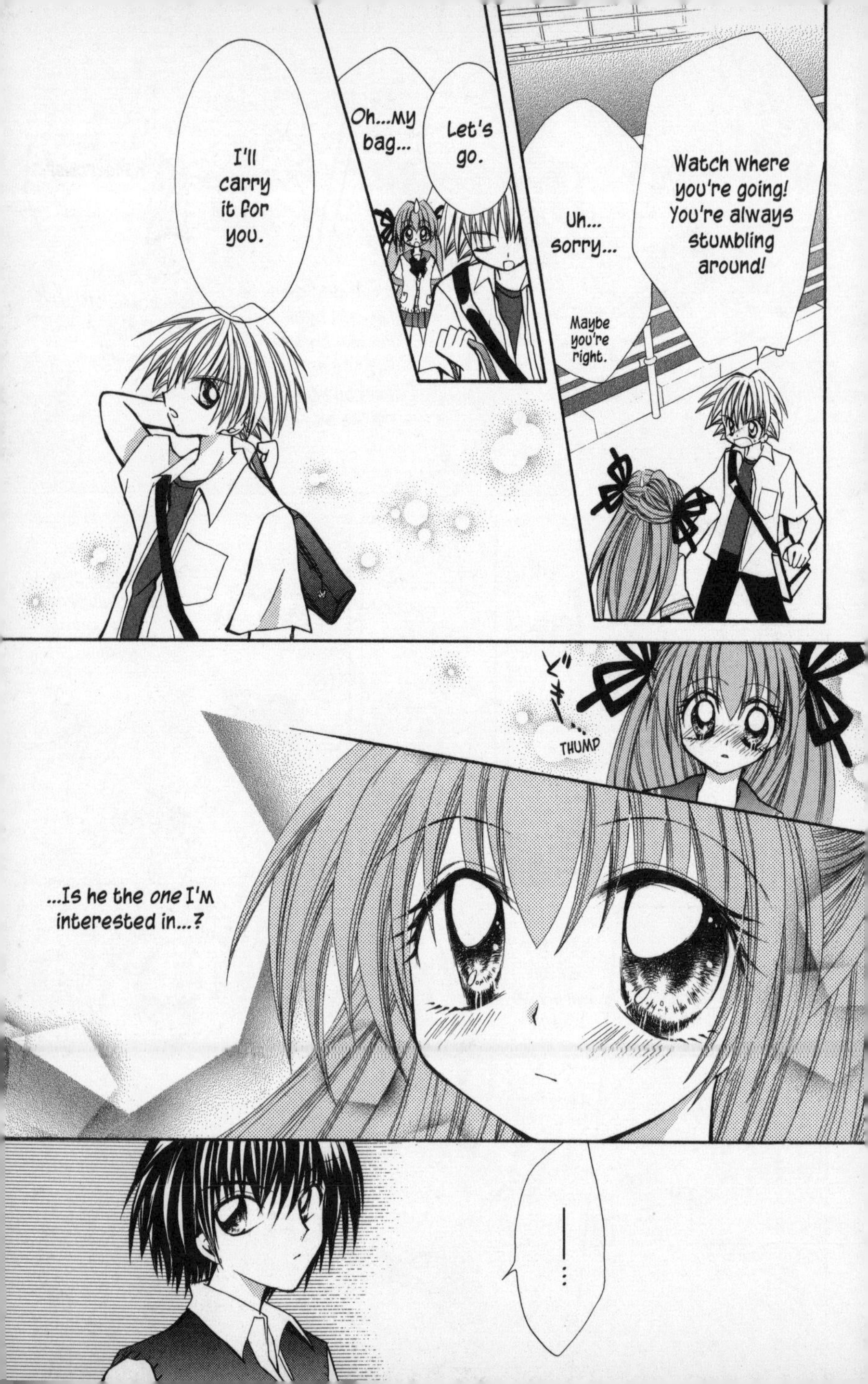
Watch where you're going! You're always stumbling around!
Uh... sorry...
Maybe you're right.
Let's go.
Oh...my bag...
I'll carry it for you.
どき
THUMP
...Is he the one I'M interested in...?
—...

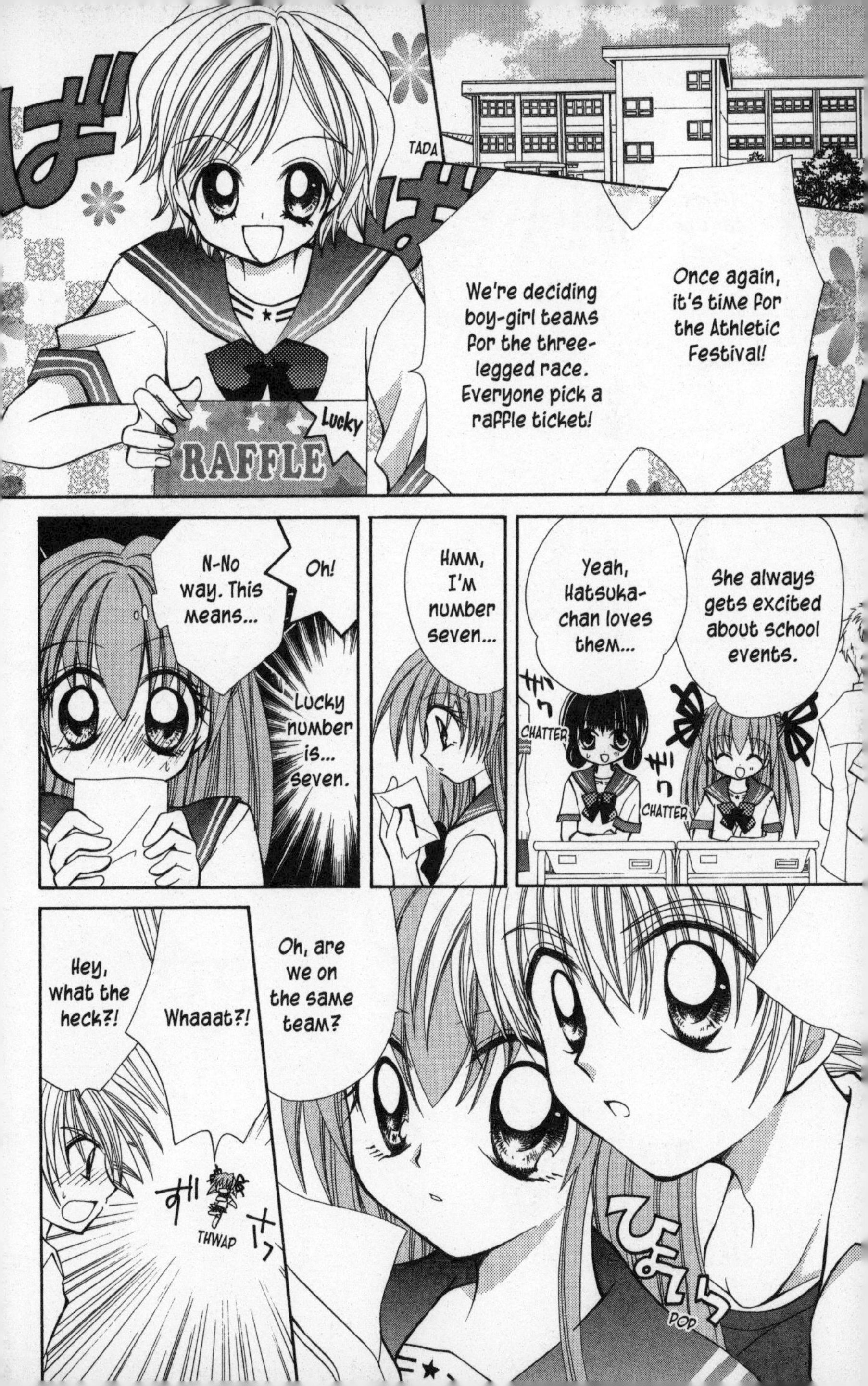
TADA
Once again, it's time for the Athletic Festival!
We're deciding boy-girl teams for the three-legged race. Everyone pick a raffle ticket!
Lucky
RAFFLE
She always gets excited about school events.
Yeah, Hatsuka-chan loves them...
CHATTER
CHATTER
Hmm, I'm number seven...
Oh!
N-No way. This means...
Lucky number is... seven.
Oh, are we on the same team?
POP
Whaaat?!
Hey, what the heck?!
THWAP

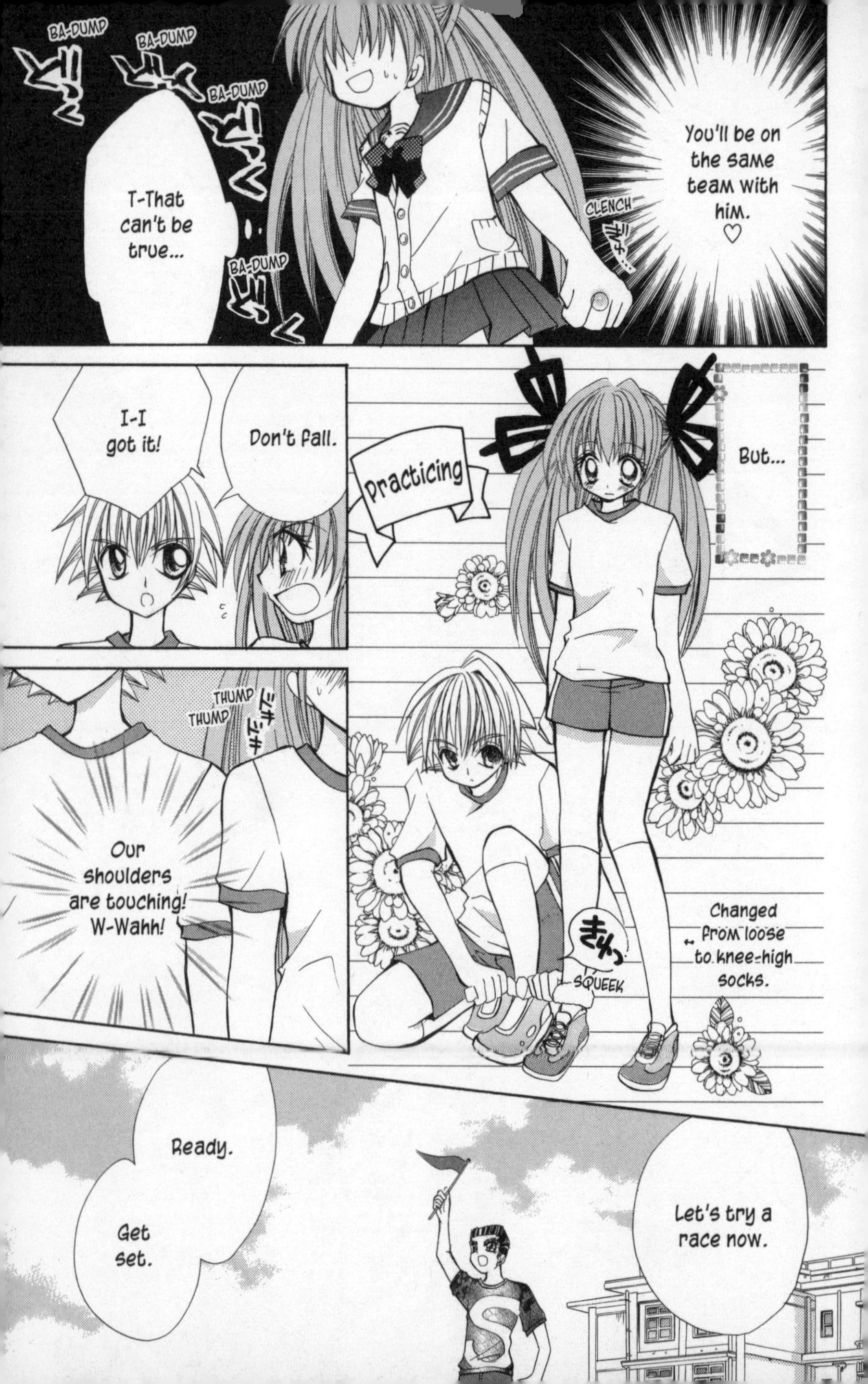
You'll be on the same team with him. ♡
CLENCH
BA-DUMP
BA-DUMP
BA-DUMP
T-That can't be true...
BA-DUMP
But...
Practicing
Changed from loose to knee-high socks.
SQUEEK
Don't fall.
I-I got it!
THUMP THUMP
Our shoulders are touching! W-Wahh!
Let's try a race now.
Ready.
Get set.

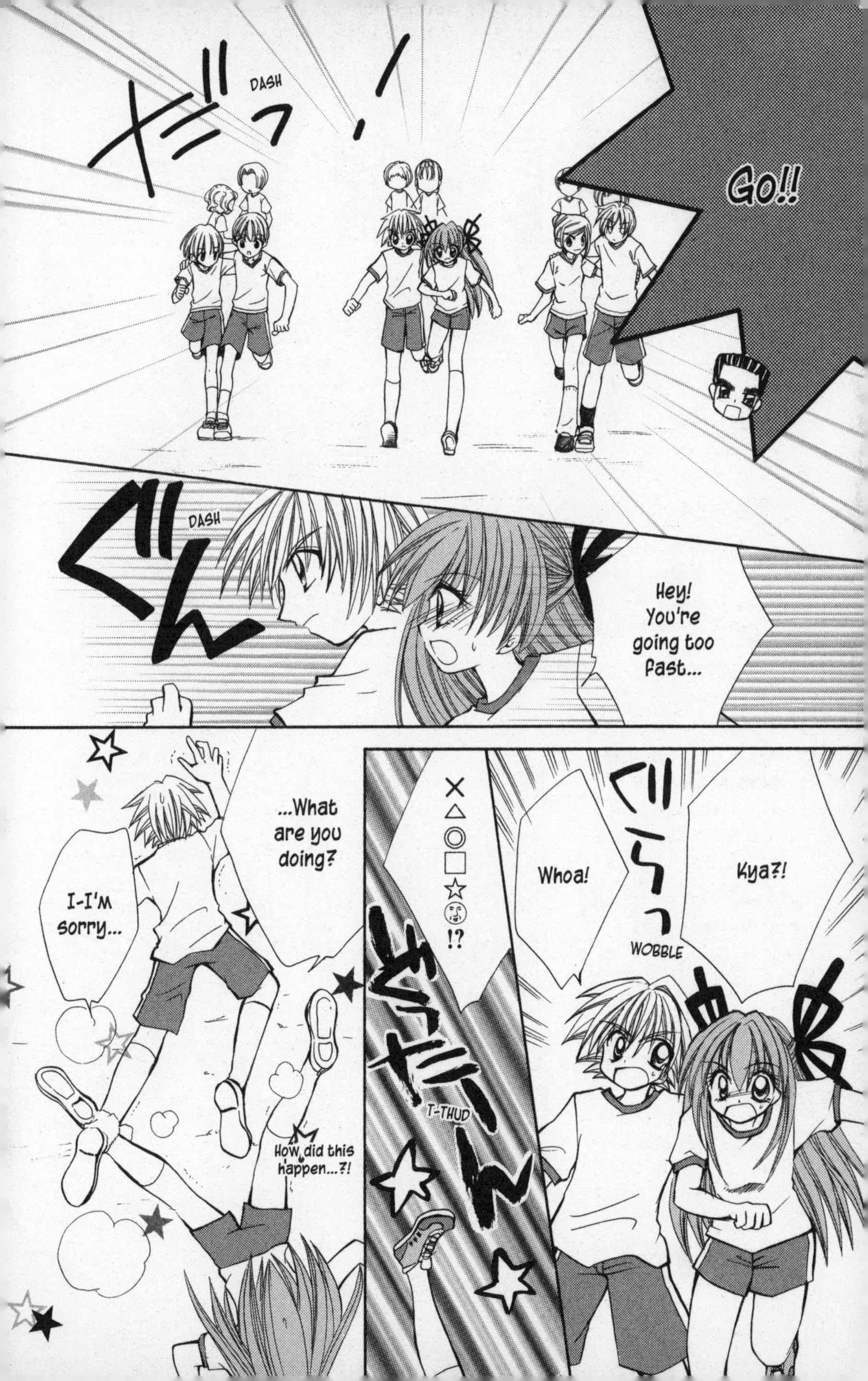
Go!!
DASH
Hey! You're going too fast...
DASH
Kya?!
WOBBLE
Whoa!
×△○□☆!?
T-THUD
...What are you doing?
I-I'm sorry...
How did this happen...?!

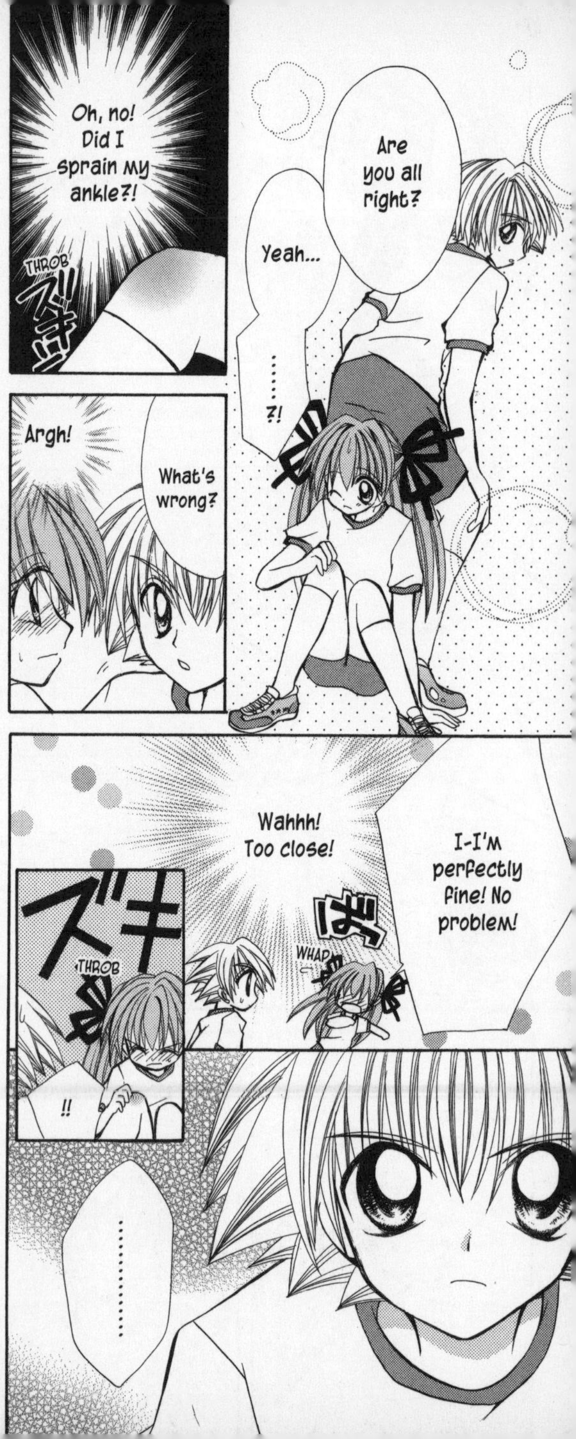
Are you all right?
Yeah...
......?!
Oh, no! Did I sprain my ankle?!
THROB
Argh!
What's wrong?
I-I'm perfectly fine! No problem!
Wahhh! Too close!
WHAP
THROB
!!
......

Q&A

Q. Have you decided on the ending?

A. I have all the details and really want to draw it now . . . It probably won't happen that way . . . But I can assure you that it'll have a happy ending. It'll be awesome if it goes as planned!!

Q. What are those things in Rokka's hair? Does she put her hair in them?

A. Those are hair accessories. Her hair isn't in there. Maybe she puts them in occasionally. (Laughs)

Q. Didn't Zero sell off his skateboard . . . ?

A. He did but Ichi bought it back for him. For details, please read page 163 of POP 9 in volume two. (It's in Ichi's line.)

Q. Are you using a fashion magazine as a reference for the characters' outfits?

A. I want to dress them in that type of outfits, but I don't really look at them when I draw. I tend to design them myself.

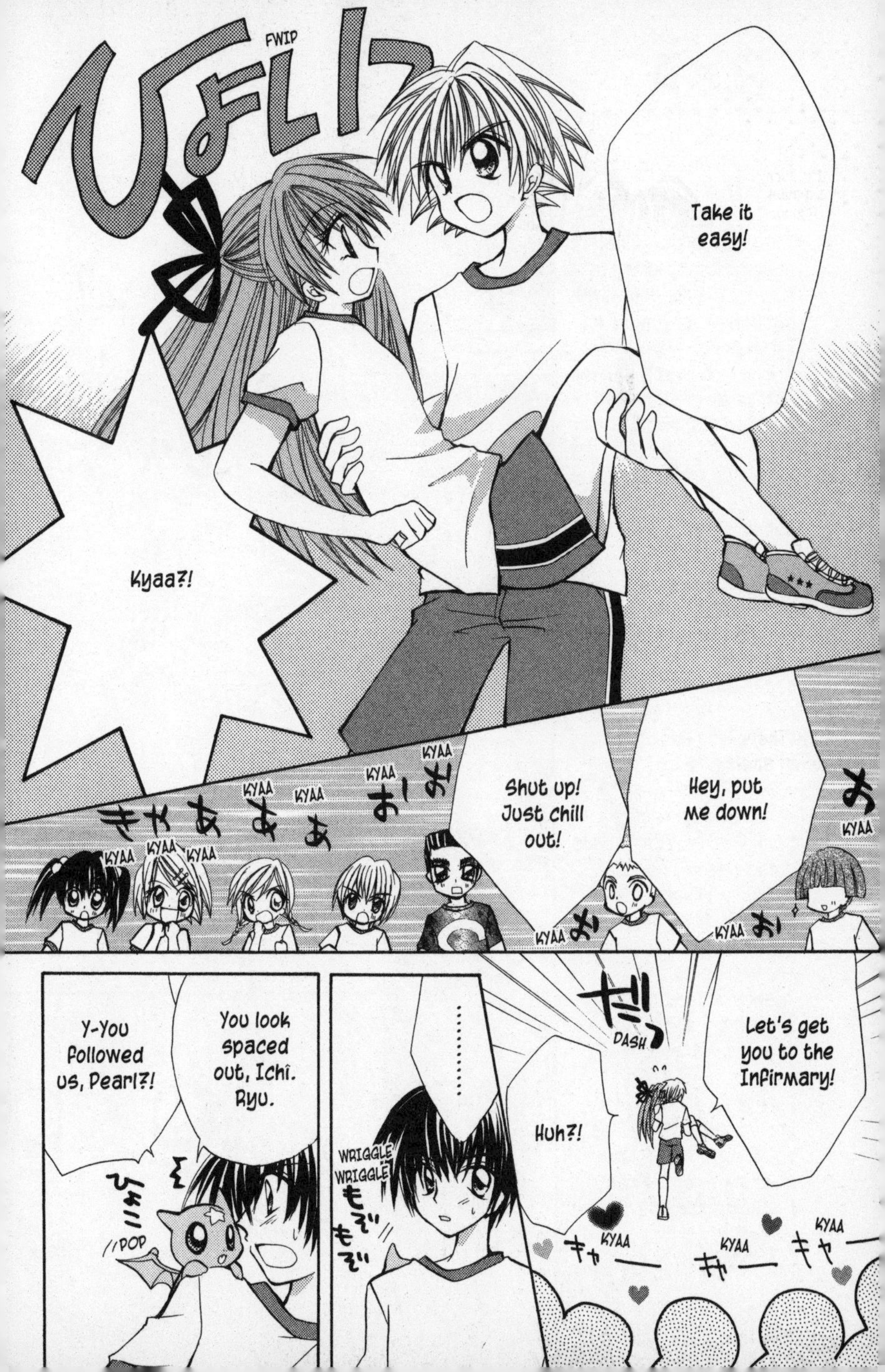
FWIP
Take it easy!
Kyaa?!
Hey, put me down!
Shut up! Just chill out!
KYAA KYAA KYAA KYAA KYAA KYAA KYAA KYAA KYAA KYAA
DASH
Let's get you to the Infirmary!
KYAA KYAA KYAA
Huh?!
....
WRIGGLE WRIGGLE
You look spaced out, Ichi. Ryu.
Y-You followed us, Pearl?!
POP

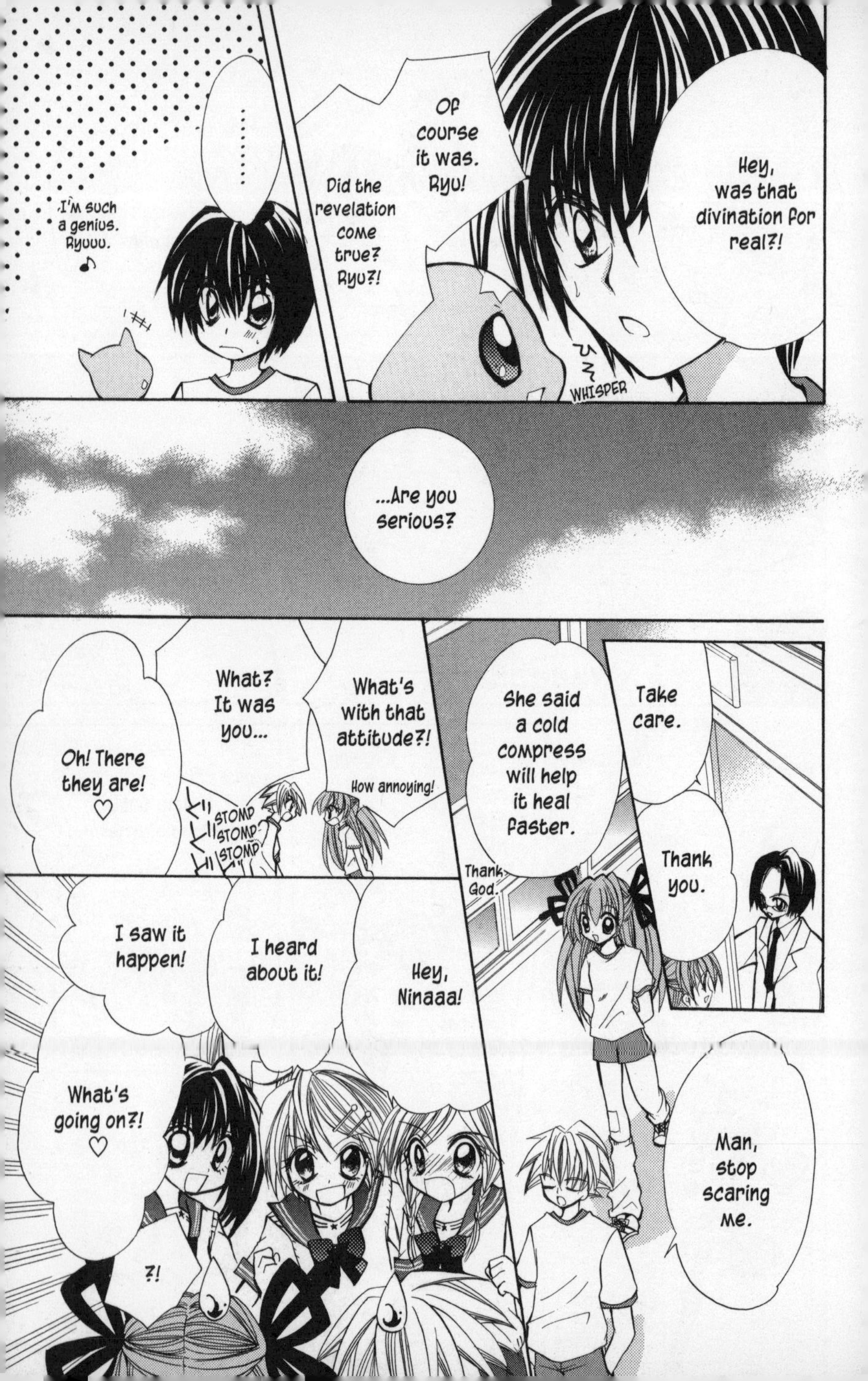

Hey, was that divination for real?!
WHISPER
Of course it was. Ryu!
Did the revelation come true? Ryu?!
……
I'm such a genius. Ryuuu. ♪
...Are you serious?
Take care.
Thank you.
She said a cold compress will help it heal faster.
Thank God.
What's with that attitude?!
How annoying!
What? It was you...
STOMP STOMP STOMP
Oh! There they are! ♡
Man, stop scaring me.
Hey, Ninaaa!
I heard about it!
I saw it happen!
What's going on?! ♡
?!

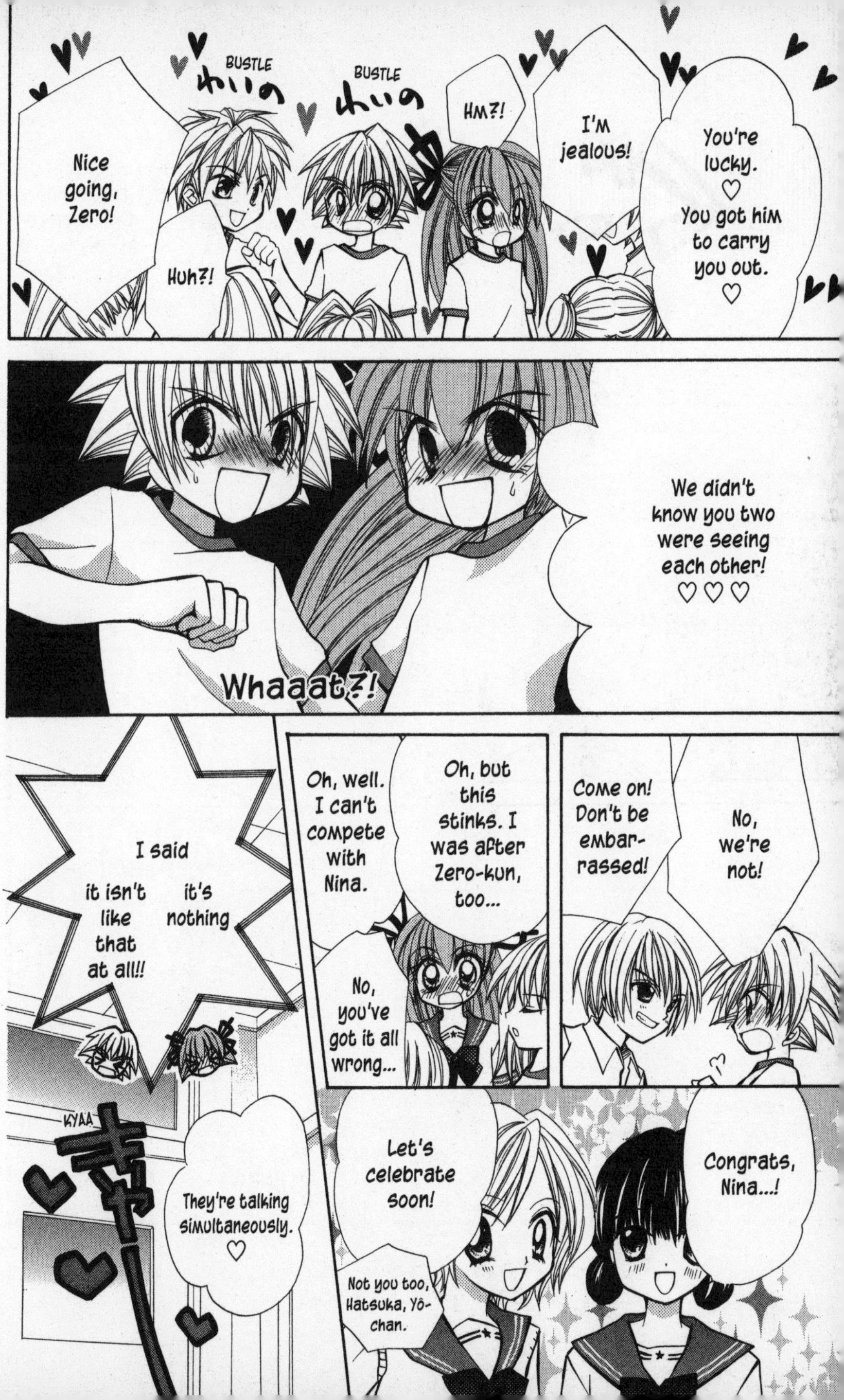
You're lucky. ♡ You got him to carry you out. ♡
I'M jealous!
HM?!
BUSTLE
BUSTLE
Huh?!
Nice going, Zero!
We didn't know you two were seeing each other! ♡ ♡ ♡
Whaaat?!
No, we're not!
Come on! Don't be embarrassed!
Oh, but this stinks. I was after Zero-kun, too...
Oh, well. I can't compete with Nina.
No, you've got it all wrong...
Congrats, Nina...!
Let's celebrate soon!
Not you too, Hatsuka, Yô-chan.
I said
it's nothing
it isn't like that at all!!
KYAA
They're talking simultaneously. ♡

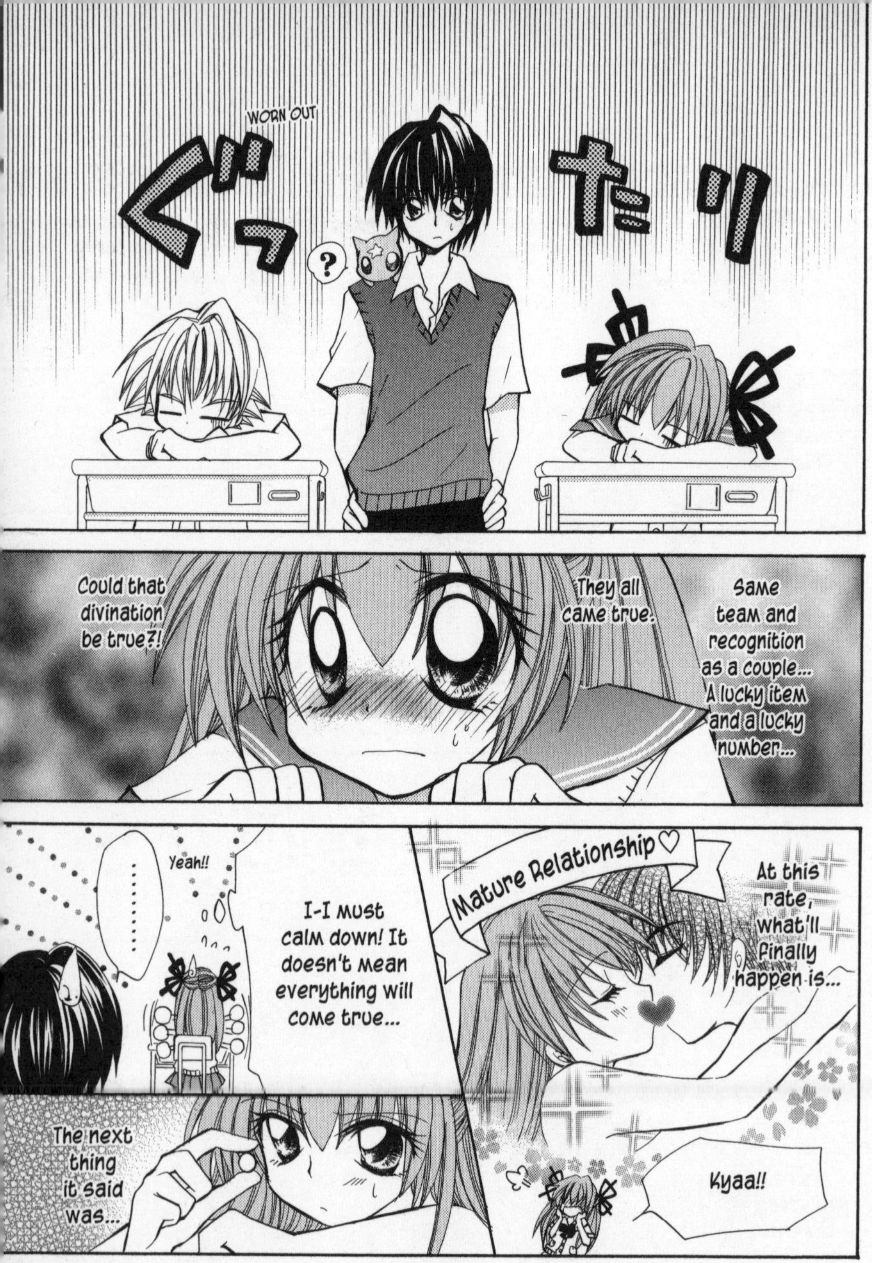
WORN OUT
?
Same team and recognition as a couple... A lucky item and a lucky number...
They all came true.
Could that divination be true?!
Mature Relationship♡
At this rate, what'll finally happen is...
I-I must calm down! It doesn't mean everything will come true...
......
Yeah!!
Kyaa!!
The next thing it said was...

A boy you think is just a friend
might suddenly ask you out. Ryu.

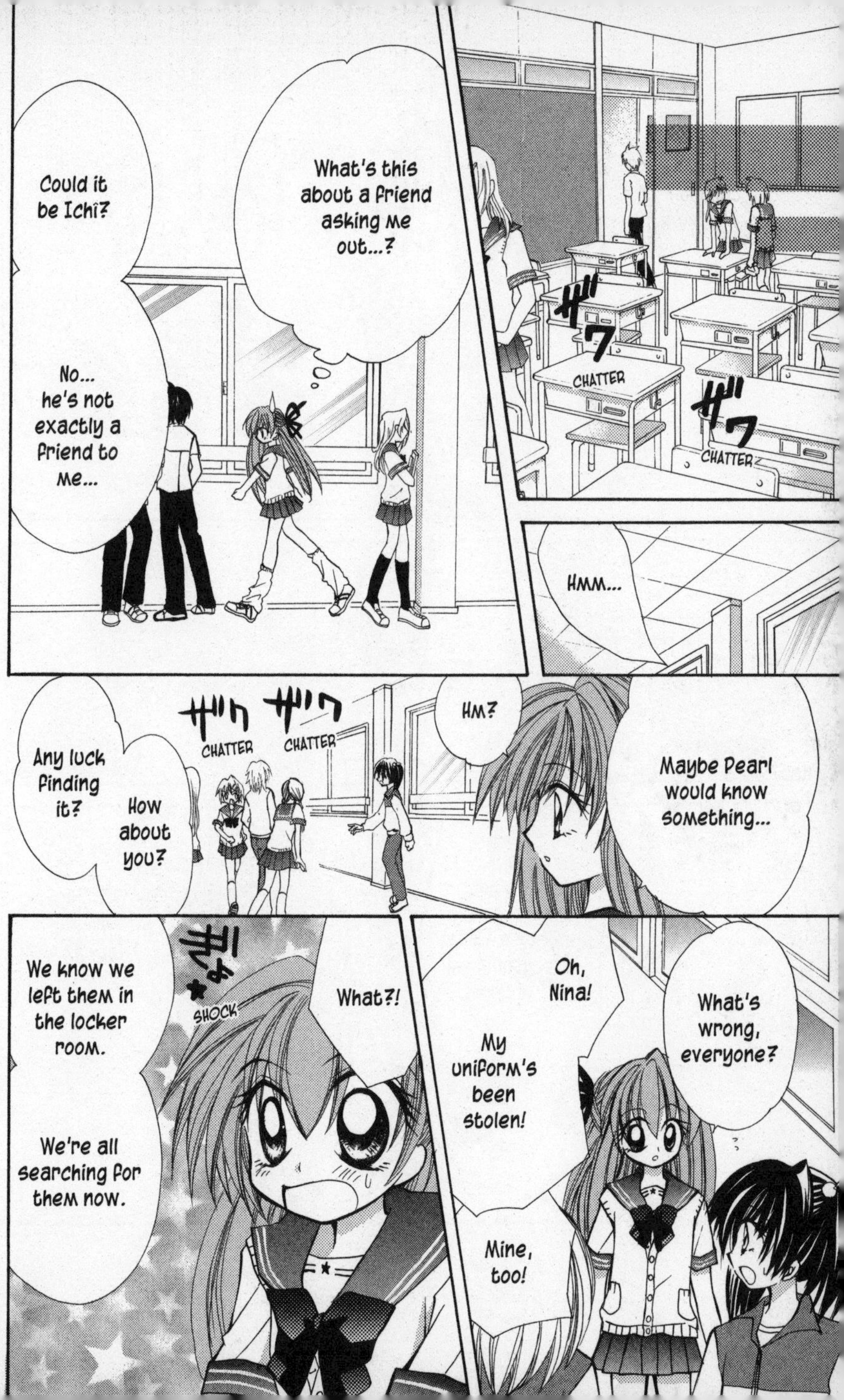
CHATTER
CHATTER
HMM...
What's this about a friend asking me out...?
Could it be Ichi?
No... he's not exactly a friend to me...
HM?
Maybe Pearl would know something...
CHATTER
CHATTER
Any luck finding it?
How about you?
What's wrong, everyone?
Oh, Nina!
My uniform's been stolen!
Mine, too!
What?!
SHOCK
We know we left them in the locker room.
We're all searching for them now.

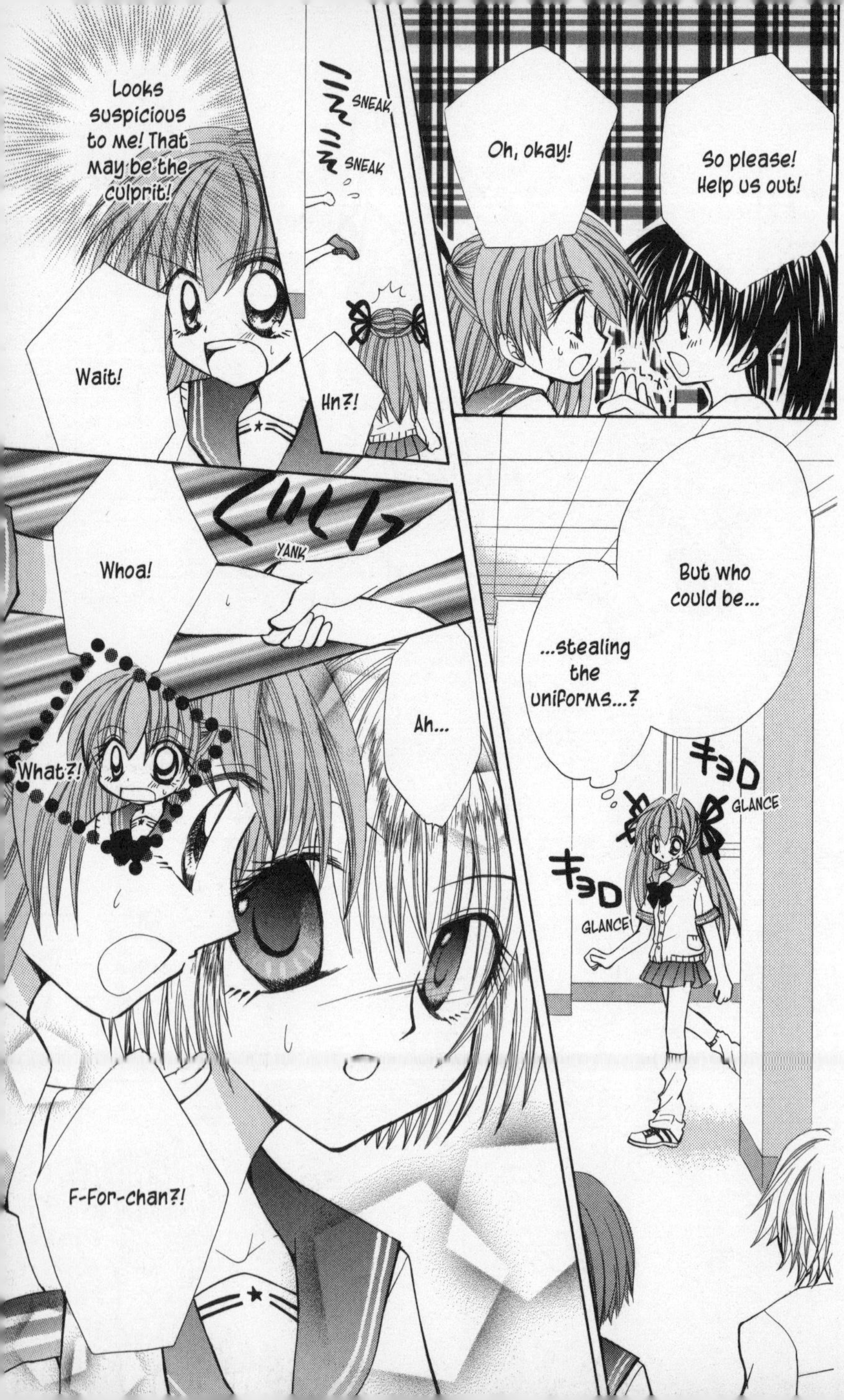
So please! Help us out!
Oh, okay!
But who could be...
...stealing the uniforms...?
GLANCE
GLANCE
SNEAK
SNEAK
Looks suspicious to me! That may be the culprit!
Wait!
Hn?!
YANK
Whoa!
Ah...
What?!
F-For-chan?!

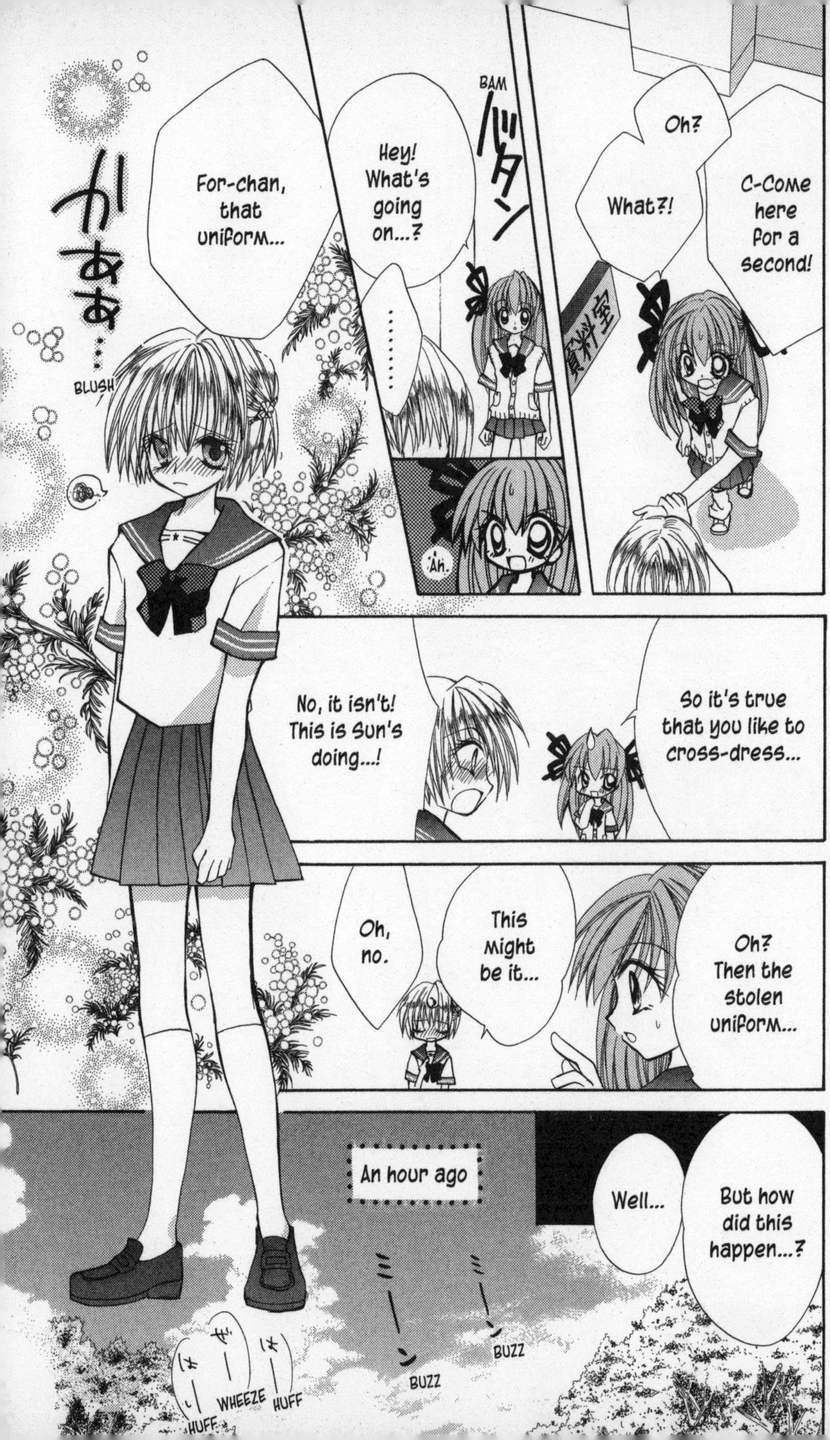
Oh?
What?!
C-Come here for a second!
資料室
BAM
バタン
Hey! What's going on...?
....
Ah.
For-chan, that uniform...
かぁぁ...
BLUSH
So it's true that you like to cross-dress...
No, it isn't! This is Sun's doing...!
Oh? Then the stolen uniform...
This might be it...
Oh, no.
But how did this happen...?
Well...
An hour ago
BUZZ
BUZZ
HUFF
WHEEZE
HUFF

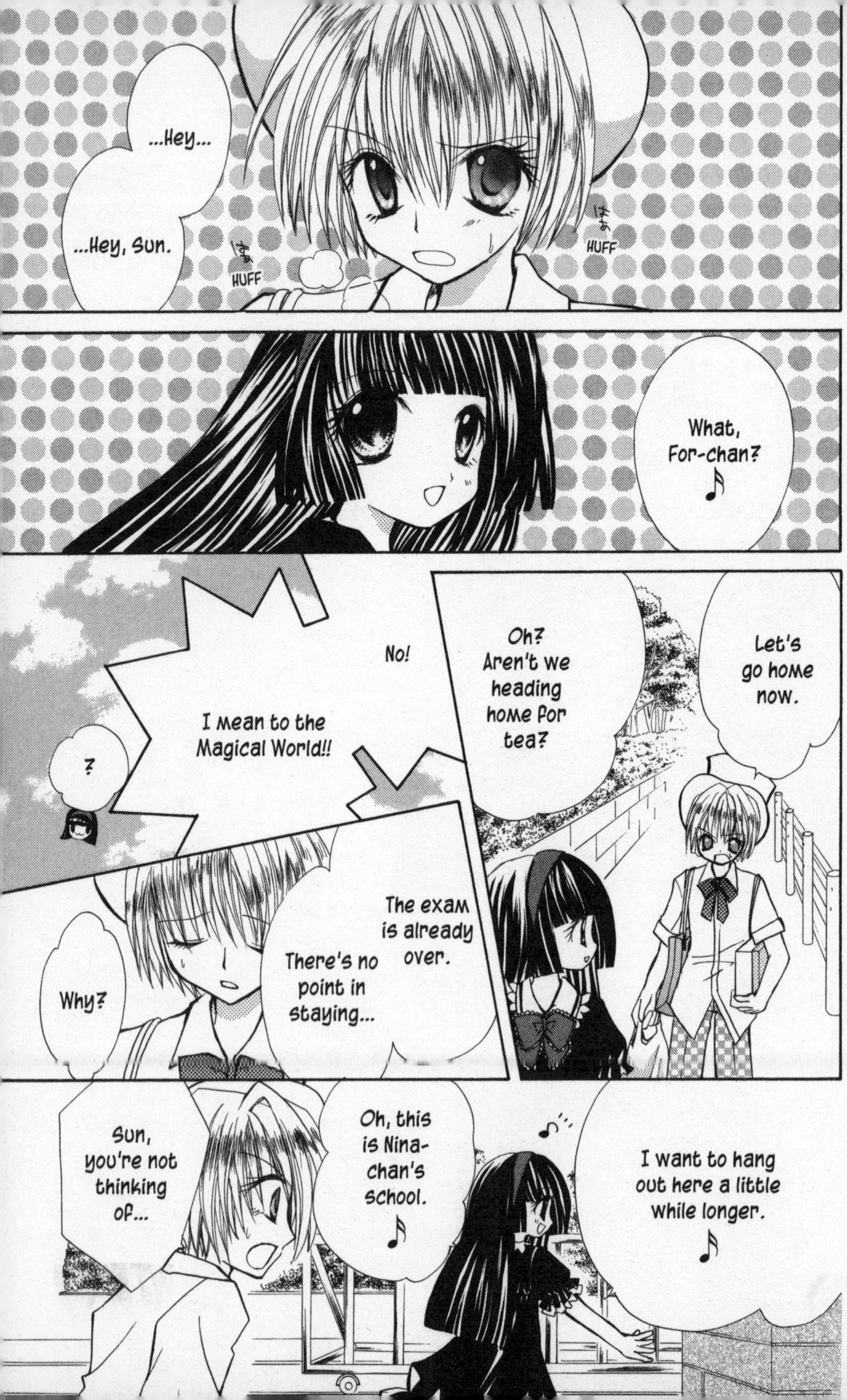
...Hey...
...Hey, Sun.
HUFF
HUFF
What, For-chan? ♪
Let's go home now.
Oh? Aren't we heading home for tea?
No!
I mean to the Magical World!!
?
The exam is already over.
There's no point in staying...
Why?
I want to hang out here a little while longer. ♪
Oh, this is Nina-chan's school. ♪
Sun, you're not thinking of...

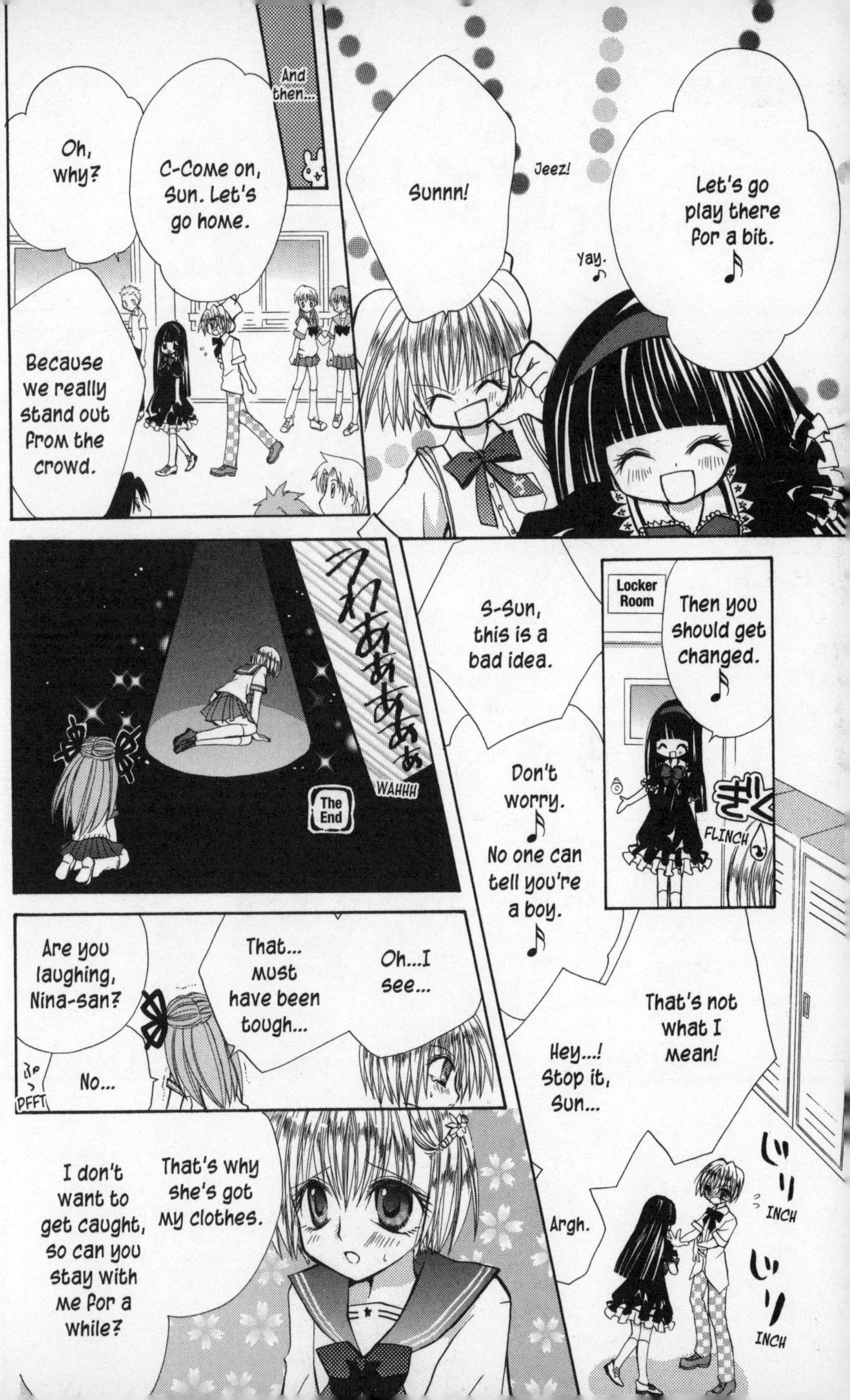
Let's go play there for a bit. ♪
Jeez!
Sunnn!
Yay. ♪
And then...
C-Come on, Sun. Let's go home.
Oh, why?
Because we really stand out from the crowd.
Locker Room
Then you should get changed. ♪
FLINCH
S-Sun, this is a bad idea.
Don't worry. ♪ No one can tell you're a boy. ♪
That's not what I mean!
Hey...! Stop it, Sun...
Argh.
INCH
INCH
WAHHH
The End
Oh...I see...
That... must have been tough...
Are you laughing, Nina-san?
No...
PFFT
That's why she's got my clothes.
I don't want to get caught, so can you stay with me for a while?

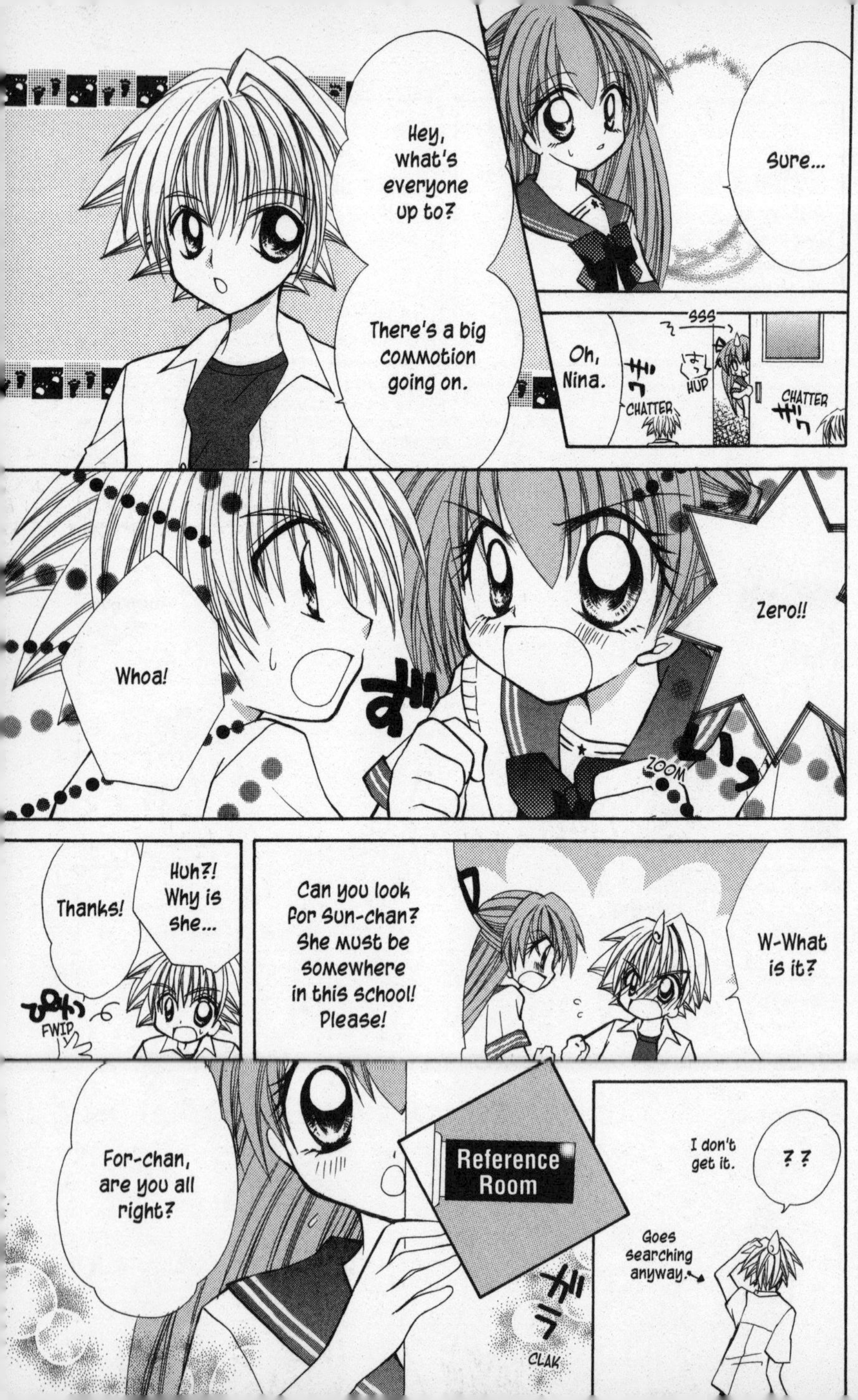
Sure...
SSS
Oh, Nina.
HUP
CHATTER
CHATTER
Hey, what's everyone up to?
There's a big commotion going on.
Zero!!
ZOOM
Whoa!
W-What is it?
Can you look for Sun-chan? She must be somewhere in this school! Please!
Huh?! Why is she...
Thanks!
FWIP
? ?
I don't get it.
Goes searching anyway.
Reference Room
For-chan, are you all right?
CLAK

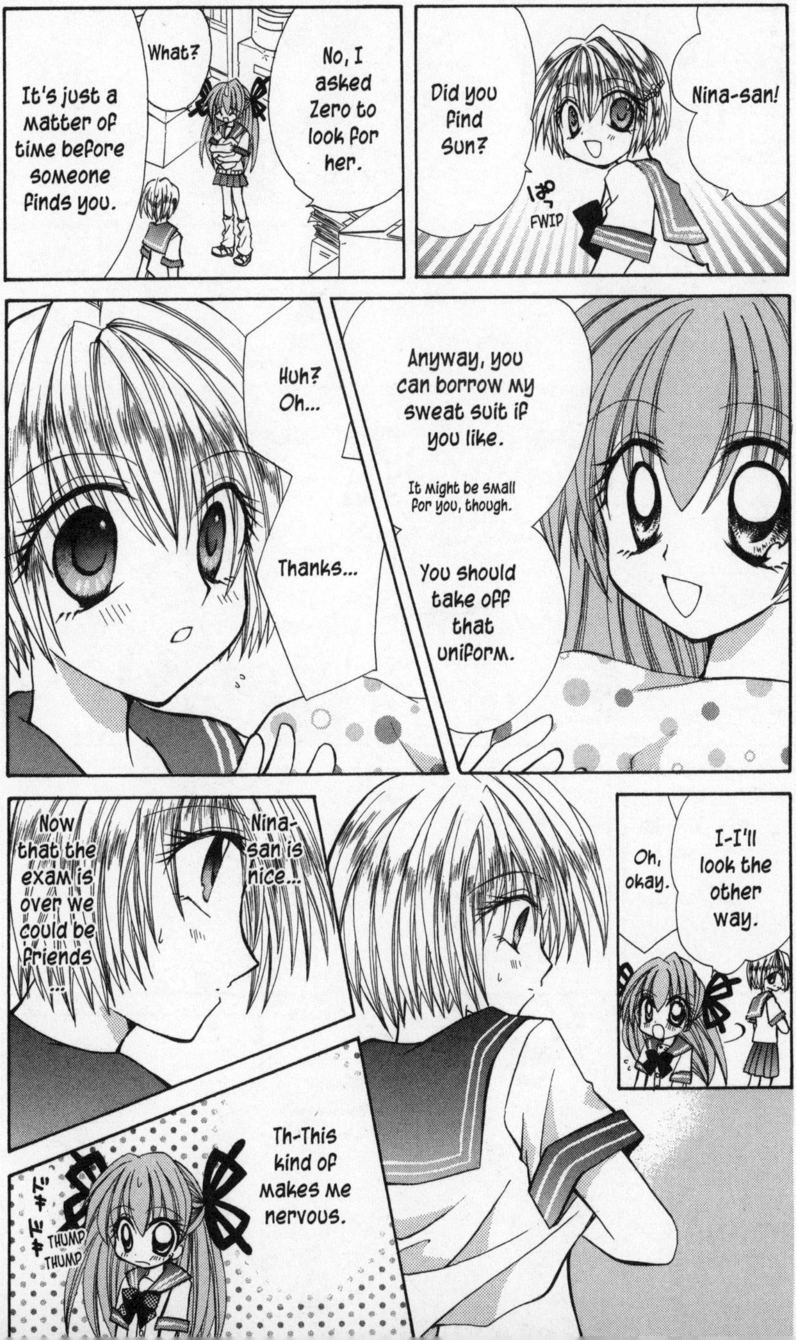
Nina-san!
Did you find Sun?
ぱっ
FWIP
No, I asked Zero to look for her.
What?
It's just a matter of time before someone finds you.
Anyway, you can borrow my sweat suit if you like.
It might be small for you, though.
You should take off that uniform.
Huh? Oh...
Thanks...
I-I'll look the other way.
Oh, okay.
Nina-san is nice...
Now that the exam is over we could be friends...
Th-This kind of makes me nervous.
ドキドキ
THUMP THUMP

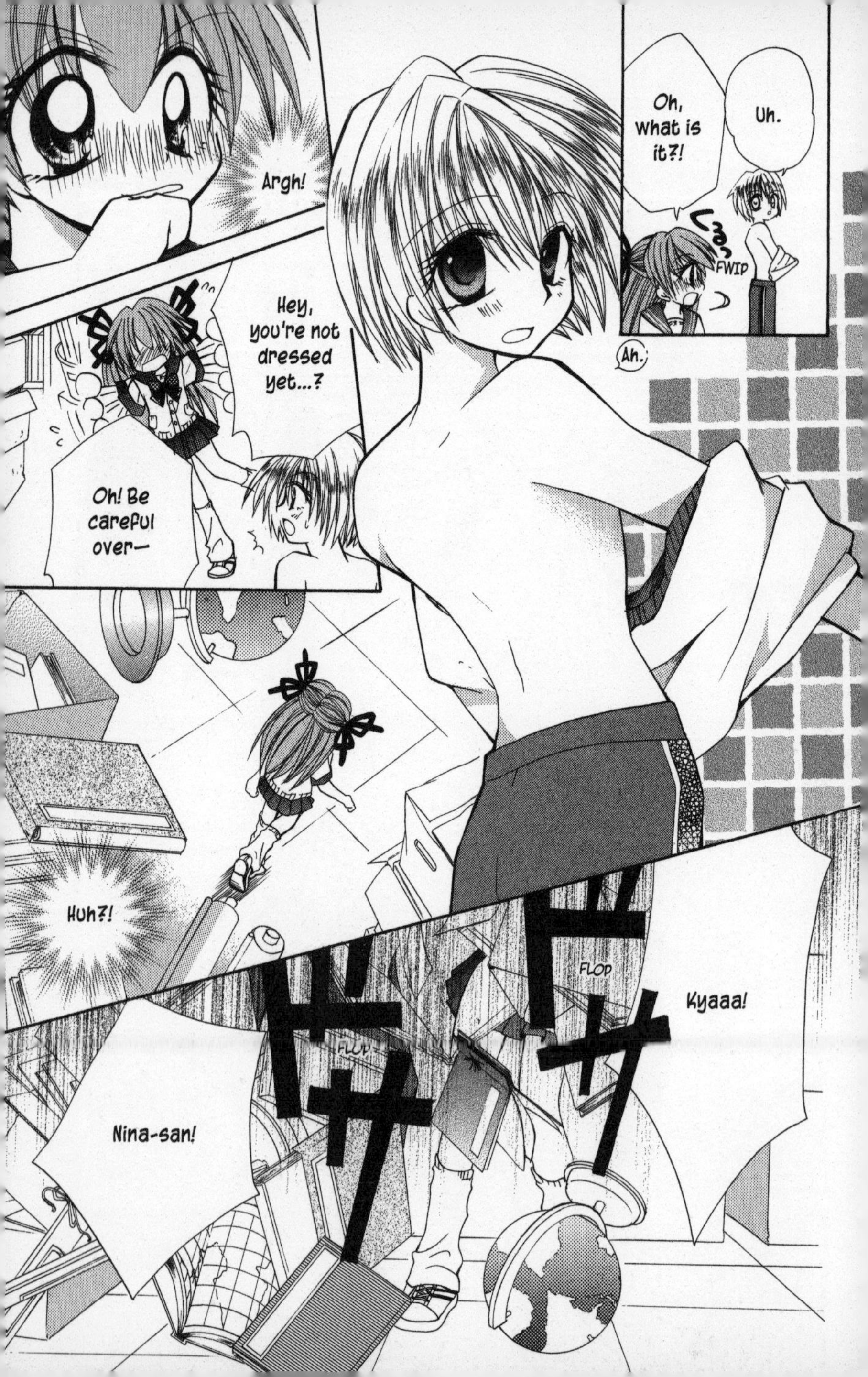

Uh.
Oh, what is it?!
くるっ
FWIP
Ah.
Argh!
Hey, you're not dressed yet...?
Oh! Be careful over—
Huh?!
FLOP
Kyaaa!
FLOP
Nina-san!

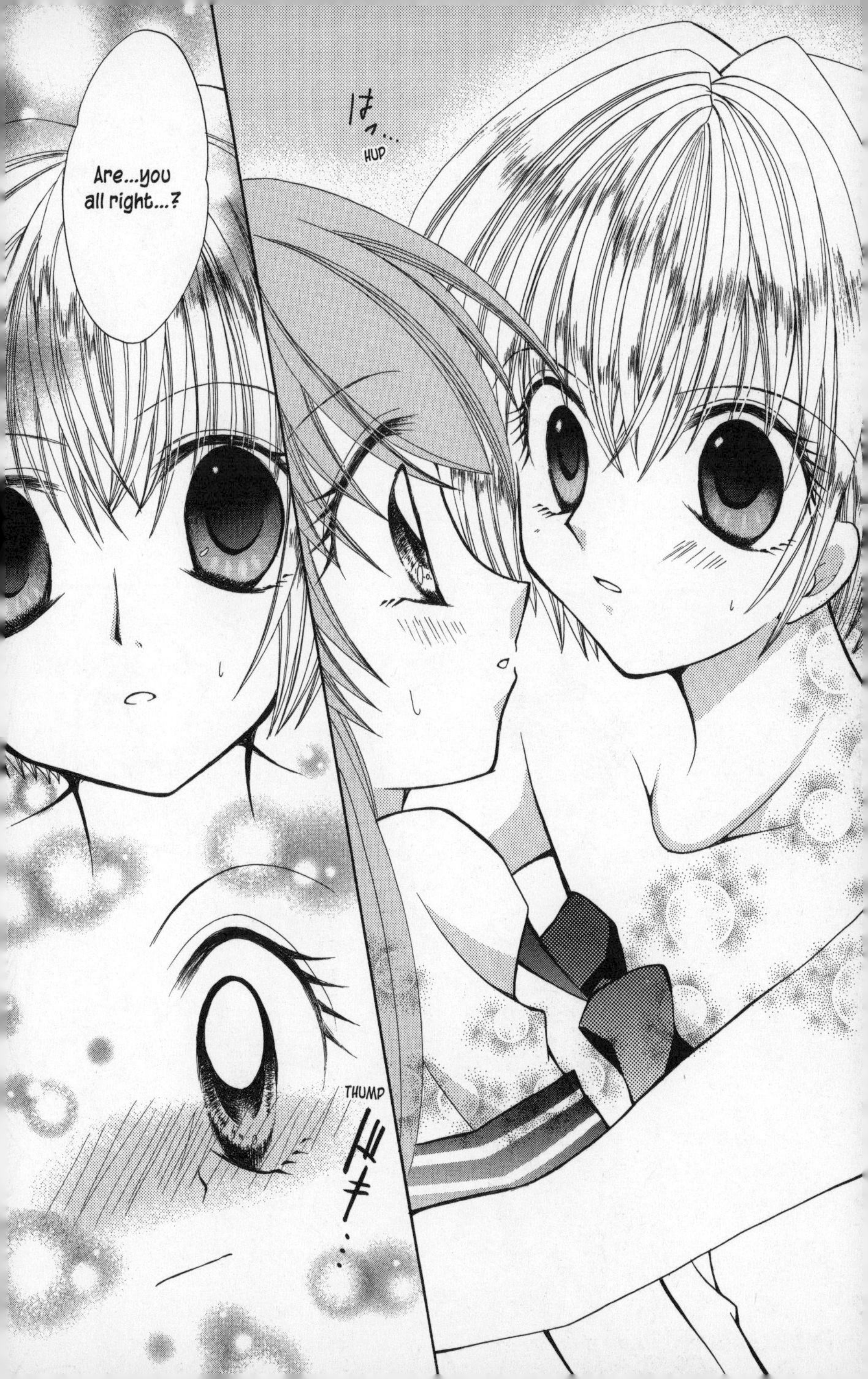

はっ…
HUP
Are...you all right...?
THUMP
ドキ…

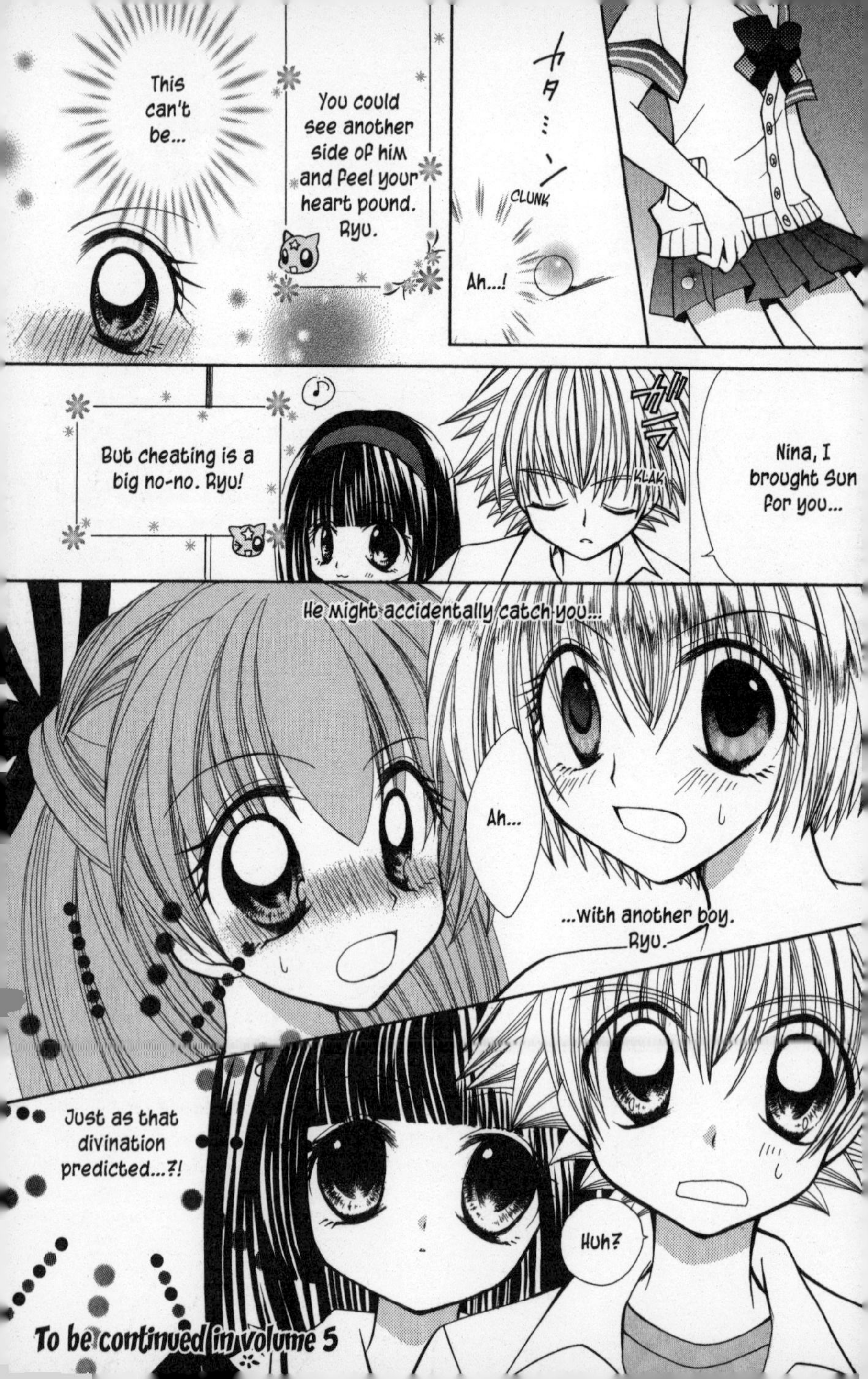
CLUNK
Ah...!
You could see another side of him and feel your heart pound. Ryu.
This can't be...
Nina, I brought Sun for you...
KLAK
But cheating is a big no-no. Ryu!
He might accidentally catch you...
Ah...
...with another boy. Ryu.
Huh?
Just as that divination predicted...?!
To be continued in volume 5

Rokka Is All Grown Up!

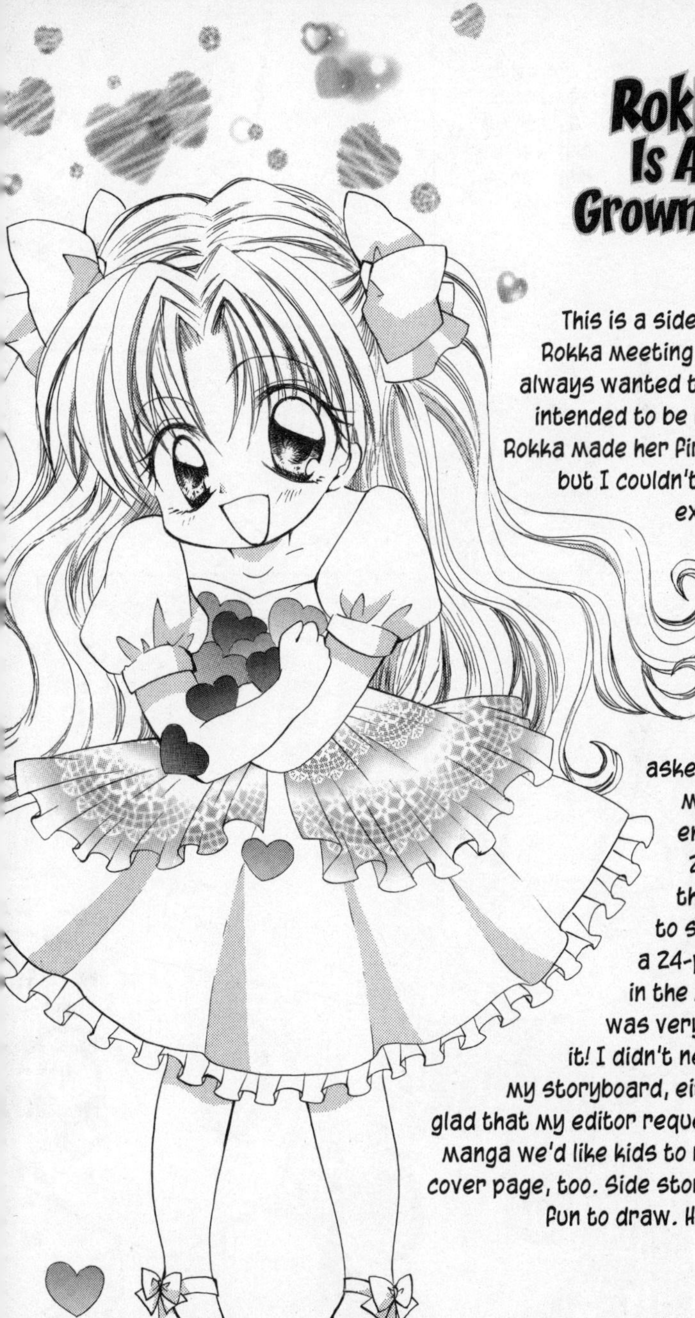

This is a side story about Rokka meeting Ichî that I've always wanted to draw. It was intended to be in POP 2 when Rokka made her first appearance, but I couldn't draw it to my expectations. I finally drew it after letting it sit for quite a while. Though I was initially asked for 16 pages, my storyboard ended up running 24 pages and I thought I'd have to shorten it. I got a 24-page allotment in the magazine and was very thankful for it! I didn't need to change my storyboard, either . . . . I was glad that my editor requested it for the manga we'd like kids to read. I like the cover page, too. Side stories are so much fun to draw. Ha ha.

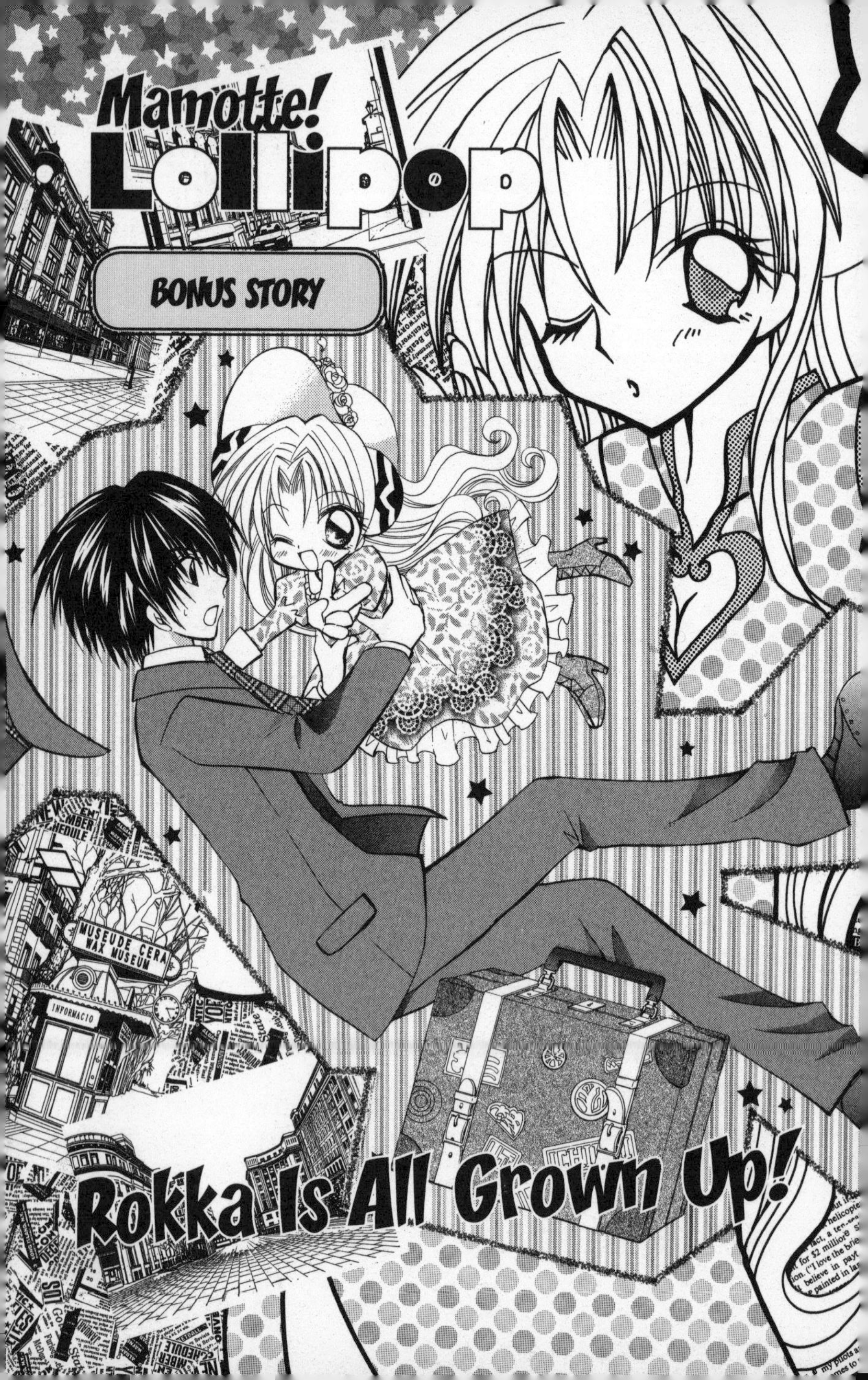
Mamotte! Lollipop
BONUS STORY
MUSEUDE CERA
WAX MUSEUM
Rokka Is All Grown Up!

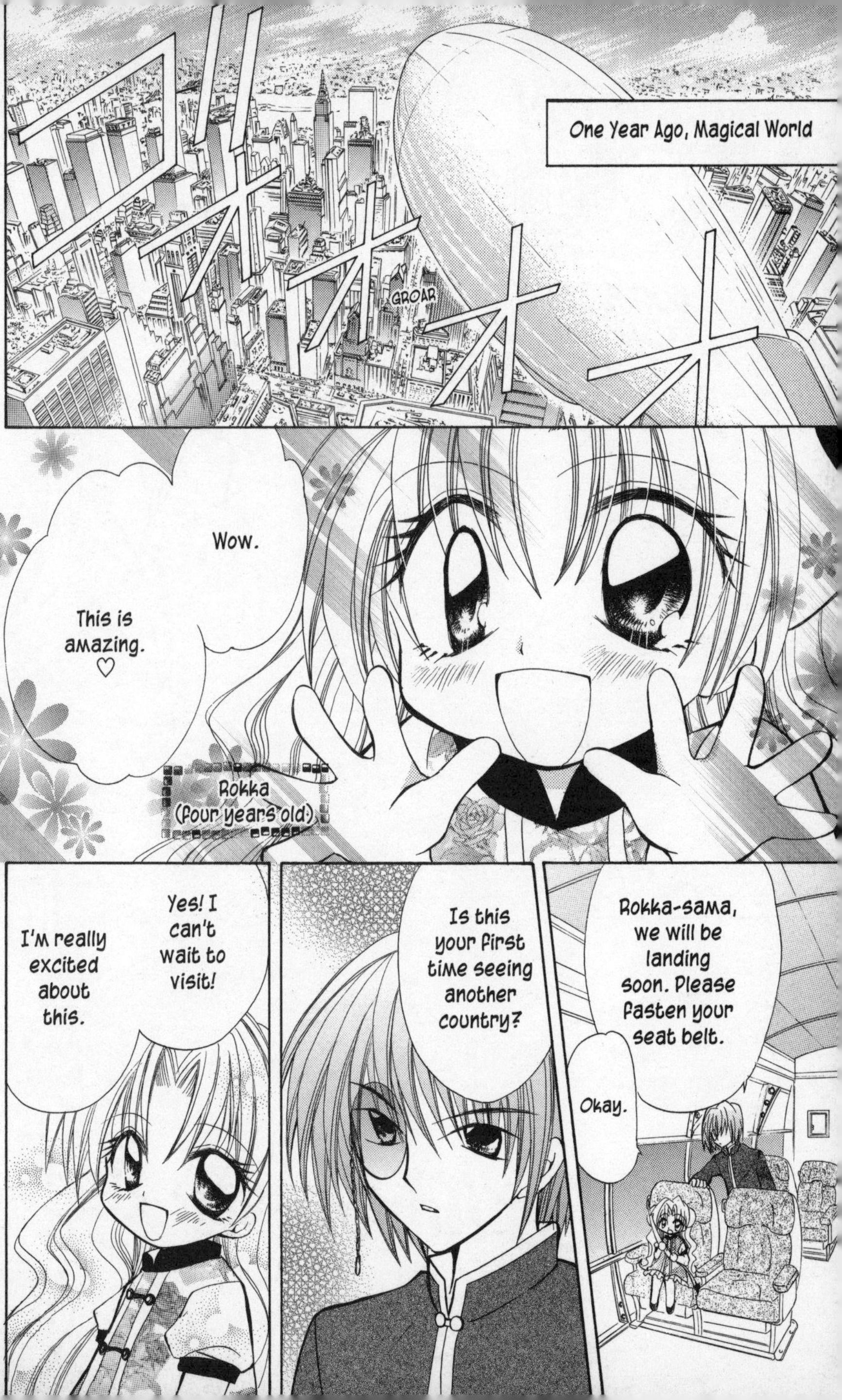
One Year Ago, Magical World
GROAR
Wow.
This is amazing. ♡
Rokka (four years old)
Rokka-sama, we will be landing soon. Please fasten your seat belt.
Okay.
Is this your first time seeing another country?
Yes! I can't wait to visit!
I'm really excited about this.

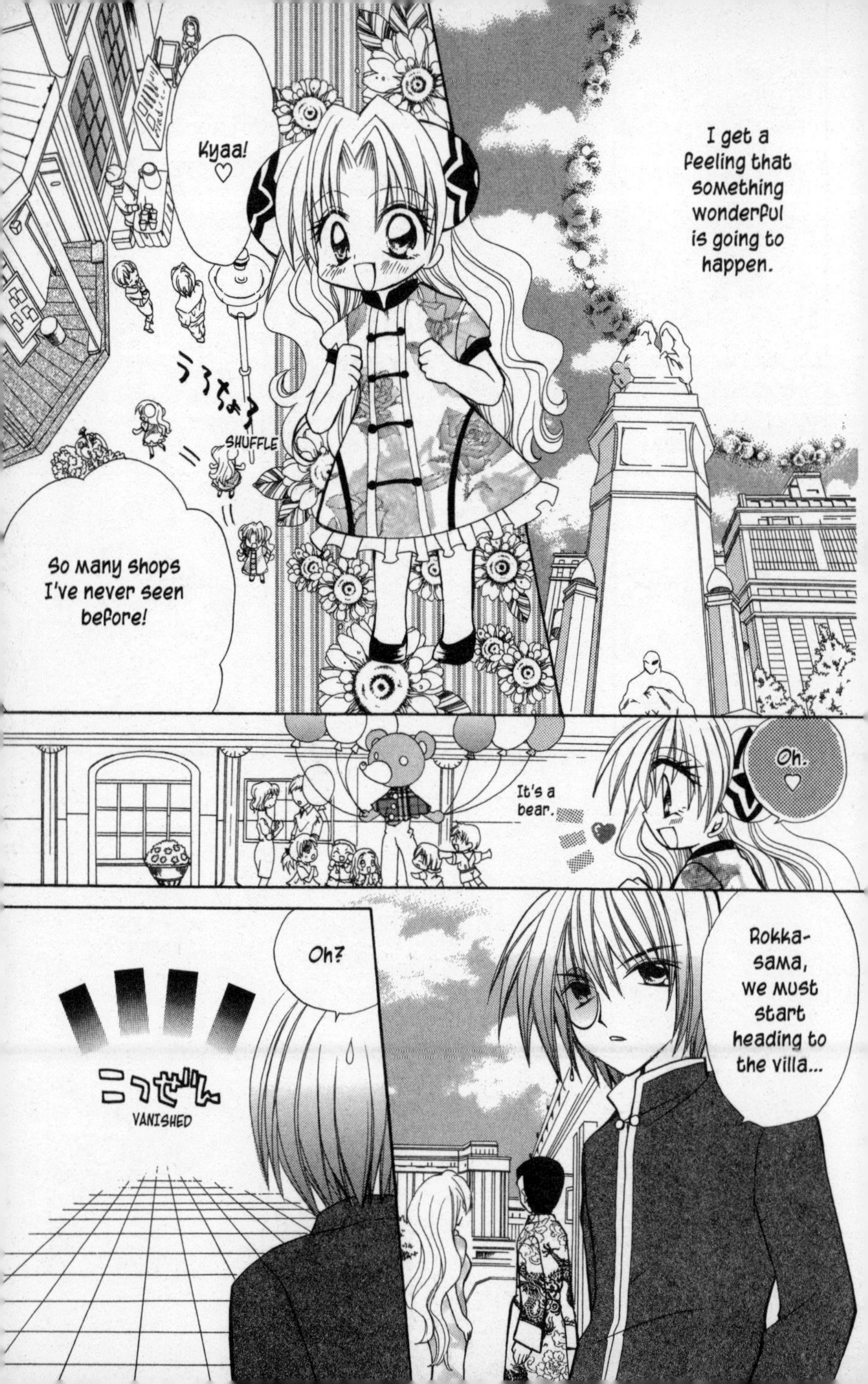

I get a feeling that something wonderful is going to happen.
Kyaa! ♡
SHUFFLE
So many shops I've never seen before!
Oh. ♡
It's a bear.
Rokka-sama, we must start heading to the villa...
Oh?
VANISHED

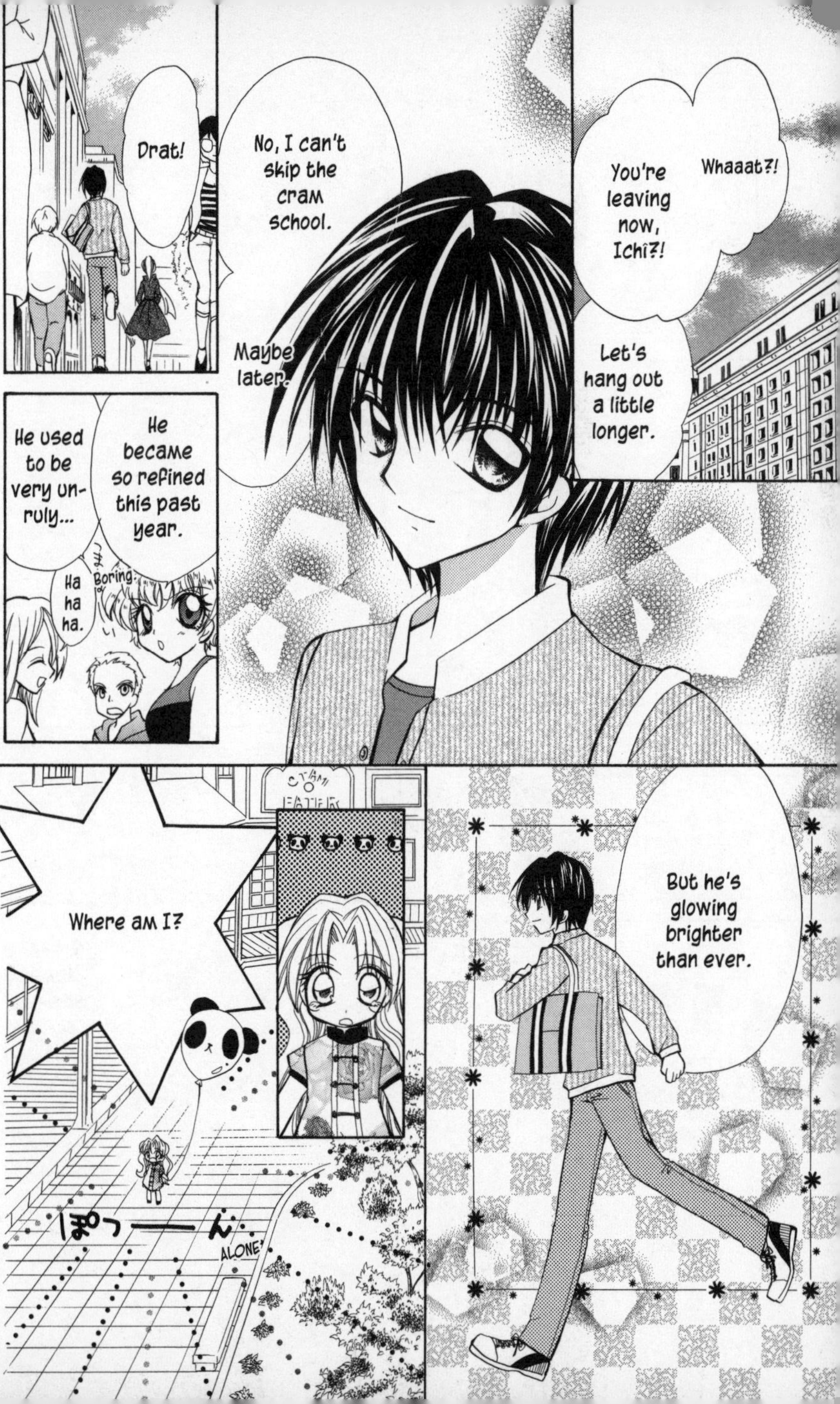

Whaaat?!
You're leaving now, Ichi?!
Let's hang out a little longer.
No, I can't skip the cram school.
Maybe later.
Drat!
He became so refined this past year.
He used to be very unruly...
Boring.
Ha ha ha.
But he's glowing brighter than ever.
Where am I?
ぽつーーん
ALONE

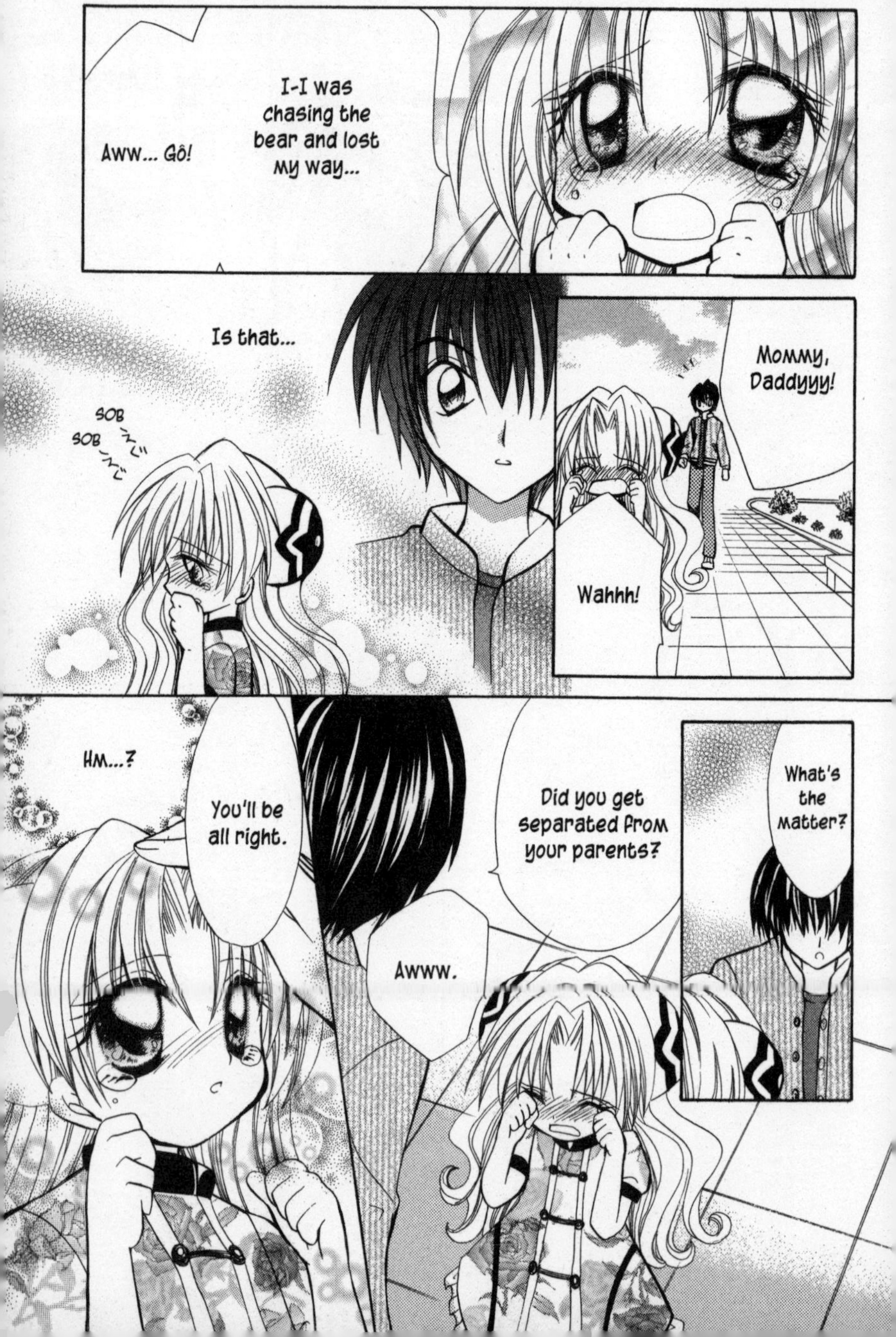
I-I was chasing the bear and lost my way...
Aww... Gô!
Mommy, Daddyyy!
Wahhh!
Is that...
SOB
SOB
What's the matter?
Did you get separated from your parents?
Awww.
You'll be all right.
Hm...?

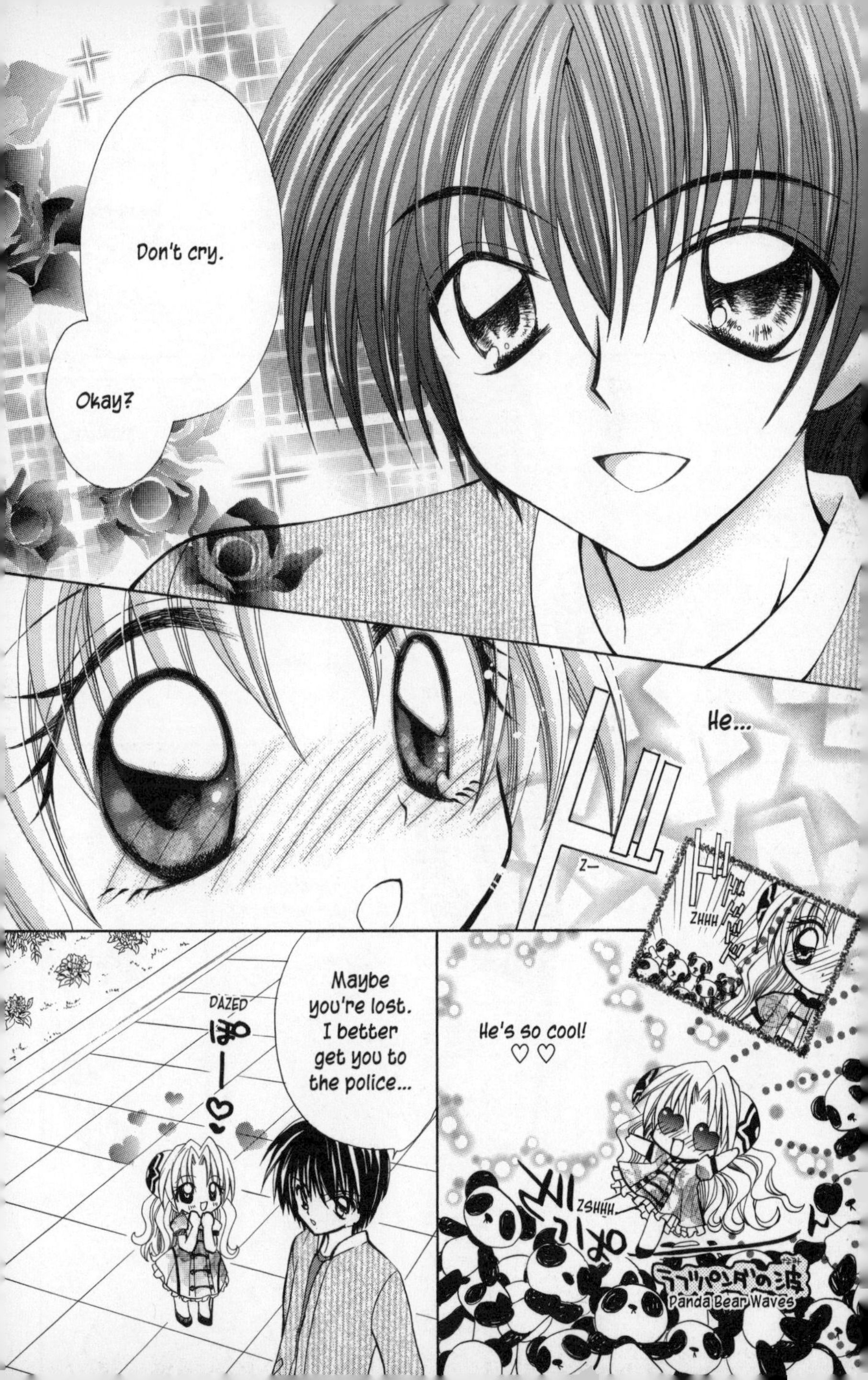
Don't cry.
Okay?
He...
Z—
ZHHH
He's so cool! ♡ ♡
ZSHHH
ラブパンダの波
Panda Bear Waves
Maybe you're lost. I better get you to the police...
DAZED
ぽー

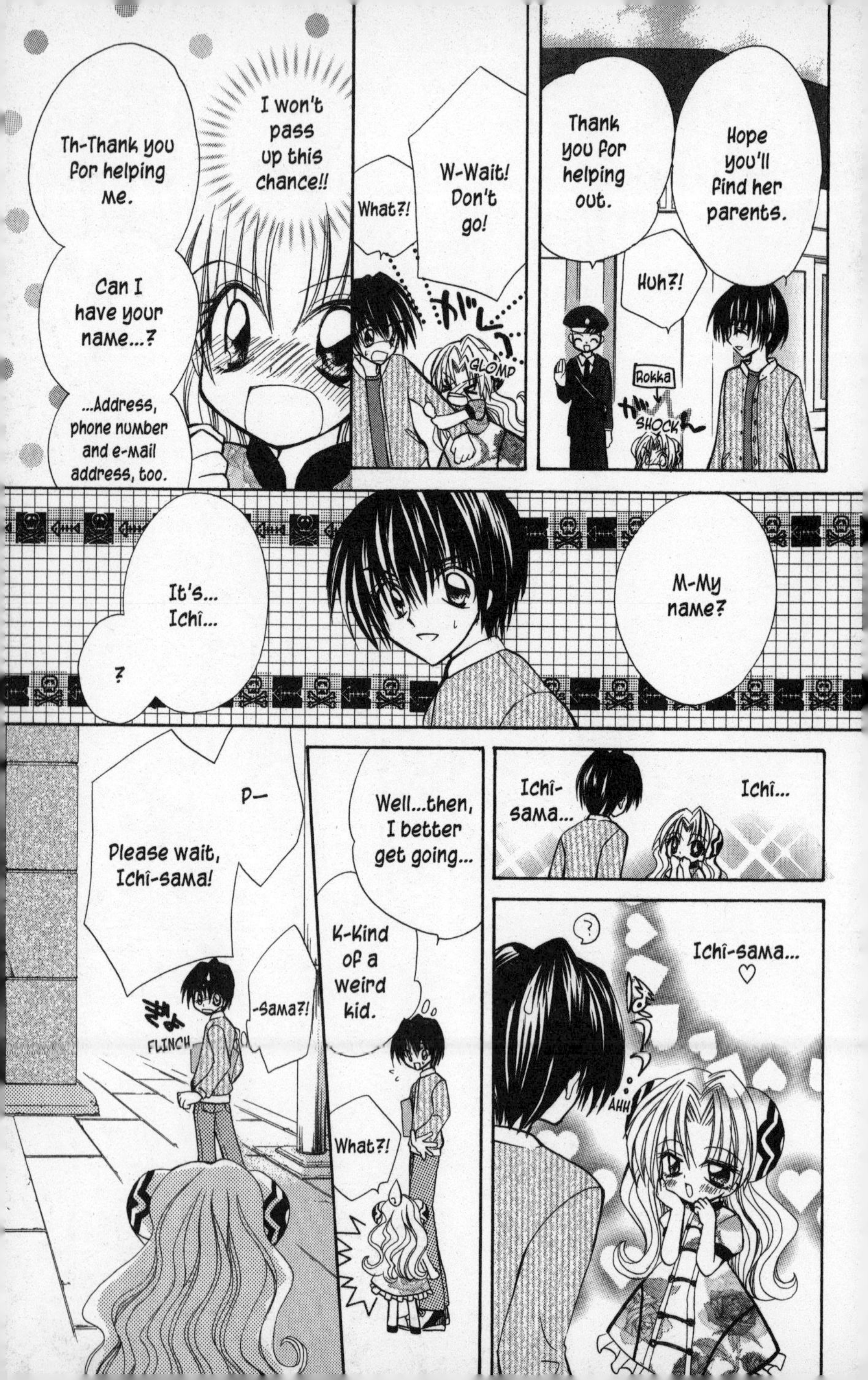
Hope you'll find her parents.
Thank you for helping out.
Huh?!
Rokka
SHOCK
W-Wait! Don't go!
What?!
GLOMP
I won't pass up this chance!!
Th-Thank you for helping me.
Can I have your name...?
...Address, phone number and e-mail address, too.
M-My name?
It's... Ichî...
?
Ichî...
Ichî-sama...
Ichî-sama... ♡
?
AHH
Well...then, I better get going...
K-Kind of a weird kid.
What?!
P—
Please wait, Ichî-sama!
-sama?!
FLINCH

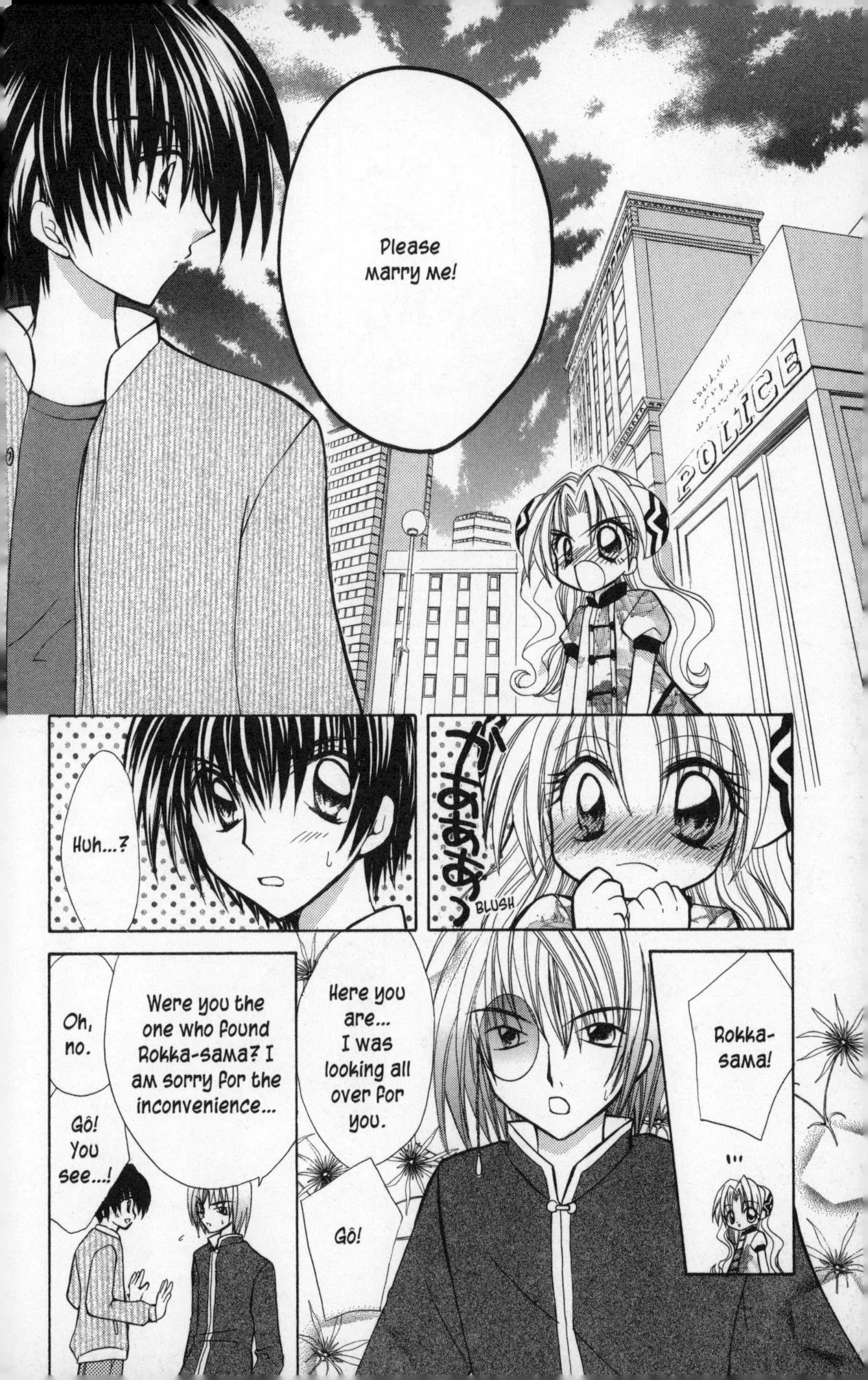
Please marry me!
POLICE
BLUSH
Huh...?
Rokka-sama!
...
Here you are... I was looking all over for you.
Gô!
Were you the one who found Rokka-sama? I am sorry for the inconvenience...
Oh, no.
Gô! You see...!

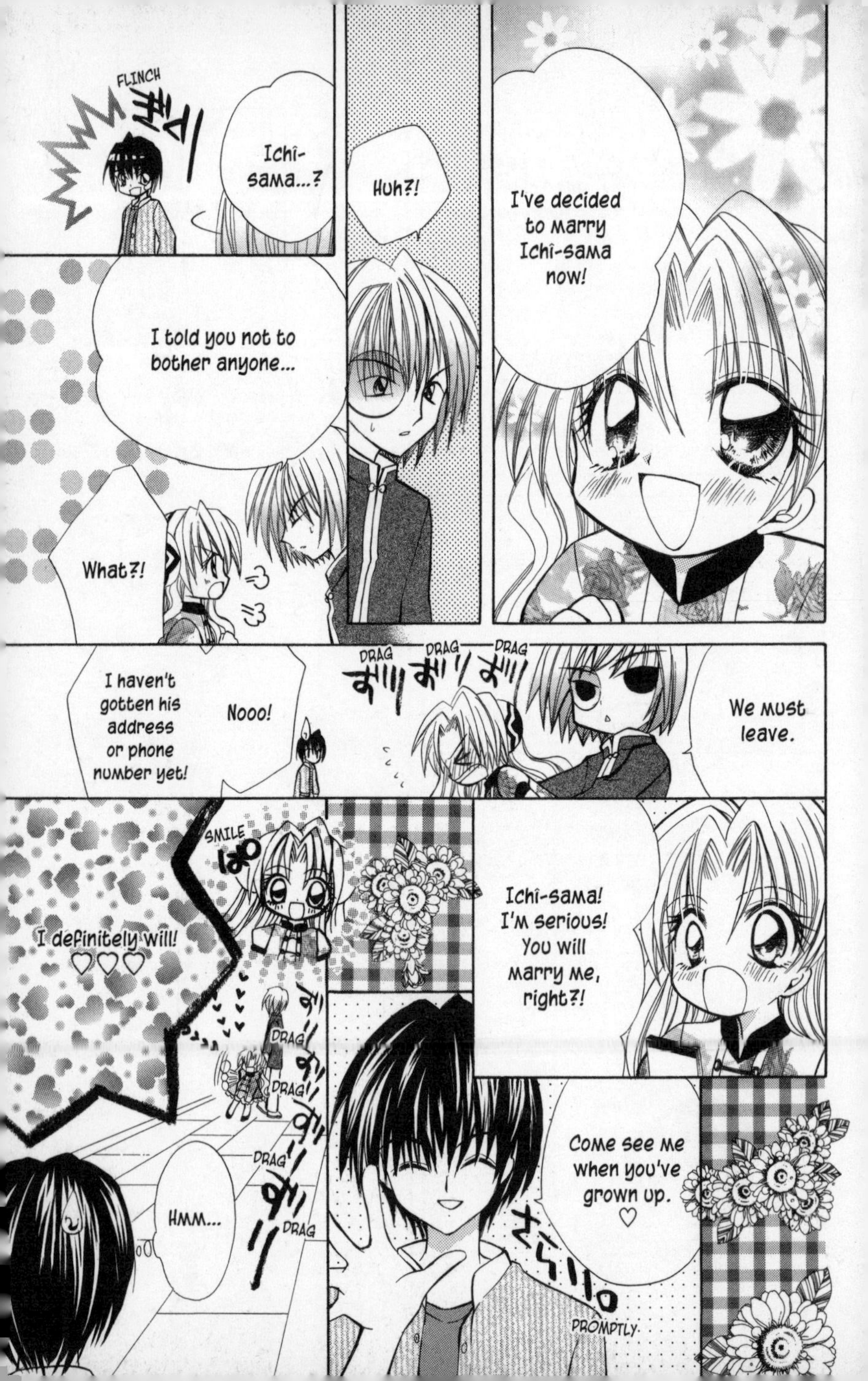
I've decided to marry Ichî-sama now!
Huh?!
FLINCH
Ichî-sama...?
I told you not to bother anyone...
What?!
We must leave.
DRAG DRAG DRAG
Nooo!
I haven't gotten his address or phone number yet!
Ichî-sama! I'm serious! You will marry me, right?!
Come see me when you've grown up. ♡
PROMPTLY
SMILE
I definitely will! ♡♡♡
DRAG
DRAG
DRAG
DRAG
HMM...

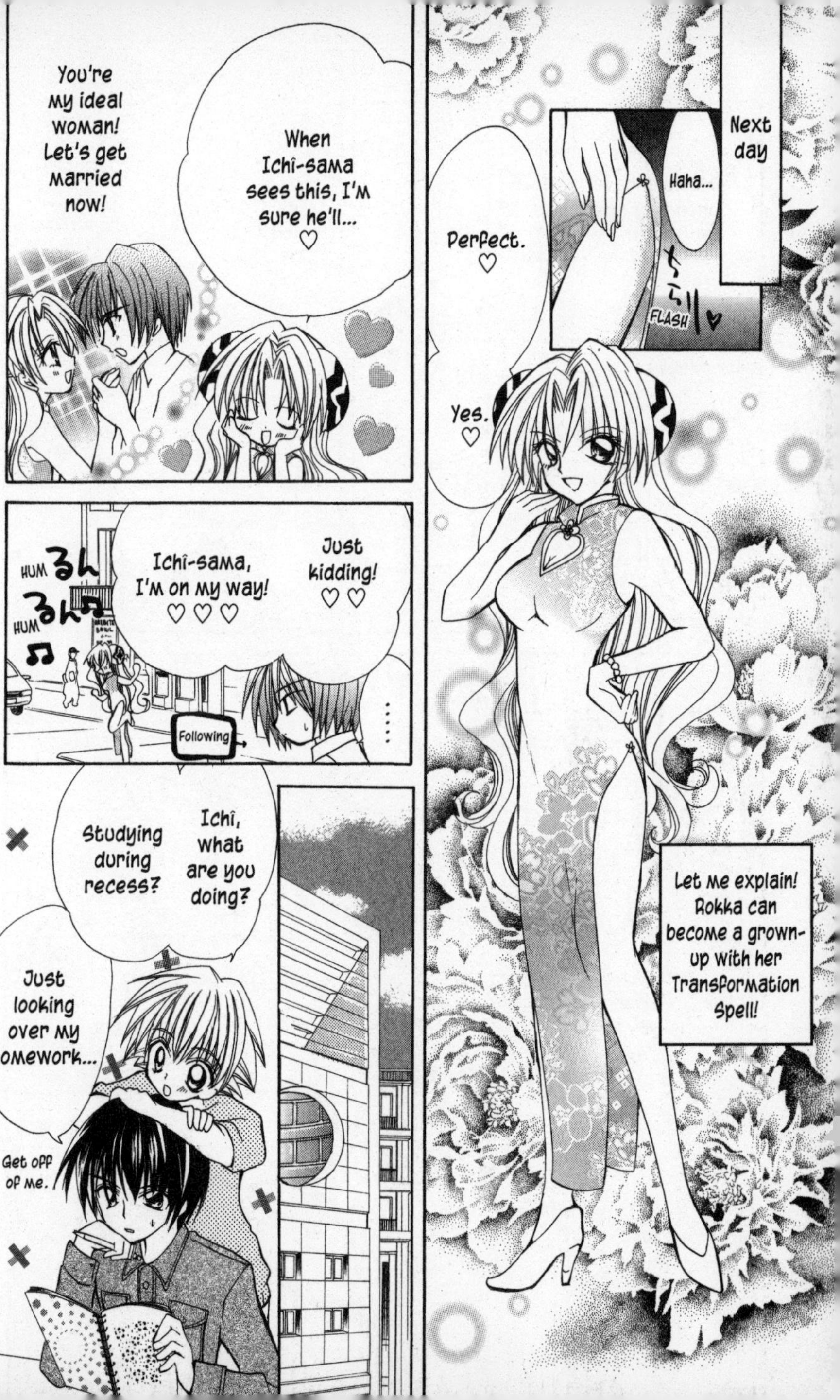
Next day
Haha...
FLASH
Perfect. ♡
Yes. ♡
Let me explain! Rokka can become a grown-up with her Transformation Spell!
When Ichî-sama sees this, I'm sure he'll... ♡
You're my ideal woman! Let's get married now!
Just kidding! ♡ ♡
Ichî-sama, I'm on my way! ♡ ♡ ♡
HUM るん
HUM るん
Following
Ichî, what are you doing?
Studying during recess?
Just looking over my homework...
Get off of me.

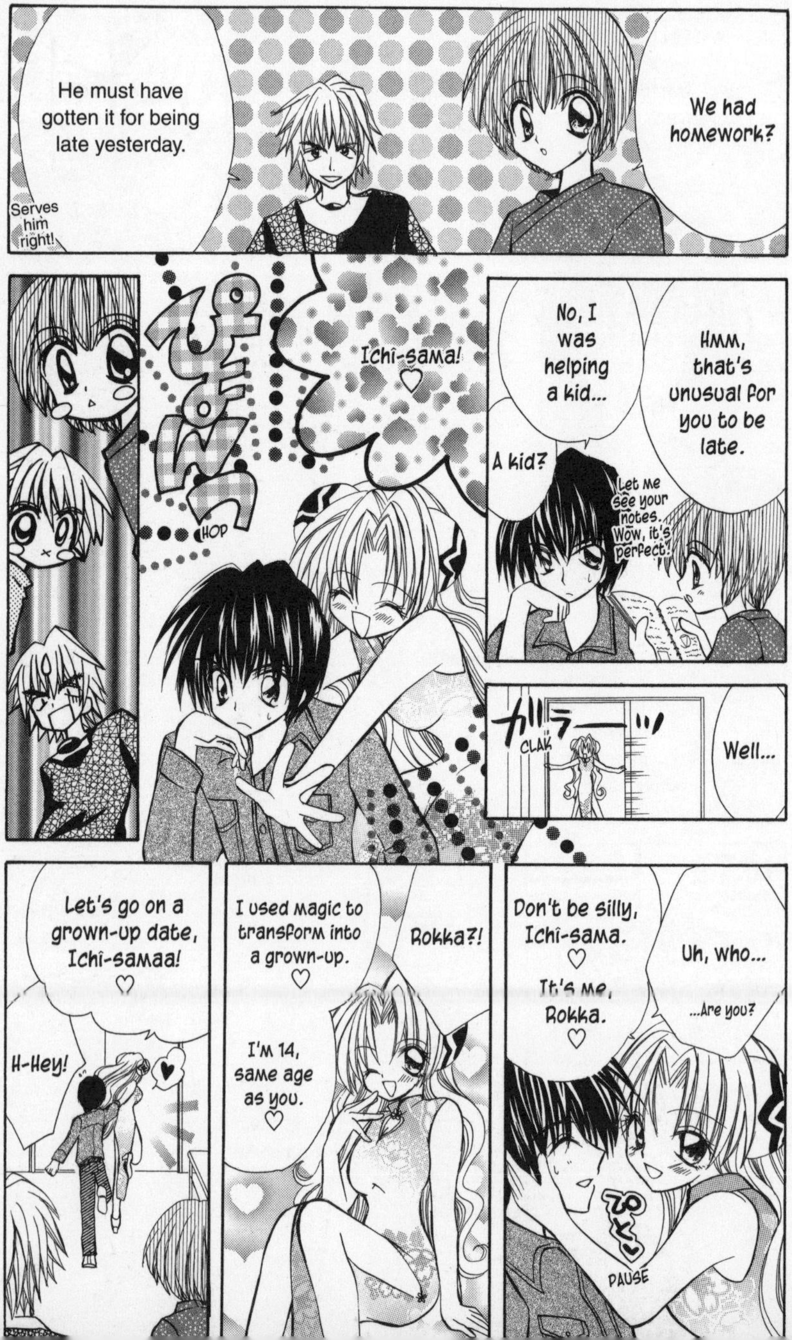
We had homework?
He must have gotten it for being late yesterday.
Serves him right!
Hmm, that's unusual for you to be late.
No, I was helping a kid...
A kid?
Let me see your notes. Wow, it's perfect!
Well...
CLAK
Ichî-sama! ♡
HOP
Uh, who...
...Are you?
Don't be silly, Ichî-sama. ♡
It's me, Rokka. ♡
PAUSE
Rokka?!
I used magic to transform into a grown-up. ♡
I'm 14, same age as you. ♡
Let's go on a grown-up date, Ichî-samaa! ♡
H-Hey!

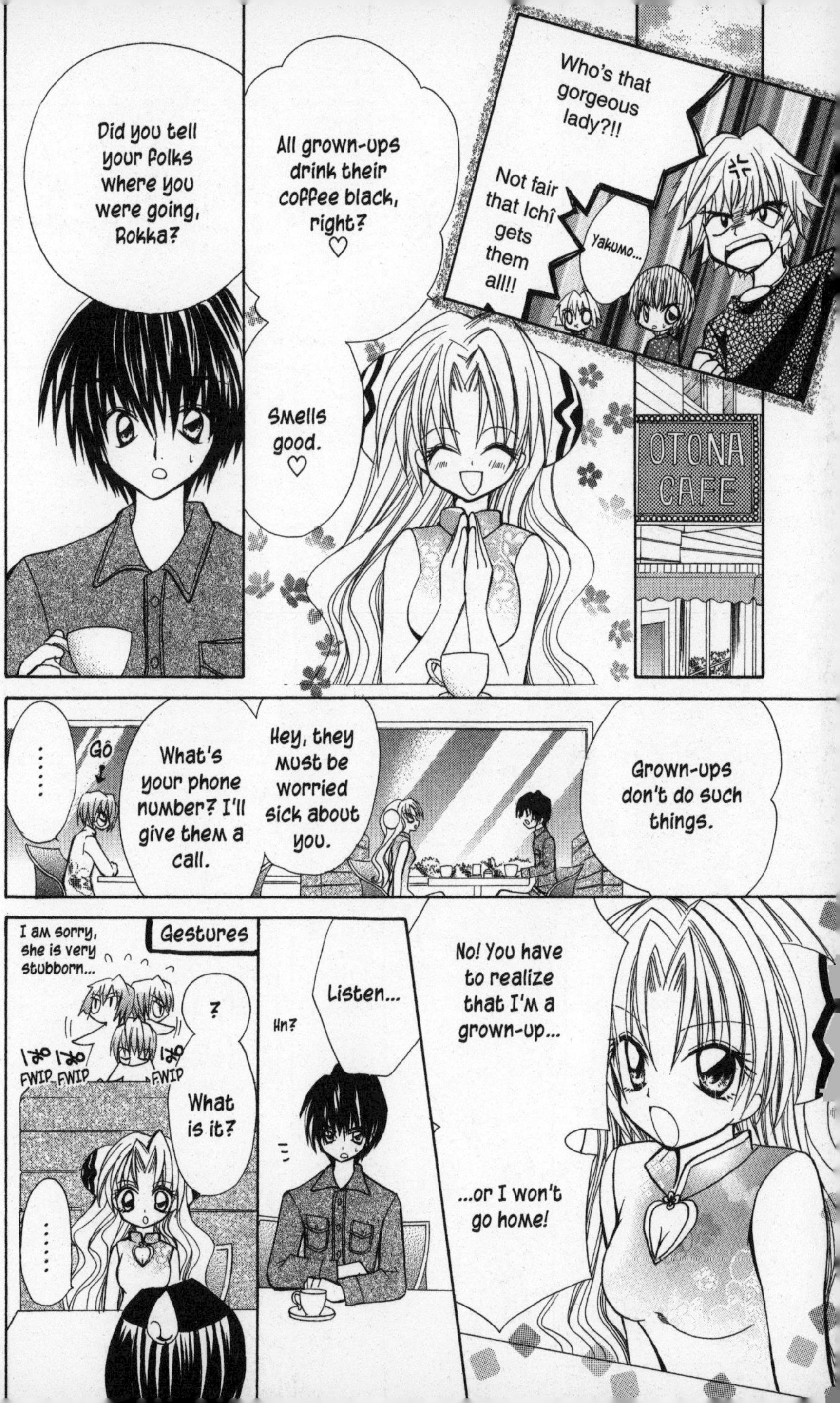
OTONA CAFE
Who's that gorgeous lady?!!
Not fair that Ichî gets them all!!
Yakumo...
All grown-ups drink their coffee black, right? ♡
Smells good. ♡
Did you tell your folks where you were going, Rokka?
Grown-ups don't do such things.
Hey, they must be worried sick about you.
What's your phone number? I'll give them a call.
Gô
......
No! You have to realize that I'm a grown-up...
...or I won't go home!
Listen...
Hn?
Gestures
I am sorry, she is very stubborn...
?
FWIP FWIP
FWIP
What is it?
......

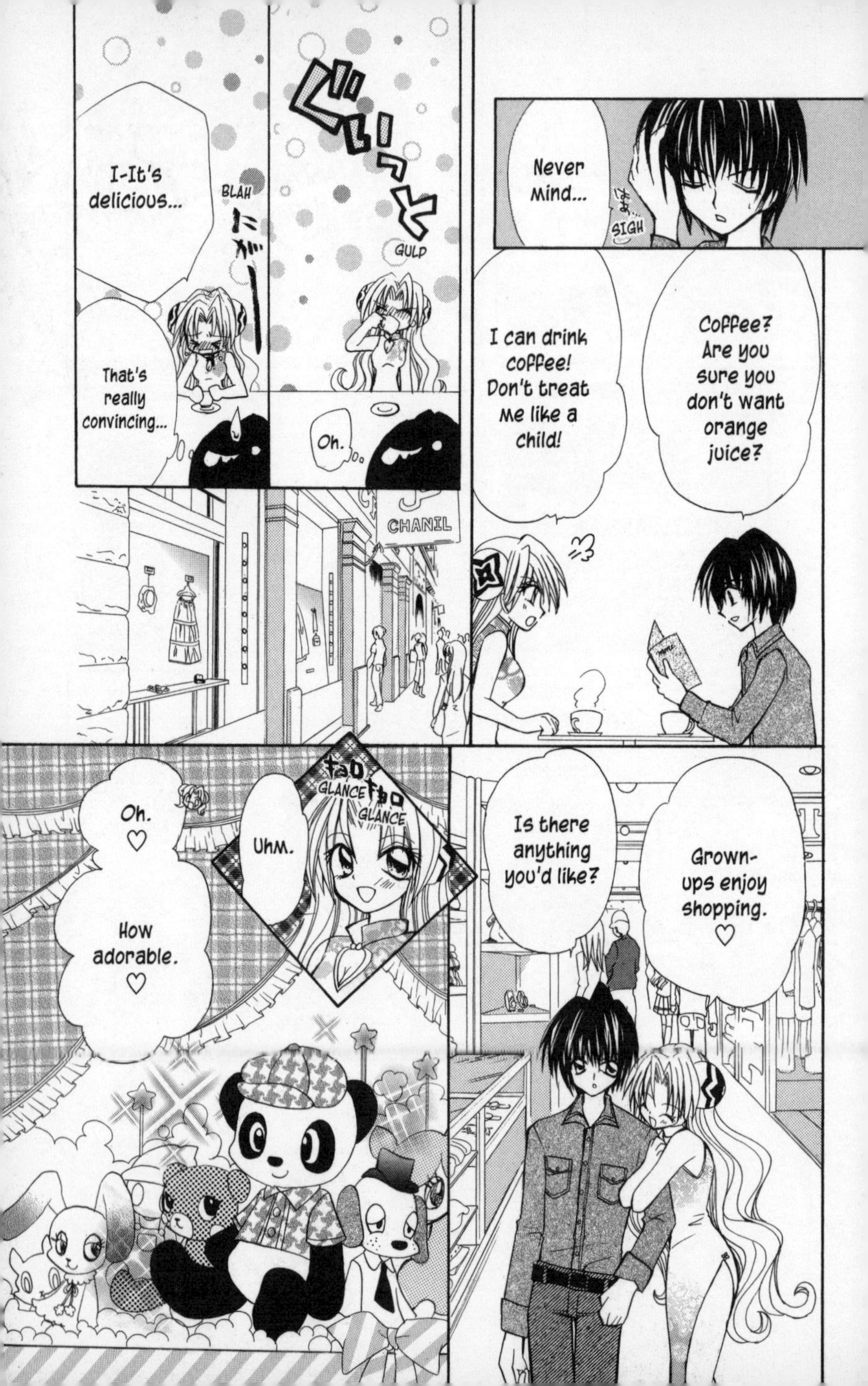
Never mind...
SIGH
Coffee? Are you sure you don't want orange juice?
I can drink coffee! Don't treat me like a child!
GULP
Oh.
I-It's delicious...
BLAH
That's really convincing...
CHANIL
Grown-ups enjoy shopping. ♡
Is there anything you'd like?
GLANCE GLANCE
Uhm.
Oh. ♡
How adorable. ♡

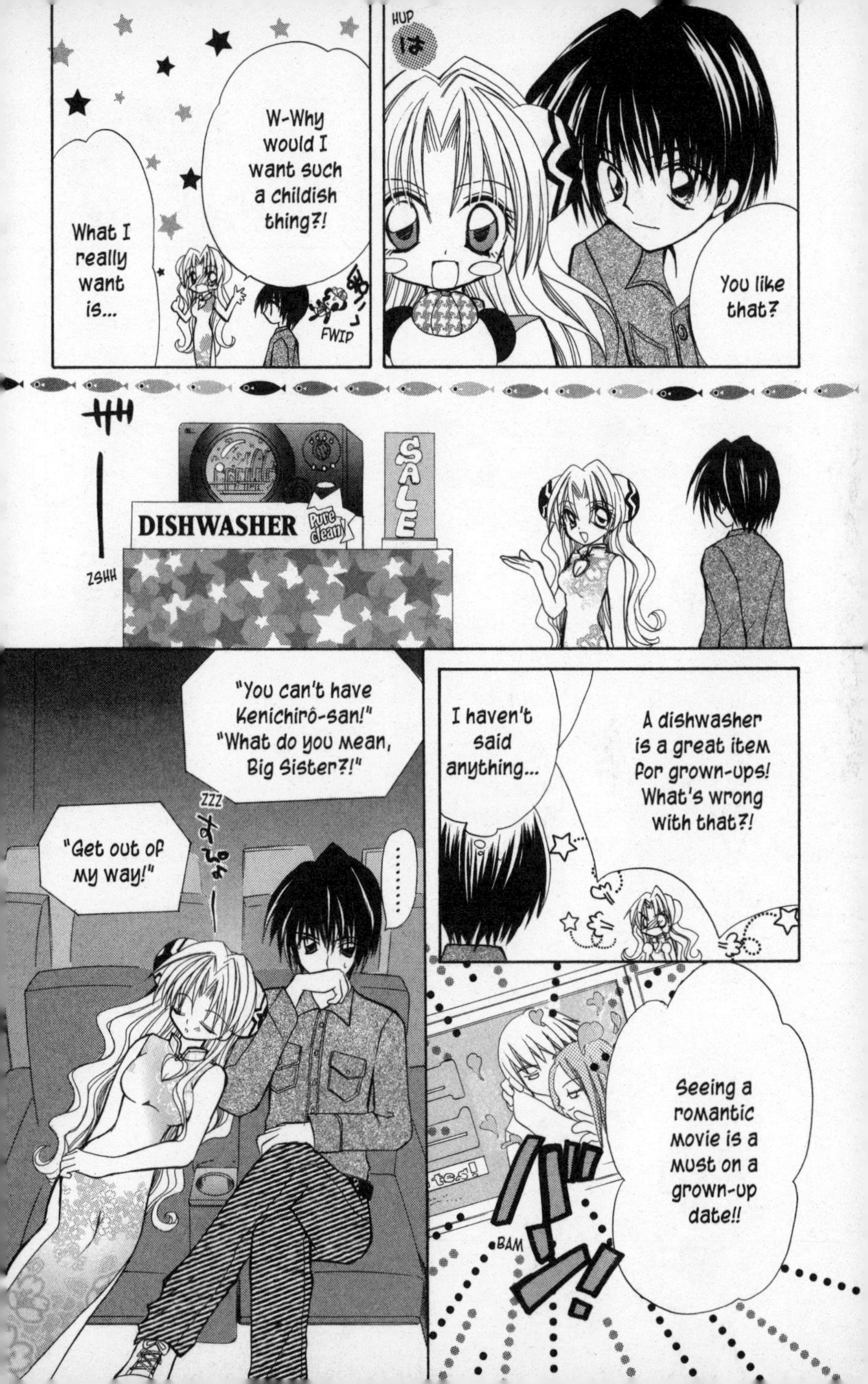
HUP
は
You like that?
W-Why would I want such a childish thing?!
FWIP
What I really want is...
ZSHH
SALE
DISHWASHER
Pure clean!
A dishwasher is a great item for grown-ups! What's wrong with that?!
I haven't said anything...
Seeing a romantic movie is a must on a grown-up date!!
BAM
"You can't have Kenichirô-san!" "What do you mean, Big Sister?!"
ZZZ
......
"Get out of my way!"

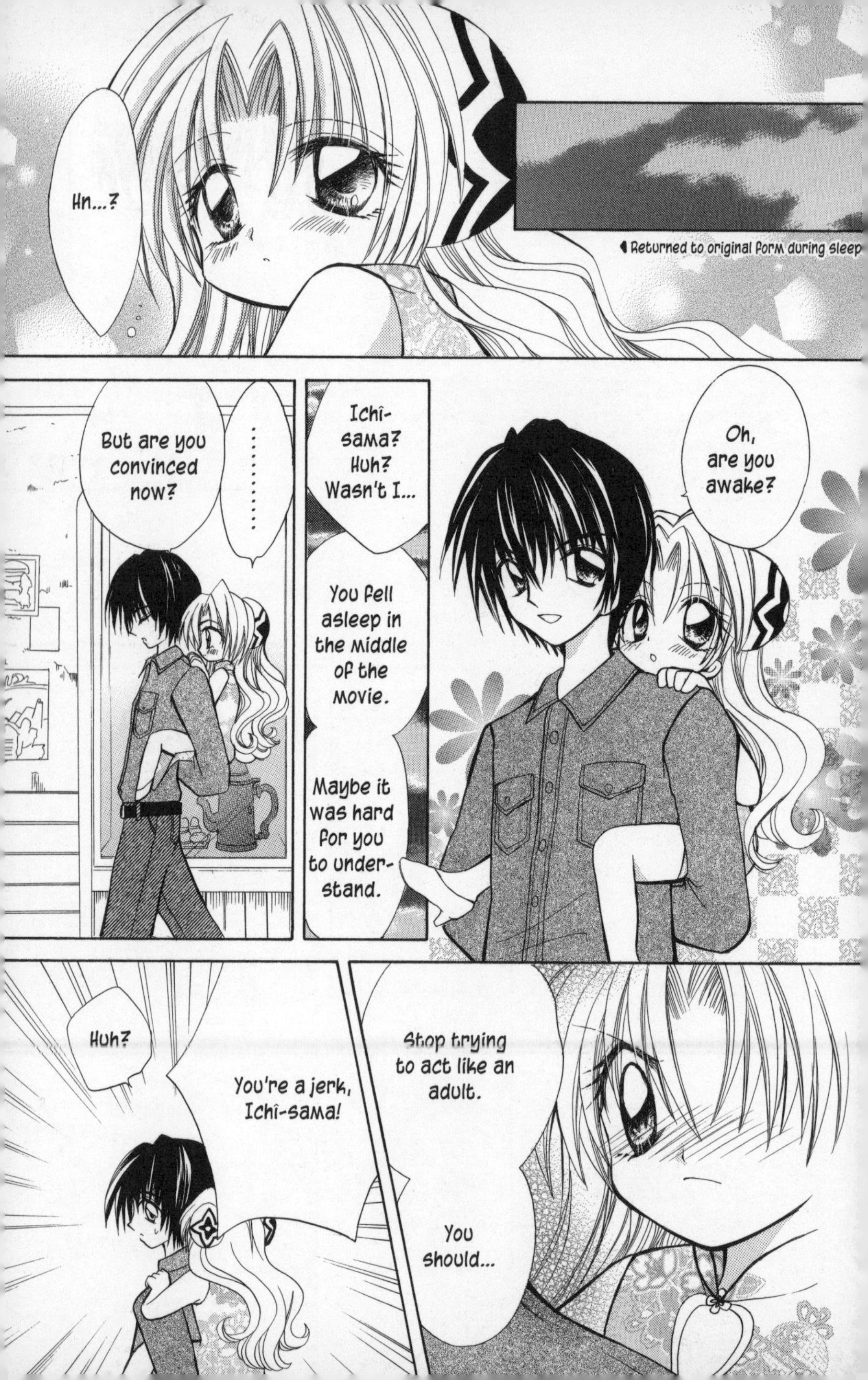
Returned to original form during sleep
Hn...?
Oh, are you awake?
Ichî-sama? Huh? Wasn't I...
You fell asleep in the middle of the movie.
Maybe it was hard for you to understand.
....
But are you convinced now?
Stop trying to act like an adult.
You should...
You're a jerk, Ichî-sama!
Huh?

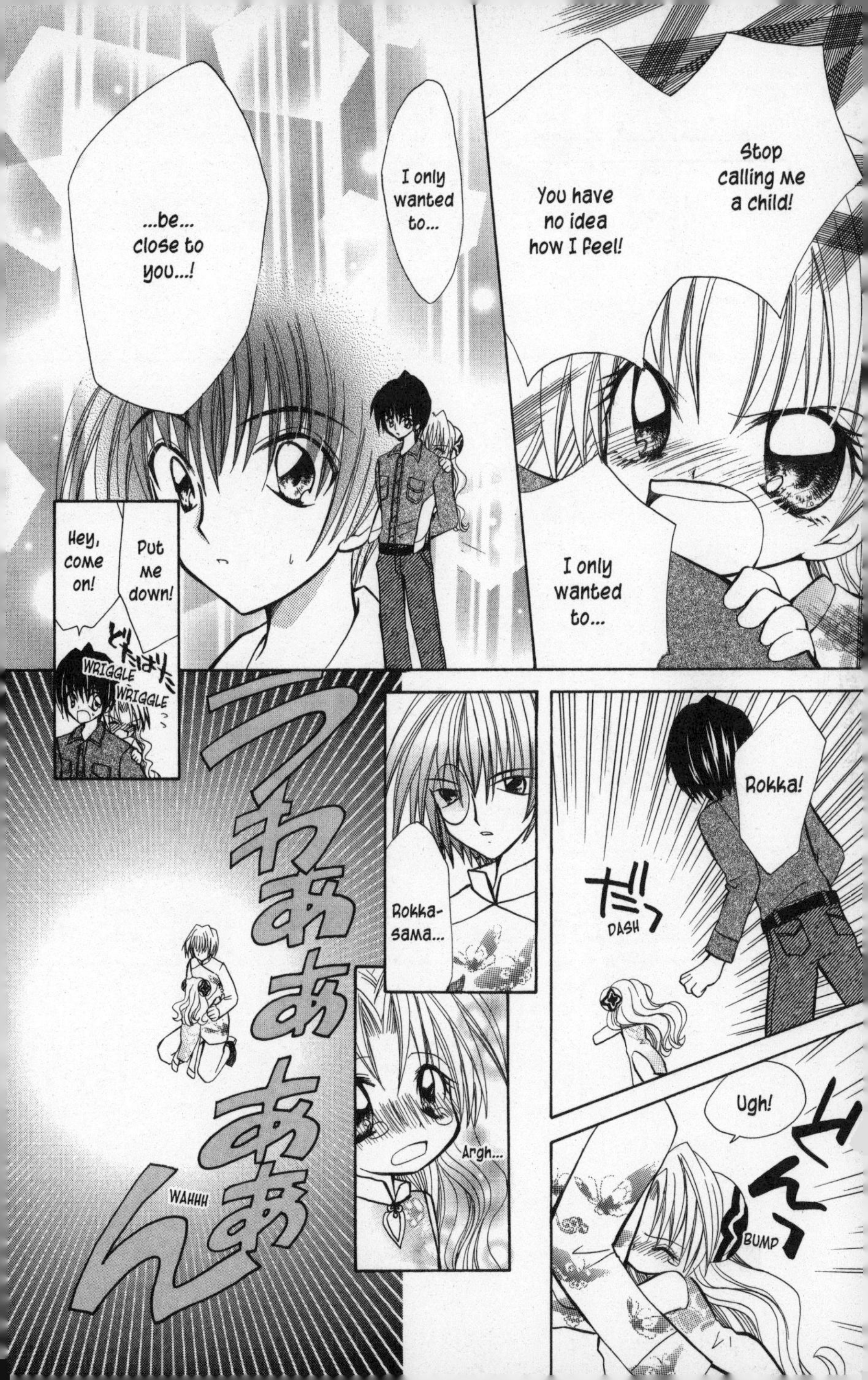
Stop calling me a child!
You have no idea how I feel!
I only wanted to...
I only wanted to...
...be... close to you...!
Put me down!
Hey, come on!
どたばた
WRIGGLE WRIGGLE
Rokka!
だっ
DASH
Ugh!
BUMP
Rokka-sama...
Argh...
うわあああん
WAHHH

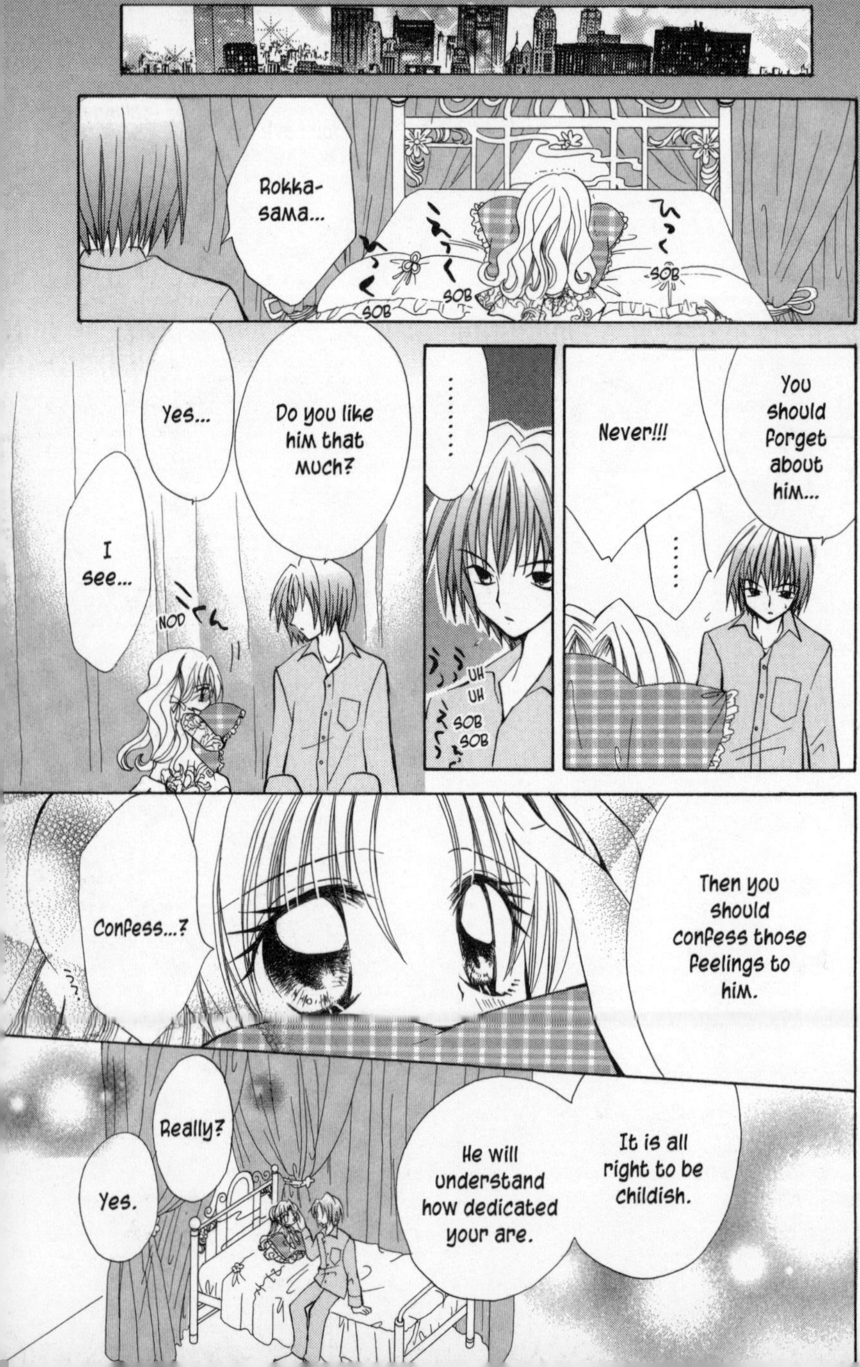
Rokka-sama...
SOB
SOB
SOB
You should forget about him...
Never!!!
......
......
UH UH
SOB SOB
Do you like him that much?
Yes...
I see...
NOD
Then you should confess those feelings to him.
Confess...?
It is all right to be childish.
He will understand how dedicated your are.
Really?
Yes.

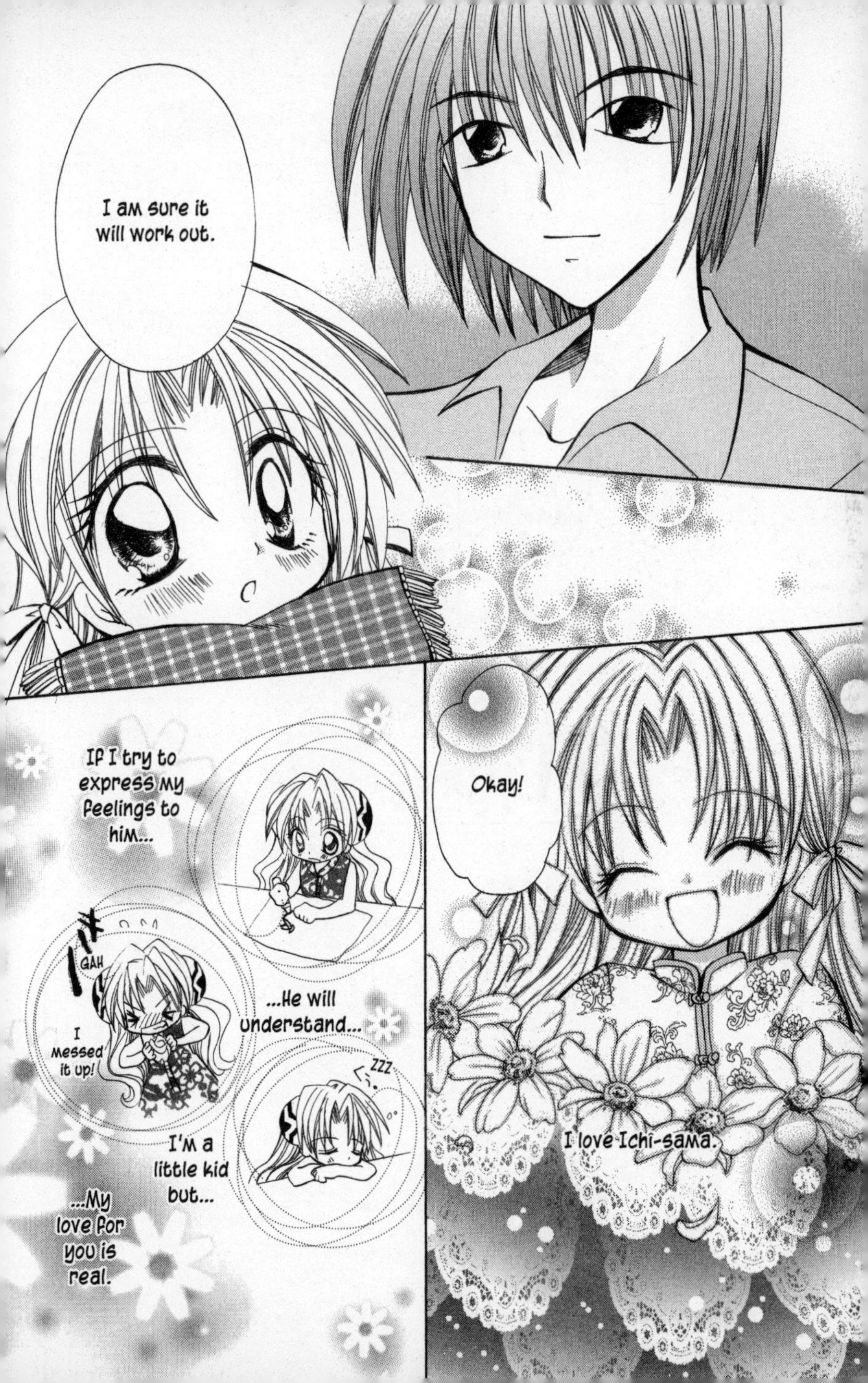
I am sure it will work out.
Okay!
I love Ichi-sama.
If I try to express my feelings to him...
GAH
I messed it up!
...He will understand...
ZZZ
I'm a little kid but...
...My love for you is real.

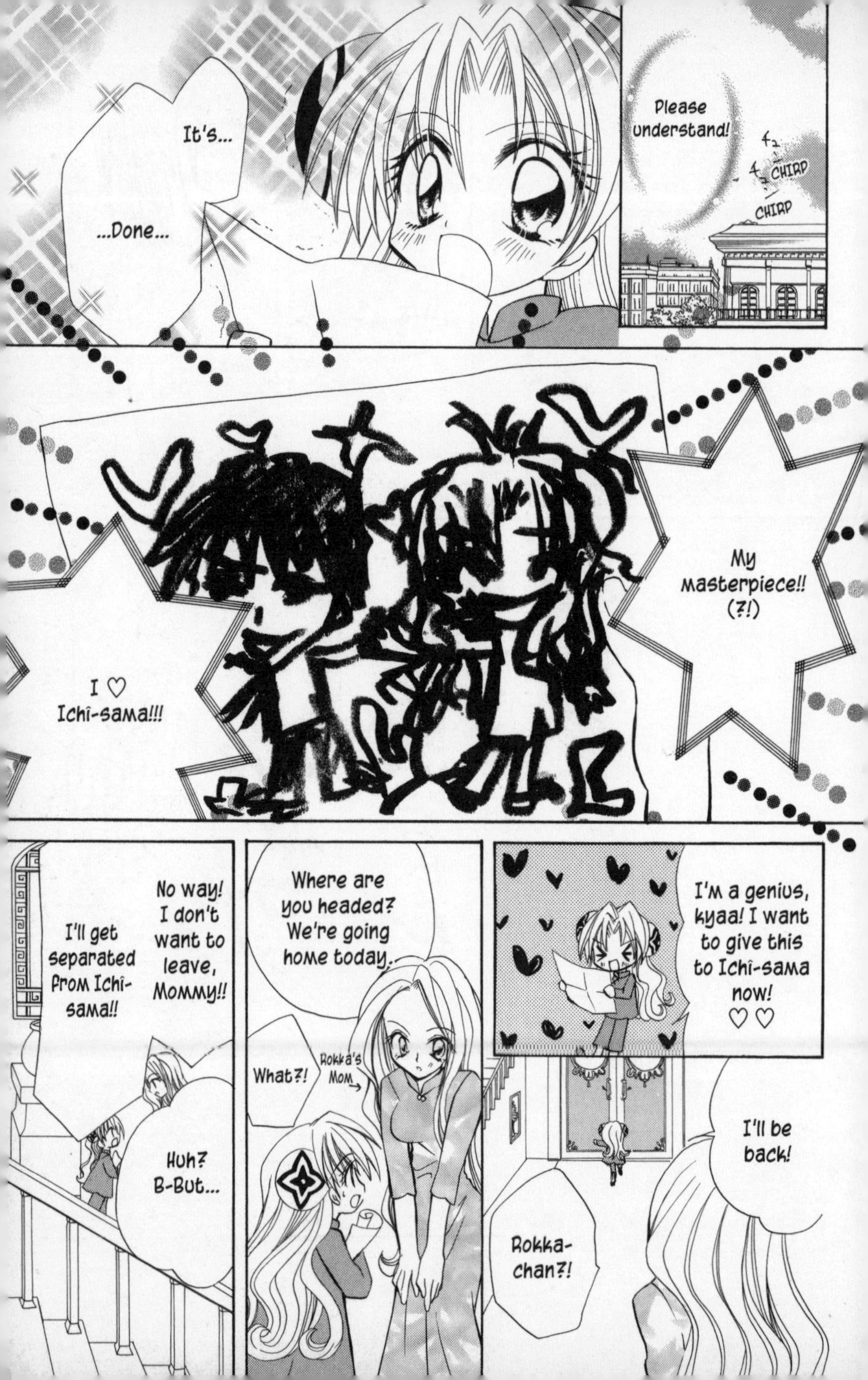
Please understand!
CHIRP
CHIRP
It's...
...Done...
My masterpiece!! (?!)
I ♡ Ichî-sama!!!
I'm a genius, kyaa! I want to give this to Ichî-sama now! ♡ ♡
I'll be back!
Rokka-chan?!
Where are you headed? We're going home today.
What?!
Rokka's Mom
No way! I don't want to leave, Mommy!!
I'll get separated from Ichî-sama!!
Huh? B-But...

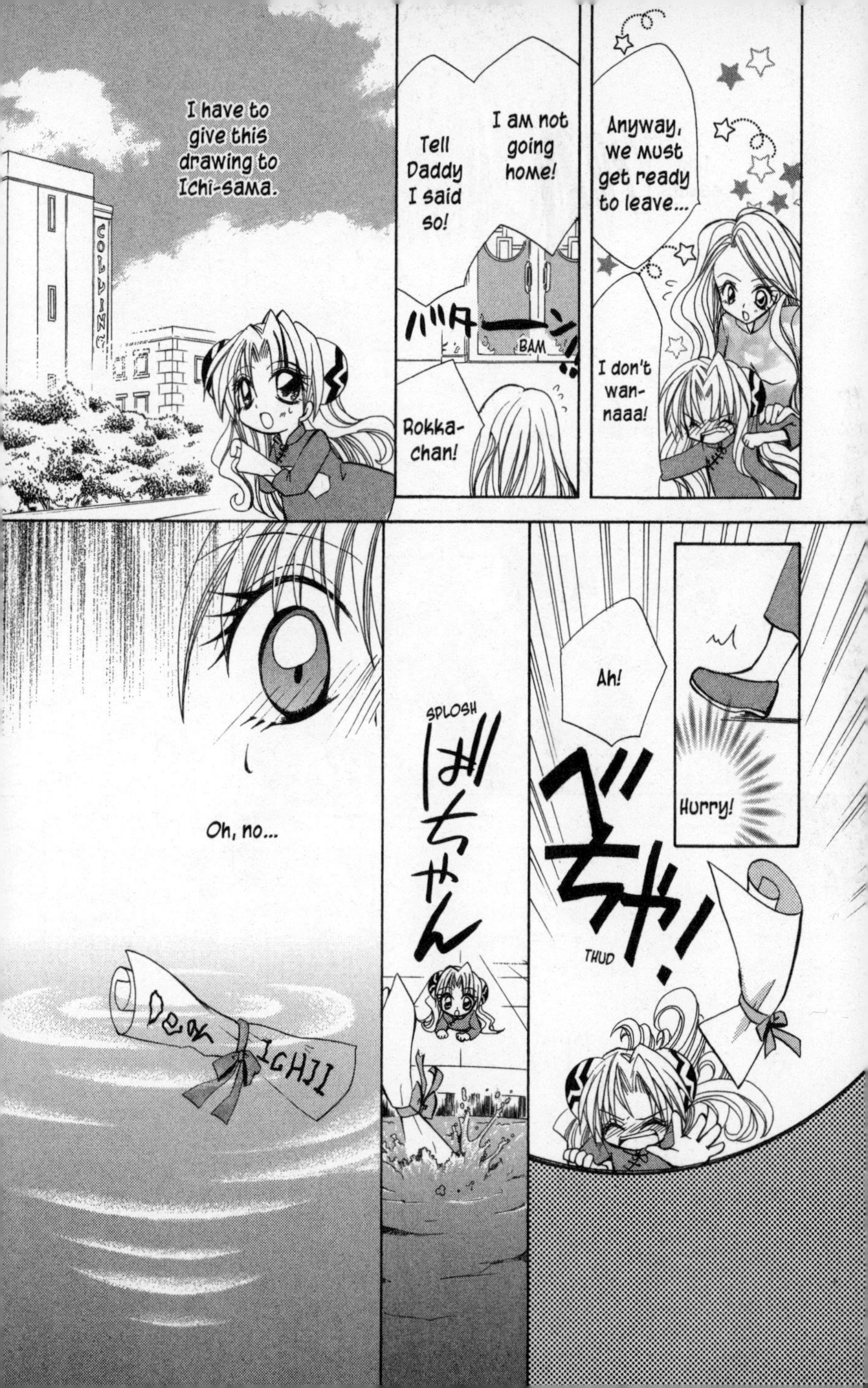
Anyway, we must get ready to leave...
I don't wan-naaa!
I am not going home!
Tell Daddy I said so!
バターン
BAM
Rokka-chan!
I have to give this drawing to Ichi-sama.
Hurry!
Ah!
べちゃ!
THUD
ぼちゃん
SPLOSH
Oh, no...
Dear ICHJI

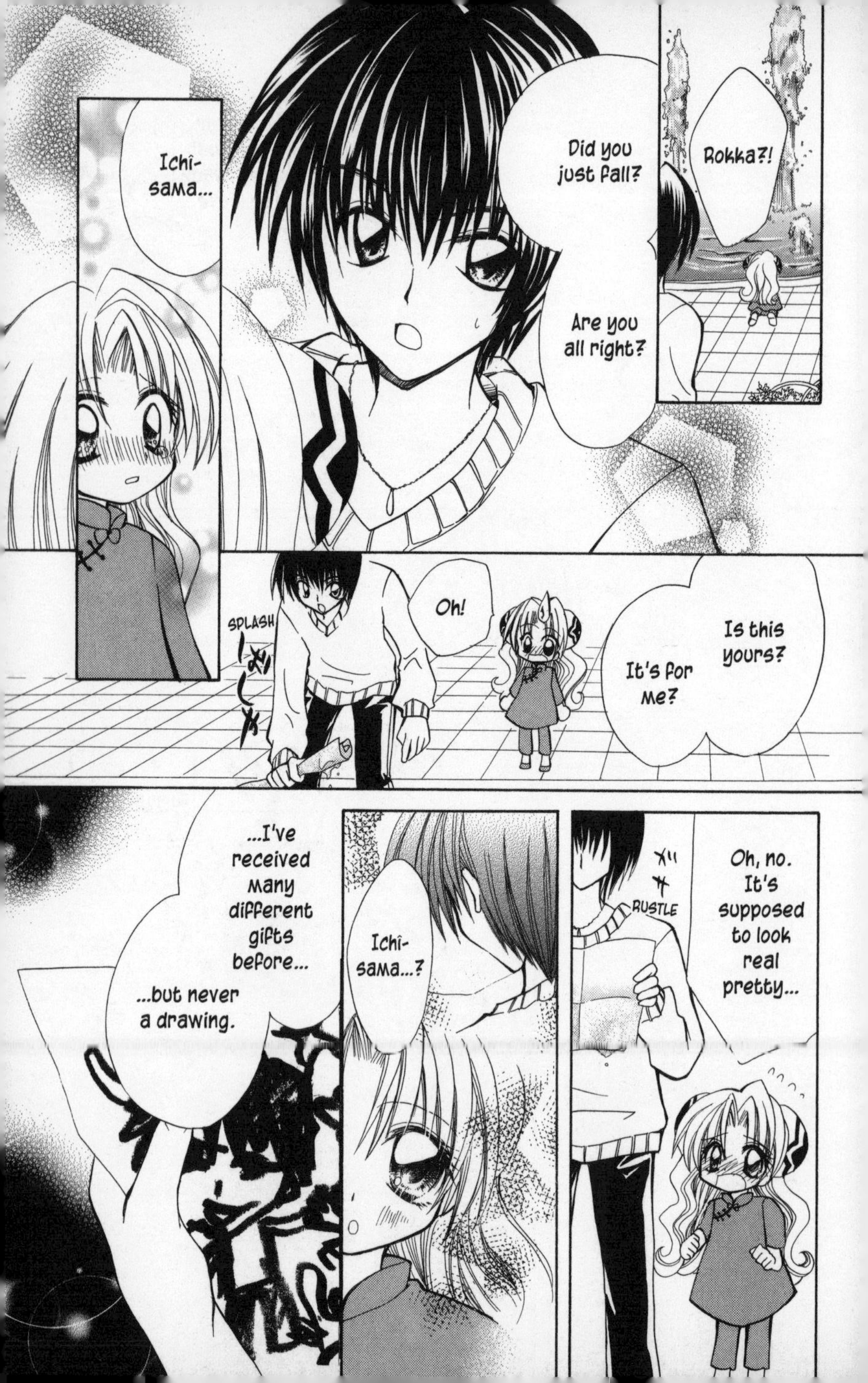
Rokka?!
Did you just fall?
Are you all right?
Ichî-sama...
Is this yours?
It's for me?
Oh!
SPLASH
Oh, no. It's supposed to look real pretty...
RUSTLE
Ichî-sama...?
...I've received many different gifts before...
...but never a drawing.

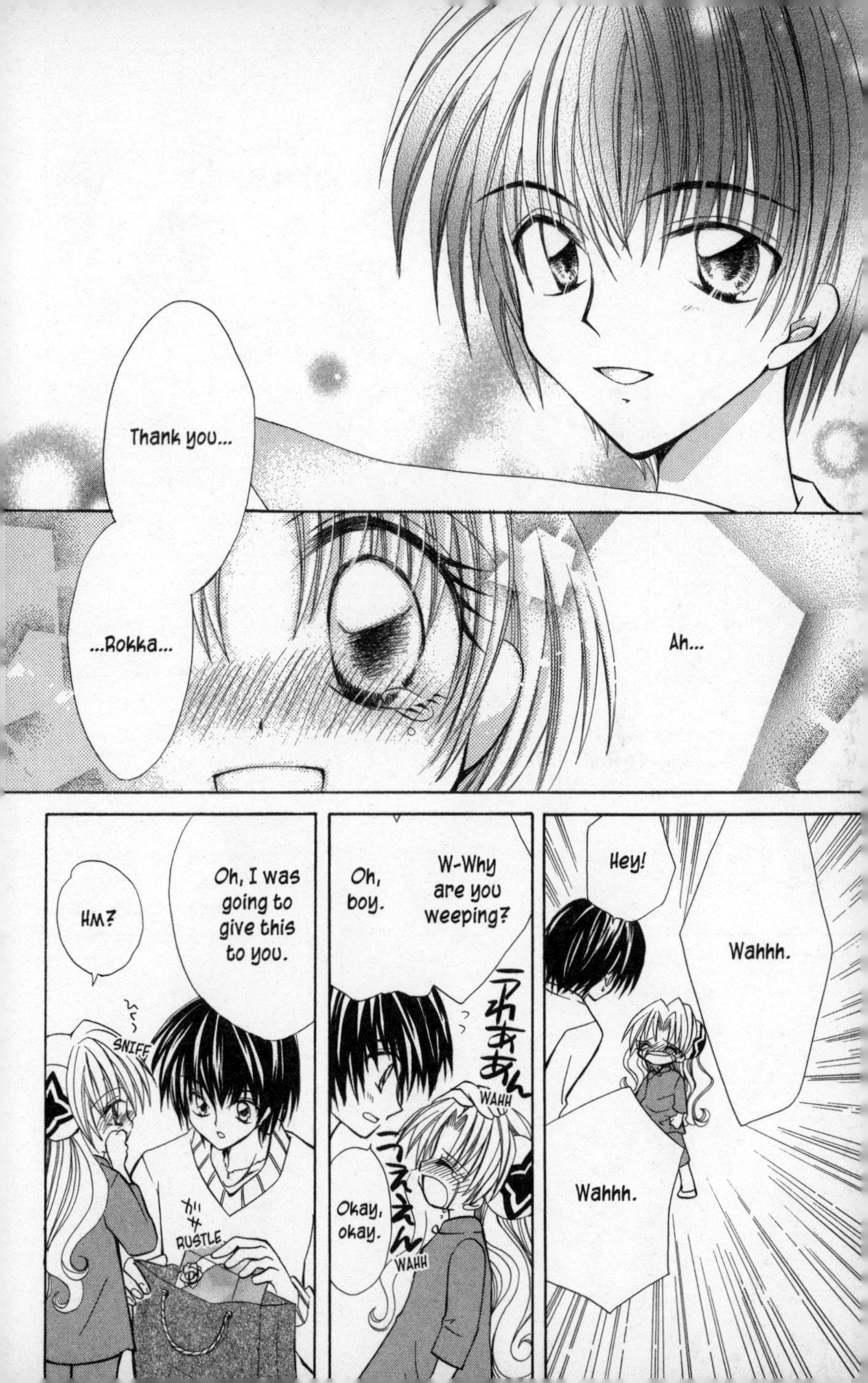
Thank you...
Ah...
...Rokka...
Hey!
Wahhh.
Wahhh.
W-Why are you weeping?
Oh, boy.
WAHH
WAHH
Okay, okay.
Oh, I was going to give this to you.
Hm?
SNIFF
RUSTLE

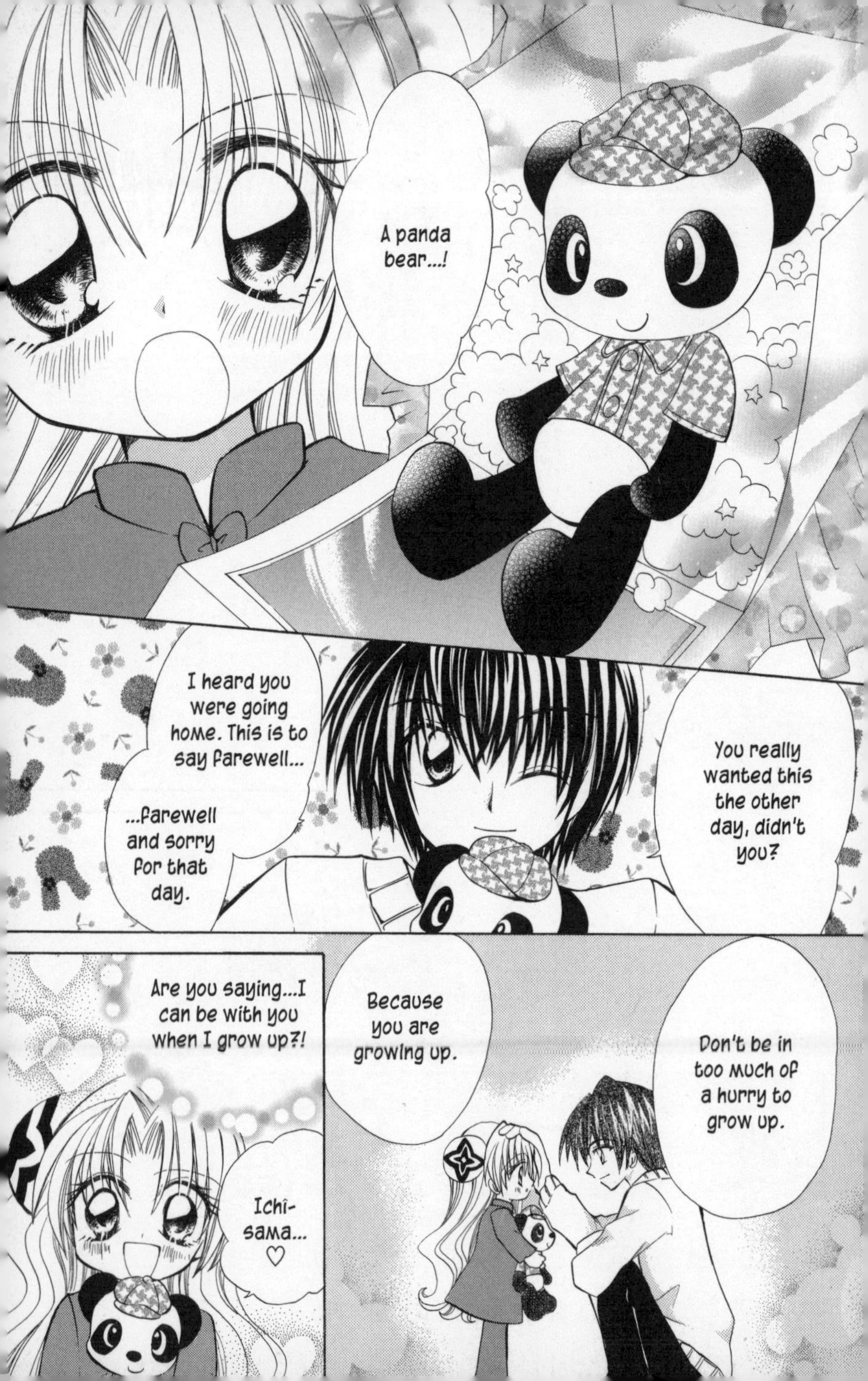
A panda bear...!
You really wanted this the other day, didn't you?
I heard you were going home. This is to say farewell...
...farewell and sorry for that day.
Don't be in too much of a hurry to grow up.
Because you are growing up.
Are you saying...I can be with you when I grow up?!
Ichî-sama... ♡

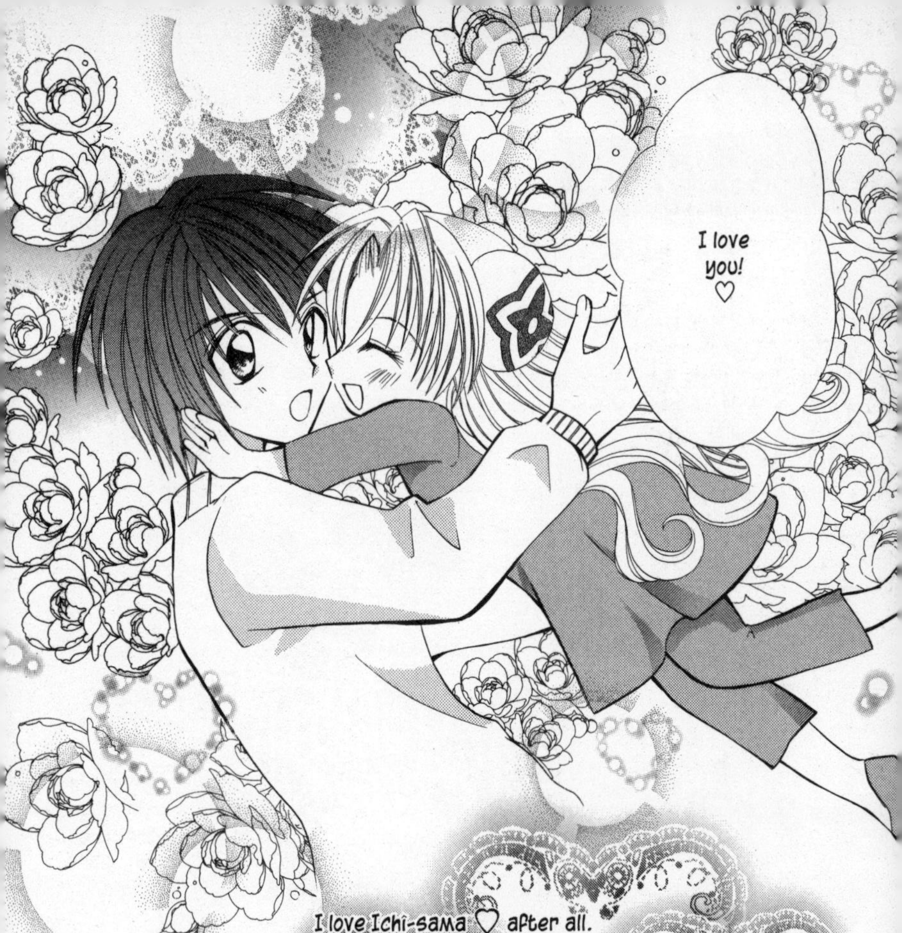
I love you! ♡
I love Ichi-sama ♡ after all.
I'll become the best woman and
come back to you someday.
You just wait. ♡

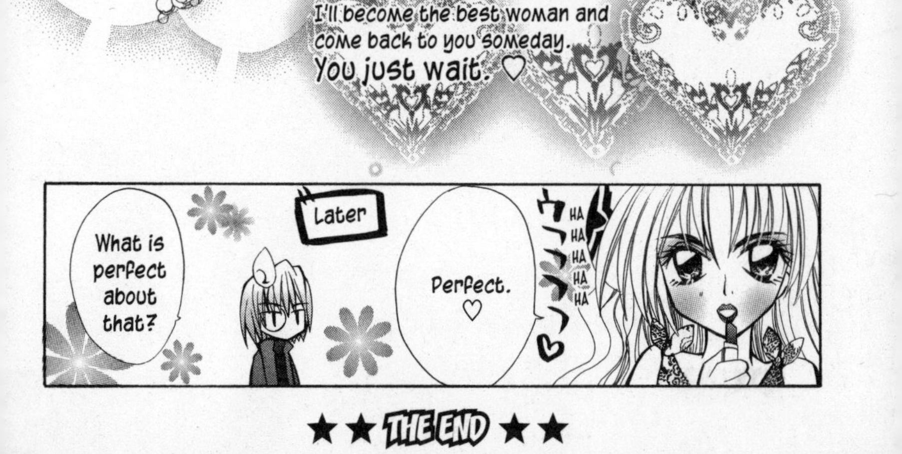
HA HA HA HA HA
Later
Perfect. ♡
What is perfect about that?

★★ THE END ★★

Mini-Theatre: TAKE 3

Nanase & Yakumo: Nanase-chan Fan Club

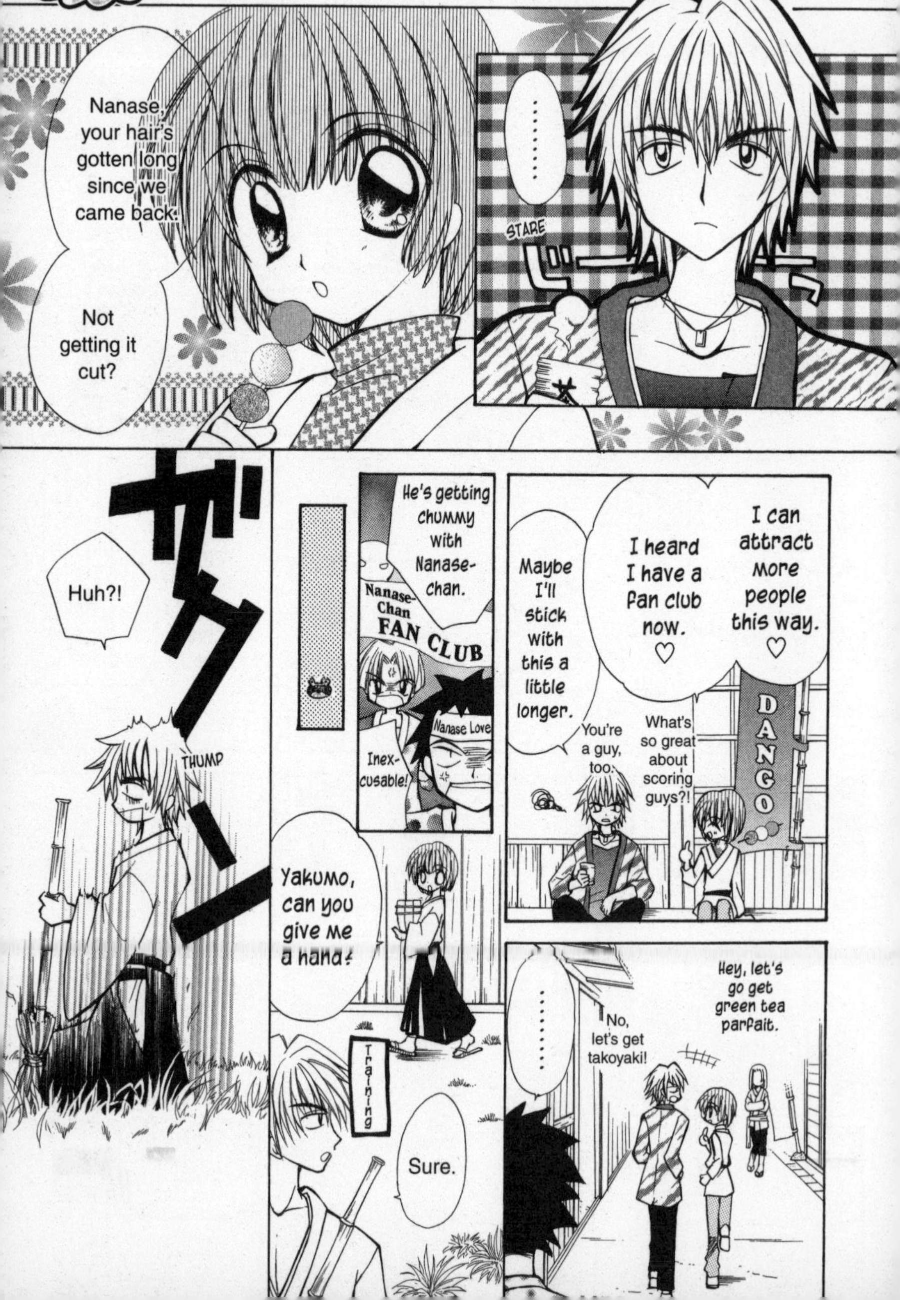
......
STARE
Nanase, your hair's gotten long since we came back.
Not getting it cut?
I can attract more people this way. ♡
I heard I have a fan club now. ♡
Maybe I'll stick with this a little longer.
What's so great about scoring guys?!
You're a guy, too.
DANGO
Hey, let's go get green tea parfait.
No, let's get takoyaki!
......
He's getting chummy with Nanase-chan.
Nanase-Chan FAN CLUB
Nanase Love
Inexcusable!
Yakumo, can you give me a hand?
Training
Sure.
Huh?!
THUMP

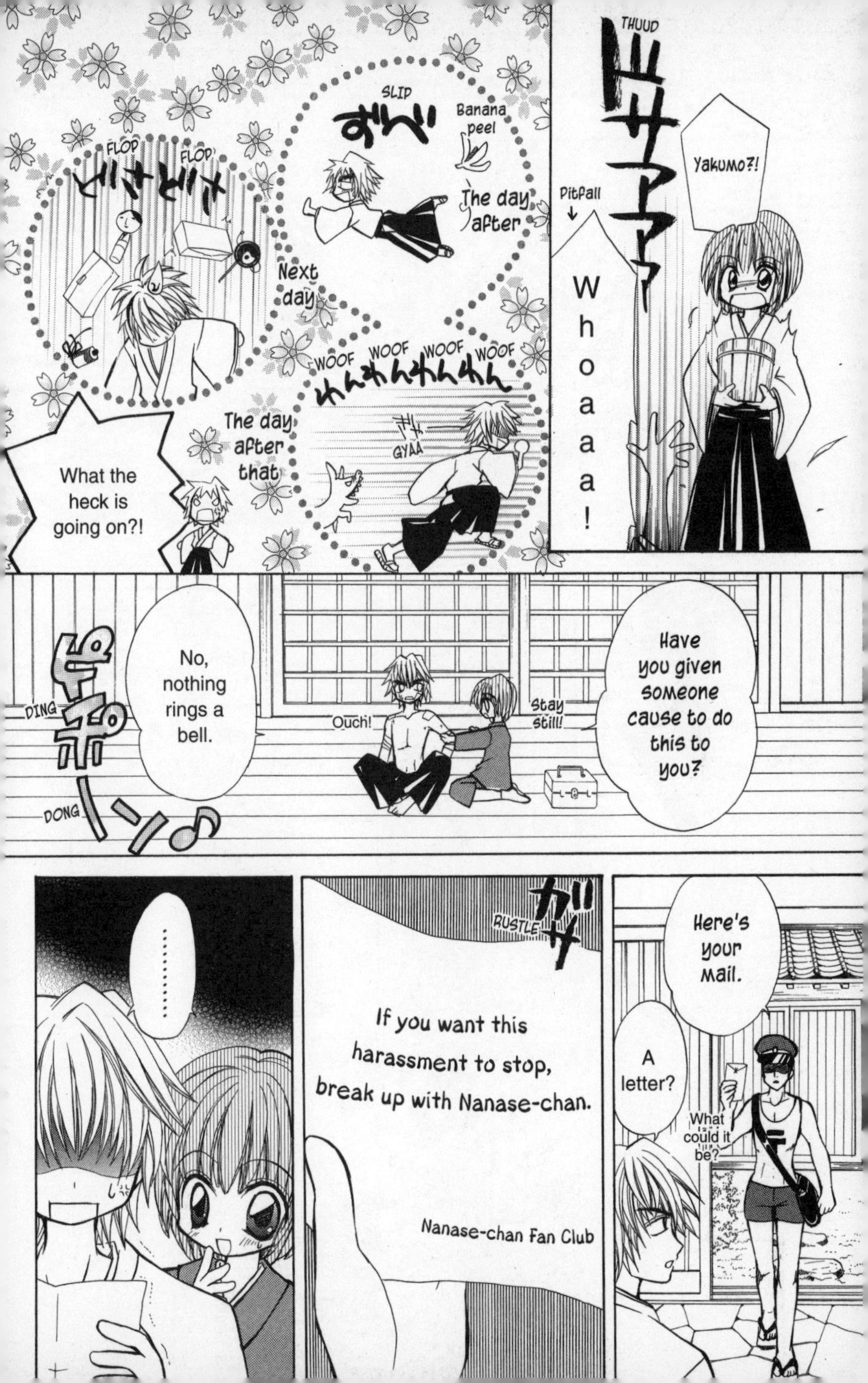
THUUD
Yakumo?!
Pitfall
Whoaaa!
SLIP
Banana peel
The day after
FLOP FLOP
Next day
WOOF WOOF WOOF WOOF
GYAA
The day after that
What the heck is going on?!
Have you given someone cause to do this to you?
Stay still!
Ouch!
No, nothing rings a bell.
DING
DONG
Here's your mail.
A letter?
What could it be?
RUSTLE
If you want this harassment to stop, break up with Nanase-chan.
Nanase-chan Fan Club
......

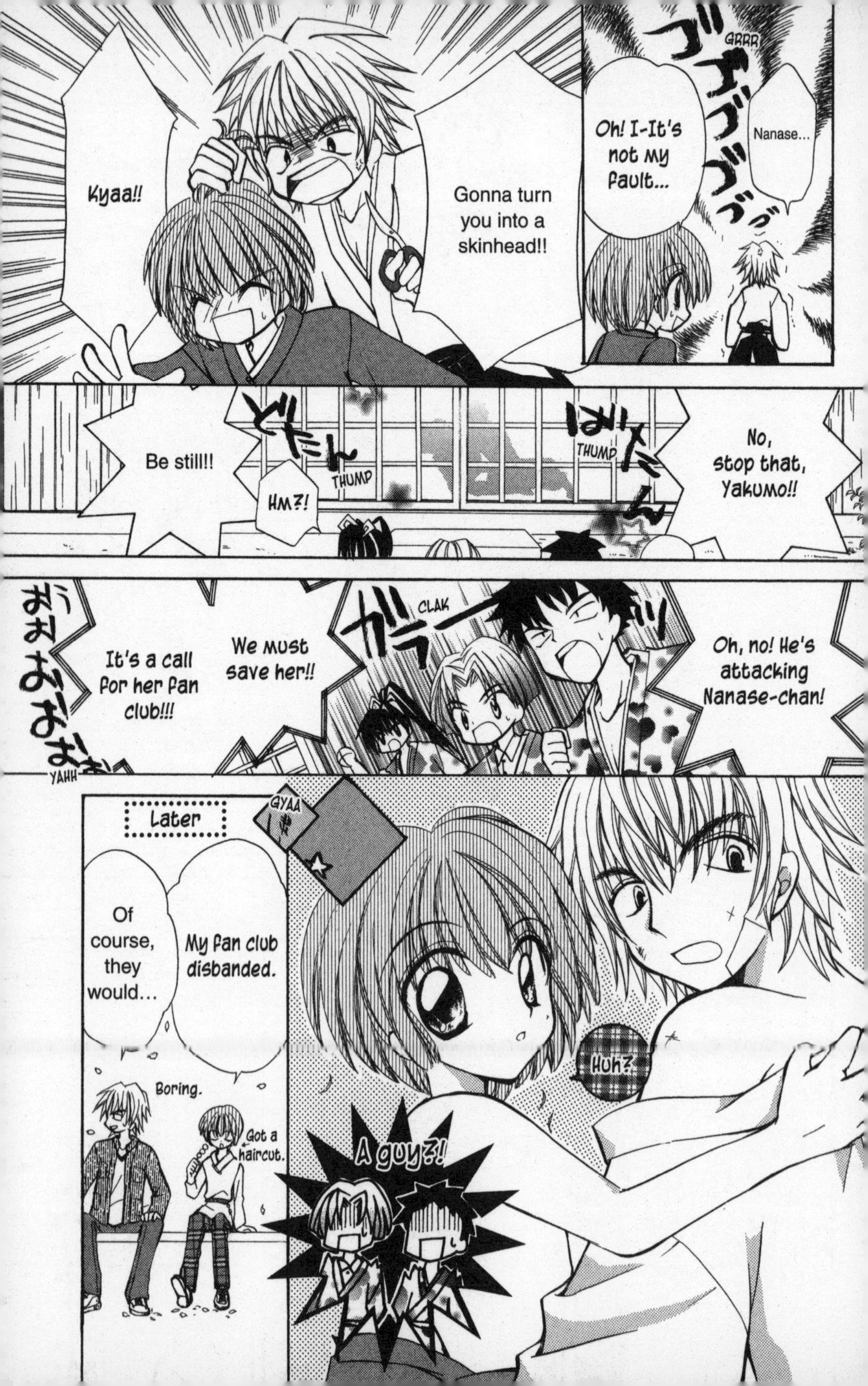
GRRR
Nanase...
Oh! I-It's not my fault...
Gonna turn you into a skinhead!!
Kyaa!!
No, stop that, Yakumo!!
THUMP
Hm?!
THUMP
Be still!!
Oh, no! He's attacking Nanase-chan!
CLAK
We must save her!!
It's a call for her fan club!!!
YAHH
GYAA
Huh?
A guy?!
Later
My fan club disbanded.
Of course, they would...
Boring.
Got a haircut.

Zero, Ichî & Nina: Afterschool Story

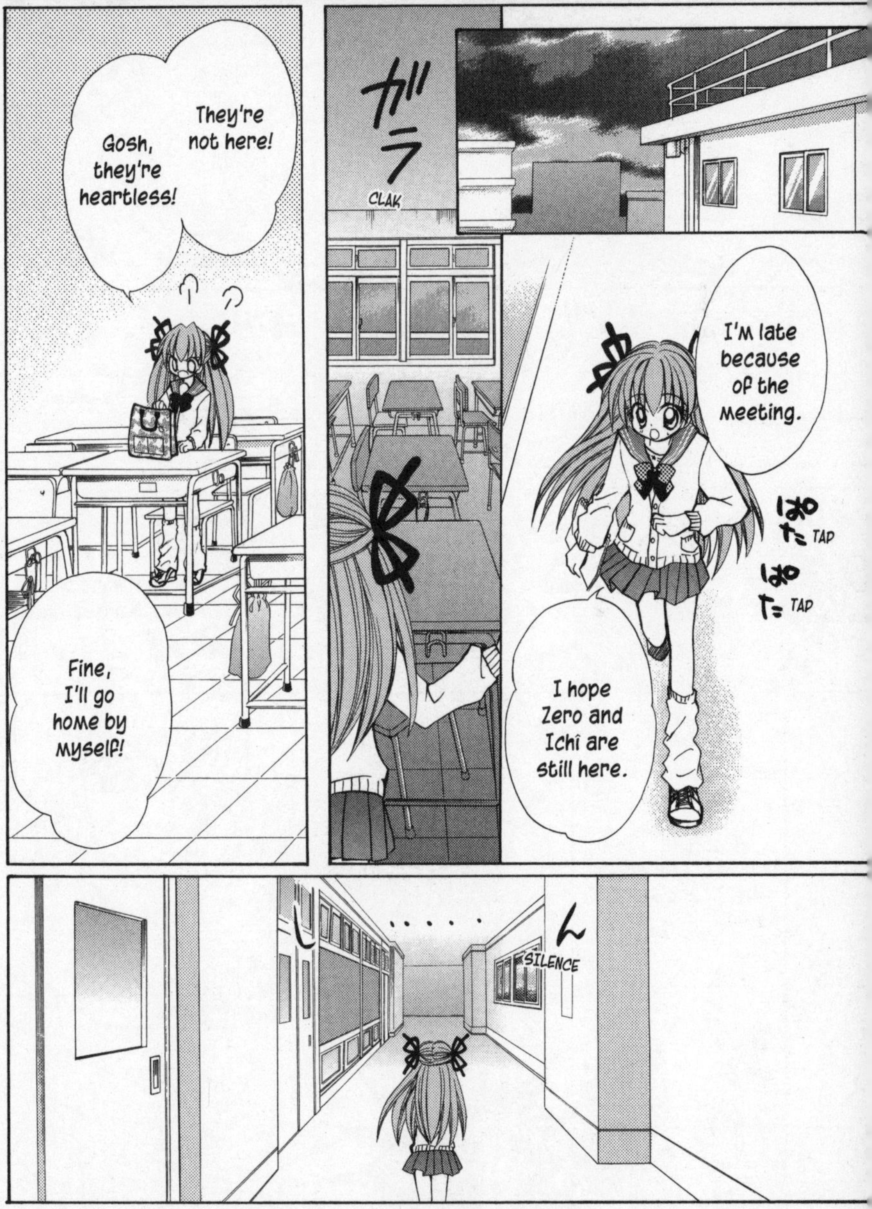
I'm late because of the meeting.
ぱた TAP
ぱた TAP
I hope Zero and Ichî are still here.
ガラ
CLAK
They're not here!
Gosh, they're heartless!
Fine, I'll go home by myself!
.....
しん
SILENCE

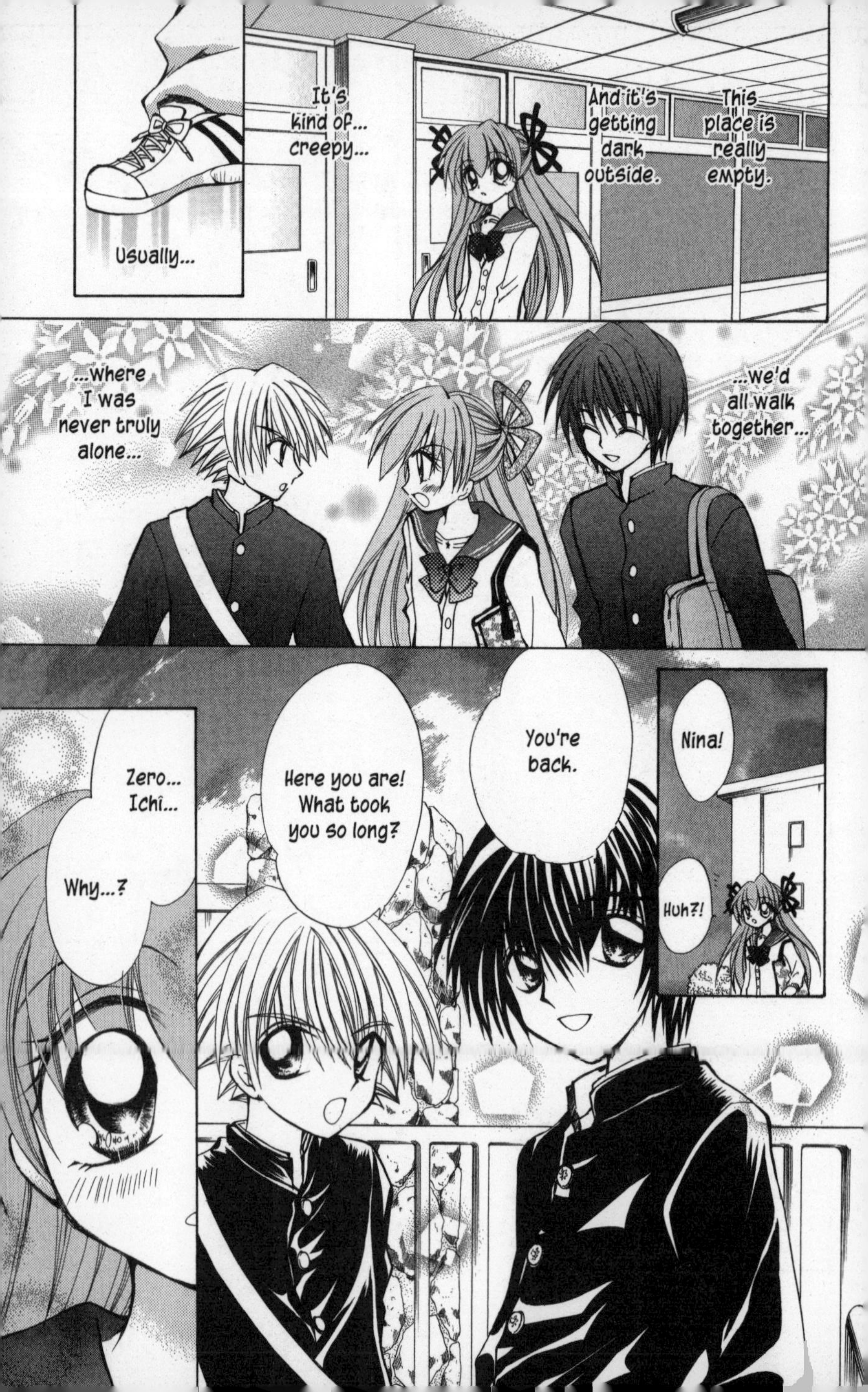
This place is really empty.
And it's getting dark outside.
It's kind of... creepy...
Usually...
...we'd all walk together...
...where I was never truly alone...
Nina!
Huh?!
You're back.
Here you are! What took you so long?
Zero... Ichi...
Why...?

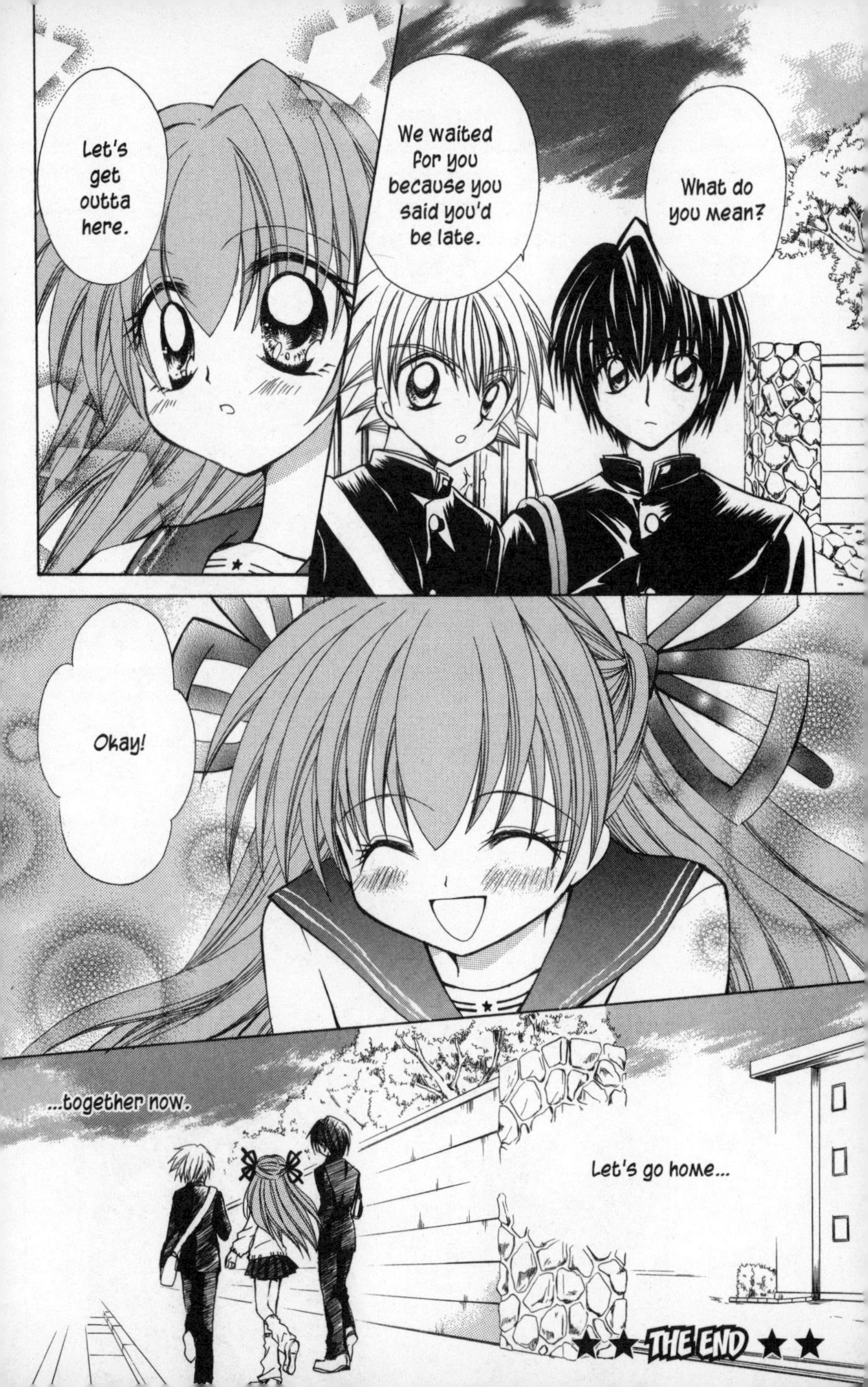
What do you mean?
We waited for you because you said you'd be late.
Let's get outta here.
Okay!
Let's go home...
...together now.
★★ THE END ★★

Mini ★ Theatre

This was a collection of bonus stories that ran in *Nakayoshi Lovely*. Actually, it was the last-minute manga that I drew in one day. (Sweatdrops) It was tough, but I really had fun drawing it. Its short length allowed me to include many characters, too! Since I could create this kind of manga at any time, I'd like to do it again.... I enjoy working with the side characters and revealing their backgrounds.

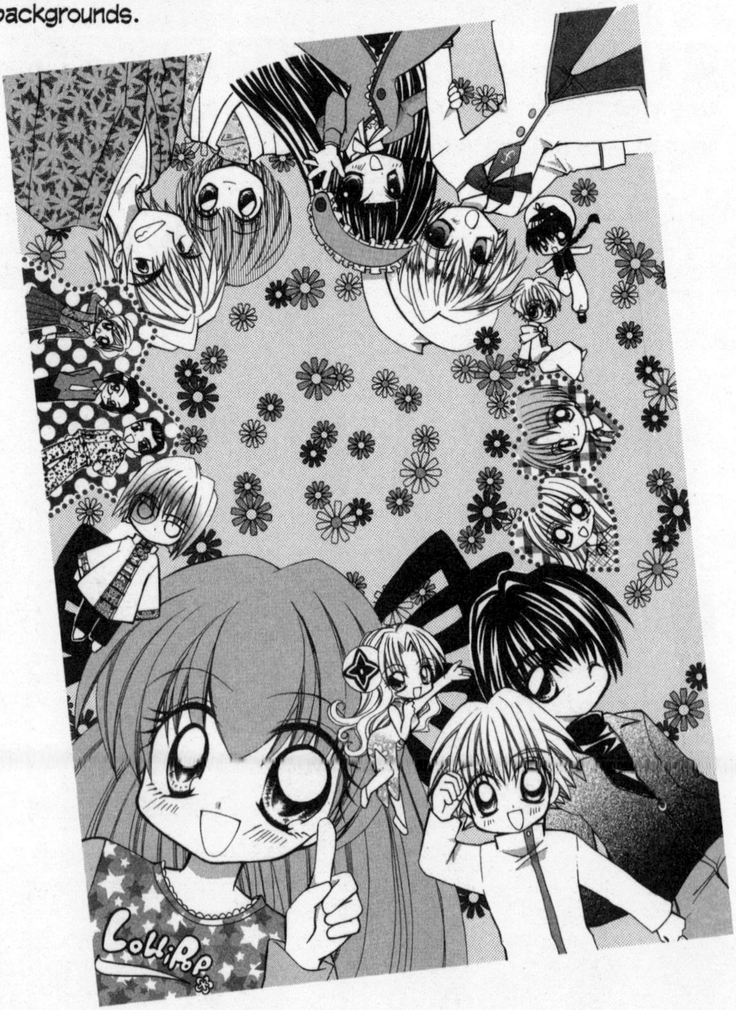

Eleven & Twelve's

Real Love Relationship Test!

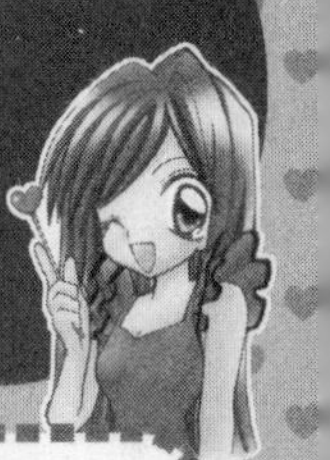

Check this out with Nina at the beach in summer!
We got this special test that'll determine your love pattern. ♥

Q1 You go to the beach with your friends. What's the color of your bathing suit?

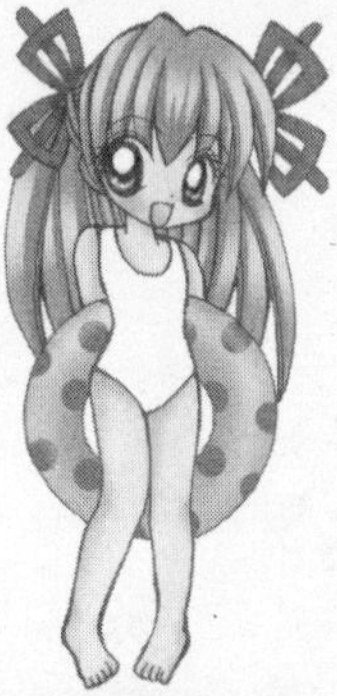

① Pink

② Light Blue

③ White

④ Black

⑤ Red

Q2 The weather is awesome! What do you want to do?

① Watermelon Splitting

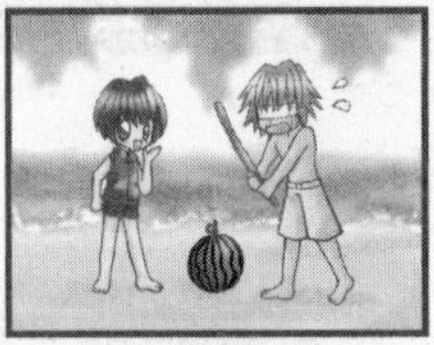

② Beach Volleyball

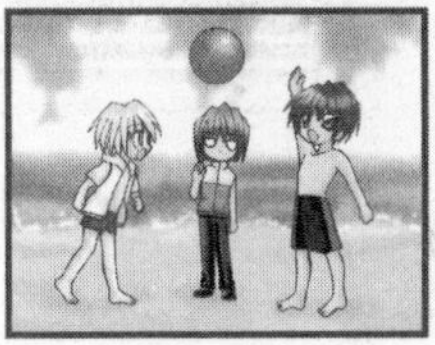

③ Swimming

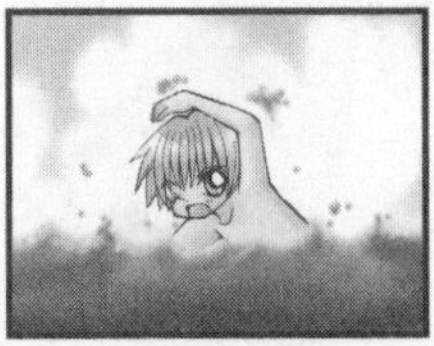

④ Sunbathing (napping)

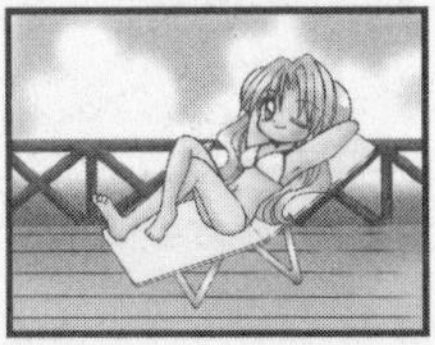

Q3 After lots of swimming and sunbathing, you get thirsty. You run into a rest area and drink barley tea. Then what do you say?

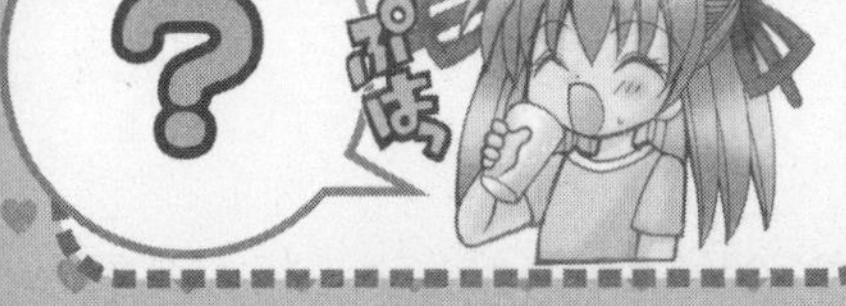
?
GASP
ぷはっ

Q4 Coincidentally, five boys you know are having shaved ice at a rest area. Now name the boy whose personality would match the following flavors of the syrup.

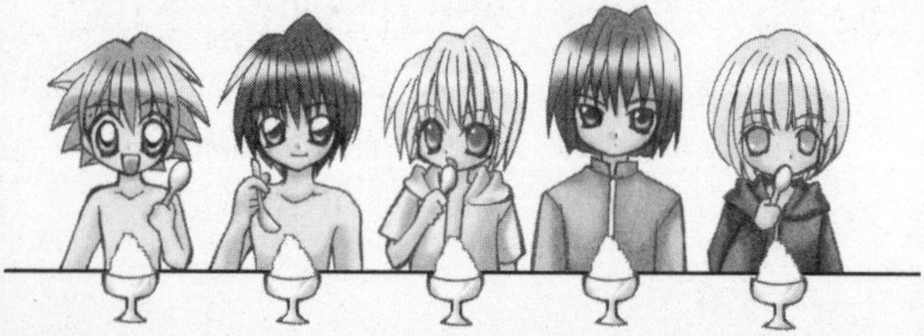

① Strawberry
② Melon
③ Lemon
④ Blue Hawaiian
⑤ Green Tea

Q5 You go out with the boys. You all decide to play in the sand, but what are you going to do?!

① Build a sand castle.
② Build a mound.
③ Bury someone.
④ Get yourself buried.

Q6 You walk on the beach and find a real cute puppy. Now what do you do?!

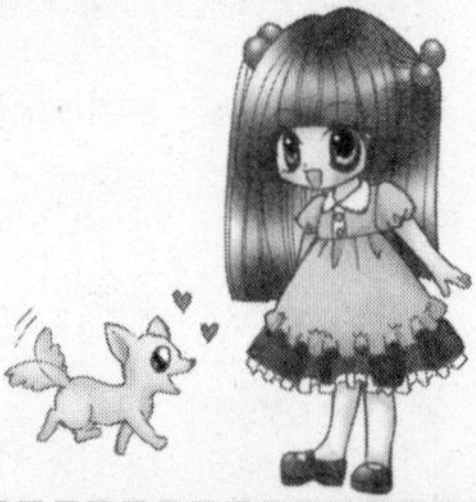

Q7 After having fun throughout the day, you notice stars in the sky. Is that a new constellation?! Pick a name for it.

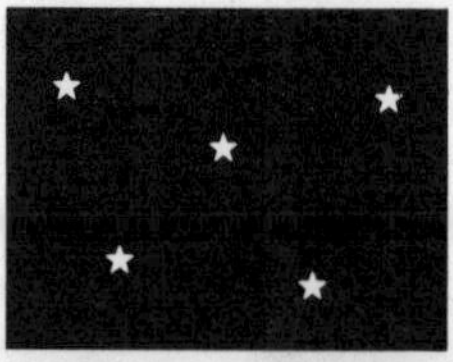

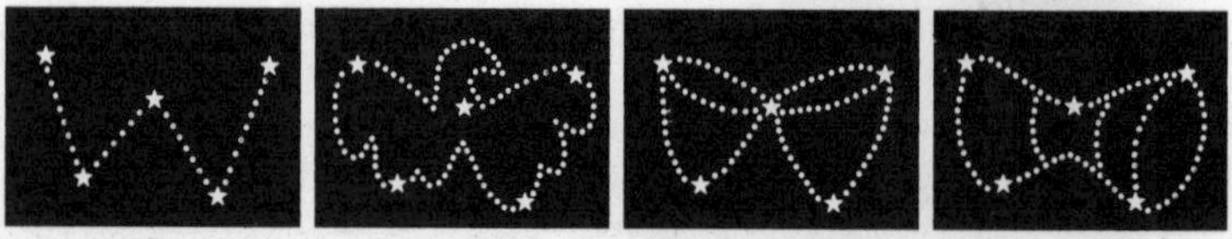

① W (Double) ② Phoenix ③ Ribbon ④ Drum

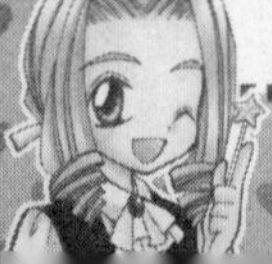

The results are on the next page.♪

Real Love Relationship Test!

Exciting Test Results

A1 Your aggression level & confession style

① **Pink,** 100% Aggressive ▶ Persistent even when he's got a girlfriend, you'd try to attract him with your femininity!

② **Light Blue,** 40% Aggressive ▶ Shrewd, you'd ask him out, but wait for him to confess his love.♡

③ **White,** 20% Aggressive ▶ Even if it's just a crush, you're relatively happy with watching him from afar.♡

④ **Black,** 60% Aggressive ▶ Preferring writing a love letter, you're practical at approaching him after gathering information.

⑤ **Red,** 80% Aggressive ▶ If he's not involved in a relationship, you'd call and confess your love to him!

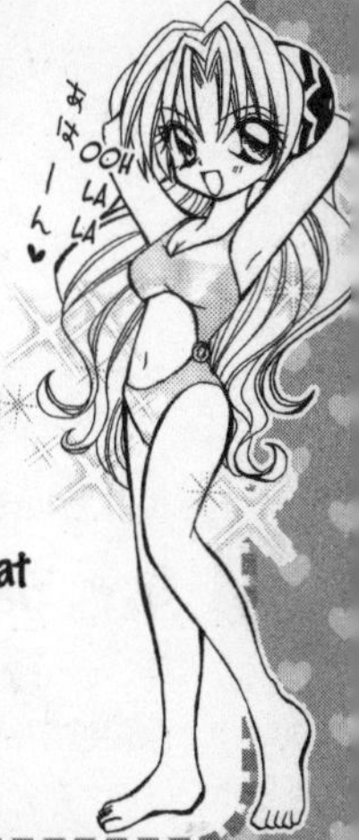
OOH LA LA

A2 Your thrilling ★ chance of getting kissed.

① **Watermelon Splitting,** 80% Aggressive ▶ You're a real thrill seeker. Are you close to kissing?!

② **Beach Volleyball,** 60% Aggressive ▶ An indirect kiss is a possibility for someone seeking a little thrill like you . . .

③ **Swimming,** 40% Aggressive ▶ Preferring less excitement, you're uncomfortable with kissing, but you can hold hands.

④ **Sunbathing,** 20% Aggressive ▶ Lacking in thrills, you won't be kissing for quite a while.♪

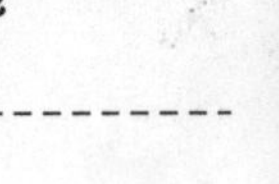
kiss

A3 This is what you'd say after your first kiss!

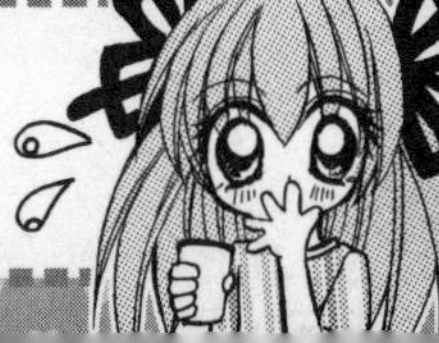

A4 What he means to you.

① Strawberry	▶	A friend.	For its pleasant taste that everyone likes, strawberry symbolizes friendship.
② Melon	▶	A lover.	Its tongue-coloring feature—his ability to change your outlook—indicates a symbol of love.
③ Lemon	▶	Someone who loves you.	Sweet and stimulating, lemon flavor indicates you're his love interest.
④ Blue Hawaii	▶	Someone you'd kiss.	Its mature taste represents a boy who excites you.
⑤ Green Tea	▶	Someone you respect.	Someone you respect. Its soothing effect shows an individual who'd accept you.

A5 Type of person you'd fall in ♡ with at first sight.

① Build a sand castle.	▶	He's full of confidence. An older reliable person.
② Build a mound.	▶	He has excellent reflexes. An athlete of your age.
③ Bury someone.	▶	Someone entertaining and the same age as you.
④ Get yourself buried.	▶	A cute younger boy who'd depend on you.

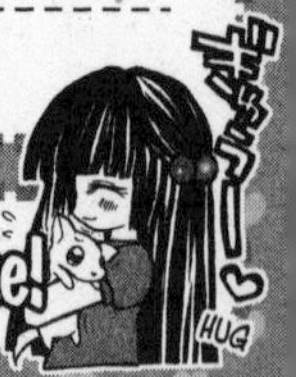
HUG

A6 It's what you want to do to someone you like!

A7 A priority in choosing your fiancé.

① W (Double)	▶	Money - Being realistic as you are, put emphasis on his fortune!
② Phoenix	▶	Tenderness - With your romantic nature, judge by his personality!
③ Ribbon	▶	Appearance - You're sophisticated, so go for a guy with good looks!
④ Drum	▶	Health - Full of energy, you should seek someone athletic!

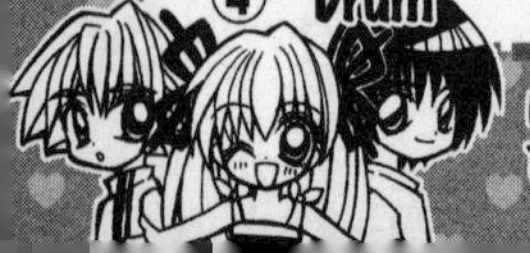

How did you do?!
Try this on your friends and other boys, too!

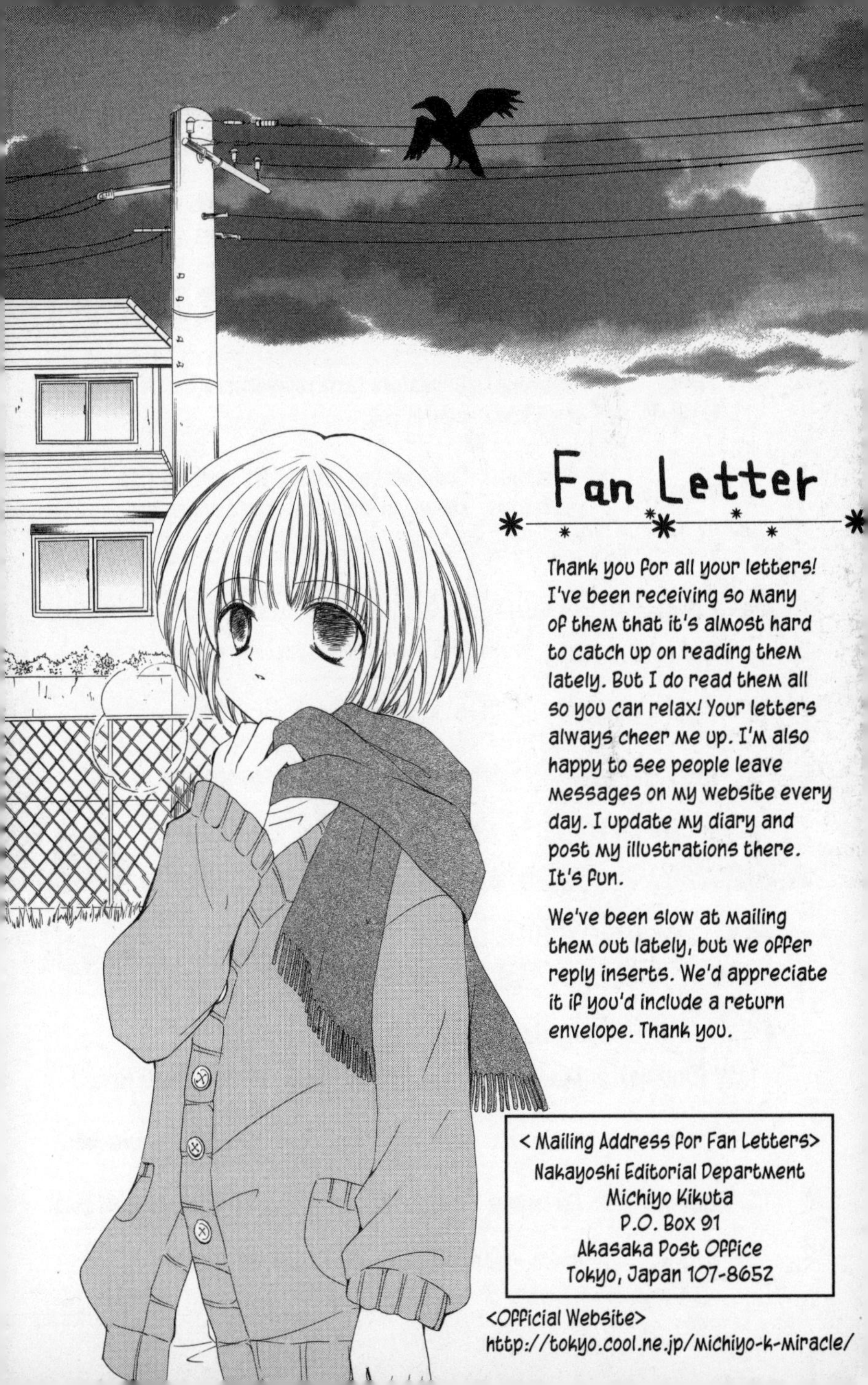

Fan Letter

Thank you for all your letters! I've been receiving so many of them that it's almost hard to catch up on reading them lately. But I do read them all so you can relax! Your letters always cheer me up. I'm also happy to see people leave messages on my website every day. I update my diary and post my illustrations there. It's fun.

We've been slow at mailing them out lately, but we offer reply inserts. We'd appreciate it if you'd include a return envelope. Thank you.

< Mailing Address for Fan Letters>
Nakayoshi Editorial Department
Michiyo Kikuta
P.O. Box 91
Akasaka Post Office
Tokyo, Japan 107-8652

<Official Website>
http://tokyo.cool.ne.jp/michiyo-k-miracle/

BYE-BYE ★

This is the last page. Thank you for reading all the way to the end. In volume 4, the Magic Exam has finally (?) ended and we got the new twist of the story! I don't know whether I'm surprised or happy that I can still continue to draw *Mamotte! Lollipop*... I seem to have grown attached to the characters after drawing them so long and I love them all! I liked them from the beginning, but I love them more than ever now. Now that I've gotten this far in the series, I think my goal is to focus on finishing drawing about them.

In the magazine, the story is already unfolding rapidly with the new characters. I hope my fans are following the new plot twist. Drawing manga is still tough, but I've somehow managed to come this far. Of course, there will be volume 5 so see you then! Bye!

2004. 8. 30

SPECIAL THANKS!

Yanomichi : Mike kaziyama : Yunori Morio ı kumi Katuoka ı Mai Sukou : Nahoru Mita : Tomo Miyakawa : Hozumix : Rui Itou : and a special guest, M. Sekiya . . . and you!

When's my turn?

It's Ichi for Volume 1. ♪

ABOUT THE CREATOR

Michiyo Kikuta

Born in Ibaraki Prefecture on February 10th. Aquarius. Blood type B. She entered and won second place in the 31st Nakayoshi New Faces Manga Award with the manga *Giniro Moyô* in the year 2000, which then made its debut in *Nakayoshi Haru-yasumi Land* (Nakayoshi Spring Break Land) in 2001. Her featured works are *Mamotte! Lollipop* and *Medical Magical*. She enjoys clothes shopping and loves sweets.

Translation Notes

Japanese is a tricky language for most Westerners, and translation is often more art than science. For your edification and reading pleasure, here are notes on some of the places where we could have gone in a different direction in our translation of the work, or where a Japanese cultural reference is used.

Title: *Mamotte! Lollipop*
Mamotte means to protect and Lollipop, as we later come to know, is a tool that will help save the heroine from danger.

Names
The characters in *Mamotte! Lollipop* have names based on Japanese numbers. For example, Zero for *zero* (zero); Ichî for *ichi* (one), Nina for *ni* (two), and Sun for *san* (three).

Kyaa and *Gyaa*
Kyaa is a girlish scream. Though it sometimes indicates fright or surprise, it's usually a scream of delight. Gyaa, on the other hand, nearly always indicates real fright, embarrassment, or pain.

Tanuki, page 19
A *tanuki* is a dog that looks just like your ordinary, garden-variety dog. It is also known as the "raccoon dog." The creator uses this word to describe to her assistants exactly how they should paste the toning on her drawings.

Sick visit, page 46

Visiting a sick friend or classmate at home is a very common Japanese custom.

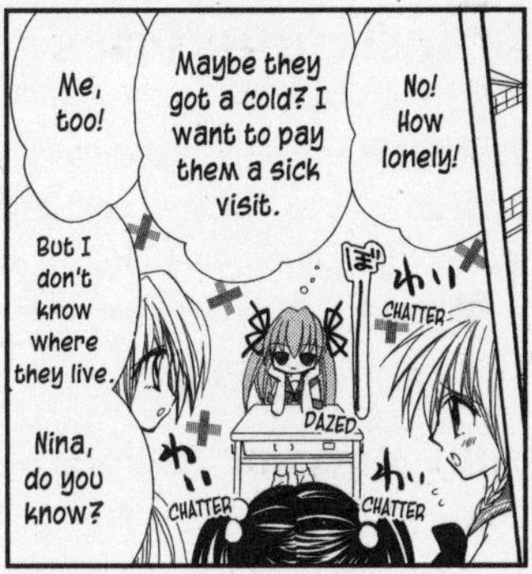
No! How lonely!
Maybe they got a cold? I want to pay them a sick visit.
Me, too!
CHATTER
DAZED
But I don't know where they live.
CHATTER
CHATTER
Nina, do you know?

K Fest, page 75

"K Fest" is an abbreviation for Kodansha Super Character Festival. This annual event celebrates popular fictional characters—and particularly, those characters who appear in the Japanese publisher Kodansha's books and manga.

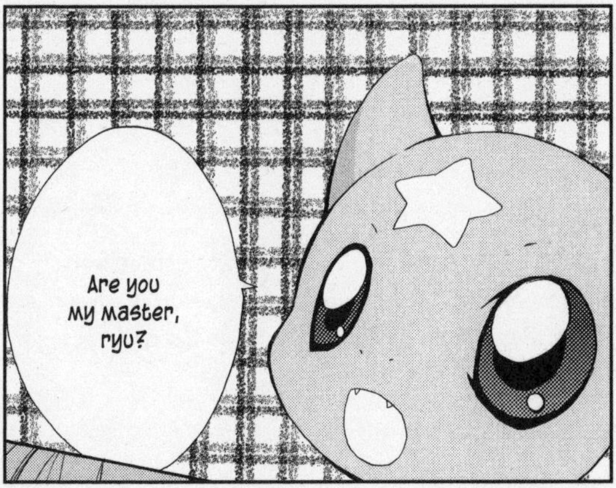
Are you my master, ryu?

***Ryu*, page 99**

Pearl has a habit of ending its sentences with the word *ryu*. It is a play on the word *ryû*, which means "dragon."

Cream Stew, page 99

This is a popular dish in Japan, almost as popular as curry. It is a stew made with cream sauce.

Let's stay friends, page 106

The actual word used is *yoroshiku*, customarily said when meeting someone for the first time. It means "nice to meet you." Since Zero and Ichî have already established a relationship with Nina, we felt "let's stay friends" best fit the context.

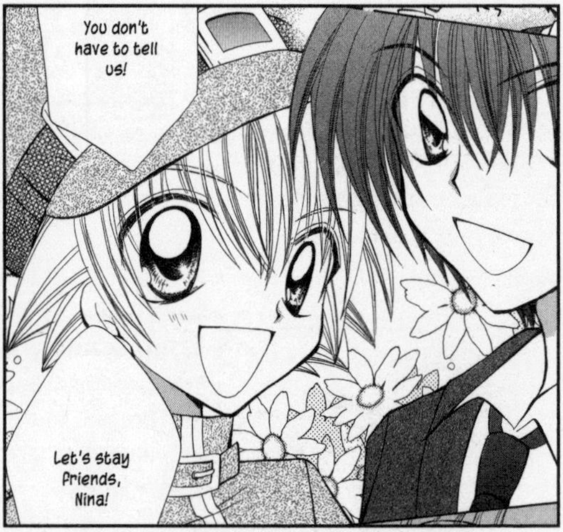
You don't have to tell us!
Let's stay friends, Nina!

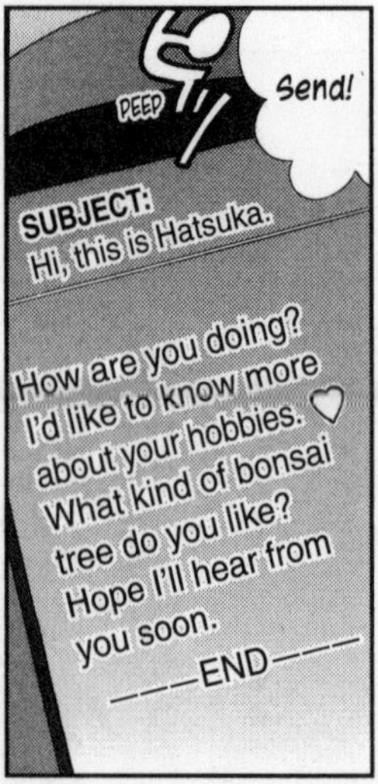
PEEP
Send!
SUBJECT:
Hi, this is Hatsuka.
How are you doing?
I'd like to know more about your hobbies. ♡
What kind of bonsai tree do you like?
Hope I'll hear from you soon.
——END——

How are you doing? I'd like to know more about your hobbies, page 108

In her first two sentences, Hatsuka is actually thanking Gô for sharing his e-mail address with her and tells him that she has decided to write him. It is typical in Japanese culture to thank someone for sharing personal information, such as an e-mail address.

Special picnic, page 109

Kuku actually says *aizuma bentô*. Literally translated, this means a "meal packed by your beloved wife." Since Kuku is not married, we have decided to replace it with the phrase "special picnic."

Ohh! I want to tell him how I feel!
Maybe I'll pack him a special picnic! ♡
GROAR

Loose socks, page 129

Loose socks, or baggy socks similar to leg warmers in appearance, are popular among young Japanese girls.

No, I can't skip the cram school.
Maybe later.

Cram school, page 150

Cram schools are specialized schools that help prepare students to pass Japan's difficult high school and college entrance examinations.

P—
Please wait, Ichî-sama!
-sama?!
FLINCH

***Ichî-sama*, page 153**

Though attaching the honorific *-sama* to a name indicates respect, Rokka is using it to express an even stronger feeling—that she practically worships Ichî.

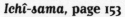

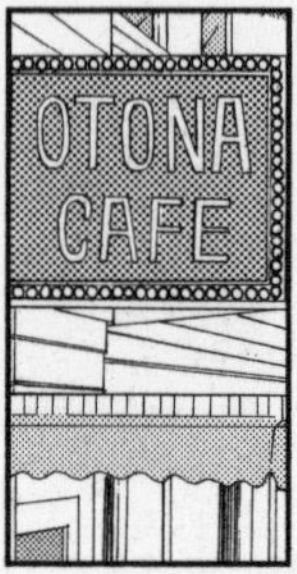
OTONA CAFE

Otona Café, page 158

The word *otona* in the name of this café means "grown-up" in Japanese.

I'll be back, page 165

Ittekimasu or "I'm leaving," literally translated, is the customary thing to say before leaving a Japanese home. We don't have an equivalent formula in English, so "I'll be back" was used as the closest replacement.

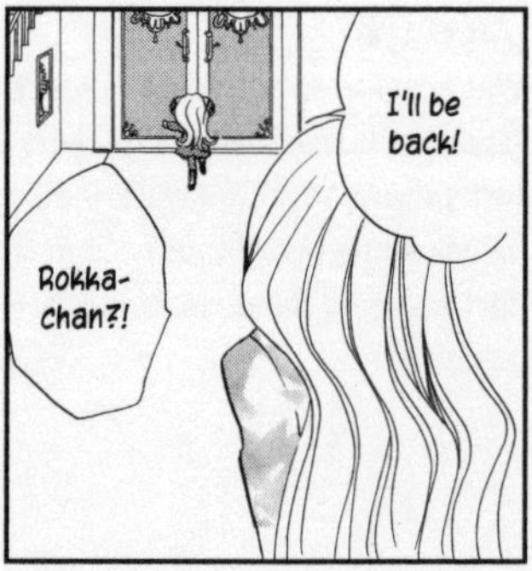
I'll be back!
Rokka-chan?!

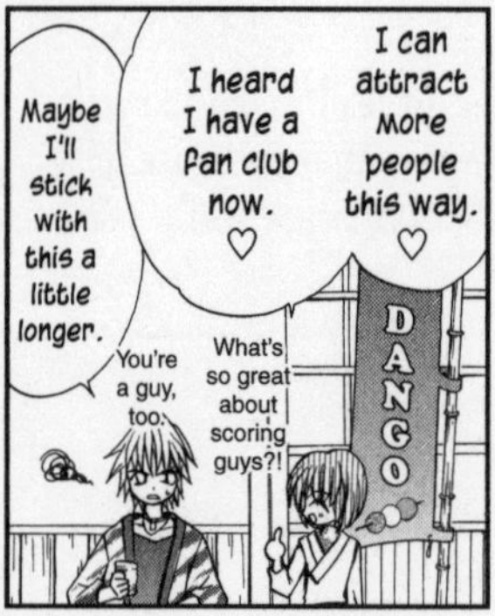
I can attract more people this way. ♡
I heard I have a fan club now. ♡
Maybe I'll stick with this a little longer.
What's so great about scoring guys?!
You're a guy, too.
DANGO

Dango, page 171

Dango is a Japanese dumpling made of glutinous rice and often served on a skewer.

Takoyaki, page 171

Takoyaki, literally translated, means "fried octopus." It is a Japanese dumpling made of diced octopus (called *tenkasu*), bits of deep-fried tempura batter, cabbage, green onion and pickled ginger, and then topped with a sweet Worcestershire-type sauce (called *okonomiyaki* sauce), mayonnaise, dried green seaweed and dried bonito flakes. Delicious!

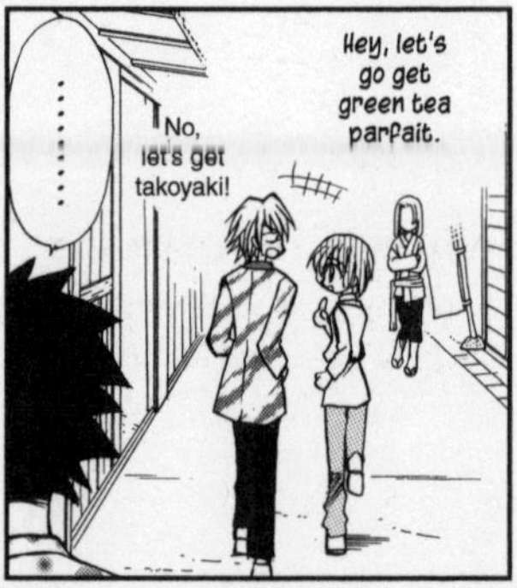
Hey, let's go get green tea parfait.
No, let's get takoyaki!
......

Lovely, page 177

Lovely is short for *Nakayoshi Lovely*, a special-edition magazine published by Kodansha, *Mamotte! Lollipop*'s Japanese publisher.

Watermelon splitting, page 178

Watermelon splitting is a favorite Japanese beach pastime. Players take turns trying to split a watermelon with a stick while blindfolded . . . but the best part is eating the watermelon after the game!

Rest area, page 178

Japanese beaches don't have public shower facilities. Instead, people pay to rent privately owned *umi no ie* or "ocean houses," where they can leave their belongings and take a shower. These houses also offer refreshments for sale.

Barley tea, page 178

Mugicha or "barley tea" is a popular iced summer drink made by brewing roasted barley.

Indirect kiss, page 180

Sharing food or drink with a person of the opposite sex—even without touching—is called an "indirect kiss" in Japan.

Preview of Volume 5

We're pleased to present you a preview from volume 5. Please check our website (www.delreymanga.com) to see when this volume will be available in English. For now you'll have to make do with Japanese!

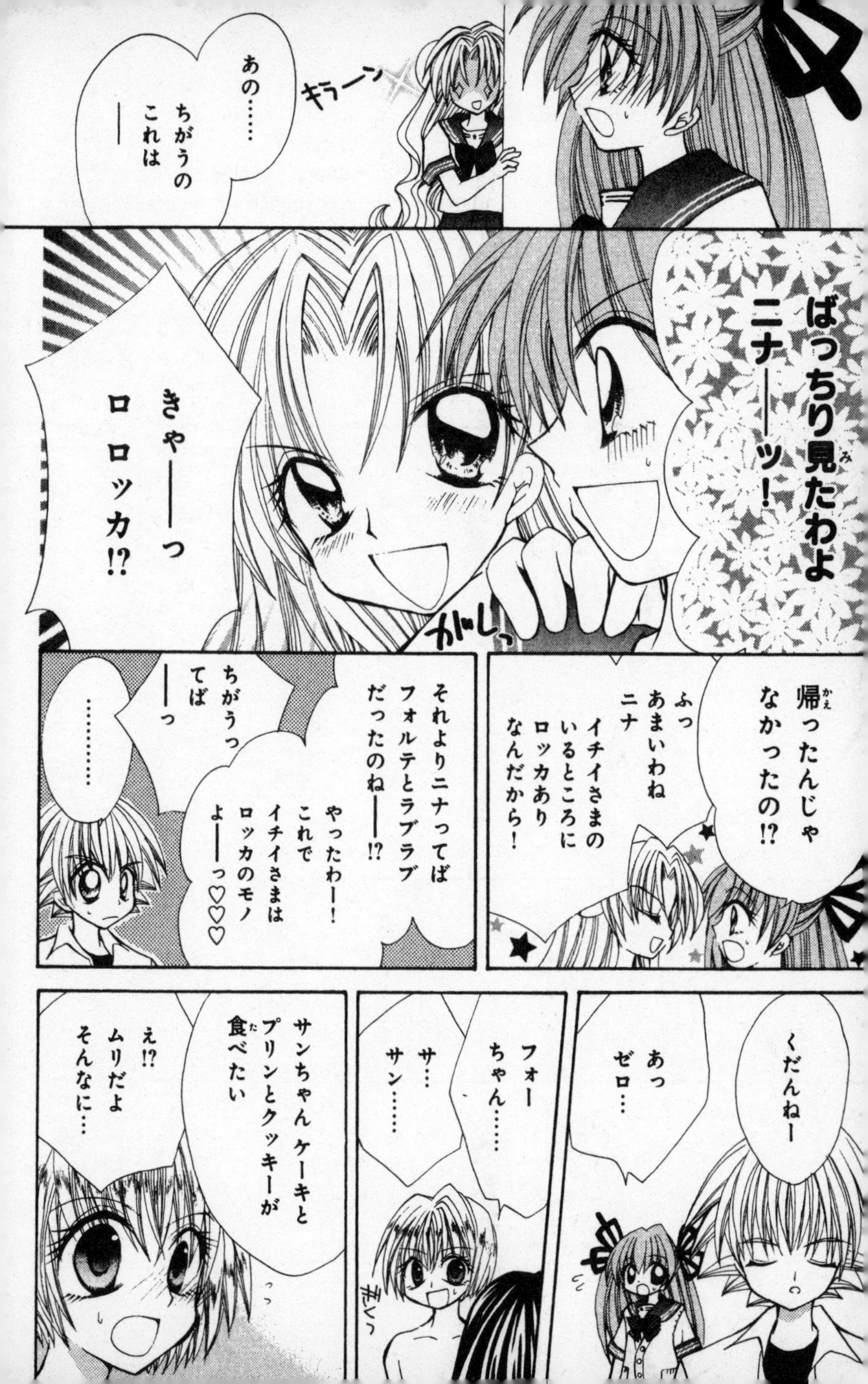
キラーン
あの…… ちがうの これは ―
ばっちり見たわよ ニナ――ッ!
ガシっ
きゃ――っ ロロッカ!?
帰ったんじゃ なかったの!?
ふっ あまいわね ニナ イチイさまの いるところに ロッカあり なんだから!
それよりニナってば フォルテとラブラブ だったのね――!?
やったわー! これで イチイさまは ロッカのモノ よ――っ♡♡♡
ちがうっ てば ――っ
……………
くだんねー
あっ ゼロ…
フォー ちゃん……
サ… サン……
ギくっ
サンちゃん ケーキと プリンとクッキーが 食べたい
え!? ムリだよ そんなに…

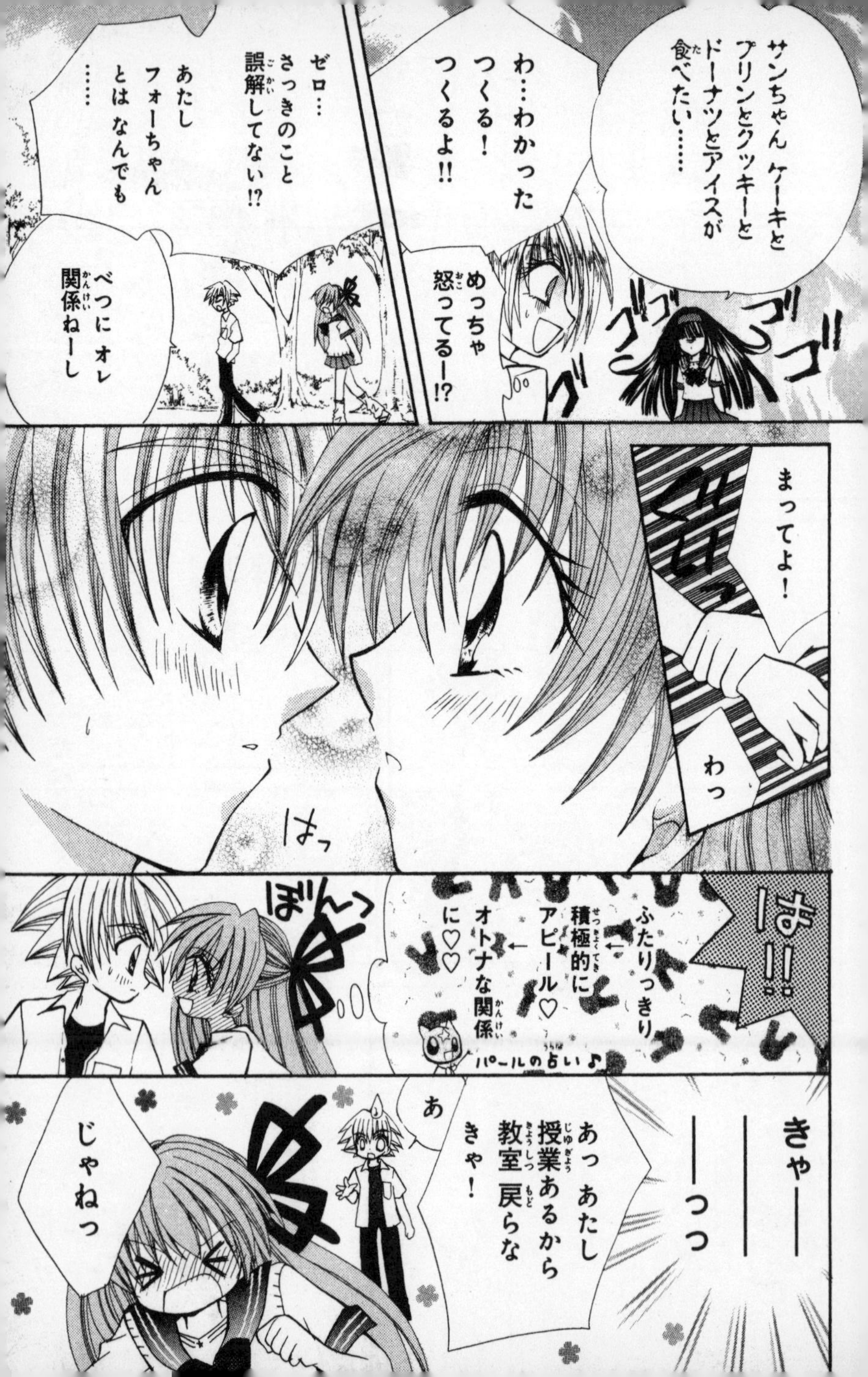

サンちゃん ケーキとプリンとクッキーとドーナツとアイスが食べたい……
ゴゴゴゴ
めっちゃ怒ってるー!?
わ…わかった つくる! つくるよ!!
ゼロ… さっきのこと誤解してない!?
あたし フォーちゃんとは なんでも ……
べつに オレ 関係ねーし
まってよ!
ぐいっ
わっ
はっ
は!!
ふたりっきり← 積極的にアピール♡← オトナな関係に♡♡
パールの占い♪
ぼんっ
きゃ―――っっ
あっ あたし授業あるから教室戻らなきゃ!
あ
じゃねっ

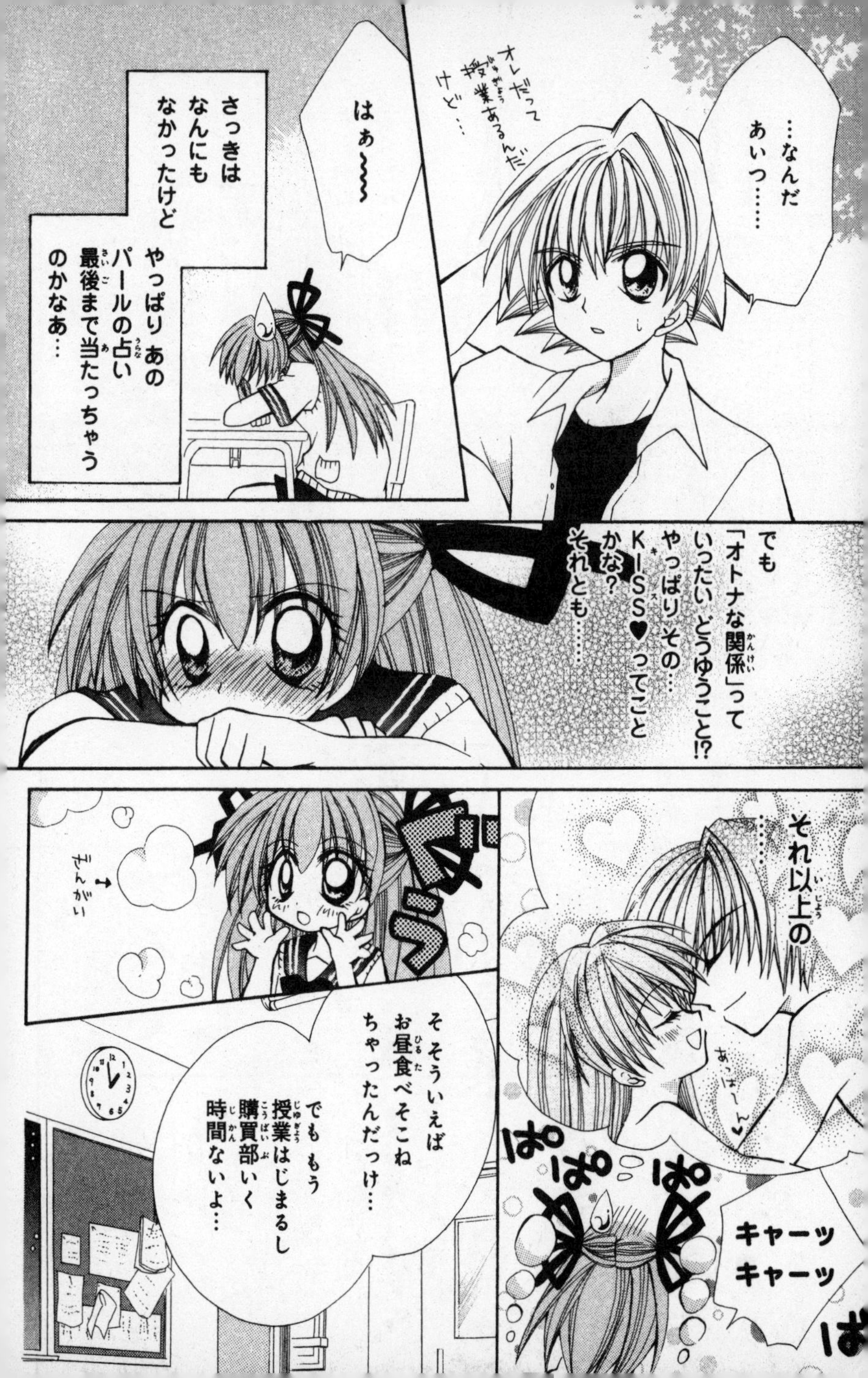

…なんだ あいつ……
オレだって授業あるんだけど…
はぁ〜〜〜
さっきは なんにも なかったけど
やっぱり あの パールの占い 最後まで当たっちゃう のかなあ…
でも「オトナな関係」って いったい どうゆうこと!? やっぱり その… KISS♥ってこと かな? それとも……
それ以上の……
あっは〜ん♥
ぱ ぱ ぱ
キャーッ キャーッ
ぱ
ぜんがい
そういえば お昼食べそこね ちゃったんだっけ…
でも もう 授業はじまるし 購買部いく 時間ないよ…

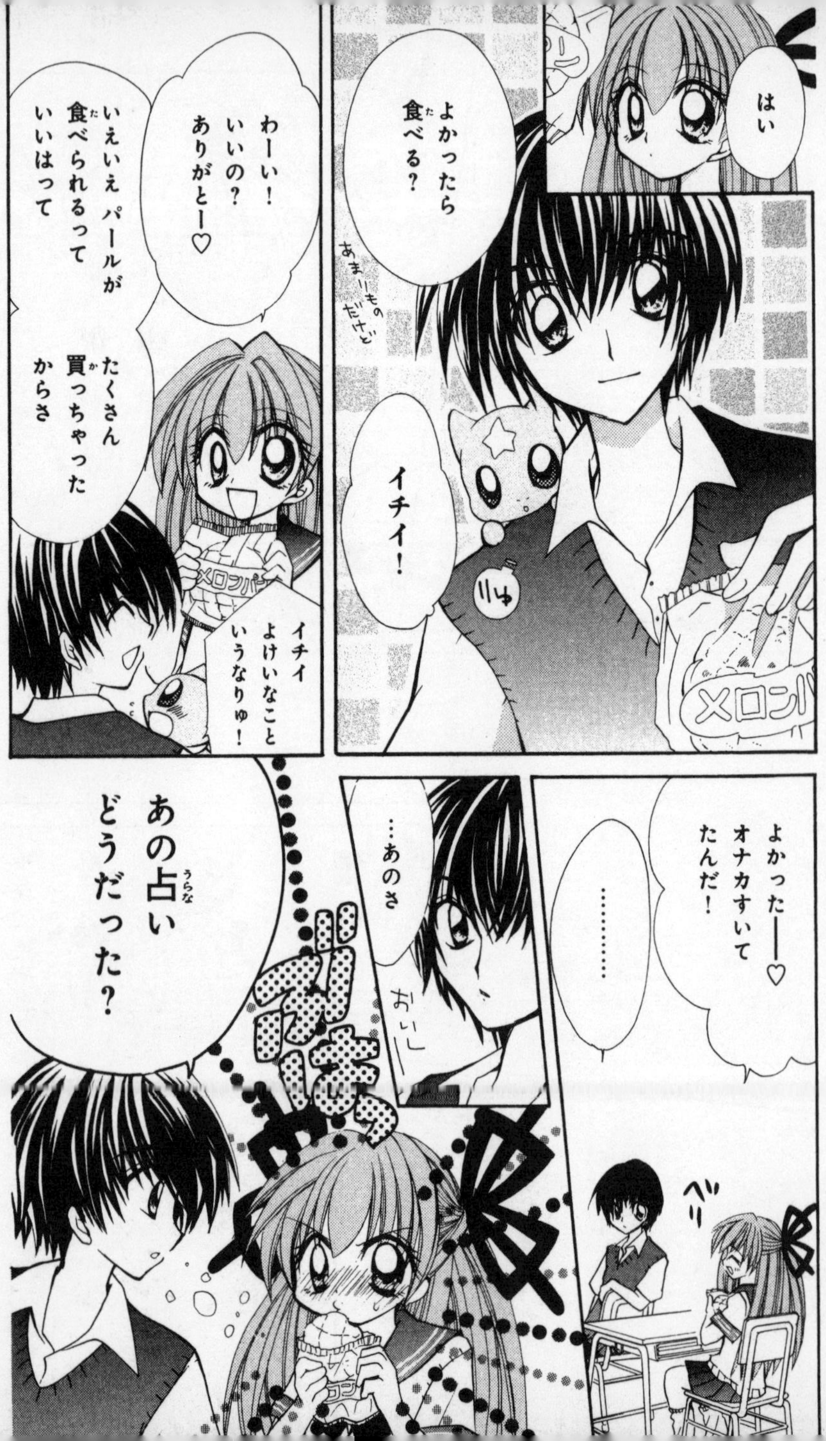
はい
よかったら食べる?
あまりものだけど
イチイ!
わーい! いいの? ありがとー♡
いえいえ パールが食べられるって いいはって
たくさん 買っちゃった からさ
イチイ よけいなこと いうなりゅ!
メロンパ
よかったー オナカすいて たんだ!
………
ペリ
…あのさ
おいし
あの占い どうだった?

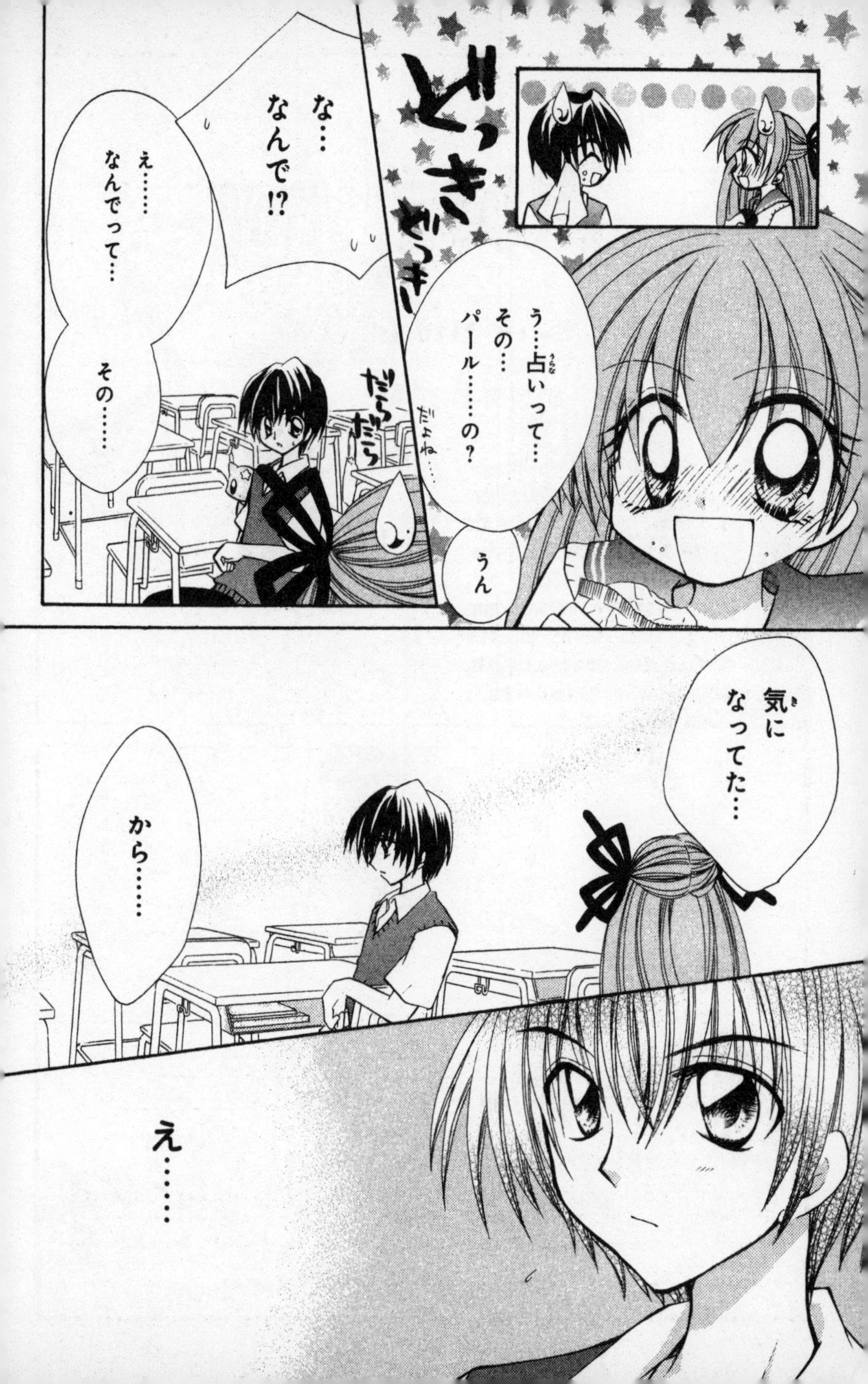
どっきどっき
う…占いって…その…パール……の？
だよね…
うん
だらだら
な…なんで!?
え……なんでって…
その……
気になってた…
から……
え……

SHIN MIDORIKAWA

NEVER STOP BELIEVING

Since ancient days, the Gaius School of Witchcraft and Wizardry has trained the fiercest swordsmen and the most powerful wizards.

Now one boy could become the greatest of them all. If he studies hard. If he is true to his friends. If he believes.

And if he survives . . .

Special extras in each volume! Read them all!

VISIT WWW.DELREYMANGA.COM TO:
• Read sample pages
• View release date calendars for upcoming volumes
• Sign up for Del Rey's free manga e-newsletter
• Find out the latest about new Del Rey Manga series

RATING T AGES 13+

DEL REY MANGA デルレイ
The Otaku's Choice.™

Aventura © 2006 Shin Midorikawa/ KODANSHA LTD. All rights reserved.

PEACH-PIT

Creators of *Dears* and *Rozen Maiden*

Everybody at Seiyo Elementary thinks that stylish and super-cool Amu has it all. But nobody knows the *real* Amu, a shy girl who wishes she had the courage to truly be herself. Changing Amu's life is going to take more than wishes and dreams—it's going to take a little magic! One morning, Amu finds a surprise in her bed: three strange little eggs. Each egg contains a Guardian Character, an angel-like being who can give her the power to be someone new. With the help of her Guardian Characters, Amu is about to discover that her true self is even more amazing than she ever dreamed.

Special extras in each volume! Read them all!

VISIT WWW.DELREYMANGA.COM TO:
• Read sample pages
• View release date calendars for upcoming volumes
• Sign up for Del Rey's free manga e-newsletter
• Find out the latest about new Del Rey Manga series

RATING T AGES 13+

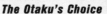 DEL REY MANGA デルレイ

The Otaku's Choice

Shugo Chara! © 2006 PEACH-PIT/ KODANSHA LTD. All rights reserved.

SHIKI TSUKAI

MANGA BY TORU ZEKU
ART BY YUNA TAKANAGI

DEFENDING THE NATURAL ORDER OF THE UNIVERSE!

The *shiki tsukai* are "Keepers of the Seasons"—magical warriors pledged to defend the planet's natural order against those who would threaten it.

When 14-year-old Akira Kizuki joins the *shiki tsukai,* he knows that it'll be a difficult life. But with his new friends and mentors, he's up to the challenge!

Special extras in each volume! Read them all!

VISIT WWW.DELREYMANGA.COM TO:
• Read sample pages
• View release date calendars for upcoming volumes
• Sign up for Del Rey's free manga e-newsletter
• Find out the latest about new Del Rey Manga series

RATING T AGES 13+

DEL REY MANGA デルレイ
The Otaku's Choice.™

Shiki Tsukai © 2006 by Toru Zeku and Yuna Takanagi / KODANSHA LTD. All rights reserved.

KITCHEN PRINCESS

STORY BY MIYUKI KOBAYASHI
MANGA BY NATSUMI ANDO
CREATOR OF ZODIAC P.I.

HUNGRY HEART

Najika is a great cook and likes to make meals for the people she loves. But something is missing from her life. When she was a child, she met a boy who touched her heart—and now Najika is determined to find him. The only clue she has is a silver spoon that leads her to the prestigious Seika Academy.

Attending Seika will be a challenge. Every kid at the school has a special talent, and the girls in Najika's class think she doesn't deserve to be there. But Sora and Daichi, two popular brothers who barely speak to each other, recognize Najika's cooking for what it is—magical. Could one of the boys be Najika's mysterious prince?

Special extras in each volume! Read them all!

RATING   T AGES 13+

VISIT WWW.DELREYMANGA.COM TO:
• Read sample pages
• View release date calendars for upcoming volumes
• Sign up for Del Rey's free manga e-newsletter
• Find out the latest about new Del Rey Manga series

 DEL REY MANGA デルレイ

The Otaku's Choice

Kitchen Princess © 2005 Natsumi Ando and Miyuki Kobayashi / KODANSHA LTD. All rights reserved.

Subscribe to

DEL REY'S MANGA
e-newsletter—

and receive all these
exciting exclusives directly
in your e-mail inbox:

• Schedules and announcements about
the newest books on sale

• Exclusive interviews and exciting
behind-the-scenes news

• Previews of upcoming material

• A manga reader's forum, featuring a
cool question-and-answer section

For more information and to sign up
for Del Rey's manga e-newsletter,
visit www.delreymanga.com

TOMARE!

W9-CEN-858

止まれ

[STOP!]

You're going the wrong way!

Manga is a completely different type of reading experience.

To start at the *beginning*, go to the *end*!

That's right! Authentic manga is read the traditional Japanese way—from right to left. Exactly the opposite of how American books are read. It's easy to follow: Just go to the other end of the book, and read each page—and each panel—from right side to left side, starting at the top right. Now you're experiencing manga as it was meant to be!